Christianity at Corinth

Christianity at Corinth

The Quest for
the Pauline Church

Edited by
Edward Adams and David G. Horrell

Westminster John Knox Press
LOUISVILLE • LONDON

Book Design by Sharon Adams
Cover Design by Mark Abrams

First Edition
Published by Westminster John Knox Press
Louisville, Kentucky

This book is printed on acid-free paper that meets the American National Standards Institute Z39.48 standard. ♾

PRINTED IN THE UNITED STATES OF AMERICA

04 05 06 07 08 09 10 11 12 13—10 9 8 7 6 5 4 3 2 1

Library of Congress Cataloging-in-Publication Data is on file at the Library of Congress, Washington, D.C.

ISBN 0-664-22478-4

Contents

Abbreviations

AB	Anchor Bible
ABSA	*Annual of the Brisith School at Athens*
AJA	*American Journal of Archaeology*
ANRW	*Aufstieg und Niedergang der römischen Welt*
ANTC	Abingdon New Testament Commentaries
BAGD	W. Bauer, W. F. Arndt, F. W. Gingrich, and F. W. Danker, *Greek-English Lexicon of the New Testament and Other Early Christian Literature.* 2nd ed. Chicago, 1979
BDAG	W. Bauer, F. W. Danker, W. F. Arndt, and F. W. Gingrich, *Greek-English Lexicon of the New Testament and Other Early Christian Literature.* 3rd ed. Chicago, 2000
BETL	Bibliotheca ephemeridum theologicarum lovaniensium
BFCT	Beiträge zur Förderung christlicher Theologie
BHT	Beiträge zur historischen Theologie
BibInt	*Biblical Interpretation*
BJRL	*Bulletin of the John Rylands University Library of Manchester*
BNTC	Black's New Testament Commentaries
BR	*Biblical Research*
BTB	*Biblical Theology Bulletin*
BZ	*Biblische Zeitschrift*
CBQ	*Catholic Biblical Quarterly*
CIG	*Corpus inscriptionum graecarum*
CIL	*Corpus inscriptionum latinarum*
CQ	*Classical Quarterly*

CSCA	*California Studies in Classical Antiquity*
Doc.Masada	H. M. Cotton, J. Geiger, *Masada II: The Yigael Yadin Excavations 1963–1965, Final Reports, the Latin and Greek Documents.* Jerusalem, 1989
DTT	*Dansk teologisk tidsskrift*
EKKNT	Evangelisch-katholischer Kommentar zum Neuen Testament
ET	English translation
EvT	*Evangelische Theologie*
Exp	*Expositor*
ExpTim	*Expository Times*
FRLANT	Forschungen zur Religion und Literatur des Alten und Neuen Testaments
HDR	Harvard Dissertations in Religion
HNT	Handbuch zum Neuen Testament
HR	*History of Religions*
HTR	*Harvard Theological Review*
HUCA	*Hebrew Union College Annual*
ICC	International Critical Commentary
IG	*Inscriptiones graecae*
Int	*Interpretation*
JAAR	*Journal of the American Academy of Religion*
JBL	*Journal of Biblical Literature*
JRA	*Journal of Roman Archaeology*
JRH	*Journal of Roman History*
JRS	*Journal of Roman Studies*
JSNT	*Journal for the Study of the New Testament*
JSNTSup	Journal for the Study of the New Testament: Supplement Series
JTS	*Journal of Theological Studies*
KJV	King James Version
LCL	Loeb Classical Library
LXX	Septuagint
NA	Nestle-Aland, *Novum Testamentum Graece*
NEB	New English Bible
NHS	Nag Hammadi Studies
NICNT	New International Commentary on the New Testament
NIDNTT	*New International Dictionary of New Testament Theology.* Ed. C. Brown. 4 vols. Grand Rapids, 1975–1985
NIGTC	New International Greek Testament Commentary

NovT	*Novum Testamentum*
NRSV	New Revised Standard Version
NTD	Das Neue Testament Deutsch
NTS	*New Testament Studies*
OCD	*Oxford Classical Dictionary*
PCPhS	*Proceedings of the Cambridge Philosophical Society*
PG	Patrologia graeca. Ed. J.-P. Migne. 162 vols. Paris, 1857–1886
P.Lond	*Greek Papyri in the British Museum*
PW	A. F. Pauly, *Paulys Realencyclopädie der classischen Altertumswissenschaft.* New edition G. Wissowa. 49 vols. Munich, 1980
RSV	Revised Standard Version
SBLDS	Society of Biblical Literature Dissertation Series
SBLSP	Society of Biblical Literature Seminar Papers
SBS	Stuttgarter Bibelstudien
SEG	Supplementum epigraphicum graecum
SNTSMS	Society for New Testament Studies Monograph Series
SNTW	Studies of the New Testament and Its World
Sup	Supplement
SVF	*Stoicorum veterum fragmenta.* H. von Arnim. 4 vols. Leipzig, 1903–1924
Tab.Vindol	*Tabulae Vindolandenses II*
TDNT	*Theological Dictionary of the New Testament.* Ed. G. Kittel and G. Friedrich. 10 vols. Grand Rapids, 1964–1976
TLZ	*Theologische Literaturzeitung*
TU	Texte und Untersuchung
TWNT	*Theologische Wörterbuch zum Neuen Testament.* Ed. G. Kittel and G. Friedrich. 10 vols. Stuttgart, 1932–1979
TynBul	*Tyndale Bulletin*
TZ	*Theologische Zeitschrift*
VC	*Vigilae christianae*
WBC	Word Biblical Commentary
WMANT	Wissenschaftliche Monographien zum Alten und Neuen Testament
WUNT	Wissenschaftliche Untersuchungen zum Neuen Testament
ZNW	*Zeitschrift für die neutestamentliche Wissenschaft*

Abbreviations of Nonbiblical Texts Referred to in Main Text and Footnotes

Aelius Aristides
Or.   *Orations*

Appian
Bell. civ.   *Bella civilia*

Apuleius
Metam.   *Metamorphoses*

Aristotle
Pol.   *Politica*

Augustine
Civ.   *De civitate Dei*

b. Qidd   Babylonian Talmud, *Qiddushin*

CD   Cairo (Genizah text of the Damascus) Document (Dead Sea Scroll)

Cicero
Agr.   *De Lege Agraria*
Fin.   *De Finibus*
Nat. d.   *De Natura deorum*
Off.   *De Officiis*
Tusc.   *Tusculanae Disputationes*

1 *Clem.*	*1 Clement*
2 *Clem.*	*2 Clement*

Clement of Alexandria
Strom.	*Stromata*

Did.	*Didache*

Dio Chrysostom
Or.	*Orations*

Dionysius of Halicarnassus
Ant. rom.	*Antiquitates Romanae*

1 En.	*1 Enoch*

Epictetus
Diss.	*Dissertations*
Ench.	*Enchiridion*

Eusebius
Praep. ev.	*Praeparatio Evangelica*

Gos. Thom.	*Gospel of Thomas*

Hermas
Mand.	*Mandates*
Vis.	*Visions*

Isocrates
Ep.	*Epistles*
Or.	*Orations*

Josephus
Ag. Ap.	*Against Apion*
Ant.	*Antiquities*
War	*Jewish War*

Jub.	*Jubilees*

Justin Martyr
Dialogue	*Dialogue with Trypho*

Juvenal
Sat.	*Satires*

M. 'Abot	Mishnah, *'Abot*
M. Neg.	Mishnah, *Nega'im*

Origen
Cels.   *Contra Celsum*

Philo
Abr.   *De Abrahamo*
Conf.   *De confusione linguarum*
Congr.   *De congressu eruditionis gratia*
Contempl.   *De vita contemplativa*
Decal.   *De decalogo*
Det.   *Quod deterius potiori insidiari soleat*
Deus   *Quod Deus sit immutabilis*
Ebr.   *De ebrietate*
Flacc.   *In Flaccum*
Fug.   *De fuga et inventione*
Gig.   *De gigantibus*
Leg. All.   *Legum allegoriarum*
Legat.   *De legatione ad Gaium*
Migr.   *De migratione Abrahami*
Mos.   *De vita Mosis*
Mut.   *De mutatione nominum*
Opif.   *De opificio mundi*
Post.   *De posteritate Caini*
Quod Omn.   *Quod Omnis Probus*
Somn.   *De somniis*
Spec.   *De specialibus legibus*
Virt.   *De virtutibus*

Plato
Ep.   *Epistles*
Phaed.   *Phaedo*
Phaedr.   *Phaedrus*
Theaet.   *Theaetetus*

Pliny the Elder
Nat.   *Naturalis historia*

Pliny the Younger
Ep.   *Epistulae*
Pan.   *Panegyricus*

Plutarch
Caes.   *Caesar*
Cat. Maj.   *Cato the Elder*
Cic.   *Cicero*

Comp. Arist. Cat.	Comparison of Aristides and Cato
Comm. not.	De communibus notitiis
Conj. praec.	Conjugalia praecepta
Is. Os.	De Iside et Osiride
Lyc.	Lycurgus
Mor.	Moralia
Plac. philos.	De placita philosophorum, libri V
Stoic. abs.	Compendium argumenti Stoicos absurdiora poetis dicere
Stoic. rep.	De Stoicorum repugnantiis

Ps.-Sallust
Ep.	Epistula

1QpHab	Pesher on Habbakuk from Qumran Cave 1 (Dead Sea Scroll)
1QS	Community Rule (Dead Sea Scroll)

Seneca
Clem.	De Clementia
Ep.	Epistles

Sextus Empiricus
Math.	Adversus mathimaticos

Socratic Ep.	Socratic Epistles

Stobaeus
Flor.	Florilegium

Suetonius
Dom.	Domitian
Tib.	Tiberius
Vesp.	Vespasian

T.Naph.	Testament of Naphtali

Tacitus
Ann.	Annals
Dial.	Dialogus de Oratoribus

Tertullian
Apol.	Apology

Xenophon
Mem.	Memorabilia

Contributors

Edward Adams
John M. G. Barclay
C. K. Barrett
Ferdinand Christian Baur
John K. Chow
Nils A. Dahl
James D. G. Dunn
Elisabeth Schüssler Fiorenza
Michael D. Goulder
Bengt Holmberg
David G. Horrell
Richard A. Horsley
Margaret Y. MacDonald
Justin J. Meggitt
Johannes Munck
Jerome Murphy-O'Connor
Terence Paige
Walter Schmithals
Gerd Theissen
Anthony C. Thiselton
Laurence L. Welborn

Illustrations

Preface

Paul's letters to the Corinthians, especially 1 Corinthians, offer a uniquely vivid portrait of the life of early Christian groups. They have therefore long been a focus for scholarly interest and have led to many attempts to reconstruct the situation at Corinth and to reenvisage the character of the Corinthian assemblies. The aim of this book is to represent the history of scholarship in this area of New Testament studies, including the most recent work, and to subject it to critical scrutiny. This is the first attempt to collect together in one volume extracts from a wide range of essays on the subject, and we hope that the book will be useful for those teaching and studying the Corinthian letters and for those undertaking research in the area. We should stress that the focus here is on the various ways in which the character of Corinthian Christianity has been reconstructed, through Paul's letters; we do not include material primarily concerned with reading Paul's Corinthian letters from theological, ethical, pastoral, or other perspectives.

The introductory essay offers a critical overview of the history of attempts to reconstruct 'Christianity at Corinth', and is intended to serve both as an orientation to the field and as a critical and suggestive review. The extracts from the history of scholarship, together with their short introductions and suggestions for further reading, provide examples of key approaches and arguments, influential proposals and counterarguments, which will give a sense of the trends, and the diversity, in this area of study. Various areas of methodological reflection and critique are further developed in the four essays with which the volume concludes.

For presentation in this volume, some of the footnotes to the essays from which the extracts are taken have been shortened or deleted. We have sought to conform all references, including biblical and other ancient references, to a common style. In addition, some typographical errors in the originals have been corrected. The original publications should be consulted in order to see the essays and their notes in full.

We would like to express our thanks to those who have helped bring this project to fruition. We are very grateful to the authors of the four specially commissioned essays (chapters 19–22) for their work in producing these chapters. We must also thank the publishers and authors who have given us permission to reproduce the extracts from previously published work. There are others, too, to whom we owe our thanks: Guy Sanders, Director of the Corinth Excavations; Nancy Bookides, Assistant Director; James Herbst and Ioulia Tzonou-Herbst; and Mary and Michael Walbank, all of whom were generous with their time and assistance, and kind in the welcome they offered us, when we spent a week at Corinth in March 2001; the British Academy, who awarded us a Small Research Grant for this project that made possible the visit to Corinth, a number of our meetings together, and other research support; Cherryl Hunt, who cheerfully undertook a range of tasks, including researching bibliography and scanning a number of extracts; Leslie McFall, who checked the reproduced material against the original publications for accuracy; John Barclay and Stephen Barton, who offered suggestions on our initial outline. We would also like to thank our own universities, King's College London and the University of Exeter, for their support of our research and for granting us research leave during which this book was brought to completion. Edward Adams records his thanks to his university department for a research grant, which helped cover the cost of indexing, and to Tyndale House Cambridge, and the Warden of the House, Bruce Winter, in particular, for hosting his study leave. David Horrell would like to thank the Alexander von Humboldt foundation, and Gerd Theissen in particular, for sponsoring his period of research in Heidelberg.

Edward Adams and David Horrell
May 2003

Frequently Cited Works

C. K. Barrett, 'Christianity at Corinth', *BJRL* 46 (1964) 269–97 = Barrett, 'Christianity at Corinth'.

S. C. Barton, 'Paul's Sense of Place: An Anthropological Approach to Community Formation in Corinth', *NTS* 32 (1986) 225–46 = Barton, 'Paul's Sense of Place'.

F. C. Baur, 'Die Christuspartei in der korinthischen Gemeinde, der Gegensatz des paulinischen und petrinischen Christentums in der ältesten Kirche, der Apostel Petrus in Rom', *Tübinger Zeitschrift für Theologie* 4 (1831) 61–206 = Baur, 'Die Christuspartei'.

J. K. Chow, *Patronage and Power: A Study of Social Networks in Corinth* (JSNTSup 75; Sheffield: Sheffield Academic Press, 1992) = Chow, *Patronage and Power*.

A. D. Clarke, *Secular and Christian Leadership in Corinth: A Socio-Historical and Exegetical Study of 1 Corinthians 1–6* (Leiden: Brill, 1993) = Clarke, *Secular and Christian Leadership*.

H. Conzelmann, *1 Corinthians* (Hermeneia; Philadelphia: Fortress, 1975) = Conzelmann, *1 Corinthians*.

N. A. Dahl, 'Paul and the Church at Corinth', in *Christian History and Interpretation* (ed. W. R. Farmer, C. F. D. Moule, and R. R. Niebuhr; Cambridge: Cambridge University Press, 1967) 313–35 = Dahl, 'Paul and the Church at Corinth'.

G. D. Fee, *The First Epistle to the Corinthians* (NICNT; Grand Rapids: Eerdmans, 1987) = Fee, *First Epistle*.

E. Schüssler Fiorenza, 'Rhetorical Situation and Historical Reconstruction in 1 Corinthians', *NTS* 33 (1987) = Fiorenza, 'Rhetorical Situation'.

M. D. Goulder, 'Σοφία in 1 Corinthians', *NTS* 37 (1991) 516–34 = Goulder, 'Σοφία'

D. G. Horrell, *The Social Ethos of the Corinthian Correspondence* (SNTW; Edinburgh: T. & T. Clark, 1996) = Horrell, *Social Ethos*.

J. C. Hurd, *The Origin of 1 Corinthians* (London: SPCK, 1965) = Hurd, *Origin*.

D. Litfin, *St. Paul's Theology of Proclamation: 1 Corinthians 1–4 and Greco-Roman Rhetoric* (SNTSMS 79; Cambridge: Cambridge University Press, 1994) = Litfin, *St. Paul's Theology*.

W. Lütgert, *Freiheitspredigt und Schwarmgeister in Korinth* (Göttingen: Bertelsmann, 1908) = Lütgert, *Freiheitspredigt*.

M. Y. MacDonald, 'Women Holy in Body and Spirit: The Social Setting of 1 Corinthians 7', *NTS* 36 (1990) 161–81 = MacDonald, 'Women Holy'.

D. B. Martin, *The Corinthian Body* (New Haven: Yale University Press, 1995) = Martin, *Corinthian Body*.

W. A. Meeks, *The First Urban Christians: The Social World of the Apostle Paul* (New Haven and London: Yale University Press, 1983) = Meeks, *First Urban Christians*.

J. J. Meggitt, *Paul, Poverty and Survival* (SNTW; Edinburgh: T. & T. Clark) = Meggitt, *Paul, Poverty*.

M. M. Mitchell, *Paul and the Rhetoric of Reconciliation: An Exegetical Investigation of the Language and Composition of 1 Corinthians* (Louisville: Westminster John Knox, 1992) = Mitchell, *Rhetoric*.

R. Morgan, 'Tübingen School', in *A Dictionary of Biblical Interpretation* (ed. R. J. Coggins and J. L. Houlden; London: SCM; Philadelphia: Trinity Press International, 1990) 710–13 = Morgan, 'Tübingen School'.

J. Munck, 'The Church without Factions', in *Paul and the Salvation of Mankind* (ET London: SCM, 1959) 135–67 = Munck, 'The Church without Factions'.

J. Murphy-O'Connor, *St. Paul's Corinth: Texts and Archaeology* (3d ed., Collegeville, Minn.: Liturgical Press, 2002) = Murphy-O'Connor, *St. Paul's Corinth*.

W. Schmithals, *Gnosticism in Corinth* (ET Nashville: Abingdon, 1971) = Schmithals, *Gnosticism*.

G. Theissen, *The Social Setting of Pauline Christianity* (ET Edinburgh: T. & T. Clark; Philadelphia: Fortress, 1982) = Theissen, *Social Setting*.

A. C. Thiselton, 'Realized Eschatology at Corinth', *NTS* 24 (1978) 510–26 = Thiselton, 'Realized Eschatology'.

B. W. Winter, *After Paul Left Corinth: The Influence of Secular Ethics and Social Change* (Grand Rapids: Eerdmans, 2001) = Winter, *After Paul Left Corinth*.

A. C. Wire, *The Corinthian Women Prophets: A Reconstruction through Paul's Rhetoric* (Minneapolis: Fortress, 1990) = Wire, *Corinthian Women Prophets*.

Introduction

The Scholarly Quest for Paul's Church at Corinth: A Critical Survey

David G. Horrell and Edward Adams

The earliest Christian communities in Corinth, known primarily from the letters of Paul addressed to them, have long been a major focus of scholarly investigation. Paul's letters to the Corinthians, especially 1 Corinthians, provide a uniquely detailed and vivid portrait of the life of this early Christian congregation,[1] a portrait that shows all too clearly that there were issues of dispute between Paul and the Corinthians, and almost certainly also among the Corinthians themselves. The particular preoccupations of scholars, and the ways in which they have sought to explain the character and disputes of the first Corinthian Christians, have varied very widely over time. In this opening essay, and in the book as a whole, we aim to illustrate this history of scholarship and to subject it to critical examination.

---

1. Paul, of course, does not use the terms 'Christian' or 'Christianity', and to apply these terms to the earliest followers of the movement that later came to be denoted by these labels is somewhat problematic and anachronistic. One must not assume that the Corinthians conceived of themselves as 'Christians' in the way that later believers did, given a period of institutional and doctrinal development. We follow convention in using the terms, in the absence of anything we consider better ('believers' is equally problematic, emphasizing belief more than is appropriate). The term 'Christian' did, after all, develop early, and within the NT period. See also the comments on this subject in Margaret MacDonald's essay below, ch. 21, pp. 285–87.

The critical survey of scholarship set out in this introduction provides a context to inform the reading of the extracts that follow, each of which represents a particular kind of approach to understanding the earliest Christian church at Corinth. The four essays that follow the extracts, by Justin Meggitt, Bengt Holmberg, Margaret MacDonald, and James Dunn, each individually offers a specific kind of critical methodological reflection relevant to understanding and assessing the extracts, and indeed the much larger body of literature dealing with earliest Christianity at Corinth. Before we begin to deal with the history of scholarly attempts to understand the Corinthian Christians, however, it is important first to present a basic sketch of the context in which these Christians lived, that of the city of Corinth in the first century C.E.

1. CORINTH IN THE FIRST CENTURY

Ancient Corinth lies on the southern side of the isthmus that links the Peloponnesian peninsula with the northern mainland of Greece and separates the Aegean and Ionian seas. It is located at the base of the rugged limestone summit, Acrocorinth, which stands 574 metres (1,886 feet) high and dominates the local landscape (see photo, p. 46). The geographical position of Corinth made it an important site of mercantile activity (as well as a place of great military significance) throughout antiquity. It commanded the land trade route between the north and south of Greece, but more importantly, lying between the two ports of Lechaeum, 3 kilometres (about 2 miles) to the north, and Cenchreae, 9 kilometres (5–6 miles) to the east, on either side of the isthmus, it controlled the major sea trade route between Asia and Italy (see fig. 1, p. 44). The voyage around the Peloponnesus was long and often dangerous. A paved road, known as the *diolkos,* was built across the isthmus in the sixth century B.C.E. to enable ships to transport their cargo between east and west without having to negotiate the difficult waters around Cape Malea at the tip of the peninsula. Merchandise could be unloaded on one side of the isthmus, dragged overland, and reloaded on the other side; light vessels could actually be dragged across. The geographer Strabo, writing around 7 B.C.E., reports that Corinth was renowned for its wealth;[2] he attributes the city's economic success to its ability to exploit the commercial potential of its strategic location.

The history of ancient Corinth is in many respects 'a tale of two cities'. The Greek city of Corinth, whose history reaches back into the eighth century B.C.E., flourished until 146 B.C.E., when it was destroyed by the Roman general, Lucius Mummius. Relations between Rome and the Achaian league, of which the city-state of Corinth was a prominent member, had always been strained.[3] The Acha-

---

2. Strabo 8.6.19–20a. Cf. Murphy-O'Connor, *St. Paul's Corinth*, 53–54.
3. For the history of relations between Corinth and Rome, see J. Wiseman, 'Corinth and Rome I: 228 B.C.–A.D. 267', *ANRW* 2.7.1 (1979) 438–548, esp. 450–62.

ians provoked outright conflict with Rome by declaring war on Sparta, Rome's ally. The armies of the Achaian league were crushed by the Romans and as a consequence Corinth was sacked and burned. Of its inhabitants, the men were slain and the women and children sold into slavery.[4] The city was refounded as a *Roman* colony just over a century later, in 44 B.C.E. Ancient testimony that the city was utterly destroyed by Mummius[5] and lay in a state of complete abandonment until its reestablishment[6] has often been taken at face value by scholars, but the archaeological data show that the destruction was far from total; many buildings survived fairly intact.[7] There is also archaeological evidence pointing to the inhabitation of Corinth from 146 to 44 B.C.E.[8] Moreover, Cicero, in the only extant account by someone with firsthand knowledge of Corinth during this period, indicates that when he visited the city in his youth, about 79–77 B.C.E., people were living among the ruins.[9] But clearly there was no formal political life in Corinth between its destruction and refounding.[10]

The colonisation of Corinth was ordered by Julius Caesar shortly before his death. The city was given the name *Colonia Laus Iulia Corinthiensis* (Colony of Corinth in honour of Julius).[11] Most of the early colonists were freedmen.[12] Whether the first colonists also included army veterans is now considered doubtful.[13] The origin of the early settlers is unclear. Many were probably Greek, but they could have originated in any part of the Roman world. The resident population of the city consisted of citizens (*cives*)—the colonists and their descendants—and resident aliens (*incolae*).[14] The latter would have included those Greeks living in and around Corinth prior to its refounding. The population grew as people migrated to the city, attracted by its economic growth. Corinth was under the control of the governor of the province of Macedonia until 27 B.C.E.,

---

4. Pausanias 7.16.1–9. Cf. Polybius 39.2; Strabo 8.6.23. See also Wiseman, 'Corinth and Rome', 462.

5. Pausanias 2.1.2; cf. the comments of Antipater of Sidon in *Greek Anthology* 9.151.

6. Strabo 8.6.23.

7. Wiseman, 'Corinth and Rome', 494. Cf. also W. L. Willis, 'Corinthusne deletus est?' *BZ* 35 (1991) 233–41.

8. Wiseman, 'Corinth and Rome', 495.

9. Cicero, *Tusc.* 3.22.53. In *Agr.* 2.87, Cicero indicates that people were farming the land in the area of Corinth.

10. Cf. C. K. Williams II, 'The Refounding of Corinth: Some Roman Religious Attitudes', in *Roman Architecture in the Greek World* (ed. S. Macready and F. S. Thompson; London: Society of Antiquaries, 1987) 26–37, here p. 27; D. W. J. Gill, 'Corinth: A Roman Colony of Achaea', *BZ* 37 (1993) 259–64.

11. The name was changed to *Colonia Iulia Flavia Augusta Corinthiensis* sometime before the end of the reign of Vespasian in response to his generosity to the city after the earthquake in the 70s C.E. (hitherto dated 77 C.E., as in Wiseman, 'Corinth and Rome', 506, but now put more generally within the decade). The original name of the colony was restored sometime after the death of Domitian. See Wiseman, 'Corinth and Rome', 506–7; and further M. E. H. Walbank, 'What's in a Name? Corinth under the Flavians', *Zeitschrift für Papyrologie und Epigraphik* 139 (2002) 251–64.

12. Strabo, 8.3.23c.

13. Murphy-O'Connor, *St. Paul's Corinth*, 64, 112.

14. D. Engels, *Roman Corinth: An Alternative Model for the Classical City* (Chicago and London: University of Chicago Press, 1990) 17.

when the senatorial province of Achaia was created. Corinth seems to have been made the administrative capital of the new province.[15] In 15 C.E., due to protests by citizens about taxation, Achaia became an imperial province.[16] In 44 C.E., however, the Emperor Claudius returned the province to senatorial control.[17]

A great deal of information about the city of Corinth in Paul's time is available to scholars. Archaeological excavations at Corinth were initiated by W. Dörpfeld, and the report of his work on the Archaic Temple was published in 1886. The American School of Classical Studies at Athens began excavations at the site in 1896. An ongoing series of volumes presenting the results of these investigations was launched in 1930.[18] The most extensive excavations have been in the centre of the Roman city—the forum and its surrounding streets and buildings—though other areas, such as the sanctuary of Demeter and Kore on the north slope of Acrocorinth, the Asklepeion, and some outlying villas, have been excavated. The archaeological, epigraphic, and numismatic data, together with ancient literary sources,[19] enable us to draw a surprisingly sharp profile of the city in the mid-first century C.E.[20] Jerome Murphy-O'Connor's *St. Paul's Corinth*, first published in 1983 and now in its third edition, is the best-known attempt to gather together the ancient literary and nonliterary materials relevant to reconstructing the urban context of Paul's mission and the church he founded.[21] A growing number of studies, most recently Bruce Winter's *After Paul Left Corinth,* make use of the archaeological evidence to illuminate the issues and disputes that arose in the Corinthian church and that Paul had to address in 1 Corinthians.[22] However, despite occasional claims that such evidence can simply be presented as 'data' (see §6 below), interpretive decisions are inevitably bound up with any use of even the most concrete archaeological evidence, and there are important methodological issues to be considered with regard to the

15. The evidence for this assumption is circumstantial: Wiseman, 'Corinth and Rome', 501.

16. Tacitus, *Ann.* 1.76.4.

17. For a brief period Corinth enjoyed freedom from Roman control. Nero granted independence to the city. This probably happened in 66 C.E., though some scholars put it in 67 C.E. The edict was revoked by Vespasian and Achaia again became a senatorial province: Wiseman, 'Corinth and Rome, 505–6.

18. *Corinth, Results of Excavations Conducted by the American School of Classical Studies at Athens.* Preliminary reports and other studies have been published in the *American Journal of Archaeology* and *Hesperia.*

19. Our principal literary source is Pausanias, who visited Corinth in 165 C.E. Pausanias, however, needs to be used cautiously for reconstructing Corinth in the mid-first century, as he is reflecting the Corinth of over a century later. Extensive rebuilding was undertaken in Corinth after the earthquake in the 70s C.E.

20. For an excellent discussion of the evolution of Roman Corinth and its buildings, see M. E. H. Walbank, 'The Nature and Development of Roman Corinth from 44 BCE to the End of the Antonine Period' (Ph.D., Open University, 1986). A revised version of part of this thesis was published as 'The Foundation and Planning of Early Roman Corinth', *JRA* 10 (1997) 95–130. For a brief account of what the centre of Corinth looked like around 50 C.E., see Murphy-O'Connor, *St. Paul's Corinth,* 24–35.

21. Murphy-O'Connor, *St. Paul's Corinth.* The best summary of the archaeology of ancient Corinth is Wiseman's essay, 'Corinth and Rome', though it needs to be supplemented by more recent archaeological studies. See also Engels, *Roman Corinth.*

22. Winter, *After Paul Left Corinth.*

handling of ancient sources in the reconstruction of early Christianity at Corinth (see ch. 19 below). The following general outline is therefore, inevitably, subject to debate at many points of detail.

Corinth was a thriving colony when Paul arrived,[23] though there remain questions as to how the ancient Greco-Roman economy should be understood and how 'thriving' it was: some ('primitivists') stress the rudimentary and agriculturally dependent character of the economy of the Roman Empire, while others see manufacturing, trade, and commerce as playing a more significant role.[24] Donald Engels mounts a controversial argument in claiming that Roman Corinth functioned as a service city (rather than a 'consumer' city), providing a wide range of goods and services for rural residents in the *Corinthia* (the surrounding countryside, with its towns and villages, controlled by the city), for those who lived in the province of Achaia, and above all, for the many traders, travelers, and tourists who came to Corinth from all over the Mediterranean world.[25]

The Isthmian games, established in 582 B.C.E. and celebrated every two years, brought large numbers of visitors to the Corinthia. The games were second in fame only to the Olympic games and, as Engels notes, 'attracted contestants and spectators from all over the central and eastern Mediterranean, as inscriptions listing the victors in the contests show'.[26] During the period of Corinth's abandonment, the Isthmian games were placed under the supervision of Sikyon, but when the city was refounded as a Roman colony, they were returned to Corinthian control (from at least 40 B.C.E.).[27] In addition to the biennial Isthmian games, there were also the quadrennial Caesarean games and the Imperial contests. The local games have frequently been seen as the background to Paul's use of athletic metaphors in 1 Cor 9.24-27.[28]

Corinth was marked by religious variety.[29] Traditional gods and goddesses of the Greek and Roman pantheons were worshiped alongside specifically

23. D. G. Romano, 'A tale of two cities: Roman colonies at Corinth', in *Romanization and the City: Creation, Transformation, and Failures* (ed. E. Fentress; JRA Sup 38; Ann Arbor: Journal of Roman Archaeology, 2000) 83–109, has argued that the Julian colony was something of a failure and that it had to be refounded during the Flavian period (reflected in the change to the name *Colonia Iulia Flavia Augusta Corinthiensis*). However, Walbank, 'What's in a Name?', disputes Romano's claims. Far from being a declining colony, she insists, 'it was a flourishing commercial and administrative centre' (p. 261).

24. See Meggitt, *Paul, Poverty,* 41–73.

25. Engels, *Roman Corinth,* 43–65. Corinth had its own light industries that provided employment for many Corinthians: lamp and pottery manufacture, bronze manufacture, and marble sculpture. See Engels, *Roman Corinth,* 33–39.

26. Engels, *Roman Corinth,* 52.

27. The sanctuary of Poseidon and the theatre at Isthma were not built until the 50s. Prior to this, the games seem to have been held in or near Corinth itself. Cf. E. R. Gebhard, 'The Isthmian Games and the Sanctuary of Poseidon in the Early Empire', in *The Corinthia in the Roman Period* (ed. T. E. Gregory; JRA Sup 8; Ann Arbor: Journal of Roman Archaeology, 1993) 78–94.

28. E.g., Murphy-O'Connor, *St. Paul's Corinth,* 13; R. Garrison, 'Paul's Use of the Athlete Metaphor in 1 Corinthians 9', in idem, *The Graeco-Roman Context of Early Christian Literature* (JSNTSup 137; Sheffield: Sheffield Academic Press, 1997) 95–104.

29. For a discussion of the evidence, see Engels, *Roman Corinth,* 92–107. On the later period, fourth to seventh centuries C.E., see R. M. Rothaus, *Corinth: The First City of Greece* (Leiden: Brill, 2000).

Corinthian deities (the heroes Bellerophon and Melikertes), uniquely Roman gods, and oriental divinities (including Isis and Serapis). Numismatic evidence indicates the popularity of Poseidon and Aphrodite; these seem to have been the favourite divinities of many ordinary Corinthians. Both deities were connected with the sea, which was so important for Corinth's economy and trade. The isthmus of Corinth had long been associated with Poseidon, and the Isthmian games were held in his honour. The old Greek city of Corinth was known as the 'city of Aphrodite', and her status as Corinth's deity was maintained in the Roman colony. Epigraphic evidence suggests that civic religion was dominated by distinctively Roman cults, including the imperial cult.[30] Roman cults were favoured by the city's elite.

In many of its outward manifestations, the city that Paul visited and in which he founded the Corinthian church had a distinctly 'Roman' character. Mary Walbank, for example, notes that 'in layout, organisation and religious practice, Corinth was a Roman colony and not simply a restoration of a Greek city'.[31] Later, it is true, a deliberate attempt to 're-Hellenise' Corinth began in the second century C.E., during the reign of Hadrian, who sought by general policy to revive the glorious past of ancient Greece. But in the mid-first century C.E., Corinth reflected, to a very significant degree, Roman patterns both in its physical appearance and its political and cultural makeup, even if Greek language and culture remained important at the popular level.[32]

On its refounding, the city was laid out according to the Roman grid system known as 'centuriation'.[33] Older Greek buildings and foundations were incorporated into the new city, but many of the new buildings, such as the Julian basilica (built in the early 20s), were designed after Roman models. The imposing and splendid Temple E, which appears to have been erected (in the first phase of its construction) between the reigns of Augustus and Caligula, is a Roman podium-style temple.[34] It may have been the temple of the Capitoline Triad,[35] or had some other close connection with imperial cult and ideology, though its precise dedication and purpose are still debated.

The administration of the city followed a Roman colonial pattern.[36] The leading officials of the city were the two *duoviri* (chief magistrates) who were elected

30. M. E. H. Walbank, 'Evidence for the Imperial Cult in Julio-Claudian Corinth', in *Subject and Ruler: The Cult of the Ruling Power in Classical Antiquity* (ed. A. Small; JRA Sup 17; Ann Arbor; Journal of Roman Archaeology, 1996) 201–14.

31. M. E. H. Walbank, 'Pausanius, Octavia and Temple E at Corinth', *ABSA* 84 (1989) 394; cf. idem, 'Foundation and Planning of Early Roman Corinth', 95–130.

32. The *Romanitas* of Corinth is heavily emphasised by Winter (*After Paul Left Corinth*, 7–22).

33. See D. G. Romano, 'Post 146 B.C. Land Use in Corinth, and Planning of the Roman Colony of 44 B.C.E.', in *The Corinthia in the Roman Period* (ed. T. E. Gregory; JRA Sup 8; Ann Arbor: *Journal of Roman Archaeology*, 1993) 9–30; Walbank, 'Nature and Development of Roman Corinth'; idem, 'Foundation and Planning of Early Roman Corinth'.

34. Engels, *Roman Corinth*, 62.

35. As argued by Walbank, 'Pausanias, Octavia and Temple E at Corinth'.

36. See Wiseman, 'Corinth and Rome', 497–500.

annually. They were called *duoviri quinquennales* every fifth year when they were responsible for taking the census and appointing *decuriones* (councilors). In addition to the *duoviri*, two aediles were elected each year; they were responsible for maintenance of public streets and buildings and managing the commercial affairs of the city. *Decuriones* were appointed from among former holders of the offices of aedile and *duovir*. A *curator annonae* seems to have been elected irregularly to deal with food shortages. The most honoured office in the city, though, was not that of *duovir* as in other Roman colonies, but that of *agonothetes*, the president of the games.

Latin was widely used for official purposes in Corinth. According to the evidence compiled in the volume of inscriptions published in 1966 by J. H. Kent, of the 104 inscriptions produced before the reign of Hadrian, 101 are in Latin and only 3 are in Greek.[37] Subsequent investigation has only slightly modified this picture: writing in 2000, Michael Dixon reports that '[a] total of six Greek texts from Corinth can be dated prior to the reign of Hadrian, four of which deal with the Isthmian games and a fifth with an Isthmian synod'.[38] Coins minted locally were inscribed in Latin.[39] Latin thus appears to have been the formal, administrative language of Corinth. However, there is little reason to doubt that Greek was commonly spoken. Ostraca have been discovered written in Greek.[40] Moreover, lead curse tablets found in the temple of Demeter and Kore are virtually all in Greek.[41] Paul, of course, wrote to the Corinthian church in Koine Greek.

The old Greek city of Corinth—known as the city of Aphrodite—had apparently gained a reputation as a centre for sexual promiscuity. Aristophanes coined the term 'to Corinthianise' (κορινθιάζομαι, i.e., to fornicate) after the city's renown for sexual laxity.[42] Plato used the phrase 'a Corinthian girl' (Κορινθίαν κόρην) to make reference to a prostitute.[43] Strabo spoke of a thousand sacred prostitutes at the temple of Aphrodite on Acrocorinth.[44] Whether the reputation ascribed to Greek Corinth genuinely reflected the reality is another matter: the accuracy of Strabo's remark, which refers in any case to the situation pre-146 B.C.E., has certainly been sharply questioned.[45] Older commentaries on Paul's

---

37. J. H. Kent, *Corinth: Results of Excavations Conducted by the American School of Classical Studies at Athens*, vol. 8.3: *The Inscriptions 1926–1950* (Princeton; American School of Classical Studies at Athens, 1966) 18–19; Engels, *Roman Corinth*, 71 with table 12, p. 172, taken from Kent.

38. M. D. Dixon, 'A New Latin and Greek Inscription from Corinth', *Hesperia* 69 (2000) 335–42. Dixon's comment shows, of course, that there were reasons why these few inscriptions were written in Greek: their connection with the Isthmia (rather than the city of Corinth) and specifically its games.

39. Winter, *After Paul Left Corinth*, 11. The mint was closed temporarily by Vespasian and reopened under Domitian.

40. Kent, *Corinth*, 8.3:19.

41. Winter, *After Paul Left Corinth*, 168–69.

42. Aristophanes, frag. 354.

43. Plato, *Rep.* 404d; Murphy-O'Connor, *St. Paul's Corinth*, 56–57.

44. Strabo 8.6.20c

45. See, e.g., Murphy-O'Connor, *St. Paul's Corinth*, 56; Fee, *First Epistle*, 3, both of whom refer to the earlier article of H. Conzelmann, 'Korinth und die Mädchen der Aphrodite. Zur Religionsgeschichte der Stadt Korinth', *Nachrichten von der Akademie der Wissenschaften in Göttingen* 8 (1967) 247–61, repr. in H. Conzelmann, *Theologie als Schriftauslegung* (Munich: Chr. Kaiser, 1974) 152–66.

Corinthian letters often assume the correctness of these representations and apply them to the Corinth of Paul's time, depicting the city as a particular hotbed of sexual licence and vice.[46] (This image of Corinth also lingers on in popular perception and preaching.) Prostitution was certainly practiced in first-century Corinth (cf. 1 Cor 6.12–20),[47] but the service was hardly exclusive to this city in the Greco-Roman world: the lewd graffiti from brothels in Pompeii and the city's erotic art are obvious examples that attest otherwise![48] In all likelihood, then, Paul's Corinth was no more sexually promiscuous than any other cosmopolitan city in the empire.

Corinth was thus a busy and flourishing city in Paul's day (though it was not one of the great urban centres of the empire),[49] a centre of trade and commerce offering a wide range of products and services to its many visitors. Paul himself was one of these visitors, a tradesperson, brought to Corinth by his own sense of calling to spread the Christian message through the cities of the Roman Empire (cf. Rom 15.14–29; Gal 1.15–16).

2. CHRISTIANITY ARRIVES AT CORINTH

Paul clearly describes himself as the founder of the Christian church(es) in Corinth: he 'laid a foundation' on which others later built (1 Cor 3.10; cf. 3.6; 4.15; 2 Cor 10.14ff.).[50] He did not do this alone, however: it emerges from both 1 Thessalonians (probably written from Corinth during Paul's first mission there)[51] and 2 Corinthians that Silvanus and Timothy also accompanied Paul during that founding visit (1 Thess 1.1; 2 Cor 1.19).

According to Acts 18, which recounts Paul's experiences in Corinth, Paul's first point of contact in Corinth was with Aquila, a Jew, and his wife Priscilla, who worked at the same trade as Paul; they were σκηνοποιοί (Acts 18.2–3). Whether this should be understood to mean 'tentmakers', as the term is rendered in most English

46. H. L. Goudge (*The First Epistle to the Corinthians* [3rd ed.; London: Methuen, 1911] xv) writes, 'It was a city of pleasure, perhaps the most immoral city in the world'. A. Robertson and A. Plummer (*A Critical and Exegetical Commentary on the First Epistle of St Paul to the Corinthians* [2nd ed.; ICC; Edinburgh: T. & T. Clark, 1914]) are aware of the distinction between the old city and the Corinth of Paul's own day, but still speak of the 'notorious immorality of Corinth' and 'its very evil reputation' (p. xiii).

47. Cf. Plutarch, *Mor.* 768a.

48. See, e.g., N. Davies, *Europe: A History* (Oxford: Oxford University Press, 1996) 190; M. Grant et al., *Eros in Pompeii* (New York: Bonanza, 1982).

49. The city, on Paul's arrival, had not yet reached its peak; it would later become the largest city in Greece. Engels (*Roman Corinth*, 33) estimates that the population of Corinth and Lechaeum was 80,000 with a further 20,000 living in the *territorium* of Corinth. This estimate may, however, be too high. Walbank estimates between 20,000 and 50,000 for the population of Corinth in the Roman period ('Foundation and Planning of Early Roman Corinth', 107).

50. For a more detailed overview of the foundation and character of the Corinthian congregation, on which some of the following is based, see Horrell, *Social Ethos,* 73–101.

51. This is the generally accepted view; see, e.g., E. Best, *The First and Second Epistles to the Thessalonians* (BNTC; London: A. & C. Black, 1972) 7, 11; W. G. Kümmel, *Introduction to the New Testament* (London: SCM, 1975) 257–60.

translations (KJV, RSV, NRSV, etc.), or 'leatherworkers', or 'makers of stage prop-erties' (i.e., scenery for the theatre), is open to some debate.[52] It is possible that Prisca[53] and Aquila were actually converts to Christianity before Paul, since they had come to Corinth having been expelled from Rome (a church to which Paul wrote but did not himself found [cf. Rom 1.10–15; 15.18–24]) due to disturbances among Jews there because of 'Chrestus' (see below). It is intriguing to ponder whether Prisca and Aquila might have introduced Christianity to Corinth, rather than the much more famous Paul, but there is little firm evidence to substantiate this idea.

When did Paul's first visit to Corinth take place? In Acts 18 two references enable us to correlate the account with external historical evidence, and thus to date Paul's visit. The first piece of evidence is the edict of Claudius, recorded by the Roman historian Suetonius (*Claudius* 25), expelling Jews from Rome who had rioted 'at the instigation of Chrestus' (probably a Latin misspelling of *Christus*, Christ) and to which Luke refers in Acts 18.2. This edict is dated by Orosius, a fifth-century ecclesiastical historian, to 49 C.E., and, until recently, this was very widely accepted as correct.[54] The second crucial reference comes in Acts 18.12, where Gallio is named as proconsul of Achaia (the province in which Corinth was located). Fragments of an inscription found at Delphi mention Gallio as procon-sul of the province and enable his proconsulship to be dated to 50–51 or 51–52 C.E. (probably the latter).[55] On the traditional dating of Claudius's edict this fits in rather well with Luke's description of Paul's eighteen-month stay in Corinth (Acts 18.1–18): Paul would have arrived shortly after the edict—say, around 49–50 C.E.—and left during Gallio's proconsulship, probably sometime in 51–52.

While most scholars still accept (or assume) this traditional dating,[56] it has been strongly challenged by Gerd Lüdemann, who argues that Orosius's date is inaccurate, and that other earlier evidence (notably from Cassius Dio) suggests that the edict was issued in 41 C.E.[57] If Lüdemann is right, then Paul's arrival in Corinth may—but *need* not—be dated to the early 40s.[58] A decision on this mat-

52. See BDAG, 928–29, and further references there. On Paul's manual labour see esp. R. Hock, *The Social Context of Paul's Ministry: Tentmaking and Apostleship* (Philadelphia: Fortress, 1980).

53. Paul names the woman first in Rom 16.3 (and cf. 2 Tim 4.19), perhaps indicating her higher social status, or importance in the church, though this order is reversed in 1 Cor 16.19. Luke calls her Priscilla, a diminutive version of the name (Acts 18.2, 18, 26).

54. See G. Lüdemann, *Paul, Apostle to the Gentiles: Studies in Chronology* (London: SCM, 1984) 2, 164–71; Murphy-O'Connor, *St. Paul's Corinth*, 152–60.

55. See Murphy-O'Connor, *St. Paul's Corinth*, 161–69, 219–21; idem, *Paul: A Critical Life* (Oxford: Oxford University Press, 1996) 15–22.

56. E.g., Bruce Winter (*After Paul Left Corinth*, 219) and Anthony C. Thiselton (*The First Epis-tle to the Corinthians* [NIGTC; Grand Rapids: Eerdmans, 2000] 28–29) follow this position without mentioning the alternative proposal and associated arguments.

57. Lüdemann, *Paul, Apostle to the Gentiles*, 164–70; also Murphy-O'Connor, *St. Paul's Corinth*, 152–60.

58. John Knox, for example, broadly accepts Lüdemann's scheme (see J. Knox, 'Chapters in a Life of Paul—A Response to Robert Jewett and Gerd Luedemann', in *Colloquy on New Testament Stud-ies: A Time for Reappraisal and Fresh Approaches* [ed. B. Corley; Macon, Ga.: Mercer University Press, 1983] 339–64), but suggests around 43 for the arrival in Corinth (p. 358); Murphy-O'Connor accepts Lüdemann's date for the edict, but maintains the view that Paul arrived in Corinth somewhat later than the edict, at the time traditionally suggested (*St. Paul's Corinth*, 159).

ter affects not only the dating of Paul's arrival in Corinth, but also the dating of 1 Thessalonians, generally agreed to have been written from Corinth during Paul's first visit there.

In general terms, we can say a number of things about the earliest Christian congregations in Corinth with a reasonable degree of confidence, though as we shall see throughout this book, much remains open to debate. For example, it is reasonably clear that the Christians at Corinth included both Jews and Gentiles, though the latter were probably in the majority (see 1 Cor 12.2; cf. 8.7). Prisca and Aquila, along with Lucius, Jason, and Sosipater (Rom 16.21),[59] and Crispus and Sosthenes (Acts 18.2, 8, 17; 1 Cor 1.1, 14; 16.19), were probably all Jews, and Paul's illustration in 1 Cor 7.18–19 also strongly implies a Jewish presence among the congregation, since otherwise it would have been without significance to them. Other literary evidence confirms the presence of Jews in Corinth at Paul's time (Philo, *Legat.* 281). And soon afterward, in the late 60s C.E., large numbers of enslaved Jews—six thousand according to Josephus—captured by Vespasian in the Jewish War in Palestine, were apparently brought to the region to assist with Nero's project to dig a canal through the Isthmus (see fig. 1, p. 44). When this project was abandoned, these slaves would probably have been sold in local slave markets, so many may have ended up in Corinth or its surrounding areas.[60] But although Luke mentions a synagogue in Corinth at the time of Paul's arrival there (Acts 18.4), archaeologists have yet to discover evidence confirming a Jewish presence in Corinth in the first century C.E.: both the lintel inscription reading [ΣΥΝΑ]ΓΩΓΗ ΕΒΡ[ΑΙΩΝ] ('synagogue of the Hebrews') and the capital from a half-column with three *menorot* and other Jewish symbols (palm branches and citron) date from considerably later, probably from the fifth century C.E. (see pictures, pp. 46–47).[61]

59. Romans is generally agreed to have been written by Paul from Corinth, so the people who send greetings in the final chapter are members of the Corinthian churches (Rom 16.21–23).

60. Josephus, *War* 3.539–40: 'Vespasian followed in due course and had them all removed to the stadium. He then gave orders for the execution of the old and unserviceable, to the number of twelve hundred; from the youths he selected six thousand of the most robust and sent them to Nero at the isthmus'.

61. For the synagogue inscription, see B. D. Meritt, *Corinth: Results of Excavations Conducted by the American School of Classical Studies at Athens,* vol 8.1: *Greek Inscriptions, 1896–1927* (Cambridge: Harvard University Press, 1931) §111, pp. 78–79; for the column piece, see R. L. Scranton, *Corinth: Results of Excavations Conducted by the American School of Classical Studies at Athens,* vol. 16: *Mediaeval Architecture in the Central Area of Corinth* (Princeton: American School of Classical Studies at Athens, 1957) 116 n. 130, who dates the capital to the fifth century. On both pieces see also F.-J. de Waele, *Corinthe et Saint Paul* (Paris: Albert Guillot, 1961) 174, 196. De Waele suggests that the synagogue inscription dates from the fifth century. The synagogue inscription is often mentioned as relevant evidence for Paul's time, sometimes with a rather vague comment about the problems of dating. See, e.g., G. A. Deissmann, *Light from the Ancient East* (ET London: Hodder & Stoughton, 1927) 13 n. 7; C. K. Barrett, *The First Epistle to the Corinthians* (BNTC; London: A. & C. Black, 1971) 2.

Dr. Nancy Bookides, Assistant Director of the Corinth Excavations, also told us of a Jewish cooking pot that had been found in the excavations northeast of the theatre but not published. The pot was recognised as Jewish by Dr. Barbara Johnson because of the construction: lid and pot were originally joined together at one edge. The purchaser thus knew the pot had not been used to cook in before, and snapped the last join of lid to pot before using it.

It is difficult to estimate with any precision the size of the Corinthian Christian community around the time of 1 Corinthians. Counting the names Paul mentions establishes a minimum, and allowing for unnamed members of households, children, slaves, and so on, Murphy-O'Connor makes a plausible estimate of somewhere 'between forty and fifty persons as a base figure'.[62] But much remains unknown: What proportion of the congregation is mentioned by name in Paul's letters? How many different groups met, and from what area did the groups come together when 'the whole church' met at Gaius's house (Rom 16.23)? Were all of these Christian groups based in Corinth itself, or were they also based in Lechaeum and Cenchreae, Corinth's two ports and likely places for Paul and others to arrive, especially, of course, if they came by ship (see fig. 1, p. 44)? There was certainly a Christian group based in Cenchreae, since Paul mentions Phoebe, a minister (διάκονος) of this congregation, in Rom 16.1–2. Furthermore, 2 Corinthians (probably a composite letter; see below) is addressed to 'the church (ἐκκλησία) of God which is in Corinth, with all the saints who are in the whole of Achaia' (2 Cor 1.1; cf. Rom 15.26; 1 Cor 16.15; 2 Cor 9.2; 11.10; 1 Thess 1.7–8). We simply do not know to what extent there were groups of Christians elsewhere in the province, but this address clearly indicates, as does the reference to Phoebe, that they were not only within the city of Corinth itself.

Despite the various uncertainties, we can be reasonably sure that the early Christians met in private homes, since Paul makes a number of references to the church in so-and-so's house (Rom 16.5; 1 Cor 16.19; Phlmn 2; cf. Col 4.15), and there shared their common meal, known as the Lord's Supper (1 Cor 11.20; cf. Acts 2.46), and worshiped together (see 1 Cor 12–14).[63] Some have suggested that meetings may have been held in 'a purpose built "club-room"', like those used for meetings by clubs and voluntary associations (*collegia*), but in the absence of concrete evidence to support this suggestion it can only remain a possibility.[64] On the other hand, even when we accept the literary evidence suggesting that meetings took place in private homes, there remain questions as to what kind of houses we should imagine the Christians meeting in; we have no concrete archaeological evidence of specifically Christian activity or meeting places in the first century at Corinth. Should we imagine the congregation meeting in a villa,[65] or in a small unit within a tenement block,[66] or in a shop or

---

62. Murphy-O'Connor, *St. Paul's Corinth*, 182.

63. On the household context of the early churches, see further C. Osiek and D. L. Balch, *Families in the New Testament World: Households and House Churches* (Louisville: Westminster John Knox, 1997); H.-J. Klauck, *Hausgemeinde und Hauskirche im frühen Christentum* (SBS 103; Stuttgart: Katholisches Bibelwerk, 1981); Barton, 'Paul's Sense of Place'.

64. C. S. de Vos, *Church and Community Conflicts: The Relationships of the Thessalonian, Corinthian, and Philippian Churches with Their Wider Civic Communities* (SBLDS 168; Atlanta: Scholars Press, 1999) 204–5.

65. So, e.g., Murphy-O'Connor, *St. Paul's Corinth*, 178–85 (see ch. 9 below).

66. Cf. R. Jewett, 'Tenement Churches and Communal Meals in the Early Church: The Implications of a Form-Critical Analysis of 2 Thessalonians 3:10', *BR* 38 (1993) 23–43; Meggitt, *Paul, Poverty*, 63–65.

workshop (or the domestic space behind or above such units)?[67] Our answer to this question depends to some extent on much debated questions about the social and economic level of the members of these congregations (see further chs. 6, 9, 17, and 19 below).

While much therefore remains unknown and open to debate, it is worth reminding ourselves that we are better informed about the church at Corinth than about any other, in the earliest years of Christianity.[68] We should not necessarily assume, however, that the Corinthian churches were by any means typical: John Barclay, in the essay extracted below (ch. 14), argues that the Corinthian and Thessalonian communities were quite different in character and theological outlook.[69] We are particularly well informed—or, perhaps one should say, less poorly informed, given the general paucity of evidence—about Christianity at Corinth in part because the extensive archaeological studies of Roman Corinth enable a comparatively full picture to be built up of the context in which the Corinthian Christians lived.[70] But the relatively large amount of information available is also, indeed largely, due to the nature and extent of Paul's correspondence with this particular church, though not all of this correspondence is extant. First Corinthians is not Paul's first letter to the Corinthians: he refers in 1 Cor 5.9 to an earlier letter, now almost certainly lost.[71] The Corinthians also wrote a letter to Paul, asking about various matters, to which Paul replies in 1 Corinthians (1 Cor 7.1). And after 1 Corinthians Paul wrote a 'painful letter', or 'letter of tears', to which he refers in 2 Cor 2.4–9 and 7.8–12, following a visit to Corinth that involved a painful and angry confrontation with some individual and led to Paul's withdrawal (2 Cor 1.23—2.11; 7.12). This painful letter may be lost, or may be largely preserved in 2 Cor 10–13.[72] The early chapters of 2 Corinthians then reflect the reconciliation that seems to have been achieved after the painful visit and letter. Many scholars think that the canonical 2 Corinthians contains at least two letters, chs. 1–9 and 10–13 seemingly reflecting two quite different situations. Some argue for a more complex partition of the letter (and in some cases, of 1 Corinthians too) and thus reconstruct a larger number of letters sent from Paul to Corinth.[73] If 2 Cor 10–13 is to be identified as the painful letter, then it was written before 2 Cor 1–9; if not, and if it was not part of the same letter as

---

67. Cf. Meggitt, *Paul, Poverty*, 65, further 62–67.

68. Cf. G. Schöllgen, 'Was wissen wir über die Sozialstruktur der paulinischen Gemeinden?' *NTS* 34 (1988) 71–82; here p. 74.

69. J. M. G. Barclay, 'Thessalonica and Corinth: Social Contrasts in Pauline Christianity', *JSNT* 47 (1992) 49–74, reprinted in *New Testament Interpretation and Methods* (ed. S. E. Porter and C. Evans; Sheffield: Sheffield Academic Press, 1997) 267–92.

70. On the history of the excavations, see above, §1.

71. It is sometimes suggested that a portion of it may be preserved in 2 Cor 6.14–7.1; see, e.g., Hurd, *Origin*, 135–37.

72. For an argument to this effect, see Horrell, *Social Ethos*, 296–312.

73. See, e.g., N. H. Taylor, 'The Composition and Chronology of Second Corinthians', *JSNT* 44 (1991) 67–87; G. Bornkamm, 'The History of the Origin of the So-Called Second Letter to the Corinthians', *NTS* 8 (1962) 258–64; Schmithals, *Gnosticism*.

chs. 1–9,[74] then, as many commentators argue, it represents a later letter still, written in response to a fresh outbreak of trouble after the apparent reconciliation for which 2 Cor 1–7 gives thanks.

Especially in 1 Corinthians, written in the early 50s in response to both oral and written communication from Corinth (1 Cor 1.11; 7.1; 11.18, etc.),[75] Paul addresses a wide range of issues in the life of the church there: factions, litigation, sexual morality, food offered to idols, spiritual gifts, and so on. This letter in particular thus provides a unique window onto the life of an early Christian community. The window, though, is hardly transparent; the picture that emerges owes much to the particular perspective of the scholar who engages in the construction of that picture. The evidence is worse than secondhand: it comes to us from a letter of Paul, written in response to information passed to him by the Corinthians. We have only one side of the conversation, as it were, and to understand it we must guess (intelligently, one hopes) at some of the things said from the other side. Moreover, any historical reconstruction inevitably reflects the perspective and convictions (implicit or explicit) of the historian. It is clear enough that the Corinthian community faced various kinds of division and tension, and a range of problematic issues, but the nature and causes of these problems are, as we shall see, subject to much debate.

3. FERDINAND CHRISTIAN BAUR (1792–1860): THE DIVISIONS AT CORINTH AND THEIR SIGNIFICANCE FOR THE HISTORY OF EARLY CHRISTIANITY

It is not difficult to determine a point at which to begin an investigation of the history of modern scholarly study of Corinthian Christianity: the publication in 1831 of F. C. Baur's lengthy essay on 'the Christ-party in the Corinthian community, the opposition of Petrine and Pauline Christianity in the early church, the apostle Peter in Rome'.[76] Admittedly, Baur draws on earlier works in his own study, and there is of course a long history of commentary on 1 Corinthians, from the early church onward. But Baur's essay forms a major landmark in the modern, critical study of the divisions in the church at Corinth, and in early Christianity

74. For arguments in favour of the unity of canonical 2 Corinthians, a minority position, see, e.g., P. Barnett, *The Second Epistle to the Corinthians* (NICNT; Grand Rapids: Eerdmans, 1997) 15–25; A. M. G. Stephenson, 'Partition Theories on II Corinthians', in *Studia Evangelica* 2 (ed. F. L. Cross; TU 87; Berlin: Akademie, 1964) 639–46; idem, 'A Defence of the Integrity of 2 Corinthians', in K. Aland et al., *The Authorship and Integrity of the New Testament* (London: SPCK, 1965) 82–97.

75. On the traditional dating, around 2–3 years pass between Paul's founding visit and the writing of 1 Corinthians, generally placed around 53–55 C.E. (see, e.g., Barrett, *First Epistle*, 5; Kümmel, *Introduction to the New Testament*, 279). Lüdemann dates 1 Corinthians to either 49 or 52 C.E., 8–11 years after the founding visit in 41 C.E. (Lüdemann, *Paul, Apostle to the Gentiles*, 263).

76. Baur, 'Die Christuspartei', repr. in F. C. Baur, *Historisch-kritische Untersuchungen zum Neuen Testament* (Ausgewählte Werke 1; Stuttgart-Bad Cannstatt: Friedrich Frommann, 1963) 1–146. See also the introduction to ch. 1 below, with suggestions for further reading there.

more generally. Indeed, the Tübingen school, of which Baur was the leading figure, was and remains enormously influential, 'the central point', Horton Harris claims, 'of nineteenth-century Biblical research'.[77]

The launching point for Baur's argument was the report concerning the 'parties' among the Christians at Corinth, whose slogans Paul reports in 1 Cor 1.12: 'I am of Paul, but I am of Apollos, etc. . . . .' Baur argues that these four slogans actually represent an essentially twofold division, between Paul and Apollos on the one hand, and Peter (Cephas) and Christ on the other. Crucial to Baur's case is his argument concerning the 'Christ' party. Baur argues that the slogan 'I am of Christ' reflects the view of the Jewish Christians that the Christ, the Messiah, belonged especially to them, and their claim that their authority depended upon a direct link with Christ, embodied especially in their chief apostle, Peter. Hence '[t]hey called themselves τοὺς Κηφᾶ ["those of Cephas"], because Peter held the primacy among the Jewish Apostles, but τοὺς Χριστοῦ ["those of Christ"], because they relied on the direct connection with Christ as the chief token of genuine apostolic authority' (p. 57 below). The Judaizers' attack on Paul, then, evident from the terms in which Paul defends himself in both the Corinthian letters (e.g., 1 Cor 9.1ff.; 2 Cor 10–13), was that he was not a genuine apostle, not truly 'of Christ' (τοῦ Χριστοῦ). The basic cause of the conflict and division at Corinth, then, was the tension and disagreement between Jewish Christians, linked with Peter, and Pauline Christians, who followed Paul's critical stance toward the law.

Baur's theory concerning the divisions at Corinth is important not only as an argument concerning the nature of the problems at Corinth. His view of the twofold division at Corinth formed the basis for a much wider theory about early Christian history. This history, Baur proposed, was dominated by an early opposition between Pauline (Gentile) Christianity and Petrine (Jewish) Christianity that was eventually reconciled in the synthesis of second-century catholic Christianity. In his works subsequent to the 1831 article, Baur sought to elaborate this thesis, placing the New Testament and other early Christian writings 'on this bilinear model of the development according to their Jewish or Gentile Christian provenance and their stage in the process of reconciliation'.[78] The terms in which Baur developed this theory, specifically the idea of a dialectic between thesis and antithesis leading to synthesis as history progresses, owe much to the philosophy of G. W. F. Hegel (1770–1831), by whom Baur was influenced, and in whose work Baur found a philosophical framework with which he could make sense of the details of early Christian history.[79] There is some debate as to whether Hegel influenced Baur at the time of the original 'Christ party' essay, but Baur certainly adopted a Hegelian perspective soon after that time, in writings dating from 1833

77. H. Harris, *The Tübingen School* (Oxford: Clarendon, 1975) 1; cf. p. v.

78. Morgan, 'Tübingen School', 711.

79. See further Harris, *Tübingen School*, 155–58; P. Addinall, 'Why Read the Bible?' *ExpTim* 105 (1994) 136–40.

to 1835.[80] To some extent both the appeal and the weakness of Baur's work lie here. He offers a grand theory that seeks to make sense of the range of texts and arguments within early Christianity, and to show how in the movement of history a synthesis emerged; this framework thus seems to give a clear and comprehensible picture within which one can understand not only the problems at Corinth, but also the whole sweep of early Christian history. However, it is perhaps precisely in this grand theory that some of the problems lie, since the theory may be accused both of ignoring the true diversity of texts and arguments within early Christianity and also of reading its particular theme of conflict into situations where it seems not to be evident.[81]

Indeed, an alternative thesis about the Corinthian situation and the Christ party was presented in 1908 by W. Lütgert, who argued precisely against Baur's twofold division between Paul and the Jewish-Christian 'nomists'. What Baur failed to see, Lütgert suggested, was that the apostolic church faced opposition from two sides, from the Jewish-Christian law-observers on one side, and from the antinomian, libertine Gnostics, the 'spiritual enthusiasts' (Schwarmgeister), on the other.[82] It is these 'enthusiasts' (Schwärmer), Lütgert argued, who formed the Christ party at Corinth and who consitituted the opposition to Paul there. Although Lütgert is rather less frequently cited than Baur, this view of Paul's opposition at Corinth has also been prominent in subsequent research (see further §4 below).[83]

Also a feature of Baur's work, and that of the Tübingen school which he led, was the radical criticism of the New Testament and early Christian documents, with many of these texts regarded as pseudonymous and as written much later than was (and is) conventionally thought.[84] In part this may be seen as influenced

---

80. Harris, *Tübingen School*, 26.

81. Cf. Harris, *Tübingen School*, 258: 'Baur *forced* the [New Testament] books into the framework by manipulating the facts and distorting the evidence, by emphasizing the details which harmonized with his views while omitting everything which did not.' Also S. Neill and N. T. Wright, *The Interpretation of the New Testament 1861–1986* (Oxford: Oxford University Press, 1988) 20–30. For more sympathetic evaluations, see Addinall, 'Why Read the Bible?' and Morgan, 'Tübingen School'.

82. Lütgert, *Freiheitspredigt*. Introducing his argument, Lütgert writes: 'Allein der Apostelkreis hatte Gegner auf beiden Seiten. Auf der einen Seite standen die Vertreter des Gesetzes, aber auf der andern Seite stand von Anfang an ein Feind, der diesem ersten diametral gegenüberstand: die Verdreher der Freiheitspredigt. Die Gemeinde stand zwischen Nomisten und Antinomisten, so wie die Reformatoren zwischen der alten Kirche und den Schwärmern' (pp. 7–8).

83. For example, Murphy-O'Connor sees Paul's opponents in 2 Corinthians as '*pneumatikoi*', spiritual people: J. Murphy-O'Connor, 'Pneumatikoi in 2 Corinthians', *Proceedings of the Irish Biblical Association* 11 (1987) 59–66; idem, *The Theology of Paul's Second Letter to the Corinthians* (Cambridge: Cambridge University Press, 1991).

84. See the summary in Harris, *Tübingen School*, 237, 259–62. Note, for example, the influence of this criticism on Friedrich Engels, for whom the work of the Tübingen school leaves the book of Revelation, dated to around 68 C.E., as 'the oldest, and the only, book of the New Testament, the authenticity of which cannot be disputed', and therefore as the most important source with which to define early Christianity (F. Engels, 'On the Book of Revelation' [1883] 207; cf. also 'On the History of Early Christianity' [1894–95] 320–33; in K. Marx and F. Engels, *On Religion* [Moscow: Foreign Languages Publishing House, 1957]), or, conversely, the stinging criticism of Heinrich Merz, from 1845 (quoted in Harris, *Tübingen School*, 6–7).

by Baur's desire to fit the texts into his grand theoretical schema, but his approach is also fundamentally shaped by a desire to approach the documents of early Christianity free from the constraints of ecclesiastical dogma, and to subject them to rational, historical, scientific criticism.[85]

In terms of the use of sources, the reader of Baur's work will notice that his primary sources are mostly early Christian writings themselves: in contrast to much more recent sociohistorical work, there is no attempt, for example, to construct a context for understanding the Corinthian church from ancient non-Christian Greek and Latin writers, despite Baur's knowledge of these classical texts.[86] Archaeological excavations only began at Corinth toward the end of the nineteenth century (see §1 above), so Baur did not of course have access to any such material directly relevant to his investigation.

Baur's work, and that of the Tübingen school as a whole, was highly controversial in its own time, and drew criticism then and in subsequent decades.[87] While some objected to the rationalistic, even atheistic, approach Baur and his colleagues took, more telling criticisms, perhaps, focused on the historical conclusions to which Baur had come. For example, J. B. Lightfoot blew a significant hole in Baur's reconstruction by demonstrating the authenticity of the letters of Ignatius; and many of Baur's very late datings for New Testament writings have also been subsequently undermined.[88] Nevertheless, many subsequent essays on the divisions at Corinth, throughout the twentieth century, have taken Baur's arguments as their starting point, though they have often sought to demonstrate why Baur was wrong.[89] Some contemporary scholars, however, notably Michael Goulder, continue to argue that something like Baur's view of the division between Petrine and Pauline Christianities makes best sense of the evidence at Corinth and elsewhere.[90] Consequently, even though Baur's views are now more often rejected than accepted, he continues to influence the agenda for studies of Corinth and of early Christian history generally.

4. CORINTHIAN 'THEOLOGY':
RELIGIOUS AND PHILOSOPHICAL PARALLELS

In the late nineteenth and early twentieth centuries, a new movement developed in the study of biblical literature. Known as the *religionsgeschichtliche Schule* ('the history of religions school'), the main aims of scholars involved in this group were

---

85. See further Harris, *Tübingen School*, 1, 241–42, etc.
86. Cf. Harris, *Tübingen School*, 18–19.
87. On Baur and the Tübingen school, and criticism of the work of the school, see esp. Harris, *Tübingen School*; Neill, *Interpretation*, 20–64; W. G. Kümmel, *The New Testament: The History of the Investigation of Its Problems* (London: SCM, 1973) 120–205.
88. See Harris, *Tübingen School*, 213–16, 261–62; further Neill, *Interpretation*, 35–64.
89. See, e.g., chs. 2, 5, and 10 below.
90. See ch. 13 below, and suggestions for further reading there.

to further the historical understanding of early Christianity by studying it in the light of its wider religious context, both Jewish and Hellenistic. This involved doing something that has become a standard method of historical research but which was controversial at the time: exploring the parallels between biblical texts and a wide range of noncanonical, non-Christian sources.[91] In contrast to more recent work on Christianity at Corinth, earlier work influenced by this *religionsgeschichtliche* approach focused on the specifically *religious* parallels rather than the wider context of social and political life in the Roman empire.

First Corinthians gives us various indications of the Corinthians' views. Most scholars agree that at various points in the letter, Paul cites Corinthian opinions or 'slogans' ('All things are lawful', 6.12; 10.23; 'Food for the stomach and the stomach for food', 6.13; 'It is well for a man not to touch a woman', 7.1; 'All of us possess knowledge (γνῶσις)', 8.1; 'No idol in the world really exists. . . . There is no God but one', 8.4; 'There is no resurrection of the dead', 15.12). Also, many accept that we can deduce Corinthian theological interests and attitudes from Paul's various critical remarks in the letter. So we may infer, for example, that the Corinthians, or some of them, thought highly of their 'wisdom' (σοφία, 1.18—3.23); that they considered themselves 'spiritual people' (πνευματικοί) and 'perfect' or 'complete' (τέλειοι), while viewing others as merely 'natural people' (ψυχικοί; cf. 2.6—3.3); that they were zealous for 'spiritual things/gifts' (πνευματικά, 14.1, 12, 37), above all 'speaking in tongues' (γλώσσαις λαλοῦντες).[92] What the slogans and watchwords mean and whether and how they fit together is heavily disputed, however. Many scholars have felt, though, that they form a consistent set of ideas and values and that this theological perspective underlies most, if not all, of the problems and controversies that Paul addresses in the letter.

Probably the most influential attempt to relate Corinthian 'theology' to particular religious and philosophical traditions has been the concern to note parallels with 'Gnosticism'. A number of scholars writing in the nineteenth century noted what they perceived as Gnostic ideas and tendencies among the Corinthian Christians. For example, F. L. Godet in his commentary on 1 Corinthians identified the alleged Christ party of 1 Cor 1.12 as 'Gnostics before Gnosticism'.[93] However, it was W. Lütgert, in the landmark study mentioned above, who developed such observations into a comprehensive theory of the nature of Paul's conflict at Corinth.[94] In direct opposition to Baur, Lütgert maintained that Paul was not battling against Jewish-Christian nomists at Corinth, but rather fighting against an assault from the other direction, from a group of 'pneumatic libertines'

---

91. See R. Morgan with J. Barton, *Biblical Interpretation* (Oxford: Oxford University Press, 1988) 124–29; Kümmel, *New Testament*, 206–25. For a brief overview, see R. Morgan, 'History of Religions School', in *Dictionary of Biblical Interpretation* (ed. R. J. Coggins and J. L. Houlden; London: SCM, 1990) 291–92.

92. For a helpful summary of Corinthian emphases, see Barclay, ch. 14 below, pp. 187–91.

93. F. L. Godet, *Commentary on St. Paul's First Epistle to the Corinthians*, vol. 1 (Clark's Foreign Theological Library, new series; Edinburgh: T. & T. Clark, 1898) 77. Cf. vol. 2 (1898), pp. 184–87.

94. Lütgert, *Frieheitspredigt*. A brief summary is given in Schmithals, *Gnosticism*, 120–2.

akin to the second-century Gnostics. In Lütgert's view, Corinthian Gnosticism developed as a corruption of Paul's gospel of freedom under Hellenistic influence. A. Schlatter, in a study published a few years after Lütgert's, similary argued that the Corinthian theology was Gnostic-like in character.[95] According to Schlatter, however, the heretical theology did not stem from Paul's own teaching, but was introduced into the Corinthian church by Jewish teachers from outside.

The interpretation of Corinthian Christianity in Gnostic terms was fueled by a growing scholarly belief that Gnosticism was a pre-Christian movement. The idea that Gnosticism was an identifiable religious phenomenon prior to and concurrent with earliest Christianity was vigorously promoted by the history of religions school in the early decades of the twentieth century. The thesis was accepted by Rudolf Bultmann and many of his pupils. It was one of Bultmann's students, Walter Schmithals, in his detailed study, *Gnosticism at Corinth*, a revision of doctoral work conducted under Bultmann (first published in 1956),[96] who gave the Gnostic explanation of Christianity at Corinth its best-known scholarly presentation (see ch. 3 below). On Schmithals's reading, virtually every 'problem' with which Paul deals in the course of his Corinthian correspondence sprang from a Gnostic source.[97] Like Schlatter, Schmithals understood the heresy to have been brought into the community by Jewish false teachers. Through an elaborate 'mirror-reading' of Paul's Corinthian letters,[98] Schmithals reconstructed the elements of a coherent Gnostic theology: a docetic Christology (expressed in the formula 'Jesus be cursed' in 1 Cor 12.3), which drew a sharp distinction between the human Jesus and the heavenly Christ; the rejection of the cross as a feature of the scheme of salvation (cf. 1 Cor 1.17—2.5); a belief in a higher 'wisdom' available only to those who are 'spiritual/pneumatic' (1 Cor 2.6—3.1); a radical devaluation of the physical body and fleshly human nature (1 Cor 6.12–30; 15); the belief that the pneumatic individual has liberty in matters of sex and food (1 Cor 5; 6.12–20; 8–10);[99] and a Gnostic eschatology, the goal of which is the redemption of the individual from the physical body. Whether the Corinthians also held to the Gnostic heavenly redeemer myth (the descent of the heavenly saviour through the aeons) was a point of contention between Schmithals and Ulrich Wilckens, another scholar who argued for a full-scale Gnosticism at Corinth.[100]

95. A. Schlatter, *Die korinthische Theologie* (BFCT, 18/2; Gütersloh, 1914). See summary in Schmithals, *Gnosticism*, 122–23.

96. Schmithals, *Gnosticism*.

97. For Schmithals, all of Paul's opponents, even those in Thessalonica and Galatia, were Gnostics. See W. Schmithals, *Paul and the Gnostics* (ET Nashville: Abingdon, 1972).

98. According to Schmithals, the two canonical Corinthian letters comprise six separate letters (Epistles A, B, C, D, E, F), reflecting different stages of unfolding developments at Corinth. For methodological reflections on 'mirror-reading', see J. M. G. Barclay, 'Mirror-Reading a Polemical Letter: Galatians as a Test Case', *JSNT* 31 (1987) 73–93.

99. Schmithals (*Gnosticism*, 230–37) argues that 1 Cor 7 provides no evidence of ascetic tendencies at Corinth. Paul's Gnostic opponents were libertines, not ascetics.

100. U. Wilckens, *Weisheit und Torheit* (Tübingen: Mohr, 1959). Cf. idem, 'σοφία', *TDNT* 7:519–22.

Wilckens claimed that 1 Cor 2.6ff. reflects such a redeemer-myth schema, but this was doubted by Schmithals.[101]

In the 1960s and 1970s, the idea of a pre-Christian Gnosticism was subjected to intense criticism. The notion, as articulated by the history of religions school, was shown to be a scholarly construct derived from an indiscriminate and historically insensitive use of primary sources. Scholars such as Robin Wilson insisted that there was no real evidence to justify talk of Gnosticism in the first century.[102] The collapse in scholarly confidence in the concept of pre-Christian Gnosticism meant that it could no longer be invoked as a possible *source* for Corinthian belief and action.[103] Schmithals's analysis of Corinthian Christianity in terms of Gnosticism came to be regarded by most critics as an anachronistic and speculative reading of the evidence on the basis of a highly dubious historical assumption.

Even so, up until quite recently, many scholars, including Gerd Theissen,[104] whose work initiated the latest phase of the quest for Paul's church at Corinth (see §6 and ch. 6 below), were happy to identify the theological outlook of the Corinthians (or in Theissen's case, the Corinthians from the higher social stratum) as 'Gnostic', or 'proto-Gnostic'. Impressed by the similarities between Corinthian emphases and the views of later 'Gnostics' (interest in wisdom and knowledge, a superior attitude, anthropological dualism, a liberal position on eating meat sacrificed to idols), such interpreters felt that it was still appropriate to use the term 'Gnosticism' or 'incipient Gnosticism' to describe Corinthian religiosity. Wilson himself maintained that 'what we have in Corinth . . . is not yet Gnosticism, but a kind of *gnosis*'.[105] According to Wilson, we find in Corinthian Christianity the beginnings of what was later to develop into full-scale Gnosticism.

In more recent scholarship, the heuristic value of the terms 'Gnosticism', 'incipient Gnosticism', or 'gnosis' as applied to Corinthian Christianity has been seriously questioned. Dale Martin, for example, points out that the specific features that the Corinthians share with later 'Gnostics' were ubiquitous in the first century: 'one could say that anyone in the first century who held certain philosophical ideas (deprecation of the body, some form of anthropological dualism) was a proto-Gnostic, but this brings one no closer to a historical reconstruction of their social location'.[106] The past decade or so has thus witnessed a sharp decline in the use of the term 'Gnostic' or 'proto-Gnostic' with reference to the

---

101. Schmithals, *Gnosticism*, 138–41.

102. R. McL. Wilson, 'Gnosis at Corinth', in *Paul and Paulinsim: Essays in Honour of C. K. Barrett* (ed. M. D. Hooker and S. G. Wilson; London: SPCK, 1982) 102–19. However, ongoing research into the origins of Gnosticism keeps open the possibility of pre-Christian roots for the phenomenon, perhaps in some branch or form of Judaism (see n. 110 below for references).

103. Conzelmann, *1 Corinthians*, 15.

104. Theissen, *Social Setting*, 132–37. He writes on p. 132, 'Even if the speculative fantasies of later Gnostics cannot be imputed to the Corinthian "gnostics", as they certainly cannot, neither can the parallels between the two be ignored.'

105. Wilson, 'Gnosis', 112. Cf. R. McL. Wilson, 'How Gnostic were the Corinthians?' *NTS* 19 (1972–3) 65–74.

106. Martin, *Corinthian Body*, 71.

Corinthians and scholars have sought other ways, or looked to other sources, to describe and explain aspects of the Corinthians' outlook, often looking outside the realm of specifically religious parallels to the wider Greco-Roman context. Peter Marshall, for example, characterises the Corinthians as 'hybrists': boastful people who considered themselves superior to others.[107]

Research on Gnosticism has taken a new turn with the appearance of Michael A. Williams's *Rethinking 'Gnosticism': An Argument for Dismantling a Dubious Category*.[108] Williams maintains that 'Gnosticism' is more a scholarly stereotype than a real historical phenomenon, a label that serves to classify as one movement groups and texts that are actually rather diverse. He points out that many of the texts and groups usually regarded as 'Gnostic' do not display the set of common characteristics alleged by scholars to be typical of Gnosticism. He argues that we should speak not of 'Gnosticism' but of 'biblical demiurgical traditions', since the essential feature of writings and movements branded 'Gnostic' is the use of biblical sources in developing the key contrast between the creator-deity and the supreme god. At the very least, this problematises any attempt to use 'Gnosticism' or 'proto-Gnosticism' as a descriptive category for Corinthian theology.[109]

The use of Gnosticism as a background to explain the Corinthians' theology has therefore fallen very much into the background, and Williams's book may contribute further to the demise of the label. However, one should note that Williams's thesis has by no means found widespread acceptance. Moreover, many scholars of Gnosticism would continue to see the phenomenon as having pre-Christian roots in Judaism, even if Gnosticism itself appears as a distinct movement only in the Christian era.[110]

When the notion of a pre-Christian Gnosticism became a questionable (and for many, untenable) basis on which to explain Corinthian Christianity, several scholars, most notably Richard Horsley, attempted to find the background to Corinthian theological perspectives in 'Hellenistic Judaism'.[111] The Corinthians'

---

107. P. Marshall, *Enmity in Corinth: Social Conventions in Paul's Relations with the Corinthians* (WUNT 2.23; Tübingen: Mohr Siebeck, 1987).

108. M. A. Williams, *Rethinking 'Gnosticism': An Argument for Dismantling a Dubious Category* (Princeton: Princeton University Press, 1996).

109. Clearly Corinthian Christianity could not be described as a 'biblical demiurgical' movement, in Williams's terms, since there is no evidence to suggest they drew a distinction between the world-maker and the highest god (cf. 1 Cor 8.4–6). But for a recent attempt at a comparison between 1 Corinthians and certain 'Gnostic' texts, notably the *Gospel of Philip*, in the light of Williams's work, see T. E. Klutz, 'Re-reading 1 Corinthians after *Rethinking "Gnosticism"*,' *JSNT* 26 (2003) 193–216.

110. See, e.g., B. A. Pearson, *Gnosticism, Judaism, and Egyptian Christianity* (Minneapolis: Fortress, 1990); P. Perkins, *Gnosticism and the New Testament* (Minneapolis: Fortress, 1993).

111. R. A. Horsley, 'Pneumatikos vs. Psychikos: Distinctions of Spiritual Status among the Corinthians', *HTR* 69 (1976) 269–88; idem, 'Consciousness and Freedom among the Corinthians: 1 Corinthians 8–10', *CBQ* 40 (1978) 574–89; idem, 'How can some of you say there is no resurrection of the dead?' Spiritual Elitism in Corinth', *NovT* 20 (1978) 203–31; idem, 'Gnosis in Corinth', *NTS* 27 (1981) 32–51; J. A. Davis, *Wisdom and Spirit: An Investigation of 1 Corinthians 1.18–3.20 against the Background of Jewish Sapiential Traditions in the Greco-Roman Period* (Lanham, New York, London: University Press of America, 1984); B. A. Pearson, *The Pneumatikos-Psychikos Terminology in 1 Corinthians* (SBLDS 12; Atlanta: Scholars Press, 1973).

enthusiasm for wisdom and knowledge seemed an obvious connection with Hellenistic Judaism, with its speculation about and veneration of wisdom, as exemplified in the *Wisdom of Solomon*. Horsley, in a series of articles published in the 1970s and 1980s, pointed to a number of parallels to Corinthian theology, including the distinction between '*pneumatikos*' and '*psychikos*', in Hellenistic Judaism as represented, above all, by Philo. In the article excerpted in this volume (ch. 8), he argues for Hellenistic-Jewish influence on the Corinthian '*gnosis*' of 1 Cor 8.1–6.

But Horsley's approach too has come under criticism. His dependence on Philo for reconstructing 'Hellenistic Judaism' is problematic. The extent to which Philo was representative of a distinct and unified 'Hellenistic-Jewish' theological movement and ethos is debatable. Also, as John Barclay has pointed out, 'the purported parallels [to Corinthian views] from Philo are from passages where Philo strives to interpret the biblical text in terms drawn from Stoic or Platonic philosophy'.[112] Without supposing any direct Philonic influence on Corinthian Christianity, Barclay argues, it is possible to assume that the Corinthians were making similar hermeneutical moves to Philo, interpreting 'Jewish' traditions as taught by Paul in terms of Greco-Roman cultural categories. As to the Corinthian interest in wisdom, much recent scholarship has moved away from locating it against a Jewish background and has connected it instead with Greco-Roman rhetoric (cf. 1 Cor 2.1–5).[113] As Johannes Munck pointed out many years ago, it is striking that in 1 Cor 1.22, Paul associates Corinthian wisdom with *Greek* cultural values, not Jewish concerns.

The concern to find a 'source' for the distinctive elements of Corinthian theology and practice reflected (and criticised) in Paul's letters has therefore turned to Greco-Roman philosophy, though there is considerable debate as to which of the available philosophies, if any, were most influential on the Corinthians. Johannes Weiss, in his commentary on 1 Corinthians published over ninety years ago, argued that the Corinthian slogans reflected Stoic influence, an argument further developed more recently by Terence Paige (see ch. 16 below).[114] Paige points to the similarity between Paul's description of the Corinthians in 1 Cor 4.8 ('Already you have all you want! Already you have become rich! Quite apart from us you have become kings! Indeed, I wish that you had become kings, so that we might be kings with you!') and claims typically ascribed to the Stoics.[115] The Stoics, according to the ancient stereotype, saw themselves as genuinely happy, wealthy, free, and fit to rule. According to Paige, the impact of Stoicism on the Corinthian congregation helps to account for the rise of an elite group of

---

112. J. M. G. Barclay, 'Thessalonica and Corinth', 65 n. 29 (below, ch. 14, p. 190 n. 19).

113. See, e.g., S. Pogoloff, *Logos and Sophia: The Rhetorical Situation of 1 Corinthians* (SBLDS 134; Missoula, Mont.: Scholars Press, 1992); Litfin, *St. Paul's Theology*. However, contrast the view of Michael Goulder (ch. 13 below).

114. J. Weiss, *Der erste Korintherbrief* (1910; repr. Göttingen: Vandenhoeck & Ruprecht, 1977), 158–59.

115. Plutarch, *Tranq. an.* 472a.

σοφοί ('wise persons') in the church with an individualistic approach to ethics, spirituality, and worship.[116] F. Gerald Downing, in his *Cynics, Paul and the Pauline Churches,* argues against a Stoic background to Corinthian thought and conduct, maintaining instead that Corinthian thinking was shaped by Cynic convictions. He argues that Stoics would never themselves have claimed to have reached the ideal of complete perfection. Cynics, by contrast, could claim that they already enjoyed the kingdom of Kronos (the golden age).[117] Another contrasting hypothesis has been proposed by Graham Tomlin, who argues that the Corinthian elite were under the sway of Epicureanism. According to Tomlin, Epicurean influence lies behind the love of wisdom (1 Cor 1, 4), sexual attitudes (1 Cor 6–7), the 'atheism' that led some in the church to attend worship freely in pagan temples (1 Cor 8–10), the liberated role of women in the congregation (1 Cor 11.2–16; 14.34–36), and above all, the dispute over resurrection (1 Cor 15).[118]

There have, then, been a wide variety of religious and philosophical traditions suggested as influences on, or at least significant parallels to, Corinthian Christianity. The very variety of proposals raises the question as to whether the textual data is substantial and clear enough to locate Corinthian theology within a specific philosophical or religious framework. When parallels are found in Gnosticism, Hellenistic Judaism, Stoicism, Cynicism, Epicureanism, and so on, we are bound at least to ask whether the Corinthians can ever be clearly located in relation to one movement or another. Parallels with various traditions can doubtless be presented, but do they indicate direct and specific influence, or to some extent the fact that the scholar in question has highlighted parallels in one set of sources rather than another? Might it be the case, as Dale Martin has suggested, that, as far as our evidence allows us to see, the Corinthians' views reflect their exposure to 'philosophical commonplaces', to 'general principles of moral philosophy stemming from Cynic and Stoic traditions'?[119] Further questions, however, are raised by Martin's analysis. While rejecting the identification of the Corinthians specifically as Stoics or Cynics, Martin maintains, as do Paige and Tomlin,[120] that their knowledge of these philosophical principles 'implies a higher-class position'.[121] The questions are first whether it is necessary to regard acquaintance with popular philosophy as a sign of high social status, and second, whether it is plau-

---

116. Others who have argued for Stoic influence on Corinthian thought and action include W. Deming, *Paul on Marriage and Celibacy: The Hellenistic Background of 1 Corinthians 7* (Cambridge: Cambridge University Press, 1995), who argues for Stoic-Cynic influence on the 'asceticism' reflected in 1 Cor 7; A. J. Malherbe, 'Determinism and Free Will in Paul: The Argument of 1 Corinthians 8 and 9', in *Paul in His Hellenistic Context* (ed. T. Engberg-Pedersen; SNTW; Edinburgh: T. & T. Clark, 1994) 231–55.

117. F. Gerald Downing, *Cynics, Paul and the Pauline Churches: Cynics and Christian Origins II* (London and New York: Routledge, 1998) 88–89; pp. 85–127 are devoted to a study of the Corinthian community against the background of cynicism.

118. G. Tomlin, 'Christians and Epicureans in 1 Corinthians', *JSNT* 68 (1997) 51–72.

119. Martin, *Corinthian Body,* 72.

120. Paige, 'Stoicism', 192 (below, ch. 16, p. 218); Tomlin, 'Christians and Epicureans', 53.

121. Martin, *Corinthian Body,* 73.

sible to consider any of the Corinthian Christians as members of higher social strata. In both cases, contemporary scholarship has, by and large, given an affirmative answer, but these views have recently been challenged by Justin Meggitt (see further chs. 6, 17, 19 below). One further question is raised by these studies of the religious and philosophical background to the Corinthians' theology: To what extent does our understanding of Paul's letters depend on a plausible construction of this Corinthian background (see ch. 22 below)? Certainly one can hardly claim that any of Paul's or the Corinthians' ideas or practices are unique without comparing them with what we know of contemporary life, yet on the other hand, the search for parallels can sometimes perhaps overshadow the distinctiveness of early Pauline or Corinthian Christianity.

5. PAUL'S GOSPEL AND ITS SUBSEQUENT (MIS)UNDERSTANDING AS THE CAUSE OF PROBLEMS AT CORINTH

Rather than look outside the Christian movement for parallels that may help to illuminate what is going on in the Corinthian churches, some scholars have sought to explain the problems at Corinth and the outlook of the Corinthian Christians by looking at Paul's own teaching, and its subsequent modifications and misunderstanding.[122]

John Hurd, for example, in *The Origin of 1 Corinthians*, works backward in time, starting with the text of 1 Corinthians, then reconstructing first the issues raised in the Corinthians' letter to Paul (1 Cor 7.1), then Paul's earlier letter (1 Cor 5.9) and original preaching at Corinth. Hurd suggests that Paul's responses to the issues raised in the Corinthians' letter are indicated with the introductory phrase περὶ δέ ('now concerning . . .': 1 Cor 7.1, 25; 8.1; 12.1; 16.1, 12).[123] He also observes that in 1 Corinthians Paul seems to respond in a more measured and calm way to issues raised in the Corinthians' letter, and more angrily to what he has heard by way of oral report.[124] Also important for his reconstruction are the citations of Corinthian opinions, or 'slogans', mentioned above, since, many scholars agree, these provide glimpses of the arguments and perspectives of the Corinthians themselves (1 Cor 6.12; 7.1; 8.1; 10.23, etc.).[125] These observations on the text of 1 Corinthians enable Hurd to attempt the task of reconstructing the issues raised in the Corinthians' letter to Paul, and to pursue the question as

122. For a recent example, see D. Wenham, 'Whatever Went Wrong in Corinth?' *ExpTim* 108 (1997) 137–41.

123. Hurd, *Origin*, 65–74. However, for a critique of Hurd's conclusions regarding the περὶ δέ formula, see M. M. Mitchell, 'Concerning περὶ δέ in 1 Corinthians', *NovT* 31 (1989) 229–56.

124. Hurd, *Origin*, 61–94, esp. 74, 82.

125. See Hurd, *Origin*, 67–68, where he tabulates the range of opinion among commentators. For further discussion, as well as the commentaries, see, e.g., J. Murphy-O'Connor, 'Corinthian Slogans in 1 Cor 6:12–20', *CBQ* 40 (1978) 391–96.

to what may have inspired this exchange of views. Hurd's argument is that the Corinthians' questions, confusion, and anger are in large part caused by changes in what Paul teaches. Initially Paul was 'enthusiastically apocalyptic'; during his founding mission to Corinth he encouraged asceticism, preached that 'all things are lawful', ate meat from the public market, and 'assured his converts that they would live to see Christ's return to earth', that the end was nigh.[126] Subsequently, under the influence of the Apostolic Decree, agreed at the Jerusalem Council after his founding visit but before his first letter to Corinth (Acts 15.20, 29), Paul changed his views and wrote a letter to Corinth (cf. 1 Cor 5.9) presenting his new teaching, which was essentially an attempt to enforce the decree in Corinth.[127] Paul now took a different line on idolatry and immorality, and his apparent change of teaching drew a vigorous response from the Corinthians in the form of their letter (1 Cor 7.1). First Corinthians itself, then, represents Paul's attempt to respond to the Corinthians' questions and criticisms, and while mediating between his former and later teaching, Paul in effect 'withdrew most of the practical regulations by which he had tried in his Previous Letter to implement the Decree'.[128]

There are, however, problems with Hurd's thesis. For one, it seems that his reconstructions become more speculative, and therefore less persuasive, the further back he goes from 1 Corinthians: Can we really be so sure that the discussions in 1 Corinthians on, say, asceticism and idol food, arose essentially because Paul originally promoted but later retracted the ideal of sexual asceticism and the freedom to eat whatever was sold in the market? And is it really plausible to imagine Paul's teaching undergoing such drastic changes in such a short period of time?[129] Hurd's argument also depends on a particular hypothesis—which may very well be correct—concerning the chronology of Paul's missionary activity, since for Hurd's thesis to work the Apostolic Decree, and the meeting at which it was agreed, have to take place *after* Paul's first visit to Corinth. This would fit into the chronologies proposed by John Knox, Robert Jewett, Lüdemann, and others, which prioritise the evidence of the epistles over that of Acts, but not into the framework provided by Acts, which places the Apostolic Council in Jerusalem prior to Paul's arrival in Corinth.[130] Moreover, Hurd proposes that Paul's initial practice and teaching were not in line with what was established in the Decree, a proposal that is not by any means universally accepted.[131] More importantly, perhaps, by focusing his attention on the reconstruction of the correspondence

126. See Hurd, *Origin*, 284, 287, and the summary on 289–95.
127. See Hurd, *Origin*, 244–70.
128. Hurd, *Origin,* 289.
129. Cf. Barrett, *First Epistle,* 7–8.
130. Cf. Fee, *First Epistle,* 13. J. Knox, *Chapters in a Life of Paul* (rev. ed.; London: SCM, 1989); R. Jewett, *Dating Paul's Life* (London: SCM, 1979); Lüdemann, *Paul, Apostle to the Gentiles.*
131. Cf. M. Bockmuehl, *Jewish Law in Gentile Churches* (Edinburgh: T. & T. Clark, 2000) 167–68. There is also debate as to whether Paul ever accepted or commended the requirements of the Decree; cf., e.g., D. R. Catchpole, 'Paul, James and the Apostolic Decree', *NTS* 23 (1977) 428–44.

between Paul and the Corinthians, Hurd appears to suggest that the problems and disagreements at Corinth arose primarily from Paul's own teaching and the Corinthians' appropriation of it. No serious attention is given to the wide range of sources, both Greco-Roman and Jewish, that might help explain the origin of some of the Corinthians' ideas and practices.[132]

Another attempt to explain the Corinthians' problems in terms of their appropriation of Paul's gospel is Anthony Thiselton's essay 'Realized Eschatology at Corinth', largely reproduced below (ch. 7).[133] In this case, however, rather than regard the problems as arising from changes in Paul's teaching, they are seen to derive from the Corinthians' distortion of the apostle's gospel. Specifically, the Corinthians have constructed a realised eschatology, in which the promises of the age to come are felt to be fully realised in the present. Thiselton argues that this imbalance in the area of eschatology provides a coherent explanation for the whole range of problems Paul confronts in 1 Corinthians. Whereas Hurd seems willing to 'blame' Paul and his changing teaching for causing the disagreements that 1 Corinthians addresses, Thiselton sides much more with those who tend to blame the Corinthians: it is their distortion of the gospel that has created the difficulties. This latter tendency, much represented in the range of works on 1 and 2 Corinthians, no doubt reflects the (often implicit) commitment of Christian scholars to Paul, and to affirming and defending his theology.[134] In some recent work, however, notably in feminist criticism, the tables have been turned (see §7 below).

While many commentators have shared or accepted, at least in part, Thiselton's explanation for the Corinthians' doctrinal errors,[135] a number of scholars have recently expressed scepticism about the realised eschatology hypothesis. Duane Litfin, for example, questions whether 1 Cor 4.8, a key verse for Thiselton, necessarily reflects an eschatological perspective on the part of the Corinthians, or only on the part of Paul.[136] Again, methodological decisions concerning the range of relevant sources, and the ideological focus adopted by the scholar, are important to understand the different arguments that emerge. Thiselton's essay focuses investigation and explanation on theological and doctrinal issues, showing how problems arise when right doctrine goes awry. Litfin, following more recent trends in scholarship, examines the views of Paul and the Corinthians in the light of practices and expectations evident in Greco-Roman sources, showing how the Corinthians are shaped by conventions common in their wider culture. Indeed, in some recent work

---

132. See the criticisms raised by J. M. Ford, 'Review of J. C. Hurd, *The Origin of 1 Corinthians*', *JTS* 17 (1966) 442–44; W. G. Kümmel, 'Review of J. C. Hurd, *The Origin of 1 Corinthians*', *TLZ* 91 (1966) 505–8.

133. Thiselton, 'Realized Eschatology'.

134. Note, e.g., the comments of C. K. Barrett (*Essays on Paul* [London: SPCK, 1982] 1, reprinted below, ch. 4, p. 80).

135. See, e.g., Barrett, *First Epistle*, 109; Fee, *First Epistle*, 172; W. Schrage, *Der erste Brief an die Korinther* (EKKNT 7.1; Zürich: Benziger; Neukirchen-Vluyn: Neukirchener Verlag, 1991) 56, 338–40.

136. Litfin, *St. Paul's Theology*, 168–69. Curiously, Litfin does not cite Thiselton in connection with this view. See further introduction to ch. 7 below.

the pendulum has clearly swung in this direction: it is the Corinthians' 'secular' context that is seen as providing the most adequate explanation for the problems Paul addresses, rather than any theological, doctrinal, or religious misconceptions.[137]

In his recent commentary on 1 Corinthians, Thiselton interestingly combines his continuing interest in theological and doctrinal matters with a focus on what can be learnt from the Greco-Roman cultural context, as explored in much recent work on Corinth (see §6 below), both reaffirming and qualifying his earlier argument:

> The triumphalism of many Christians at Corinth was certainly encouraged and supported by an overrealized eschatology which in turn led to a distorted view of what constitutes 'being spiritual,' or a 'person of the Spirit.' I stand by my conclusion of 1978. . . . *Nevertheless I now perceive how this theological misperception combined with the seductive infiltration into the Christian church of cultural attitudes derived from secular or non-Christian Corinth as a city.*[138]

What remains apparent here is the judgment that, whether through theological error or secular influence, the Corinthians are misguided and mistaken, and that Paul's voice offers a right and necessary corrective.

6. SOCIOHISTORICAL AND SOCIAL-SCIENTIFIC PERSPECTIVES ON CORINTHIAN CHRISTIANITY

Since the early 1970s there has been a renewed interest in sociohistorical perspectives on early Christianity. Given the information available, and the character of the Pauline correspondence, it is not surprising that the Corinthian churches, and 1 Corinthians in particular, have been a frequent focus for such work. Indeed, a broadly sociohistorical approach has dominated research into Christianity at Corinth in recent decades. An interest in the social history of early Christianity is not, of course, by any means new: such scholarly endeavour can be traced back, as Ralph Hochschild has shown, to at least the middle of the nineteenth century, when Wilhelm Weitling and Friedrich Lückes published contrasting works on the early church.[139] Weitling's 1846 book presented a radical,

---

137. Cf., e.g., Winter, *After Paul Left Corinth*, 25–28, and further §6 below. The term 'secular', used for example in the subtitle of Winter's book, should be subject to a caveat: the notion of a 'secular' public sphere, distinct from the (privatised) realm in which religion operates, is a thoroughly modern invention (on which see J. Milbank, *Theology and Social Theory* [Oxford: Blackwell, 1990]). In the ancient world, religion was thoroughly woven into all areas of life, including the public and political (see further R. Horsley, ed., *Paul and Empire: Religion and Power in Roman Imperial Society* [Harrisburg, Pa.: Trinity Press International, 1997]).

138. Thiselton, *First Epistle*, 40. For further discussion and critique, see D. G. Horrell, 'Review of A. C. Thiselton, *The First Epistle of Paul to the Corinthians*', *JBL* 121 (2002) 183–86.

139. See R. Hochschild, *Sozialgeschichtliche Exegese* (Göttingen: Vandenhoeck & Ruprecht; Freiburg: Universitätsverlag, 1999) 45–63.

human Jesus calling people to live in a community of equality and freedom, and depicted the early church as a form of communism, practising the community of goods. Lückes, on the other hand, presented the early church as a kind of free association (*freier Verein*) more in tune with the developing structures of his own 'civic society' (*bürgerliche Gesellschaft*). Although these early works have had virtually no impact on the subsequent scholarly literature, their different perspectives are to some extent paradigmatic for subsequent sociohistorical analyses of the character of the earliest churches: scholars continue to present reconstructions of the early church—ranging from the egalitarian, countercultural community to the community in which well-to-do benefactors are prominent—which may reflect their own contemporary political commitments and thus (implicitly or explicitly) claim the early Christian movement as an ally and paradigm.[140] Indeed, there was extensive discussion of social questions about early Christianity in the late nineteenth and early twentieth centuries, in scholarly works from both theologians and from members of the socialist movement (notably Friedrich Engels and Karl Kautsky), closely related to the societal upheavals that characterised the period.[141]

For various reasons, in the middle decades of the twentieth century, interest in social questions about early Christianity waned.[142] An important stimulus to the revival of interest in the 1970s and beyond, aside from the important wider societal stimuli,[143] was the publication in 1960 of Edwin Judge's *The Social Pattern of the Christian Groups in the First Century.* Judge's book has proved important in connection with studies of the Corinthian Christians, particularly in generating debate about their social and economic location.[144] For, in contrast to Adolf Deissmann's view of the early Christians as coming from the lower classes, Judge argued that '[f]ar from being a socially depressed group . . . if the Corinthians are at all typical, the Christians were dominated by a socially pretentious section of the population of the big cities'.[145] The contrasting views of

---

140. Cf. Hochschild, *Sozialgeschichtliche Exegese,* 54. For example, one might perhaps contrast Richard Horsley's picture of the ἐκκλησία at Corinth (see ch. 18 below) with Bruce Winter's portrait of the early Christians as 'benefactors and citizens', in *Seek the Welfare of the City: Christians as Benefactors and Citizens* (Grand Rapids: Eerdmans, 1994) and *After Paul Left Corinth,* the former work dedicated to 'a modern-day Christian benefactor and citizen'.

141. Cf. Hochschild, *Sozialgeschichtliche Exegese,* 96. For key works by Engels, see Marx and Engels, *On Religion*; and by K. Kautsky, see *Der Ursprung des Christentums: Eine historische Untersuchung* (1910; republished Hannover: Dietz, 1968); ET, *Foundations of Christianity: A Study in Christian Origins* (London: Orbach & Chambers, 1925).

142. For an analysis of the history of research, and the reasons for this decline in interest, see G. Theissen, *Social Reality and the Early Christians* (Edinburgh: T. & T. Clark, 1993) 1–29; Hochschild, *Sozialgeschichtliche Exegese*; S. C. Barton, 'The Communal Dimension of Earliest Christianity: A Critical Survey of the Field', *JTS* 43 (1992) 399–427.

143. On which see Barton, 'Communal Dimension', 399–406.

144. Theissen, for example, comments: 'This little book deserves a place of honor in the history of modern sociological exegesis' (*Social Reality,* 19 n. 23).

145. E. A. Judge, *The Social Pattern of the Christian Groups in the First Century* (London: Tyndale Press, 1960) 60.

Deissmann and Judge provided the starting point for Gerd Theissen's influential study of 'social stratification' in the Corinthian church (on which see further below, and ch. 6).

Along with the renewed interest in social history came a wide variety of attempts to use models, theories, and approaches from the social sciences in studies of the early church.[146] Most notable among the early studies are the series of essays on Corinth published in the 1970s by Gerd Theissen.[147] In these essays Theissen drew on a wide range of historical evidence—literary, inscriptional, archaeological, and so on—and on various social-scientific theories to construct a picture of the social composition of the Corinthian community and to explain the origins of some of its divisions and disagreements. The foundational study is of 'social stratification' in the Corinthian community, reproduced in part in chapter 6 below, where Theissen argues that the Corinthian Christians came from a variety of social strata: the majority from the lower classes, an influential minority from the upper classes. The social diversity Theissen saw encompassed within the congregation then served as the key to explaining some of the problems faced at Corinth. The party divisions owed a good deal to divisions among households, whose well-to-do heads had offered support and hospitality to one missionary or another. These prominent members of the community were 'competing for influence within the congregation'.[148] The divisions at the Lord's Supper (1 Cor 11.17–34) were essentially divisions along social class lines, with the wealthy receiving higher quality and quantity of food, and the poor going without.[149] The diverse convictions regarding the eating of meat offered to idols (1 Cor 8.1—11.1) also reflected class-specific behaviour: since the wealthy ate meat often, they did not firmly link it with occasions of cultic feasting, whereas the poor ate meat only rarely, and then as part of cultic celebrations, and now, as Christian converts, found such meat unacceptable.[150] Theissen saw Paul's solution to these problems in his promotion of an ethos of 'love-patriarchalism', an ethos quite distinct from the ethical radicalism of the Synoptic tradition. 'This love patriarchalism', Theissen writes, 'takes social differences for granted but ameliorates them through an obligation of respect and love, an obligation imposed upon

---

146. For a discussion of the various types of approach and a representative selection of essays, see D. G. Horrell, ed., *Social-Scientific Approaches to New Testament Interpretation* (Edinburgh: T. & T. Clark, 1999); also idem, 'Social Sciences Studying Formative Christian Phenomena: A Creative Movement', in *Handbook of Early Christianity: Social Science Approaches* (ed. A. J. Blasi, J. Duhaime, and P.-A. Turcotte; Walnut Creek, Calif.: AltaMira Press, 2002) 3–28.

147. The essays, originally published in various journals, were collected together with essays on the Jesus movement from a sociological perspective in G. Theissen, *Soziologie des Urchristentums* (Tübingen: Mohr Siebeck, 1979, 2nd ed. 1983, 3rd ed. 1988). The essays on Corinth were translated by John Schütz in Theissen, *Social Setting*.

148. Theissen, *Social Setting*, 57; see further 55–57.

149. Theissen, *Social Setting*, 145–74, reprinted in Horrell, *Social-Scientific Approaches*, 249–74. See also ch. 9 below.

150. Theissen, *Social Setting*, 121–43. Note the criticisms of J. J. Meggitt, 'Meat Consumption and Social Conflict in Corinth', *JTS* 45 (1994) 137–41; also idem, *Paul, Poverty*, 107–18.

those who are socially stronger. From the weaker are required subordination, fidelity and esteem.'[151]

Theissen's groundbreaking studies provided important material for Wayne Meeks's broader study of the social world of the Pauline Christians, *The First Urban Christians*, also a landmark study in the use of social-scientific perspectives.[152] And despite disagreements and counterarguments,[153] Theissen's work continues to set an agenda for studies of the Corinthian church.

Although the work of Theissen and Meeks has done an enormous amount to stimulate further sociohistorical studies of the Corinthian churches, there has not by any means been unanimity over issues of method and approach. Even among those who draw on social-scientific perspectives there is debate concerning the appropriate way in which to do this, with some arguing for a more rigorously model-based approach using models drawn largely from cross-cultural anthropology, and others arguing for a more eclectic use of theory and a more interpretive approach to the evidence.[154] A more significant difference lies between those who advocate the use of social-scientific methods and models and those who reject or avoid them. Judge is prominent among those who are critical of the use of social-scientific resources and who stick instead to the task of surveying and analysing primary historical data. Criticising Bengt Holmberg's use of sociological theory in *Paul and Power*, Judge accuses Holmberg of falling prey to a 'sociological fallacy', namely that 'social theories can be safely transposed across the centuries without verification'. Before importing 'social models that have been defined in terms of other cultures', Judge insists, the 'painstaking field work', the analysis of the available ancient evidence, must be 'better done'.[155] Similar arguments are mounted by those, such as Andrew Clarke and Bruce Winter, who follow Judge's call to engage in 'the proto-sociological work of historical description' (see further ch. 20 below).[156]

---

151. Theissen, *Social Setting*, 107; see further pp. 107–10, 138–40, 163–64. This notion, though not the term itself, is drawn by Theissen from E. Troeltsch, *The Social Teaching of the Christian Churches*, vol. 1 (ET London: Allen & Unwin, 1931) 72–78.

152. Meeks, *First Urban Christians*.

153. For example, for criticism of the love patriarchalism thesis, see Horrell, *Social Ethos*; for criticism of the social stratification thesis, see Meggitt, *Paul, Poverty*.

154. Prominent proponents of the model-based approach are B. Malina and J. H. Neyrey (see, e.g., B. Malina and J. H. Neyrey, *Portraits of Paul: An Archaeology of Ancient Personality* [Louisville: Westminster John Knox, 1996]; J. H. Neyrey, *Paul in Other Words* (Louisville: Westminster John Knox, 1990). Meeks represents the more eclectic, interpretive approach (see *First Urban Christians*, 1–7). For overviews that draw attention to the important differences of approach see n. 146 above and D. B. Martin, 'Social-Scientific Criticism', in *To Each Its Own Meaning: An Introduction to Biblical Criticisms and Their Application* (ed. S. L. McKenzie and S. R. Haynes; Louisville: Westminster John Knox, 1993) 103–19. For the two sides of the debate, see most recently D. G. Horrell, 'Models and Methods in Social-Scientific Interpretation: A Response to Philip Esler', *JSNT* 78 (2000) 83–105; and P. F. Esler, 'Models in New Testament Interpretation: A Reply to David Horrell', *JSNT* 78 (2000) 107–13.

155. E. A. Judge, 'The Social Identity of the First Christians: A Question of Method in Religious History', *JRH* 11 (1980) 201–17; here p. 210; B. Holmberg, *Paul and Power: The Structure of Authority in the Primitive Church as Reflected in the Pauline Epistles* (Lund: Gleerup, 1978).

156. Clarke, *Secular and Christian Leadership*, 5; see pp. 3–6; also Winter, *After Paul Left Corinth*, xiii.

On the other hand, those who promote and defend the use of the social sciences attack the apparent empiricism that underpins Judge's approach, the notion that one can collect data, innocent of the influence of models and theories. 'It is impossible', Philip Esler maintains, 'to collect facts without . . . already subscribing to a whole range of theoretical presuppositions'.[157] The use of social-scientific models, therefore, serves both to render explicit the framework with which the researcher is operating and to provide a theoretical context within which the various bits of ancient data may be rendered meaningful.

To some degree both these arguments carry weight. It is certainly the case, to side in part with Judge, that the model or theory chosen may, indeed will, shape the way in which evidence is interpreted, and that an anachronistic model embodying cultural assumptions or social institutions alien to first-century Corinth will result in a failure to appreciate the past as 'a foreign country'.[158] However, this is one reason why critics who use social-scientific perspectives argue, albeit in various ways, for models that avoid the dangers of anachronism, or for theoretical frameworks that inform and guide an investigation, but do not predetermine what will be found or how it will be seen. On the other hand, to side with Esler, to claim to seek only to present data in a descriptive way is at best naïve, failing to recognise the theoretical presuppositions guiding the work, and at worst tendentiously ideological, concealing interests and commitments beneath a veil of disinterested objectivity.[159]

There are, then, various approaches and trends in current sociohistorical and social-scientific research into Corinthian Christianity, with no neat classificatory boundaries to define where any particular piece of work fits. However, in contrast to much earlier work on the Corinthian church, from Baur onward, one common characteristic of social and historical research is the serious engagement with a wide range of ancient evidence, archaeological and literary, in the attempt to reconstruct and to understand the Greco-Roman context in which the Corinthian Christians lived. It is not the parallels to be found in the history of religions that are seen as most crucial, but rather the sources relating to everyday 'secular' life.[160] Bruce Winter, for example, argues that 'the problems which arose subsequent to Paul's departure [from Corinth] did so . . .' not because of the Corinthians' Gnostic beliefs, realised eschatology, or confusion over Paul's changing teaching, but ' . . . partly because the Christians were "cosmopolitans", i.e. citizens of this world and, in particular, citizens or residents of Roman Corinth'.[161]

why they left

---

157. P. F. Esler, *Community and Gospel in Luke-Acts: The Social and Political Motivations of Lucan Theology* (SNTSMS 57; Cambridge: Cambridge University Press, 1987) 15; cf. M. Y. MacDonald, *The Pauline Churches: A Socio-historical Study of Institutionalization in the Pauline and deutero-Pauline Writings* (SNTSMS 60; Cambridge: Cambridge University Press, 1988) 25–26.

158. The phrase is taken from the opening line of L. P. Hartley's novel, *The Go-Between* (London: Hamish Hamilton, 1953): 'The past is a foreign country: they do things differently there.'

159. Cf. further Horrell, *Social Ethos*, 27–28; idem, 'Review of B. W. Winter, *After Paul Left Corinth*', *JTS* 53 (2002) 660–65.

160. But for a caveat concerning the use of the term 'secular' in this context, see above, n. 137.

161. Winter, *After Paul Left Corinth*, 27; see pp. 25–28.

Indeed, in this particular type of approach, though not by any means in New Testament studies generally, the Greco-Roman evidence takes centre stage, rather than the range of Jewish texts important for understanding Paul himself. Winter explicitly makes the point that his aim is to study the Corinthians' background, and not that of Paul, and stresses the predominantly *Roman* character of first-century Corinth.[162]

In this quest to understand the urban context of the first Corinthian Christians, archaeology is indispensable, and while findings at Corinth itself are naturally of primary importance, discoveries from other urban centres of the Roman Empire are also highly relevant. The extent and nature of the use of archaeological information varies, of course, from study to study, and there are important methodological and hermeneutical questions to consider (see ch. 19 below]).[163] A number of scholars, for example, make use of the evidence from statues and portraiture to develop a picture of the kinds of head covering that were customary for men and women in Roman society; this picture can then help to illuminate Paul's convoluted argument about head coverings in 1 Cor 11.2–16.[164] The excavations of the sanctuary of Demeter and Kore, and of the Asklepeion, at Corinth have been especially relevant to attempts to understand the possible settings for ritual dining Paul envisages when discussing the eating of 'idol food' in 1 Cor 8–10.[165] And countless Corinthian inscriptions are of particular relevance: those commemorating the building of the meat and fish market (cf. 1 Cor 10.25),[166] or the laying of the theatre pavement by Erastus (cf. Rom 16.23 [see photo, p. 47]),[167] or various benefactions by wealthy Corinthians, and so on.[168] In recent years, the range of archaeological (and literary) evidence relating to the imperial cult, at Corinth and elsewhere, has also come to be a focus of attention (see below).

A good deal of recent social-historical work on Corinth, notably by Peter Marshall, John Chow, Andrew Clarke, Bruce Winter, and others, has used ancient

162. Winter, *After Paul Left Corinth*, xii, 11, 20–22.

163. See also the discussion in R. E. Oster, 'Use, Misuse and Neglect of Archaeological Evidence in Some Modern Works on 1 Corinthians (1 Cor 7,1–5; 8,10; 11,2–16; 12,14–26)', *ZNW* 83 (1992) 52–73.

164. E.g., R. E. Oster, 'When Men Wore Veils to Worship: The Historical Context of 1 Corinthians 11.4', *NTS* 34 (1988) 481–505; G. Theissen, *Psychological Aspects of Pauline Theology* (Edinburgh: T. & T. Clark, 1987) 158–67; D. W. J. Gill, 'The Importance of Roman Portraiture for Head-Coverings in 1 Corinthians 11:2–16', *TynBul* 41 (1990) 245–60; Winter, *After Paul Left Corinth*, 121–41.

165. Among the many monographs seeking to reconstruct the sociohistorical background to 1 Cor 8–10, see J. Fotopoulos, *Food Offered to Idols in Roman Corinth* (WUNT 2.151; Tübingen: Mohr Siebeck, 2003); P. D. Gooch, *Dangerous Food: 1 Corinthians 8–10 in Its Context* (Waterloo, Ont.: Wilfred Laurier University Press, 1993); D. Newton, *Deity and Diet: The Dilemma of Sacrificial Food in Corinth* (JSNTSup 169; Sheffield: Sheffield University Press, 1998); W. L. Willis, *Idol Meat in Corinth: The Pauline Argument in 1 Corinthians 8 and 10* (SBLDS 68; Chico, Calif.: Scholars Press, 1985).

166. For the relevant inscriptions, see A. B. West, *Corinth: Results of Excavations Conducted by the American School of Classical Studies at Athens,* vol. 8.2: *Latin Inscriptions 1896–1926* (Cambridge: Harvard University Press, 1931) §§124–25, pp. 100–104; Kent, *Corinth,* 8.3, §321, pp. 127–28.

167. For the Erastus inscription, see Kent, *Corinth,* 8.3, §232, pp. 99–100; and further ch. 17 below.

168. For examples, see West, *Corinth,* 8.2, §132, pp. 107–8; Kent, *Corinth,* 8.3, §160, p. 75.

Greco-Roman sources to construct a picture of customs and practices associated with patronage, benefaction, litigation, dining, and so on, and sought to show how these customs influenced the behaviour of at least some members of the Corinthian congregation (see ch. 15 below).[169] From this perspective, the conflict between Paul and the Corinthians is essentially one between 'the worldly outlook of the Corinthians and Paul's own Christ-centred perspective'.[170] An important facet of this reconstruction in many cases is the view that at least some of the Corinthians were members of the wealthy elite, the upper stratum of Corinthian urban society, who carried over the secular customs of patronage, benefaction, and so on, into the life of the church. Paul is then often seen to present a challenge to these influential Corinthians, refusing their patronage, criticising their behaviour at the community's meal, and denying their access to secular courts.[171] Some who are less confident about identifying the higher status Corinthian Christians as 'elite' have nonetheless also seen Paul as siding with the socially weak and upsetting the expectations of the better-off members of the congregation.[172] Crucial to most of these proposed reconstructions is the view of the Corinthian congregation as containing a mix of socioeconomic strata, a view that has recently been challenged by Justin Meggitt (see further chs. 6, 17, 19 below). Indeed, Meggitt challenges the way in which New Testament scholars have used ancient (elite) sources to reconstruct the socioeconomic context of the nonelite urban Christians Paul addresses, calling for an approach oriented more to understanding ancient 'popular culture' (see ch. 19 below).

Another direction in recent research represents a much more overtly political engagement with Paul and the Corinthian church. While Laurence Welborn related the slogans recorded in 1 Cor 1.12 to the slogans of ancient politics (see ch. 10 below), Richard Horsley and others, in a number of recent publications, have been investigating the wider theme of the relation between the Pauline congregations and the Roman imperial order (see ch. 18 below).[173] Drawing on work on the imperial cult by ancient historians such as Simon Price,[174] Horsley outlines the ways in which imperial domination was sustained—through the power of cult,

169. J. K. Chow, *Patronage and Power: A Study of Social Networks in Corinth* (JSNTSup 75; Sheffield: Sheffield Academic Press, 1992); Clarke, *Secular and Christian Leadership*; Winter, *Seek the Welfare of the City*; idem, *After Paul Left Corinth*; Marshall, *Enmity in Corinth*; T. B. Savage, *Power Through Weakness: Paul's Understanding of the Christian Ministry in 2 Corinthians* (SNTSMS 86; Cambridge: Cambridge University Press, 1996); A. C. Mitchell, 'Rich and Poor in the Courts of Corinth: Litigiousness and Status in 1 Corinthians 6.1–11', *NTS* 39 (1993) 562–86. See further ch. 15 below.

170. Savage, *Power Through Weakness*, 188; cf. also 99.

171. See Chow, *Patronage and Power*, 167–87; Clarke, *Secular and Christian Leadership*, 109–27; Winter, *After Paul Left Corinth*, 106–9.

172. E.g., D. B. Martin, *Slavery As Salvation* (New Haven and London: Yale University Press, 1990); idem, *Corinthian Body*; Horrell, *Social Ethos*.

173. R. A. Horsley, ed., *Paul and Empire*; idem, *1 Corinthians* (Nashville: Abingdon, 1998); idem, ed., *Paul and Politics: Ekklesia, Israel, Imperium, Interpretation* (Harrisburg, Pa.: Trinity Press International, 2000).

174. S. R. F. Price, *Rituals and Power: The Roman Imperial Cult in Asia Minor* (Cambridge: Cambridge University Press, 1984).

images, and patronage, as well as by the more brute forms of oppression. Viewed in the context of this imperial system, and specifically of the imperial cult, Paul's language about Christ as the one true Lord, to whom all worship belongs, takes on new nuances. Indeed, many of the terms Paul uses both of Christ and of the Christian congregations were also used in imperial, political contexts (κύριος, υἱὸς θεοῦ, εὐαγγέλιον, πολίτευμα, etc.).[175] Thus Horsley sees Paul as engaged in a thoroughly political and countercultural project, establishing radically alternative ἐκκλησίαι with new patterns of social relationships, throughout the cities of the Roman Empire. The Corinthian church serves, for Horsley, as an example of such an alternative ἐκκλησία.[176] One's response to this model of the Corinthian church will probably depend to some extent upon one's own political and ecclesial convictions and commitments. There are questions to be raised about the extent to which it may represent a somewhat idealised view of Paul and his communities, a reflection of contemporary political aspirations and commitments, perhaps, as well as of the ancient evidence.[177] Nevertheless, Horsley's work also forcefully raises questions about the extent to which other interpretive perspectives also promote their own (implicit) political convictions, and about the ways in which modern presuppositions have led scholars to assume a division between religion and politics that is thoroughly anachronistic in the ancient world (see further ch. 18 below).

~ In much, though by no means all, of this sociohistorical research, the portrait of Paul that emerges, implicitly or explicitly, is positive: he challenges the practices of the wealthy on behalf of the poor; he labours to establish alternative communities that stand in opposition to the brutal Roman Empire. Whether this positive evaluation emanates from underlying theological convictions or from sociopolitical ones is hard to say, perhaps a measure of both. It is also interesting to ponder whether, in at least some cases, the shift in focus from religious or theological ideas to social and political ones nonetheless results in a picture with a familiar structure: rather than focus on Gnostic tendencies or realised eschatology as the Corinthian error that Paul strives to correct, now it is the secular practices of the wealthy or the prevalent imperial ideology that represent the Corinthian failings and the target of Paul's critique. In either case, Paul is the guardian of theological, social, or political correctness in face of the Corinthians' obduracy and error.[178] In turning next to feminist approaches to the Corinthian

---

175. See, e.g., N. T. Wright, 'Paul's Gospel and Caesar's Empire', in Horsley, ed., *Paul and Politics*, 160–83; P. Oakes, *Philippians: From People to Letter* (SNTSMS 110; Cambridge: Cambridge University Press, 2001) 129–74.

176. R. A. Horsley, '1 Corinthians: A Case Study of Paul's Assembly as an Alternative Society', in Horsley, ed., *Paul and Empire*, 242–52, reproduced in ch. 18 below.

177. Albert Schweitzer's famous comments on those whose reconstructions of the historical Jesus in fact bear the image of their own reflection remain relevant, though not only, of course, to Horsley's work. See A. Schweitzer, *The Quest of the Historical Jesus* (London: SCM, 2000 [ET of 1913 edition]) 6.

178. Cf. further C. Briggs Kittredge, 'Corinthian Women Prophets and Paul's Argumentation in 1 Corinthians', in Horsley, ed., *Paul and Politics*, 103–9.

correspondence, however, we meet a strand of modern scholarship in which the tendency to favour Paul and to criticise the Corinthians has been questioned and, sometimes, firmly reversed.

7. (RE)DISCOVERING THE CORINTHIAN WOMEN AND (RE)READING PAUL'S RHETORIC: CONTEMPORARY HERMENEUTICAL CONCERNS

A major development in recent New Testament scholarship has been the rise of feminist interpretation. The best-known and groundbreaking feminist study is Elisabeth Schüssler Fiorenza's *In Memory of Her: A Feminist Theological Reconstruction of Christian Origins* (London: SCM), first published in 1983 and reprinted with a new introduction in 1995. Fiorenza's aim is to reconstruct a history of early Christianity in which women's contributions and their struggles for equality against patriarchal domination are recovered from texts written largely from a male perspective and in which women are often silenced and excluded. Through their commitment to exposing and critiquing patriarchy, both in the texts and in their subsequent interpretation, feminist scholars have brought issues of gender and patriarchalism in Paul's letters to the fore. First Corinthians in particular has attracted the attention of feminist scholars because the letter indicates the active involvement of women in meetings of the assembly. Indeed, in 1 Corinthians issues concerning the roles and relations of women and men are dealt with more than in any other of Paul's letters.

First Corinthians 11.2–16 shows that Corinthian women, as well as men, enjoyed the freedom to pray and prophesy in gatherings of the church for worship.[179] However, Paul is concerned to tell them that in doing this women must keep their heads covered (probably with a veil or other head covering, possibly with their long hair);[180] men, on the other hand, must not cover their heads when they pray or prophesy. Exactly what was happening at Corinth, and why, is extremely difficult to reconstruct, and Paul's argument itself is one of his more obscure and convoluted. It may be that in removing their head coverings, some of the women were indicating their emancipation from traditional gender distinctions and roles.[181] While Paul does not here attempt to curb the rights of women to participate vocally in worship, he insists on the importance of the head covering, either to retain a clearly marked distinction between men and

179. For fuller discussion and references, see Horrell, *Social Ethos*, 168–76.

180. In favour of hairstyle rather than veils as the issue here, see J. Murphy-O'Connor, 'Sex and Logic in 1 Corinthians 11:2–16', *CBQ* 42 (1980) 484–90; Fiorenza, *In Memory of Her*, 227; A. Padgett, 'Paul on Women in the Church: the Contradictions of Coiffure in 1 Cor 11:2–16', *JSNT* 20 (1984) 70. Against this see D. R. MacDonald, *There Is No Male and Female* (HDR 20; Philadelphia: Fortress, 1987) 86–87; B. Byrne, *Paul and the Christian Woman* (Homebush, NSW: St Paul Publications, 1988) 39–40.

181. Cf. Theissen, *Psychological Aspects*, 165.

women,[182] or to prevent the Christian meeting from resembling those of the more ecstatic cult groups known in Corinth,[183] or to exclude (male) sexual desire from intruding into the ecclesial meetings.[184] If 1 Cor 14.34–35 is authentic to the letter, then Paul there *does* require women to keep silent, in a way which is difficult to harmonise with 11.2–16. Various attempts have been made to explain the force of these instructions in a way that retains their coherence within the same letter, but there are strong reasons to regard 14.34–35 as a later interpolation.[185]

The evidence that 11.2–16 provides for the participation of women in congregational worship has been a starting point for the recent exploration of the wider involvement of women in church life and in the issues Paul addresses at Corinth. Margaret MacDonald, in an article part of which is reprinted in chapter 12 below, argues that the women prophets of 1 Cor 11 were the main supporters of the sexual asceticism about which Paul feels so uneasy in chapter 7.[186] She contends that the women were influenced by the (possibly) dominical tradition reflected in Gal 3.26–28, with its assertion that 'there is neither male nor female', and sought to express their newfound equality in Christ through the practice of celibacy.[187]

Antoinette Wire, in *The Corinthian Women Prophets,* has most fully developed the argument that women were involved in most of the issues with which Paul deals in 1 Corinthians. Wire postulates the existence in the Corinthian church of a group of female prophets with a coherent proto-feminist theological outlook.[188] According to Wire, these women are Paul's 'opponents' throughout the letter.

As Fiorenza attempts to recover the history of women's involvement in early Christianity from records in which that contribution is often masked and obscured, so both MacDonald and Wire engage in a style of exegesis that seeks to uncover the (at least partly) hidden story of women's involvement in activity and disputes at Corinth. In terms of what Paul explicitly says in 1 Cor 7, there are few overt signals that women were playing the leading role in the situation to which he is responding. The way in which the Corinthian slogan is formulated in v. 1 ('It is good for a *man* not to touch a woman') might suggest that those within the congregation who were urging sexual abstinence were men. The

182. Cf. Fee, *First Epistle,* 497–98; L. A. Jervis, "But I want you to know . . .": Paul's Midrashic Intertextual Response to the Corinthian Worshippers (1 Cor 11:2–16)', *JBL* 112 (1993) 235–38.

183. Cf. Fiorenza, *In Memory of Her,* 227–30; R. Kroeger and C. Kroeger, 'An Inquiry into the Evidence of Maenadism in the Corinthian Congregation', *SBLSP* 14 (1979) 2:331–38. Against this interpretation, see Theissen, *Psychological Aspects,* 163–65.

184. F. Watson, *Agape, Eros, Gender: Towards a Pauline Sexual Ethic* (Cambridge: Cambridge University Press, 2000) 40–89; further idem, 'The Authority of the Voice: A Theological Reading of 1 Cor 11.2–16', *NTS* 46 (2000) 520–36.

185. See Horrell, *Social Ethos,* 184–95.

186. MacDonald, 'Women Holy'.

187. On the dominical saying that may underlie this text, see D. R. MacDonald, *There Is No Male and Female*; further ch. 12 below.

188. Wire, *Corinthian Women Prophets.*

precise problem Paul tackles in 7.25–38, 'concerning virgins', is notoriously difficult to determine, but most scholars assume that the basic issue is whether
betrothed couples should go ahead with their marriages. If this is the case, Paul's
wording would seem to suggest that it was the engaged men who were disinclined
to marry rather than the female virgins: it is the *man* who has to decide whether
to marry or to stay as he is. But according to MacDonald and Wire, although
Paul frames the discussion of 1 Cor 7 from the male point of view, there is evidence to suggest that he is obscuring the more uncomfortable reality (for him)
that women were in fact the main proponents of the ascetic viewpoint in the
church. With almost monotonous regularity, Paul balances his address to the men
with exhortations to the women. He envisages women in every scenario he discusses, and twice (7.10–13, 39–40) gives more attention to women than men.
This careful and indeed strained attempt at gender balance, for MacDonald and
Wire, reflects a gender *imbalance* in the reality of the situation being addressed:
Paul is especially concerned to include the women in his exhortations because he
knows that they were the real perpetrators of the ascetic movement.

As a result of the work of Fiorenza, MacDonald, Wire, and others, many now
accept that women were prominent within Corinthian Christianity, though
whether they were quite as influential as these scholars contend, either within the
supposed 'ascetic movement' in the congregation or more generally in the Christian community, has been debated.[189] One may also question whether Paul's discourse is as heavily and specifically directed toward the Corinthian women as
Wire argues. Given that feminist scholars seek to recover the contribution of
women from behind (patriarchal) texts that marginalise and muzzle that contribution—and acknowledge the need to use 'historical imagination' in doing
so[190]—there will always be some debate as to how far the reconstruction represents historical reality or the creativity of the interpreter.

Wire's reading of 1 Corinthians in particular raises the important question of
how the interpreter uses Paul's text to build a profile of the church at Corinth.
Traditionally, scholars have gone about the task of reconstructing the situation in
Corinth by following the clues that Paul himself provides in the course of his
argumentation: his direct references to events in Corinth, his citation of
Corinthian slogans, his polemics against wisdom and knowledge, and so on. In
doing so, they have largely employed a 'hermeneutic of trust'; that is, they have
supposed that Paul is presenting Corinthian beliefs and practices honestly and
fairly. Wire, however, treats Paul's rhetoric with a great deal of suspicion; rather
than regarding it as a mirror that reflects the Corinthian situation accurately, she
takes the view that to a considerable extent Paul tries to conceal the true nature

189. Caution is expressed by J. M. Gundry-Volf, 'Controlling the Bodies: A Theological Profile
of the Corinthian Sexual Ascetics (1 Cor 7)', in *The Corinthian Correspondence* (ed. R. Bieringer; Leuven: Leuven University Press, 1996) 519–41. See also A. S. May, ' "The Body for the Lord": Sex and
Identity in 1 Corinthians 5–7' (Ph.D. thesis, University of Glasgow, 2001).

190. Fiorenza, *In Memory of Her*, 60–61.

of events at Corinth. In her reading of the text, she thus endeavours to bring to the fore what Paul, in his style of arguing, tries to suppress.

In many respects, Wire's work can be seen as an implementation of Fiorenza's interpretive programme (though Wire does not present it as such), as set out in the influential essay extracted in ch. 11 below. Fiorenza is critical of interpreters who unquestioningly accept Paul's characterisation of the Corinthians as foolish, immature, arrogant, divisive, and so on, and assume that in the debate between Paul and his readers he is right and they are wrong.[191] She calls for a much more critically oriented reading of Paul's portrayal of the situation, utilising the resources of literary and rhetorical criticism. She distinguishes between 'the historical argumentative situation' and 'the implied or inscribed rhetorical situation': the actual situation in Corinth and Paul's rhetorical presentation of it. The goal, as she sees it, is to read Paul's text 'in such a way that we move from the "world of the text" of Paul to the actual world of the Corinthian community' (see further ch. 11 below).[192]

Both Fiorenza and Wire approach 1 Corinthians with a high degree of suspicion about Paul's presentation of the situation in Corinth. Yet both are remarkably optimistic about the ability of rhetorical criticism to see through Paul's misleading argumentation and to uncover what was *really* happening in Corinth. The question is raised, therefore: Can one be deeply suspicious of the view of the situation portrayed in the text and yet remain hopeful of being able to reconstruct from that same text the situation as it really was?

Alert to this problem, Dennis Stamps proposes an approach to the situation in Corinth that has no pretensions about its capacity to say what was really taking place in Corinth.[193] His mode of analysis focuses, like Fiorenza's, on the 'rhetorical situation' of 1 Corinthians. For Fiorenza, the rhetorical situation is historically conditioned. That is, the rhetorical situation of 1 Corinthians is constrained, as she sees it, by the historical realities. And so, by careful and critical analysis, she believes, the interpreter can move from the inscribed situation to the historical one. Stamps, however, wants to draw a firm line between the two types of 'situation'. For him the rhetorical situation is strictly the *entextualized* situation: 'the rhetorical situation exists as a textual or literary presentation with the text or discourse'.[194] The entextualized situation, he insists, 'is not the historical situation which generates the text and/or which the text responds to or addresses; rather, at this level, it is that situation embedded in the text, and created by the text, which contributes to the rhetorical effect of the text.'[195] In isolating the

191. E. S. Fiorenza, 'Rhetorical Situation and Historical Reconstruction in 1 Corinthians', *NTS* 33 (1987) 386–403; here, pp. 389–90 (see below, ch. 11).

192. Fiorenza, 'Rhetorical Situation', 388.

193. D. Stamps, 'Rethinking the Rhetorical Situation: The Entextualization of the Situation in New Testament Epistles', in *Rhetoric and the New Testament: Essays from the 1992 Heidelberg Conference* (ed. S. E. Porter and T. H. Olbricht; JSNTSup 90; Sheffield: JSOT Press, 1993) 193–209.

194. Stamps, 'Rethinking', 199.

195. Stamps, 'Rethinking', 199.

inscribed rhetorical situation, Stamps takes up a narrative model—the approach offered by Norman Petersen in his book *Rediscovering Paul*.[196] The interpretive strategy involves transforming the letter into a narrative, that is, deriving from the letter an ordered sequence of events (as Paul presents them) relating to Paul and the Corinthians. What Stamps seeks to uncover in his exploration of the rhetorical situation is 'the story of the relationship between Paul and the Corinthians told from the temporal perspective of the time of writing and from the point of view of the sender.'[197]

It should be noted that Stamps himself does not repudiate the attempt to engage in historical reconstruction, but rather proposes an alternative which does not involve the problematic move from text to historical reality. It remains to be seen whether this approach will become a significant one. That such an alternative has been offered, however, brings up an uncomfortable question. Are our primary data, Paul's Corinthian letters, so biased and distorted that they constitute dubious historical sources? Is Paul's perspective on events at Corinth so hopelessly skewed that 1 Corinthians is of no practical use in reconstruction of the real situation? Such a thoroughgoing scepticism seems unnecessary; no scholar has as yet taken such a deeply pessimistic line. Paul must have known that if he wanted to achieve his aims in writing, he must present the situation in a way that was at least credible to his readers.[198] Nevertheless there are profound problems in supposing that we can ever rediscover, let along redescribe, some objective 'real situation' which Paul's letters reflect. Historians have become increasingly aware of the extent to which all descriptions of the past are partial and contested renarrations, shaped by the presuppositions and theoretical commitments of the researcher. Thoroughgoing scepticism about historical reconstruction is, we believe, unwarranted; but equally to be rejected is any naïve supposition that we can provide a full and unbiased description of 'how it actually happened' (*wie es eigentlich gewesen*).[199] One of the key contributions of feminist scholarship has been to highlight the ways in which the interests and ideological commitments of scholars have been implicated in their supposedly neutral descriptions of early Christianity, a topic further explored by Margaret MacDonald in chapter 21 below.

Most contemporary scholarship on Corinthian Christianity does reflect, albeit in varied ways, a confidence about the ability of interpreters to use Paul's text to reconstruct, at least partially, the historical situation at Corinth. Other historical sources, along with modern theoretical tools (such as social-scientific approaches), are widely used to further illuminate the context which Paul addresses. Some scholars adopt a naïvely descriptive approach, aiming simply to provide 'data' (cf. pp. 29–30 above), while others are more aware of the theo-

---

196. N. R. Petersen, *Rediscovering Paul: Philemon and the Sociology of Paul's Narrative World* (Philadelphia: Fortress, 1985).

197. Stamps, 'Rethinking', 209.

198. See Barclay, 'Mirror-Reading a Polemical Letter'.

199. This phrase originates in the famous statement defining the task of the historian made by German historian Leopold von Ranke (1795–1886).

retical and ideological dimensions inevitably tied up in such work. Feminist scholars in particular stress the need to read Paul's text suspiciously, but, as we have seen, they nevertheless remain confident that the situation at Corinth can be reconstructed—often against the grain of Paul's presentation of it—and are convinced that this reconstruction is an important part of the task of recovering women's history from its patriarchal marginalisation.

For the most part, historical reconstruction of the church at Corinth has been conducted to illuminate Paul's discourse itself: the primary goal has been a fuller understanding of the text of 1 and 2 Corinthians—a reflection of the status of these texts as Christian Scripture. The underlying assumption here is that the task of historical reconstruction is necessary to the interpretation of the letters. This historical reconstruction of the situation that prompted the text to be written has traditionally—at least since the rise of historical criticism—been seen as crucial to the exegesis of any New Testament text, especially the Pauline letters.[200] Recently, however, this key assumption has been called into question by those advocating a more theological reading of the letters and querying whether post-Enlightenment historical criticism offers the best way to interpret them. Francis Watson, for example, questions 'the hermeneutical assumption that interpretation must be controlled by a hypothetical "background" reconstructed by the interpreter—even where the text itself is silent about any such background.'[201] He offers a theologically oriented reading of 1 Cor 11.2–16 that is acutely aware of (unresolved) debates on the 'background' of the text but is not in any way controlled by these discussions. Richard Hays, in his commentary on 1 Corinthians, insists that his interest lies in the theological message of the letter, analysis of which, he claims, is not dependent on a reconstruction of the letter's occasion. He comments, 'As we work through the letter, we will build up some cumulative impressions of what Paul's original readers might have thought, but these impressions will remain sketchy and hypothetical; they will not be used to construct a systematic picture that will in turn govern our reading of the text.'[202]

Neither Watson nor Hays calls into doubt the legitimacy of the 'quest' for the historical church at Corinth (though Watson is sceptical about its results), but they do question its value for the theological exposition of 1 Corinthians, and other letters likewise. These theologically oriented approaches, like Stamps's form of rhetorical criticism, indicate ways in which studies of Paul's Corinthian letters could proceed and develop in considerable independence from studies of archaeology, historical background, or other attempts to reconstruct the context of the earliest churches in Corinth. A key question, however, is whether such readings

---

200. See, e.g., C. M. Tuckett, *Reading the New Testament* (London: SPCK, 1987) 55.

201. F. Watson, *Agape, Eros, Gender,* 45 n. 4. Cf. further idem, 'The Authority of the Voice'; idem, *Text, Church and World: Biblical Interpretation in Theological Perspective* (Edinburgh: T. & T. Clark, 1994); idem, *Text and Truth: Redefining Biblical Theology* (Edinburgh: T. & T. Clark, 1997).

202. R. B. Hays, *First Corinthians* (Interpretation; Louisville: John Knox Press, 1997) 8.

are likely to misconstrue the meaning and message of the text through failing to take seriously enough its historical setting (cf. ch. 22 below).

8. KEY ISSUES AND DEBATES

It should be abundantly clear from the previous survey that scholarship on Christianity at Corinth has moved through many diverse phases in which different aspects of the background, character, and literature of Corinthian Christianity have been highlighted. What should also be clear is that at the present time a wide range of diverse and sometimes incompatible approaches coexist and compete, a situation that is characteristic of contemporary biblical studies as a whole. There can be no simple fusion of these various approaches, and consequently no easy merger of their research agendas and questions. However, a number of different and important areas for future research and discussion can be highlighted.

For those who seek to be historians of early Christianity, and Christianity at Corinth in particular, it goes without saying that the range of sources—literary, archaeological, and so on—that can illuminate the ancient context are essential. However, it is not sufficient simply to gather data, to sample relevant literary sources, to cite archaeological reports. As Justin Meggitt argues in chapter 19 below, there are important questions to be asked not just about *which* sources of information should be drawn on, but also about *how* the available evidence should be used. Despite the persistence of some claims merely to be gathering and presenting 'data' relevant to understanding the Corinthian church, it should be clear that there needs to be careful and critical discussion concerning how to go about constructing an appropriate framework of interpretation, such that ancient evidence can be appropriately used to reconstruct a context for understanding the first urban Christians of Corinth. Meggitt argues for an approach that draws on the studies of 'popular culture' developed by historians. Even if one disagrees with his argument, it should at least establish the need for further discussion of the ways in which the ancient evidence should be 'read'. Meggitt insists that such discussion must be interdisciplinary, that New Testament scholars must interact not only with work done in Classics and Ancient History, but also with the approaches developed by other historians. The result may be more future research which is not only rich in its use of the available ancient evidence but also theoretically informed.

Questions about theory and method have also loomed large in debates among those who seek some kind of sociohistorical approach to reconstructing Christianity at Corinth. As we have seen, approaches range from those that eschew any use of modern social-scientific theories or models to those that adopt a strongly model-based method. There are, perhaps, dangers in either extreme: the danger of naïve empiricism at one end, the danger of fitting data to a predetermined model on the other. These are issues discussed by Bengt Holmberg in chapter 20. Holmberg stresses the need for a careful use of the available ancient evidence; no social-scientific model can substitute for that. He also highlights the ways in which different theoretical convictions guide the interpretation of ancient source material, and thus illustrates the need for explicit critical discussion of these interpretive frameworks. And in reviewing the debate about the use of 'models' in social-scientific interpretation, Holmberg illuminates the fundamental philosophical foundations of various methods: 'social-scientific perspectives or toolboxes usually come with an ontology of their own, even if this is not visible to begin with. Those who want to use these toolboxes must be prepared eventually to grapple with the underlying philosophical issues about the nature of social reality' (p. 271). Again what is highlighted is the need not only for a detailed engagement with the relevant ancient evidence—though that is certainly essential—but also for methodological discussion of the various theoretical frameworks employed.

With the realisation that no writing of history is neutral, that all interpreters write from a particular perspective, come questions about the interests and ideologies that (generally implicitly) shape particular presentations of Christianity at Corinth. One of the significant developments in recent scholarship, brought about especially by feminist criticism, is rendering visible and subjecting to critical scrutiny these various interests and ideologies. This is the subject of Margaret MacDonald's essay (ch. 21), which examines 'the implicit ideological influences on Corinthian scholarship'. In Baur's work, for example, MacDonald finds a negative portrayal of Judaism that needs critical questioning. In terms of wider trends, MacDonald examines the tendency of Corinthian scholarship in the 1950s and 1960s to place Paul 'at the centre'—to focus interest on recovering Paul's thought, with an implicit (and sometimes explicit) commitment to the superiority of the apostle's viewpoint. Similarly, she notes, scholarship of the 1960s and 1970s tended to presume 'that the *ekklesia* of first-century Corinth represents "Christianity"' (p. 285); the Corinthians are an instantiation of the religion we know as Christianity, and thus what the apostle Paul addresses to them is read as addressed to 'Christians'. Subsequent scholarship has subjected both these ideological influences to criticism: there has been a tendency to remove Paul from his pedestal, to drop the presumption that his perspective is by definition right and that of the Corinthians wrong, and also to stress the distinctiveness of this particular *ekklesia* of converts rather than see them, anachronistically, as an embodiment of what came to develop, after the split from Judaism and a process of institutional development, into 'Christianity'. In more recent scholarship MacDonald describes a tendency to place 'society at the centre', or 'women at the centre', leading to new emphases, respectively, on the Corinthian *ekklesia* in its contemporary sociopolitical context and on the value of the Corinthians' viewpoint (specifically that of the Corinthian women) over against that of Paul. While MacDonald finds much of value in these current directions in scholarship, she also identifies ways in which these approaches too prioritise certain ways of 'looking' at the Corinthian *ekklesia*, and may well neglect important aspects of the Corinthian context and background, such as the Jewish thought world. But what emerges as most vital from MacDonald's essay is the need for 'self-critical reading of the Corinthian correspondence', for scholarship attuned to the ways in which ideology and interests shape the interpretive endeavour.

It goes without saying (almost) that the reason for the expenditure of such large amounts of scholarly time and energy investigating the origins of Christianity at Corinth lies in the importance of Christianity as a world religion and the canonical status of the letters Paul wrote to Corinth. In other words, for many people it is the better understanding of Paul's texts, as well as a better understanding of Christian origins, that is the overarching aim for all such work. This of course explains the tendency MacDonald identifies to prioritise and privilege Paul's voice and perspective. While for many years the historical-critical method, generally presented as a detached, objective, scholarly endeavour, was unquestioningly accepted as the best way to shed light on these texts—constructing a historical background against which the text could then be read—this paradigm for biblical studies has in recent decades been dethroned. Some forms of rhetorical and theological approaches now aim to engage directly with the text as text, interpreting it without the use of a reconstructed 'con-text' deemed to represent the historical reality. There will no doubt continue to be divisions in biblical studies on this point, with many scholars insisting on the importance of historical and sociohistorical work (with or without the use of contemporary theories and models), and others arguing that a literary or theological appreciation of the text is by no means dependent on such historical hypotheses. James Dunn's essay (ch. 22) serves in part as an argument for the importance of historical context as a means to interpret the text: Dunn insists that 'the language of the text is the language of a whole society. And we today will only begin to understand the use of the language *in* the text if we understand the use of the language *of* the text, that is, the language in its vocabulary, syntax, and idiom as it was familiarly used and heard by the writer and listeners to the text' (p. 296). Nevertheless, Dunn shows how the various reconstructions of the 'context' of 1 Corinthians, from Baur onward, can illuminate various aspects of the text's meaning, without any one being *the* correct reconstruction. Indeed, Dunn shows how contemporary developments (such as the charismatic movement) can generate new interest in, and resonance with, aspects of Paul's text, such that the task of reading and interpreting never ends, but forms a dialogue between text and reader in which new meanings are discovered again and again.

Thus the task of reconstructing earliest Christianity at Corinth will continue in diverse ways. While some branches of New Testament scholarship may eschew historical reconstruction, exploring ways to read Paul's texts without proposing particular historical hypotheses, others will continue to make use of the wide range of ancient evidence in order to reconstruct a setting in ancient Corinth with which to better understand Paul and the Corinthians and thus to make sense of the letters that remain as testimony to their dialogue. The range of specific areas where such research may continue are too many to mention, from the imperial cult to domestic space, from dining practices to popular philosophical ideas and worldviews. One general area in which there does seem to be a convergence of opinion, unsurprising, perhaps, given the general collapse of the illusion that scholarship can ever be simply objective and disinterested, is in recognising the need for critical and theoretical reflection, on the ways to use and interpret ancient evidence (Meggitt), on the ways to employ social-scientific resources (Holmberg), and on the interests and ideologies that shape scholarship (MacDonald).

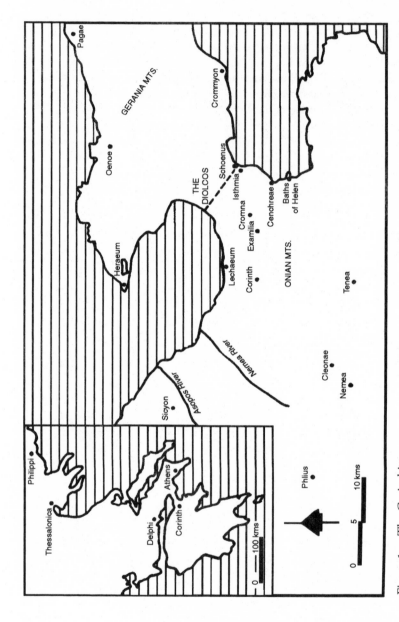

Figure 1. The Corinthia
(Reproduced with permission from The Liturgical Press)

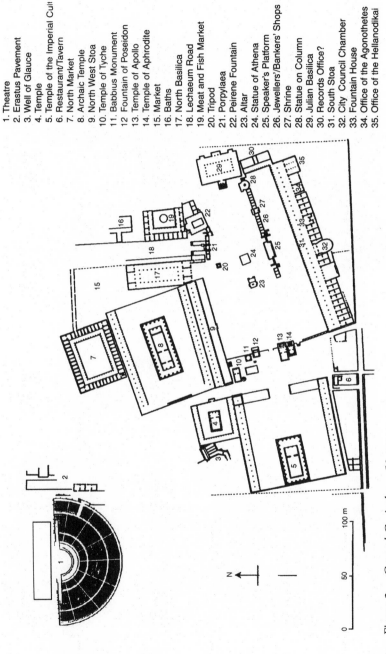

1. Theatre
2. Erastus Pavement
3. Well of Glauce
4. Temple
5. Temple of the Imperial Cult
6. Restaurant/Tavern
7. North Market
8. Archaic Temple
9. North West Stoa
10. Temple of Tyche
11. Babbius Monument
12. Fountain of Poseidon
13. Temple of Apollo
14. Temple of Aphrodite
15. Market
16. Baths
17. North Basilica
18. Lechaeum Road
19. Meat and Fish Market
20. Tripod
21. Porpylaea
22. Peirene Fountain
23. Altar
24. Statue of Athena
25. Speaker's Platform
26. Jewellers'/Bankers' Shops
27. Shrine
28. Statue on Column
29. Julian Basilica
30. Records Office?
31. South Stoa
32. City Council Chamber
33. Fountain House
34. Office of the Agonothetes
35. Office of the Hellanodikai

Figure 2.   Central Corinth ca. 50 C.E.
(Reproduced with permission from The Liturgical Press)

Photo 1. The Archaic Temple and Acrocorinth

Photo 2. The Synagogue inscription, now located in the courtyard of the Corinth Museum.

Photo 3.   The capital piece from a half-column, almost certainly from a synagogue, now located in the courtyard of the Corinth Museum.

Photo 4.   The Erastus inscription, *in situ* northeast of the theatre.

PART I
EXTRACTS FROM THE HISTORY OF SCHOLARSHIP ON CHRISTIANITY AT CORINTH

Chapter 1

The Two Epistles to the Corinthians[*]

Ferdinand Christian Baur

INTRODUCTION

There is one publication from the nineteenth century that is still regularly cited in discussions of the divisions at Corinth: Ferdinand Christian Baur's lengthy 1831 article on 'the Christ party in the Corinthian community, the opposition of Petrine and Pauline Christianity in the early church, the apostle Peter in Rome'. This essay stands head and shoulders above other contributions from the time in terms of its continuing influence in scholarship. A somewhat shortened version of the early part of the article was included in Baur's book on Paul, a section of which is reproduced here. Baur (1792–1860) developed the argument, earlier proposed by J. E. C. Schmidt, that the groups at Corinth to which Paul refers in 1 Cor 1.12 were essentially divided along a single fault line, that between Peter and Paul, with the Apollos group on Paul's side and the Christ group on Peter's.

Baur's view of the division at Corinth was the foundation stone for his reconstruction of early Christian history, a history dominated, Baur argued, by the

[*]Extracted from F. C. Baur, *Paul: The Apostle of Jesus Christ*, vol. 1 (ET of 2nd ed.; Edinburgh and London: Williams and Norgate, 1873) 267–320, here pp. 269–81.

opposition between Pauline (Gentile) Christianity and Petrine (Jewish) Christianity which was eventually synthesised in second-century catholic Christianity. In his works subsequent to the 1831 article, Baur sought to elaborate this thesis, showing how the various documents of early Christianity fitted into this Hegelian model of the progress of history. The radical criticism of the New Testament which Baur and his Tübingen school developed (including his late dating of many of the New Testament and other early Christian writings) came under sustained criticism, and Baur's proposals are now rarely accepted, at least in the form in which he proposed them. His grand but simple theory of historical development in the early church is too tidy to do justice to the diversity of perspectives and voices within early Christianity. However, whether in agreement or disagreement, a good deal of study of the history of early Christianity continues to operate in the shadow of Baur and on the lines of the agenda he established.

(For further detail, see the introductory essay above, section 3.)

Further Reading

See also chapter 13.

Baur, 'Die Christuspartei', repr. in F. C. Baur, *Historisch-kritische Untersuchungen zum Neuen Testament* (Ausgewählte Werke 1; Stuttgart-Bad Cannstatt: Friedrich Frommann, 1963) 1–146.

F. C. Baur, *The Church History of the First Three Centuries* (ET; 2 vols.; London: Williams and Norgate, 1878, 1879).

F. C. Baur, *Paul: The Apostle of Jesus Christ* (ET; 2 vols.; Edinburgh and London: Williams and Norgate, 1873, 1875).

H. Harris, *The Tübingen School* (Oxford: Clarendon, 1975).

W. G. Kümmel, *The New Testament: The History of the Investigation of Its Problems* (London: SCM, 1973), part IV, pp. 120–205.

Morgan, 'Tübingen School'.

In the first Epistle the Apostle treats of a series of circumstances which at that early period had a special interest for a church still in its infancy. The chief matter with which he concerned himself was the party spirit which existed in the Corinthian Church through the influence of the Judaising opponents. It had split into several parties, which were called by names denoting their several opinions (1.12). The names Paul, Apollos, Cephas and Christ betoken as it seems so many different parties. Very naturally the party of Paul is first placed before us. The Corinthians had not deserted the Apostle, they had only divided themselves into parties, and those members of the Church who had remained most faithful to the Apostle, as we see from the contents of both the Epistles, still continued to form an overwhelming majority. When different parties were formed in Corinth it cannot be wondered at that one of these should be called by the name of Apollos. Apollos was, according to the Apostle, undoubtedly his fellow-worker in the cause of the Gospel at Corinth, and if, as is related of him (Acts 18.24), he had attained such eminence through Alexandrine education and literary acquirements, it may easily be understood how there might be many persons in Corinth, who owing to the peculiarly Greek spirit of his discourses became so prepossessed in his favour that they gave him a certain precedence over the Apostle Paul. But why did not the favourable reception which other like-minded teachers met with from a portion of the Church, appear to the Apostle as indicating such a dangerous party spirit, and one so earnestly to be opposed? Some other circumstances must have occurred therefore before the expressed predilection for Apollos could have been considered by the Apostle as a token of a doubtful tendency in the Church. We must seek for the peculiar cause of division and schism in the names of the two other parties. With the name of Peter, an opposition to Paul is naturally connected. As far as we know, Peter himself was never at Corinth, but under the authority of his name a Jewish Christian element had, without doubt, been introduced into a Church consisting almost entirely of Gentile Christians. In this sense only can the Apostle mean to affix the name of Cephas or Peter to one of these parties. We should have expected that the Apostle would have taken as the subject of his objection, the principles propagated by the Judaising opponents, but the contents of his Epistle do not carry out this expectation. The Jewish doctrines of the absolute value of the Mosaic law, and the necessity of its observance for salvation, are no where combated as they are in the Epistles to the Galatians and the Romans, and there is no mention made of the law, and all that depends upon it. It is vain throughout the whole of both the Epistles to the Corinthians, to look for any trace which may help to bring us into a closer knowledge of the real existence of these parties, only the last chapter of the second Epistle leaves us in no doubt whatever that this opposition had by no means ceased. At the conclusion of the Epistle (2 Cor 11.22), the Apostle so openly unveils the Judaism of his opponents, and describes them as false with such sharp words, with all the authority of a born Jew who had become a teacher of Christianity, that we are easily enabled to understand the reason of his polemic against them; but we are no nearer to the desired explanation of their principles. The Judaism of his opponents appears here in a new form, and we may ask whether by means of these party relations we cannot see deeper into the fourth of these parties described by the Apostle—the so-called party of Christ. Here we come also to a most difficult question, which we must endeavour as far as possible to answer if we wish to arrive at a clear understanding of the circumstances of the Corinthian Church, and the position of the Apostle in it.

Who were these οἱ τοῦ Χριστοῦ? Amongst the interpreters and critics who in modern times have directed their attention to this question, Storr and Eichhorn have advanced theories which exhibit a natural opposition to each other, inasmuch as whilst the one adheres too closely to something special, the other on the contrary loses himself in generalities, but both have a common ground of agreement in neither relying on a decided point of support in the contents of the Epistle, nor in even giving a clear idea of the subject. According to Storr, οἱ τοῦ Χριστοῦ were those members of the Corinthian Church who had made the Apostle James the chief of their party as being the ἀδελφὸς κυρίου, in order that through this material relationship of the head of their sect to Jesus, they might claim for it a precedence which would exalt it over the Petrine party. The Apostle indeed might have had good reasons for hinting at this carnal idea of relationship to Christ, in the expression Χριστὸν κατὰ σάρκα γινώσκειν (2 Cor 5.13); but if Storr cannot bring forward anything else in support of his theory than that the Apostle speaks of the 'brethren of the Lord' (1 Cor 9.5), and speaks of James especially with Peter (15.7), of what value is such an hypothesis? According to Eichhorn, οἱ τοῦ Χριστοῦ may have been the neutrals who stood apart from the strife of parties; they did not depend on Paul, nor Apollos, nor Peter; but only on Christ. In order to give some sort of colouring to the idea of these neutrals, Pott endeavours to establish Eichhorn's theory, by a comparison of the passage 1 Cor 3.22, where Paul, after enumerating the schisms in the Corinthian Church which he had before denounced, brings forward as the main point of his argument the words πάντα ὑμῶν ἐστιν, εἴτε Παῦλος, εἴτε Ἀπολλῶς, εἴτε Κηφᾶς, πάντα ὑμῶν ἐστιν, ὑμεῖς δὲ Χριστοῦ, and does this in such a manner that we must look upon the views and doctrines of the Χριστοῦ ὄντες as those approved of by the Apostle himself. These same οἱ τοῦ Χριστοῦ are meant in 1.12, whilst in 3.22 the Apostle asserts that the Corinthians themselves τοῦ Χριστοῦ εἶναι, and he wishes to point out to the followers of the sects, the doctrines of the true Teacher, to which οἱ Χριστοῦ already had given their adherence. The sources from which they derived their Christian doctrine were equally the teachings of Paul, Apollos, and Peter; but in order to avoid any appearance of sectarianism they did not distinguish themselves by the name of the teacher who first instructed them in the principles τοῦ εἶναι Χριστοῦ, but simply called themselves τοῦ Χριστοῦ. In both the passages quoted above, there a Χριστοῦ εἶναι is indeed spoken of, but, as a more correct comparison will easily show us, in a very different sense. In the passage, 1.12, the words ἐγὼ δὲ Χριστοῦ are merely the indications of a sect, just as the three sentences immediately preceding them point out as many other sects. These words cannot however be taken as referring to the adherents of a so-called Party of Christ, were the Apostle to be understood as wishing to indicate it, as alone possessing a divine unity bestowed by Christ, in opposition to those sects and the other sectarian divisions and distinctions lying outside them. Therefore if οἱ Χριστοῦ were the neutrals, the neutrals themselves were nothing else than a sect, as Neander also supposes them to have been. 'They may indeed have maintained that they were Christians in a false sense; very probably the conceit of the Corinthians caused some to come forward, in these disputes as to whether the teachings of Paul or Peter or Apollos were the only true and perfect ones, who thought and asserted that they were better acquainted with Christianity than Paul, Peter or Apollos— some who out of verbal or written tradition, interpreted to suit their own foregone theories and opinions, made a Christ and a Christianity for themselves, and who now in their arrogant zeal for freedom wished to make themselves independent of the authority of the selected and enlightened witnesses of the Gospel, professing to have as perfect a system of doctrine as they had, and who in their presumption called themselves disciples of Christ as a distinction from all

others.' This view again can only be received as a modification of that of Eichhorn. What, after all this, are we to think of the peculiar characteristics of this
so-called Party of Christ? If they wished to set up a Christ and a Christianity of
their own in opposition to the chiefs of the other sects, to whose authority the
adherents of those sects submitted, their relation to Christ must have been
brought about in some way similar to that which had been the case with the other
sects, and we cannot see if they claimed to have a more perfect doctrine than others and to know Christianity better than Paul, Apollos and Peter, how they could
have made good their claim to this precedence with any better success than any
other of the sects. Therefore either οἱ Χριστοῦ were no sect to be classed with
the other sects mentioned with them, or they indeed formed a sect, but a sect of
which we must at the same time perceive we have at this day no data by which
to form a clear conception of its tendencies and peculiarities.

In order to arrive at a clearer understanding as to the probability of the last
mentioned point, it seems to me that the theory which J. E. Chr. Schmidt has
given, in a treatise on 1 Cor 1.12, is not without importance; namely, that there
were really but two parties, one that of Paul and Apollos, and the other, as
Schmidt expresses it, that of Peter and of Christ. Taking into consideration the
acknowledged relation in which Paul and Peter, one as the Apostle to the Gentiles, the other to the Jews, really stood towards each other, or at least the relation
in which they were thought to stand towards each other by the chief parties of
the oldest Christian Church, there can be no doubt that the chief difference lay
between the two sects which called themselves after Paul and Cephas. It follows
that the two other parties, that of Apollos and that of Christ, differed less from
each other, than from the former, of Paul and Apollos, and the relation also of
the parties of Paul and Apollos must be viewed in the same light. We see from
many passages that Paul placed Apollos completely on his own side and considered him as an authorized fellow-worker with himself in the preaching of the
Gospel, and we find nothing in the contents of either of these Epistles of the
Apostle, which would lead us to suppose that there was any important difference
between them. Still I will not deny, what is generally believed, that the Apostle,
in the passage in which he speaks of the distinction between the σοφία κόσμου
and the σοφία θεοῦ, had the party of Apollos especially in view, but on the other
hand it must be granted, that the mental tendency here pointed out must have
been more or less the ruling one in the Corinthian Church as a whole. The Apostle represents it as still fettered in this σοφία τοῦ κόσμου, and the yet deeper
and more thorough sense of the real Christian life in the inward man, he represents as a feeling which in the present state of their spiritual life, the Corinthians
had yet to attain. Although therefore the predominance of this mental tendency,
especially in so far as it consisted in an over-estimate of the outward forms of
teaching, as opposed to its quality and the nature of the doctrine itself, divided
the party of Apollos from that of Paul, and although the adherents of these parties set the teachers who were at their head, in a relation to each other which the
teachers themselves in no way recognized, the difference cannot have been so

essentially and dogmatically fixed that the two parties of the adherents of Peter, could not be reckoned as one sect; and if we look at the matter from this side, we can very well imagine that the relation between the party of Cephas and that of Christ may have been a similar one. Even if both sects must be considered as one and the same in the chief point, this does not at all affect the relation which must have subsisted between the parties of Paul and Apollos. The Apostle may also have intended to multiply the names, in order to depict the overbearing party-spirit in the Corinthian Church, which expressed itself in the multiplication of sectarian names, which indeed indicated different colours and shades of party opinion, although not exactly different parties (1 Cor 1.12). Let us, therefore, first investigate the question wherein the chief opposition consisted between the parties of Peter and Paul.

In the above named treatise, Schmidt finds the chief cause of the difference between the two parties in the presumption, which led the Jewish Christians to consider themselves true Christians, and which would scarcely allow them to reckon the Gentile Christians as real Christians. Among the first Christians there was a party which arrogated Christ to itself in a special manner—this was the Jewish Christian party. Christ, the Messiah, came in the first place for the sake of the Jews, to whom alone he had been promised; the Gentiles might thank the Jews that Christ had come into the world. Among such proud men as these Jewish Christians, would not the presumption arise that Christ, the Messiah, belonged to them alone? Exactly in this manner the presumption did arise, as we see from 2 Cor 10.7. They called themselves τοὺς τοῦ Χριστοῦ—disciples of Christ—disciples of the Messiah,—or, changing slightly the name, Χριστιανούς. If these Christians were Jewish Christians no doubt can arise that they formed one party with the sect of Peter. But if we agree with this, something else must have lain at the root of such a presumption on the part of the Jewish Christians, because it is quite incredible that they as Jewish Christians with such a presumption, which excluded the Gentile Christians from a participation in the Messianic salvation, should have gained an entrance into a Church consisting for the greater part of Gentile Christians. Therefore, however rightly Schmidt may see the ground of this opposition between the parties of Peter and of Paul, in the claim that the Petrine party made to be oἱ τοῦ Χριστοῦ, we may still enquire how this may be more exactly and certainly determined than has hitherto been done.

In order to answer this question, we shall certainly not be proceeding on an arbitrary assumption, in supposing that the chief accusation which the opposite party brought to bear against Paul would have been recognised in some way in these Epistles of the Apostle. But the vindication of the apostolic authority constitutes a chief portion of the contents of these Epistles—this authority not being willingly yielded in its full sense to the Apostle Paul by his opponents. They would not recognise him as a real and genuine Apostle, on the ground of his not being in the same sense as Peter and the rest of the Apostles, τοῦ Χριστοῦ, and not like these having been in the same direct connection with Jesus during his life on earth? Peter himself had no share in the party which went by his name in

Corinth, as it must be concluded, from what we have already seen, that Peter was never in Corinth at all; but it may well be supposed that the false Apostles who went about calling themselves by the name of Peter, eventually extended their travels to Corinth.

In the second Epistle, in which especially Paul speaks openly against these opponents, and directly contends with them, he calls them plainly ψευδαπόστολοι, ψευδάδελφοι, ἐργάται δόλιοι, μετασχηματιζόμενοι εἰς ἀποστόλους Χριστοῦ (2 Cor 11.13). They also wished to be the true ἀπόστολοι Χριστοῦ, or to be in the closest connection with them, and in this sense to be Χριστοῦ ὄντες. The special zeal of the Jewish Christians for the Mosaic law may also in this last respect be essentially the actuating motive, but since in a Church of Gentile Christians, such as was the Corinthian, they could not expect a favourable reception, if they had immediately brought forward their principles, they fell back on the special ground of their Judaistic opposition, they attacked the apostolic authority of the Apostle, and endeavoured in this way to work against him. According to this supposition, the relation of the party of Peter to that of Christ seems very simple and natural. Just as those of Paul and of Apollos did not essentially differ; so these two were not different parties, but only one and the same party under two different names, so that each name only denoted the claim which that party made for itself. They called themselves τοὺς Κηφᾶ, because Peter held the primacy among the Jewish Apostles, but τοὺς Χριστοῦ, because they relied on the direct connection with Christ as the chief token of genuine apostolic authority; and on this very account would not recognize Paul, who had been called to be an Apostle in a perfectly unusual and peculiar manner, as a genuine Apostle, enjoying the same privileges as the others, and thought they ought to place him at least far down in the ranks of Apostles.

On this account also their designation, evidently intentionally chosen, was τοῦ Χριστοῦ not τοῦ Ἰησοῦ or τοῦ κυρίου. The idea of the Messiah must be brought forward as the complete actuating organ of the Messianic happiness and blessing of the higher life, whose principle is Christ, in order to indicate all that those who belonged to this name had received from the most direct tradition, from an outward and actually experienced connection with the person of Jesus as the Messiah.

We must now endeavour as much as possible to establish the view here brought forward, by extracts from some principal passages of the two Epistles. Perhaps indeed the first apologetic section, in which the Apostle gives a vindication of his apostolic authority and work (1 Cor 1.4), contains some indications that he may have had in his mind those adherents of the party of Peter who claimed to be considered as τοὺς τοῦ Χριστοῦ. When the Apostle maintains with all his energy (1 Cor 2.26), ἡμεῖς δὲ νοῦν Χριστοῦ ἔχομεν (so far as the divine πνεῦμα is the principle of his Christian consciousness)—when he desires his readers to remember that they have to look on him as ὑπηρέτης Χριστοῦ (1 Cor 4.1)—when he asserts that he as the least of the Apostles is willing to consider himself as a μωρὸς διὰ Χριστόν (1 Cor 4.10), in so far as on good grounds they hold themselves as φρόνιμοι ἐν Χριστῷ; when, he reminds them that although they might have μυρίους παιδαγωγοὺς ἔχειν ἐν Χριστῷ, they could not have πολλοὺς πατέρας (1 Cor 4.15); in all passages such as these it is tolerably clear that he referred to the sects which he had just before mentioned; those parties who in the Apostle's opinion wished to make themselves known in an obnoxious manner, and in a perfectly peculiar sense as οἱ τοῦ Χριστοῦ ὄντες, and these special references lie behind the general apologetic tendency of all this section of the Epistle. In any case, an important passage of this section is to be found 9.1ff. The Apostle with a sudden transition here speaks in his own person, while still very closely connecting the portion of his Epistle, beginning in 9.1, with the contents of the chapter immediately preceding, and he skillfully avails himself of the opportunity thus offered for an apologetic discourse. In the foregoing eighth chapter then, the Apostle had discussed the cause of the question which had been laid before him, about the use of meat offered to idols at the participation in the Gentile sacrificial feasts, and had given his opinion that cases might arise when it would be necessary to give up, out of consideration for others, what according to a man's own views he would be perfectly justified in maintaining. He puts this idea in such a manner as to give himself an opportunity of considering many things alleged to his disadvantage by his opponents in a light which with regard to his apostolic call can only appear as a voluntary renunciation. As an Apostle he had also certain rights of which he as well as the other Apostles might avail himself of; but that he had never done so because a higher consideration had bidden him make no use of them, Οὐκ εἰμὶ ἐλεύθερος; οὐκ εἰμὶ ἀπόστολος; οὐχὶ Ἰησοῦν Χριστὸν τὸν κύριον ἡμῶν ἑόρακα; am I not free ? am I not an Apostle ? and truly an Apostle as well as any other Apostle? have I not seen the Lord Jesus Christ? Wherefore the appeal to the ἑορακέναι Ἰησοῦν Χριστὸν, τὸν κύριον ἡμῶν, as a vindication of the ἀπόστολος εἶναι, if his opponents did not deny him the real apostolic character, because he had not seen the Lord as they, or rather the Apostle at the head of their party had done, and had not lived in direct communion with him? This also must be the genuine token of the Χριστοῦ εἶναι. But that these opponents of the Apostle belonged also to one class with the adherents of the party of Peter is clear from the following words, μὴ οὐκ ἔχομεν ἐξουσίαν ἀδελφὴν γυναῖκα περιάγειν, ὡς καὶ οἱ λοιποὶ ἀπόστολοι καὶ οἱ ἀδελφοὶ τοῦ κυρίου, καὶ Κηφᾶς (1 Cor 9.5). The Χριστοῦ εἶναι held good in all these cases in the sense already discussed; it held good for the Apostles in general who had enjoyed communion with Jesus, it availed in a narrower sense for the ἀδελφοὶ Κυρίου, inasmuch as they stood in a still nearer connection to the Lord as his relatives; and it held good in the narrowest sense for Peter, inasmuch as Jesus himself had assigned him a certain precedence over the other Apostles, and he represented the whole relation between Jesus and the others in the most complete manner in his own person. But Paul thought that he himself, in the full consciousness of his apostolic dignity, and the rights and claims connected with it, ought not to take a secondary place, even to Peter. In token that he possessed the same rights as the other

Apostles, and especially the right to live at the expense of the churches to whom he preached the Gospel, the Apostle appeals first, to what holds good in law and custom in common life (vv. 7, 8); secondly, to a precept of the Mosaic Law, which indeed primarily referred to animals needed for the use of man, but which might equally be applied to the greatest things as to the least (vv. 9–12); and thirdly, to the customs prevailing in the Mosaic sacrificial worship (v. 13). But however well grounded his claim to be an Apostle might be on these accounts, still he had never made any use of them, because such a practice did not seem to him to be consistent with the plan of the Gospel, and would place himself in a mercenary light. Accordingly, living constantly in the consciousness of the chief aim to which he had devoted himself, he subjugated his whole personality to the interests of others and the regard to be paid to them, and his carnal nature he held in such subjection that it was forced to yield to the power of his spirit (vv. 15–17). This whole section contains indeed a most ample refutation of the supposition that the opponents of the Apostle had ascribed the humility and unselfishness with which he preached the Gospel in the churches, to the self-evident consciousness of the Apostle, which did not allow him to dare to place himself in a situation to assume the same rights as the other Apostles. On account of this demeanour indicating only weakness and want of self-confidence, they thought they themselves had the less cause to be obliged to keep back the selfish and self-seeking πλεονεξία (2 Cor 12.14) of which the Apostle elsewhere accuses them. But the more these charges were connected with the chief attack on his apostolic dignity the more it must have seemed to the Apostle to be for his interest to vindicate himself from them, and to place his behaviour in its true light. As here the Apostle' s apology refers in its main point to the ἑορακέναι 'Ιησοῦν Χριστὸν, τὸν κύριον ἡμῶν; without explaining more clearly the peculiar nature of this ἑορακέναι he expresses his desire of holding fast in general to all that placed him on a level with the other Apostles. And he says also that as in any case a peculiar material revelation of the Lord could be predicated of himself, he accordingly (1 Cor 15.8) declares in the same connection, that the Lord had appeared to him also as to the other Apostles. Just as the important exposition of the doctrine of the resurrection which follows seems to demand an equally authentic attestation of the chief points on which it relies, namely, that Jesus rose from the dead, and was really seen as so risen, so the theory cannot be excluded, that with regard to the chief points in which his opponents wished to involve the question of his apostolic authority, the Apostle evidently made use of the opportunity which here naturally offered itself, of placing himself in the same position with the disciples who were associated with Jesus during his life, and of vindicating his apostolic call by the criterion of a direct material appearance of the Lord.

Chapter 2

The Church without Factions: Studies in I Corinthians 1–4[*]

Johannes Munck

INTRODUCTION

For well over a hundred years F. C. Baur's thesis that the church at Corinth was characterised by the opposition of two factions, mirroring the dialectic between Pauline (Gentile) and Petrine (Jewish) Christianity in the early church as a whole, set the agenda for much of the scholarly discussion of Corinthian Christianity. In this essay, Johannes Munck contests Baur's historical reconstruction. As part of a larger critique of Baur's views, Munck denies the presence of a Judaizing group or any other distinct faction in the Corinthian church. Munck contends that Paul was addressing a problem of 'bickerings' in the congregation, not of parties with discrete theological and ethical positions. In the first section (I), extracted below, Munck argues that the only reference to 'factions' in the letter (1 Cor 11.19) occurs in an eschatological context. The factions of which Paul

*Extracted from J. Munck, 'The Church without Factions: Studies in I Corinthians 1–4', in *Paul and the Salvation of Mankind* (London: SCM, 1959) 135–67; here pp. 135–39, 148–54. Originally published as 'Menigheden uden Partier', *DTT* 15 (1952) 215–33. Reprinted by permission of SCM Press, 9–17 St Albans Place, London, N1 0NX.

here speaks are those that lie ahead for the church; they do not belong to the current experience of the Corinthian church. Paul does refer to divisions in the church (e.g., 1 Cor 1.10; 11.18), but what the apostle has in view are cliques and squabblings. In the next part of the essay (sections II–IV, not included here), Munck goes on to argue that the alleged factions of 1 Cor 1–4 play no part in the rest of the letter. In section V, printed below, he offers his own interpretation of what 1 Cor 1–4 discloses about conditions in Corinth, claiming that there can be no question of a Jewish basis to the problems in Corinth, that the church as a whole enjoyed sophistic wrangles, that the internal bickering was over personalities, not theological matters, and that the church was profoundly influenced by the Hellenistic milieu of the day. The rest of the essay argues that the Corinthians, because of their Hellenistic outlook, misunderstood the gospel, their leaders, and their own position.

The essay is important not only as a sustained critique of Baur's construction of the situation at Corinth but also as an early statement of the view that Hellenistic or Greco-Roman values and practices lie behind the situation Paul addresses in 1 Cor 1–4. In this respect Munck's essay anticipates a widespread trend in recent scholarship. His contention that the bickerings at Corinth reflect customs attested in the wider culture has been developed in detailed studies by Laurence Welborn (see ch. 10 below), Andrew Clarke, Bruce Winter, and others. His claim that the controversy between Paul and the Corinthians over wisdom had to do in part with the rhetorical conventions of that age has been echoed by Duane Litfin and Stephen Pogoloff. Nevertheless, many would also suspect that in his desire to refute Baur, Munck underplays the extent of division and conflict in the church at Corinth (for examples see chs 4 and 5 below).

Further Reading

W. Baird, "'One Against the Other": Intra-Church Conflict in 1 Corinthians', in *The Conversation Continues: Studies in Paul and John: In Honour of J. L. Martyn* (ed. R. R. Fortna and B. R. Gaventa; Nashville: Abingdon, 1990) 116–36.

Clarke, *Secular and Christian Leadership.*

J. D. G. Dunn, *1 Corinthians* (New Testament Guides; Sheffield: Sheffield Academic Press, 1995) 27–45.

Litfin, *St. Paul's Theology.*

S. M. Pogoloff, *Logos and Sophia: The Rhetorical Situation of 1 Corinthians* (SBLDS 134; Atlanta: Scholars Press, 1992).

L. L. Welborn, 'On the Discord in Corinth' (ch. 10 below).

B. W. Winter, *Philo and Paul among the Sophists* (SNTSMS 96; Cambridge: Cambridge University Press, 1997) 10–11, 147, 185, etc.

The foundation of Ferdinand Christian Baur's work on the history of primitive Christianity was laid in an article that he wrote on the factions in the church at Corinth. In it we already meet the characteristic features that we mentioned above as the *historical* side of the Tübingen School theory. The four factions in Corinth mentioned in 1 Cor 1.12ff are narrowed down, on the basis of our common knowledge of Paul and Peter in their mutual relations, to two—a Petrine, in the form of the Cephas and the Christ faction, and a Pauline, composed of the Paul faction and the Apollos faction. In other words, Baur again finds here the two main factions that he constructed within the whole Church (not only in Corinth), that is the Jewish Christian and the Gentile Christian, with their own particular views about the two apostles.

Instead of that view of conditions in Corinth and of a contrast between Petrine and Pauline Christianity—a contrast hiding behind those conditions and of decisive importance for the whole of primitive Christianity—we shall offer another and, we hope, a convincing exegesis of the texts that have hitherto been used as evidence for Baur's views, and shall try in doing so to refute the assumptions and conjectures of Baur and later scholars. For this purpose we wish not only to show that that conception rests on an exaggeration of certain much less serious party contrasts in the Gentile Christian church in Corinth—the commentators are gradually coming to recognize this—but to make it clear in the course of our argument that the first letter to the church in Corinth does not speak of factions among the Christians there, but that the texts that have hitherto been used as evidence for that assumption mention only disunity and bickerings.

First it must be shown that it can be clearly seen, from the terms that Paul uses about the situation in Corinth, that it is not a question of factions. The Greek word for faction, αἵρεσις, is used in 1 Cor 11.19: 'For factions among you must come in order that those who are genuine among you may be recognized.' There is a saying of Jesus of later tradition[1] which reads, for example in Justin, *Dialogue* 35.3, ἔσονταῖ σχίσματα καὶ αἱρέσεις.[2] This saying of Jesus may be older than Paul and may have been used by the latter in 1 Cor 11.19; or it may have its origin in this remark of Paul's; in any case Paul intends the verse to be taken eschatologically. In the last days, which are not far off, many in the Church will fall away, and thereby endanger the Church's continued existence (Matt 24.10f; cf. Acts 20.30).[3] αἵρεσις is also thought of eschatologically in the other two cases where the word is used in letters (in Acts it refers to the Jewish sects—Sadducees, Pharisees, and Christians), namely in enumerating the works of the flesh in Gal 5.19–21, where we find one after the other διχοστασίαι, αἱρέσεις, φθόνοι, and in 2 Peter 2.1 αἱρέσεις ἀπωλείας.[4] The divine purpose (ἵνα after δεῖ in 1 Cor 11.19) behind these heavy afflictions that will come on the Church consists in the recognition of those who are genuine. The many, as is shown in Matt 24.10f par., will fall away and be seduced, their love growing cold; and it is of the few that we read further on, 'But he who endures to the end will be saved.' So

---

1. A. Resch, *Agrapha* (TU 30.3, 4; 1906).
2. See also J. Jeremias, *Unknown Sayings of Jesus*, 59–61.
3. Cf. my article 'Les discours d'adieu', 159ff.
4. This refers to the false teachers of the last days; cf. 'discours d'adieu', 161f.

the disputes over the Lord's Supper open out to the apostle a sinister prospect, for he recognizes here the first signs of coming tribulations, which, however, remain hidden from the unconcerned Corinthians. The explanation of this verse must therefore start from the recognition that the apostle looks on suffering as the Christian's natural lot—a view that is expressed not only in 1 Corinthians, but even more strongly in 2 Corinthians.[5]

The last clause in v. 19, 'in order that those who are genuine among you may be recognized' (ἵνα [καὶ] οἱ δόκιμοι φανεροὶ γένωνται ἐν ὑμῖν), is probably also in itself an eschatological statement.[6] We not only find it said in the New Testament that Christians are destined to afflictions (1 Thess 3.3) and that 'we' must through many tribulations enter the kingdom of God (Acts 14.22), but we read in James 1.12, 'Blessed is the man who endures trial, for when he has stood the test (δόκιμος γενόμενος) he will receive the crown of life. . . .' Resch quotes as Agraphon 90 a saying of Jesus,[7] which reads in the Old Latin fragment of the *Didascalia* edited by Hauler, 'vir, qui non est temptatus, non est probatus a D(e)o'[8] (cf. the Greek form in Nilus, ἀνὴρ ἀπείραστος ἀδόκιμος παρὰ [τῷ] Θεῷ).[9] This saying, which is also discussed by Jeremias (pp. 56–59), has in its form no resemblance to the last clause in 1 Cor 11.19. But if we are right in taking the first clause of the verse to mean that factions and divisions must of divine necessity visit the Church in the last days, the verse's second clause has as its content the same line of thought as the saying of Jesus just quoted. Affliction is necessary. He who has experienced nothing of the kind has not proved himself genuine. Therefore we see that the divine aim of affliction is that those who prove themselves genuine will emerge from it victorious. But the rest succumb to temptation and fall away.

So it is not as yet a matter of factions; they are part of the future misfortunes, of the Messianic sufferings, which the apostle to the Gentiles has already encountered, but which the Corinthians have so far been spared.[10] On the other hand, we are told of divisions, σχίσματα, in the church. In John's Gospel we read in three places that a σχίσμα arose, among the people (7.43), the Pharisees (9.16), and the Jews (πάλιν, 10.19). In these passages the word does not imply a lasting separation, but means that some people want or think something in which others cannot concur. We find it in 1 Cor 1.10; 11.18; 12.25. σχίσματα (or σχίσμα in 12.25, though some important manuscripts have the plural) may signify here a division that is not of such short duration; and this is confirmed by the fact that the apostle wishes to define his attitude to it from a distance. In the

---

5. 1 Cor 4.8ff; 7.28; 2 Cor 4.7ff; 6.3ff; 11.23ff.
6. See *Epistula Apostolorum* 36 (47) (TU 43, p. 111): 'Thereby shall the elect be known, that they, being plagued with such afflictions, come forth.'
7. Resch, *Agrapha*, 130–32. With this we should also compare Agraphon 68 (pp. 89f).
8. E. Hauler, *Didascaliae Apostolorum Fragmenta Veronensia Latina* I (1900) 17, lines 19f.
9. PG 79, 896D. Resch quotes the passage as Nilus, *Peristeriae* 4.6, but it is in 10.6.
10. Whereas the Corinthians, according to 1 Corinthians, have not yet suffered, 2 Cor 1.6f is evidence that they now 'endure the same sufferings'.

text that we investigated earlier, 11.18ff, it is a question of happenings at the common meal, where the church members fall apart into cliques for eating and drinking. The commentators usually relate the separation ὃς μὲν πεινᾷ ὃς δὲ μεθύει to the poor and the rich.[11] No one thinks that this might refer to the factions that are supposed to be in the church, and that these factions take the Lord's Supper separately and so cause grievous division.

The same holds good for 12.25. It is true that here Paul is not speaking directly of the relations in the church at Corinth. He tells a parable of the human body and the relation of its members to each other, applying it to the Corinthian church (which is the body of Christ) and the church members' mutual service with the gifts of the Holy Spirit where among other things the thought is of Christians endowed with charismatic gifts, who are to have at heart the welfare of those who have received no such spiritual gift of grace. We therefore cannot be certain that each separate feature of the parable refers to the conditions at Corinth. But if we do so, and relate vv. 24f directly to the unhappy conditions there, then we have to think of the church members who did not share in the gifts of the Holy Spirit. God has given greater honour to these people than to those endowed with charismatic gifts, so that there may be no cleavage(s) in the body, and the different parts may care for each other in the same way. If (as must not be too readily assumed) this is the correct interpretation, then the real state of affairs is that there is no split in the church, whereas we can see by the detailed statements in ch. 14 what might indicate such a split. But it is all so uncertain that we must regard σχίσμα as a temporary division among the church members.

The third passage in which Paul speaks of σχίσματα is in 1.10. After the greeting and thanksgiving (1.1–9) he exhorts the church to be united and to avoid dissensions among themselves. It is justifiable to give σχίσματα the same meaning here as in 11.18 and 12.25, where the thought was of cliques at the Lord's Supper and cliques based on the apparently unequally distributed gifts of the Spirit. It is therefore a question, not of factions, but simply of divisions among church members for nontheological reasons. We must agree with Lietzmann in his interpretation of τὸ αὐτὸ λέγειν as *consentire*, and on the other hand reject the view of Heinrici and Schmiedel, who think that the passage is concerned with 'credal declarations' because of λέγει in v. 12.[12]

In v. 11 Paul describes the prevailing condition as ἔριδες. On this Bachmann remarks pertinently (p. 56), 'Not only the plural (which is apparently less usual with Paul; cf. e.g. Titus 3.9) but also the explanation that follows in v. 13 show that ἔριδες is meant to include antagonisms working themselves out in words, that is, bickerings; thus the idea is much more restricted than that of σχίσματα, and this is confirmed at the same time by the precision with which in this case (though not in v. 10) the ἔριδες are described as actually present. Paul therefore

---

11. It would be more prudent to speak of the more prosperous.
12. Lietzmann and G. Heinrici *ad loc.;* P. W. Schmiedel, 'Die Briefe an die Thessalonicher und an die Korinther', *Hand-Kommentar zum NT II* (1893), on 1 Cor 1.10–13.

takes care not to describe the σχίσματα as already present. But he indicates clearly enough by the context that at least they will come if the ἔριδες do not go.'

Paul therefore describes the conditions that he is combating not as factions but as bickerings, arising because the individual church members profess as their teacher Paul, Apollos, Cephas, or Christ, and exclude the others.

So far our inquiries have given us only negative results. The expressions that Paul uses in 1 Cor 1–4 about the unhappy conditions in the church show that he is not writing about factions: and in fact outside these chapters we hear nothing about the supposed factions. But not even here are we enlightened about the points of view of the four 'factions'; we learn nothing even about the 'Apollos faction' from Paul's argument. But what does 1 Cor 1–4 tell us about? We now have to estimate what Paul's argument in these first chapters tells us about the situation.

1. It is not a question of Jewish wisdom. In the passage 1.18ff people have claimed to see, in the fact that Paul is not speaking here only of the Greek striving after wisdom, but also has the Jews in mind in vv. 22–24, evidence that the argument is directed against the Alexandrian Jew Apollos. It is therefore not a purely Greek phenomenon with which Paul is concerned here, but something that is of importance for the Jews too.

It may be observed here, however, that it is in vv. 22–24 where it is supposed to be proved that the argument against false wisdom is of importance for the Jews too, that the Jews are characterized as people who do not strive for wisdom; for v. 22 reads, 'For Jews demand signs and Greeks seek wisdom' (ἐπειδὴ καὶ Ἰουδαῖοι σημεῖα αἰτοῦσιν καὶ Ἕλληνες σοφίαν ζητοῦσιν). This passage, therefore, cannot contain any argument against Jewish wisdom.

In vv. 19f Paul lays it down that what passes for wisdom in this world, and all sorts of wise men, are already destroyed. By his work of salvation (σταυρός) and the preaching of the Cross (λόγος) God has characterized the world's wisdom as foolishness. For as in its worldly wisdom the world did not recognize God in the works of creation (1.21) which testified to his wisdom, God determined to save, by the foolishness of preaching, those who believe. As in Rom 1.20f and 10.3ff we see the disobedience of the Gentiles to the Creator, and the disobedience of the Jews who strive to plead their own righteousness. Christ is the turning-point in history, in whom God shows mankind a new way, because the one hitherto taken has been shown to be impassable. This new way is a way of salvation, just as the Gentiles thought that their wisdom and philosophy were. Salvation now comes by faith. And yet Jews and Greeks go on behaving just as before, the Jews for their part demanding signs (1.22). 'We wish to see a sign from you', the Jews said to Jesus (Matt 12.38; 16.4). If Jesus had revealed himself in glory, the Jews might have believed that he was the Messiah. But the Messiah on the cross was foolishness to all except those on the way of salvation. The Greeks for their part sought salvation, as always, through philosophy; they sought wisdom, and the Gentiles who have just been converted in Corinth go on doing the same thing. But we Christians—and no doubt you Corinthians too, Paul continues in v. 23—preach Christ crucified. This preaching must seem blasphemy to the Jews. Here the force of the miraculous and the sublimity are lacking; the Messiah dies on the cross like any criminal, abandoned by God and man. And the preaching must sound like foolishness to the Gentiles, because salvation is to be found only in worldly wisdom. But to us, Jews and Greeks, who have heard God's call, the Crucified One is the power of God, though the Jews rejected him because of his weakness; and he is the wisdom of God, though the Greeks saw in his person and in his work only foolishness (1.24).

If, in a context concerned with converted Greeks, Paul brings the Jews too into his treatment of the Christ-event by which the world's wisdom became foolishness, he does so because he is speaking of man's salvation and its effect on the two species of which the human race consists, Jews and Greeks. By v. 26 the Jews have already disappeared from the train of thought.

2. Paul's argument is directed, not against the persons whose names are invoked, nor against the factions that have gathered round them, but against the church as such.

It is usual to suppose that the attacks in individual texts refer to the factions—the above-mentioned 1.18ff, for instance, to the Apollos faction, or 3.10–17 (as used to be the case) to the Cephas party. In neither case is it likely that any such controversy was behind it. In connection with Paul's treatment of the supposed factions it is a matter of marked indifference to him what the different faction leaders represented, or what was preached by the leaders who were invoked. It is not those leaders, but only the Corinthians' attitude towards them, that Paul is attacking. At bottom it is only the word 'I', in the sentences 'I belong to Paul' etc., against which he argues.

It is the church itself that loves those wrangles in which the church members exalt themselves by supposing that their wisdom has been taken over from one of the great Christian sophists, one of those close and well known to them, Paul and Apollos, or one of those known by what Paul has told them, Peter, the apostle to the Jews, or by the Lord and Master himself, Christ.

Besides 1.18ff, 3.10–17 in particular has been regarded as a polemic against other teachers. From 3.5 onward Paul has been speaking about the Christian leaders and the way they should be regarded. As God is everything, we must make no distinction between those people; but at the judgment each of them will receive his reward according to his efforts.

This last idea, which is in contrast to the Corinthians' hasty judgment on the Christian teachers, leads Paul to mention the judgment on the Corinthians themselves. Thanks to his apostolic gift of grace, Paul, as a wise architect, has laid the foundation in Corinth, but others are continuing to build on it. But each of them must take care how he continues to build (3.10). Paul therefore does not contrast himself with the other Christian leaders who have performed a task in Corinth after him. That would indeed be in complete contradiction to all the earlier argument of the chapter, which is concerned to show that there was no distinction in relation to the Christian teachers, and that none ought to be made. On the other hand, the Corinthians and the apostle are contrasted with each other. The apostle has laid the proper foundation, for which no other can be substituted; but it is of decisive importance how the Corinthians continue to build on it. It will be seen on the day of judgment what they are building, whether the material is precious or worthless (3.10–12). Paul reminds them that a day will come when everything will be revealed and a righteous judgment can be pronounced. What is the use of the Corinthians' hasty and foolish judgments on their leaders? Christ's incorruptible judgment will soon bring the real conditions to light (3.13). Three different things may happen to the Corinthians: (1) The good architect, whose work stands the test, will reap the reward of his labour. That reward is not salvation, but is added to salvation. Just as salvation comes from grace, so the reward will be given from grace, but the reward is in proportion to the good, well-tried work. (2) If, on the other hand, the work of the individual architect does not stand the test, he goes without his reward; but he is to be saved 'as through fire.' (3) But because the church in Corinth is God's temple in which God's Spirit lives, God will destroy those who seek to destroy his temple (3.14–17).

4.15 too, which speaks of countless guides, is meant for the Corinthians themselves, who have tried to continue Paul's work in their own way.

3. Paul is not arguing in chs. 1–4 against false doctrine. As we shall see later, the Corinthians' wrong conception of the Gospel as wisdom is connected with their misunderstanding of other points; but there is no dogmatic controversy in the first four chapters. We saw in the above treatment of the 'factions' that it was impossible to get a clear picture of their points of view. That is connected with the fact that Paul is not arguing against the individual factions and their false teachers, since there are no factions and since the Corinthians' shortcomings in respect of their bickerings are regarded in this section as primarily ethical failures. The usual attempts to find a Judaizing movement behind the factions, and Peterson's efforts to see Jewish contrast between true and false wisdom, must therefore be rejected.

4. The Corinthians regarded the Christian message as wisdom like that of the Greeks, the Christian leaders as teachers of wisdom, themselves as wise, and all this as something to boast about. Paul asserts, on the contrary, that the Gospel is foolishness, that the Christian leaders are God's servants whom God will judge, that the Corinthians are of the flesh and therefore without wisdom, and that none of this redounds to the glory of any human being, but that he who boasts is to boast of the Lord.

First Cor 1–4 shows us something taken from a Hellenistic *milieu* which has received the Gospel, but which introduces into the Gospel certain elements of that *milieu* which falsify the Gospel. In others of Paul's letters too we find such misunderstandings and falsifications in people's outlook on the Gospel and its preachers. Dibelius has rightly pointed out, with reference to 1 Thess 2, that the Christian preachers, like the better of the itinerant philosophic preachers of the time, were early compelled to draw a sharp dividing line between themselves and the many itinerant teachers who tried by all means to satisfy their craving for applause, riches, and fame.[13]

In Colossians we meet a church that received the Gospel much as the Corinthians did, adding to it and falsifying it by their existing pagan ideas. They venerate the cosmic powers and teach asceticism, and describe these additions to the Gospel as 'philosophy'. 'Philosophy' is used, as so often, to describe a religious doctrine or cult. It is not only in the simple circles where Christianity gains entrance at that time, that religion appears as philosophy. It is, indeed, a sign of the time that philosophy turns with its preaching to the public at large. If we look at all the representatives of various philosophic trends, we find, beside the philosophers of the schools proper, numerous writers and preachers who are only loosely connected with their philosophic school, but who take part in speech and writing in the religious debate of their time.[14]

The *milieu* to which we are introduced in 1 Cor 1–4 reflects processes that we know from literature and the upper classes. It is a question here, not simply of philosophy, but of a mixture of philosophy and sophistry, typical of that age. When Christianity becomes combined later in Alexandria with the highest civilization of the time, it first meets sophism in its more philosophic form in the person of Clement, before it finds in Origen a representative who matches the learned philosophers of the schools. In the simpler circles in Corinth we meet a more popular brand of mixture of philosophy, religion, and rhetoric.

It is a question of something that is philosophy or wisdom by name, but Christian life by content, as the Corinthians experience it in the firm consciousness of being rich, free, and equal to anything. To describe that experience they use the most imposing expressions that they know from their Greek *milieu*. That new, overflowing life is wisdom, and they have received it from a teacher of wisdom; and in their childish vainglory each boasts of having had the best and most eminent teacher of wisdom. And because they know only the popular philosophy and the professional orator or sophist, who understood how to captivate a Greek audience by his learning and eloquence, the outward form is conclusive for them. The apostle, who has not forgotten the apprehension with which he began to preach about Christ in Corinth, suddenly sees himself compared with a professional sophist who, with painted face and theatrical gestures, invites an audience of a thousand people to suggest to him a theme on which to improvise.

It is clear from the conjunction of 'word' and 'wisdom' that we have here Hellenistic features of Greek complexion. Wisdom appears in the guise of rhetoric (1.17, 20; 2.1, 4, 13). In Jewish wisdom literature such a high valuation of form is unknown. The same may be said of Philo of Alexandria, who, as we saw above, is even supposed to be the source of the Hellenistic Jewish philosophy and allegorical interpretation of Scripture of Apollos and his faction. If we examine what

---

13. M. Dibelius on 2.5 and the excursus after 2.12.

14. We are thinking here of men like Apuleius and Maximus of Tyre, Plutarch and Dio of Prusa (Dio Chrysostom).

Philo says about word and wisdom, we find that, as with Clement of Alexandria later, his attitude to rhetoric is twofold: on the one hand he thinks that the art of rhetoric is necessary like all the other branches of higher instruction, and on the other hand he sharply condemns empty sophistical talk.[15]

This seems to suggest that we must not look for the origin of the Corinthians' striving after wisdom in connexion with Jewish philosophy and scriptural interpretation from Alexandria.

We should rather suppose, on the contrary, that the acceptance of the Gospel led the Corinthians to feel rich and wise in the possession of new life and spiritual gifts. That feeling was expressed in their calling Christianity a kind of wisdom, its leaders teachers of wisdom, and themselves—this was the most important thing for them—wise men who had drawn on that wisdom through the Christian leaders. The poor, insignificant Corinthians, with neither distinguished ancestry nor pagan wisdom to support them, had become so rich through the new proclamation that they seized on the Greek terminology that was there for them, and used it to express their new glory. They did not realize that by the very use of that wisdom terminology they were betraying the message that was their wealth, and that the feeling of being up on the pinnacle and pitying the others was a betrayal of Christ and his apostles.

15. Philo condemns the sophists: *Det.* 72–74; *Post.* 86–88, etc. But at the same time he thinks that the art of rhetoric is necessary: *Det.* 39, 41–44; *Ebr.* 48f, etc. Philo's ideas of the relation of the word to knowledge and action are to be found in *Det.* 125–37. Like Philo, Clement of Alexandria rejects the art of sophistry; see *Strom.* 1.3 and 8; but rhetoric, like other philosophy, is useful for the fear of God and wisdom; *Strom.* 1.5–7.

Chapter 3

The Corinthian Christology[*]

Walter Schmithals

INTRODUCTION

Walter Schmithals's study, which developed out of a doctoral dissertation (accepted in 1954) under Rudolf Bultmann in Marburg, is the most influential exposition of the Gnostic interpretation of Corinthian Christianity. The case had been advanced in various forms before (most notably by W. Lütgert in *Freiheits-predigt*), but not with such vigour and exegetical thoroughness. In the volume, Schmithals first gives an account of Gnosticism, which he takes to be a pre-Christian phenomenon. Then he argues for a radical rearrangement of the Corin-thian correspondence. According to Schmithals, the two canonical Corinthian letters comprise six separate letters, each reflecting a different stage of the devel-opment of the crisis. Schmithals maintains that Paul faced a singular opposition in Corinth, Jewish Gnosticism, a 'heresy' that was brought into the community

*Extracted from W. Schmithals, *Gnosticism in Corinth: An Investigation of the Letters to the Corinthians* (trans. John E. Steely; Nashville: Abingdon, 1971) 124–30. Originally published as *Die Gnosis in Korinth: Eine Untersuchung zu den Korintherbriefen* (FRLANT 48; Göttingen: Vandenhoeck & Ruprecht, 1956). Reprinted by permission of Vandenhoeck & Ruprecht, 37070 Göttingen.

from outside. In the main part of the book, Schmithals examines in detail the Corinthian theological perspective. Every element of the Corinthian theology (including their claim to 'gnosis', their anthropological dualism, their view of the sacraments, their concept of liberty, and their eschatology), claims Schmithals, fits into a coherent Gnostic framework. One specific and intriguing example of Schmithals's argument, reproduced below, is his contention that the cry 'Let Jesus be accursed', referred to in 1 Cor 12.3, reflects a Gnostic Christology: the Corinthians, argues Schmithals, drew a sharp distinction between the man Jesus and the heavenly being Christ, regarding the former with contempt (the commentator Godet had come to a similar conclusion many years before).

Schmithals's reconstruction of Corinthian theology seems speculative and anachronistic, reading back into the Corinthian situation ideas and practices from a somewhat later period. In the 1960s and 1970s, the notion of an identifiable pre-Christian Gnosticism came under heavy fire; many scholars now consider that the evidence for first-century Gnosticism is lacking, and most would agree that the evidence for specifically Gnostic influence upon the Corinthians is rather slight. Nevertheless, until quite recently, some have still been prepared to speak of Gnostic or proto-Gnostic tendencies among the Corinthians, since aspects of the Corinthians' religiosity appeared to anticipate second-century developments that came to be known as Gnostic. In most recent scholarship, however, there has been a distinct move away from the use of such categories in the analysis of Corinthian Christianity. It is now more common to seek to understand Corinthian beliefs and practices in the light of the ideas and customs known from Roman society and culture more generally. Indeed, Bruce Winter's recent analysis of the curse formula in 1 Cor 12.3 provides a good example of such an interpretation, which contrasts sharply with that of Schmithals.

Further Reading

R. A. Horsley, 'Gnosis in Corinth' (ch. 8 below; and see literature cited there).
T. E. Klutz, 'Re-reading 1 Corinthians after *Rethinking "Gnosticism"*', *JSNT* 26 (2003) 193–216.
Martin, *Corinthian Body*.
U. Wilckens, *Weisheit und Torheit* (Tübingen: Mohr Siebeck, 1959); for a summary of Wilckens's view, see 'σοφία', *TDNT* 7:519–22.
R. McL. Wilson, 'Gnosis at Corinth', in *Paul and Paulinism: Essays in Honour of C. K. Barrett* (ed. M. D. Hooker and S. G. Wilson; London: SPCK, 1982) 102–4.
R. McL. Wilson, 'How Gnostic were the Corinthians?' *NTS* 19 (1972–73) 65–74.
Winter, *After Paul Left Corinth*, 164–83.

We begin with an investigation of a brief section, 1 Cor 12.1–3, and in fact especially v. 3. The conception of the pneuma in Corinth in general will be considered only later. Our section stands in Epistle B, in the larger context in which Paul answers the community's letter, and indeed Paul begins here with περὶ δὲ τῶν πνευματικῶν the treatment of a new theme. Thus what follows has reference to events in the Corinthian community. Here some obviously in pneumatic speech, and thus surely in the assembly of the community, must have said 'ἀνάθεμα Ἰησοῦς'. The community is not sure as to whether such an expression could occur ἐν πνεύματι θεοῦ and requests Paul to give information on the matter.

So much for the outward course of events. It is almost universally acknowledged that this is the way matters stood, so that we need no longer tarry at this point. Indeed the text allows us no other interpretation at all. At the most one can ask whether the community's letter also somewhere mentioned the term κύριος Ἰησοῦς. I should not assume so, since this primitive Christian confession appears in no way problematical. Paul will rather have set forth more sharply the negation in the first part in itself by means of a positive statement in the latter part of the verse.

Who, we now may ask, can have cried out 'ἀνάθεμα Ἰησοῦς' in the assembly of the community? The most obvious answer is: some non-Christian who takes part in the worship, also falls into ecstasy, but in this condition gives powerful expression to his rejection of the Christian faith by means of the ἀνάθεμα Ἰησοῦς. It is attested in 1 Cor 14.23 that ἄπιστοι took part in pneumatically stimulated gatherings. Since ἀνάθεμα in the sense appearing here is only Jewish usage,[1] we should assume that Jews are involved. Schlatter thinks accordingly that here Paul is referring to the synagogue's denunciation of Jesus. But the cursing must have occurred in the Christian service of worship. Then the reaction of the community to these incidents nevertheless is most unusual, indeed is in essence incomprehensible. It is considered possible in the very community which is founded upon the confession κύριος Ἰησοῦς that an unbaptized Jew curses Jesus ἐν πνεύματι θεοῦ, and Paul is asked in the most official way how this is the case. If this actually did develop in this way, the community in Corinth must in a real sense have consisted of νήπιοι (1 Cor 3.1), not only of νήπιοι ἐν Χριστῷ. I consider such an occurrence to be ruled out as a possibility.

Now of course some explain that for the Corinthians ecstasy as such appeared to prove an utterance ἐν πνεύματι θεοῦ and that for this reason their inquiry of Paul is understandable. But we must answer that such pneumatic manifestations as emerge in the community in Corinth are throughout not specifically Christian. They were widespread in the Hellenistic-syncretistic religions of the primitive Christian era and from that source only temporarily found admittance into the early church. This can be abundantly documented.[2] Precisely Corinth was a converging point of all possible kinds of cults, among them those of Isis, of Serapis, and of Melikertes (Paus. 2.1.3; 2.3; 4.7). The consciousness that heaven and earth are filled with θεοί and κύριοι which dwell in men as πνεύματα or impersonally as πνεῦμα was common not only to the *uneducated* men of that

1. J. Behm in *TDNT* 1:354; Lietzmann on Rom 9:3; Kümmel in Lietzmann's commentary on Corinthians, p. 61, 1.12.
2. Cf. in Lietzmann's commentary the excursus on speaking in tongues and the bibliography given there.

time and is presupposed even by Paul (1 Cor 8.5). Admonitions to test the spirits and to distinguish among them emerge everywhere. I recall only 1 John 4.1: Ἀγαπητοί, μὴ παντὶ πνεύματι πιστεύετε, ἀλλὰ δοκιμάζετε τὰ πνεύματα εἰ ἐκ τοῦ θεοῦ ἐστιν. Here in 1 John what we have is not a late development; for Paul also presupposes 'the gift of recognizing whether it is the divine or the human or a demonic spirit that speaks forth from the enraptured one' (Lietzmann, *An die Korinther*, p. 61) as something self-evident and well known to the Corinthians, when he speaks of the διακρίσεις πνευμάτων (1 Cor 12.10).[3] Even if some naïve Corinthians out of amazement over the unaccustomed pneumatic manifestations had regarded these *eo ipso* and thus unconditionally Christian, so that to them even the ἀνάθεμα 'Ιησοῦς of unbaptized Jews could appear as the cry of the Christ speaking in them (2 Cor 13.3), still it is utterly inconceivable that the community in all seriousness wrote to Paul in this sense.

But in any case the situation is such that the community has reservations about denying the Christianity of the ecstatics, even though they curse Jesus. Thus they must with good reason have appeared to her as Christians. Since the pneumatic endowment as such did not assure their Christianity even in the eyes of the Corinthians, one is compelled to admit that we are dealing here with people whose confession of Christ, in spite of the curses pronounced against Jesus, could not be flatly denied. Only under this assumption does the community's question make sense at all.

But how could a good Christian curse Jesus? Some have indeed thought that during the ecstasy, conceptions from the pre-Christian period which had been suppressed were released from the subconscious. But this appears to me to be a somewhat questionable use of modern psychoanalysis. Yet even granting that a member of the community in ecstasy cries out ἀνάθεμα 'Ιησοῦς from some sort of complexes of the subconscious, still nothing is gained thereby for the solution of our problem. For if the Jesus who was cursed was the preached and cultically venerated Kyrios, the question as to whether such a curse can be spoken in the πνεῦμα θεοῦ is incomprehensible in *any* case. As little as a congregation of today whose preacher entered the pulpit and spoke against Christ in the worst terms and cursed him would inquire at the meeting of the synod whether this preacher had indeed spoken in a Christian way, just so little could Jesus at that time be cursed, even in the highest ecstatic excitement, and the hearers still regard it as possible that this curse is spoken in the name of God, the Father of the one cursed, even according to however profound a set of theological and psychoanalytical reflections.

Thus, since in no case could ecstasy excuse a cursing of Jesus on the part of baptized people, it is to be presumed that one certain understanding of Christianity—precisely the one disputed in Corinth—did not rule out an ἀνάθεμα

---

3. Cf. 1 Cor 14.37. Otherwise, of course, *Did.* 11.7.

'Ιησοῦς. But since on the other hand no one at that time could have been called a Christian or could have appeared as such to the Corinthians without a confession of the proclaimed Christ, there results the paradoxical fact that there were in Corinth people for whom it was not a contradiction to confess the Χριστός and to cry ἀνάθεμα 'Ιησοῦς.

Now such 'Christians' are in fact not unknown to us. They also appeared in the communities to which 1 John is addressed, and asserted ὅτι 'Ιησοῦς οὐκ ἔστιν ὁ Χριστός (1 John 2.22). Naturally a Jew could also make this assertion, but the pseudo-prophets (1 John 4.1) against whom 1 John is directed did not at all deny that the Messiah had already appeared. When they denied Jesus, they were only disputing that the Messiah had come 'in the flesh' (4.2). Thus they were Gnostics who rejected a close connection between the heavenly Pneuma-Christ and the man Jesus. They apparently held the teaching that Christ had taken up residence in Jesus at the baptism, yet without thereby having been bound up with the flesh of the latter. This emerges in 1 John 5.6. Thus they confessed Christ, but not Jesus as the Christ, and must have given this a sharp emphasis over against the church's teaching.

But now it is Gnostics of a similar sort *also* who cry out ἀνάθεμα 'Ιησοῦς in Corinth in the congregational gatherings. Since because of the ἀνάθεμα it probably was a group of Jews involved here, these were surely the Hebrews of 2 Cor 11.22 whom Paul later so personally fought. They qualify as Christians, i.e., they confess 'Christ,' whom Paul proclaims as the Son of God. But that this Christ is born ἐκ γυναικός (Gal 4.4), that he thus is ὁ 'Ιησους—this they deny, and in ecstasy they express this denial in the harsh words ἀνάθεμα 'Ιησοῦς.

That the community asks Paul for information in *this* case is understandable. Still it appears on this question to have been a matter only of a doctrinal dispute within the church. Perhaps people in Corinth would have taken no offense at all at the Gnostic thesis if it had been propounded only ἐν νοΐ; for the distinction of Χριστός κατὰ σάρκα and Χριστός κατὰ πνεῦμα is familiar to Paul also,[4] and for this reason is to be presupposed for the Corinthian community. Only the ecstatic ἀνάθεμα 'Ιησοῦς, which made a sharp separation out of the distinction and with the radical rejection of the cross contained therein overturned the base of the Pauline theology, will have appeared to them doubtful. We do not know how the inquiry of the Corinthians was framed. We cannot even say whether Paul understood that the cursing of Jesus applied only to the Χριστὸς κατὰ σάρκα, although I should assume that he did. In any case it is to be assumed that the question was also discussed in Corinth ἐν νοΐ, so that there people quite correctly understood the curse as an anathematizing of the earthly manifestation of

4. Rom 1.3; 9.5. In making this distinction Paul undoubtedly stands in the Gnostic tradition. Of course he was guarded against any ἀνάθεμα 'Ιησοῦς by the fact that the cross of Christ stood at the very center of his theology. But for the rest the Pauline Christology makes use of the Gnostic schema.

the redeemer. Otherwise the inquiry to Paul would still be incomprehensible. The evidence for such a doctrinal treatment of the problem is not difficult to produce.

But first let us present still another interesting parallel to the ἀνάθεμα Ἰησοῦς from later Gnosticism. In his debate with Celsus, Origen tells (*Contra Celsum* 6.28) of Gnostics who 'admit no one to their fellowship who has not first cursed Jesus.'[5] He wants to prove that these people (the ones involved are the Ophites, whose doctrines Celsus was citing as Christian in his polemic against Christianity) in no case can be Christians since in fact they curse Jesus. But in this he is undoubtedly incorrect. The Ophites of course regarded themselves as Christians, and consequently one cannot make any accusation against Celsus when he adduces their speculations in the presentation of Christianity. Since he was personally acquainted with the Gnostics, there can be no doubt on this point. Thus the curse did not apply to the heavenly Pneuma-Christ but to his earthly dwelling, the *man Jesus*. It was the custom in one Ophite sect to admit no one who had not first cursed this Jesus, probably with the intention—and to this extent Origen was correct in his protest against Celsus—of erecting a clear barrier to the catholic church. One does not need to assume that there were direct connections between the Ophites of Celsus and the Corinthian Gnostics. But this much may be certain, that *both* cases of cursing are to be ascribed to the basic tendency of Gnostic Christology, sharply to separate the man Jesus and the heavenly spiritual being Christ, and to regard the former as without significance.[6]

Irenaeus 1.31.1 offers a convenient parallel *in substance* to the Gnostic ἀνάθεμα in a note about the Cainites. These confess Esau, Korah, the Sodomites, and others in whom the creator God, in spite of his hatred, could not find any weakness, since the Sophia took to herself the celestial part which stemmed from her. The betrayer Judas also knew this, they teach, '*et solum prae ceteris cognoscentem veritatem, perfecisse proditionis mysterium; per quem et terrena et caelestia omnia dissoluta dicunt.*' Thus here the betrayal of Jesus as the sarkic part of the redeemer is glorified similarly to the cursing of him. Parallels of this kind can be brought forward in abundance. The rejection of the Χριστὸς κατὰ σάρκα was expressed in various ways, some stronger, some weaker. But it should be unnecessary here to adduce further quotations for the presentation of the generally familiar Gnostic Christology.

The fact that in later Gnosticism people frequently were concerned also somehow to make a positive evaluation of the man Jesus is to be traced back to the influence of the Great Church. The essential distinction between Jesus and Christ was steadily maintained, even if the conceptual distinction was occasionally erased. Thus Irenaeus (3.16.1) relates of the Valentinians: 'They indeed confess with their tongues one Christ Jesus, but they divide him in their teaching.' But

---

5. 'ἐαν μή ἀρᾶς θῆται κατὰ τοῦ Ἰησοῦ.'

6. People may have appealed here to a passage like Deut 21.23 as an exegetical basis for such anathematizing: κεκατηραμένος ὑπὸ θεοῦ πᾶς κρεμάμενος ἐπὶ ξύλου. The Corinthian Gnostics could even refer with some justification to utterances of Paul such as Gal 3.13.

these later developments do not alter the fact that the man Jesus who was born of Mary and into whom the celestial Christ, without flesh and impassible (cf. Iren. 3.16.8), has descended, is for the genuine Gnostic deserving of scorn and therefore can be cursed confidently. A positive attitude toward him would be a sign that the person making such a judgment still is living under the power of the evil world (cf. Iren. 1.24.4). Thus the Christology of the Corinthian 'Christians' which is expressed in the ἀνάθεμα Ἰησοῦς in 1 Cor 12.3 is the genuinely Gnostic Christology.[7]

In conclusion it may be pointed out that the Jesus of the Gnostics in Corinth was the same historical person who was venerated by the primitive church as Lord. A pure Docetism is ruled out by the personal execration just as it is by the general consideration that in a time when there still were numerous people living who had known Jesus personally, the reality of his earthly appearing could not be denied. And the statement of Valentinus that Jesus was a being of the psychical world of aeons which exists between *Sarx* and *Pneuma* is a late attempt to evade the ἀνάθεμα Ἰησοῦς without however coming into conflict with the basic Gnostic dogma, the rejection of the sarkical sphere.

7. I was somewhat surprised when, long after completing the present work, I found in the old commentary by F. Godet (1886) an exposition of 1 Cor 12.3 which corresponds to that given above even down to details. . . . Godet's exposition, pursued entirely independently and proceeding from essentially different presuppositions, was for me a confirmation of the exegesis attempted above.

Chapter 4

Christianity at Corinth[*]

C. K. Barrett

INTRODUCTION

In this essay, originally delivered as a T. W. Manson memorial lecture in 1963, C. K. Barrett presents a survey of (then) recent scholarship, much of it German, on the problems and conflicts in the Corinthian church. In the opening section of the essay, reproduced here, Barrett sketches the literary problems confronting the student of the Corinthian correspondence before proceeding to consider the primary piece of evidence concerning the divisions at Corinth: 1 Cor 1.12. Unlike Johannes Munck (see ch. 2 above), who argued that the church at Corinth was not actually *divided* into separate parties, Barrett thinks that the four slogans do reflect the existence of four groups, each with their own distinct theological emphases and ideas. By arguing for four groups Barrett also distances himself here from those—such as F. C. Baur (see ch. 1 above) and more recently Michael Goulder (see ch. 13 below)—who argue that there is really only a twofold division at Corinth, between the Paulines and the Petrines. Each of the four groups,

*Extracted from C. K. Barrett, 'Christianity at Corinth', *BJRL* 46 (1964) 269–97, here pp. 269–75. Reproduced by courtesy of the Director and Librarian, the John Rylands University Library of Manchester.

Barrett suggests, may have developed their own views on subjects such as 'wisdom', and this Barrett explores in the next section of the essay, where he goes on to discuss the interpretation of Paul's references to 'wisdom' and 'knowledge' (the first term being especially prominent in 1 Cor 1–3 and not elsewhere in Paul). Finally, he considers the identity of the opponents in 2 Cor 10–13. Overall, the essay serves as a critical survey of key issues in studies of Corinthian Christianity, as represented in the scholarship of the 1950s and 1960s. It will be evident elsewhere in this book how scholarship has developed since, with new approaches and a focus on new concerns.

Further Reading

C. K. Barrett, *Essays on Paul* (London: SPCK, 1982).
C. K. Barrett, *The First Epistle to the Corinthians* (2nd ed.; BNTC. London: A. & C. Black, 1971).
J. A. Davis, *Wisdom and Spirit: An Investigation of 1 Corinthians 1.18–3.20 against the Background of Jewish Sapiential Traditions in the Greco-Roman Period* (Lanham, New York and London: University Press of America, 1984).
B. Witherington III, *Conflict and Community in Corinth: A Socio-Rhetorical Commentary on 1 and 2 Corinthians* (Grand Rapids: Eerdmans, 1995).

Not the least of the merits of this subject is that it enables me to build on the work of T. W. Manson himself.[1] I shall do my best to observe the warning of 1 Cor 3.10, and take heed how I build. But the subject has other merits. If Romans gives us the most systematic presentation of Paul's theology, it is nevertheless from the Corinthian epistles that we gain the most complete and many-sided picture of how Paul believed that his theological convictions should be expressed in the life of a Church. To say this is not to claim that the Corinthian Church was a paragon of all Churches; there was often a wide divergence between what happened in Corinth and what Paul thought ought to happen. But both pictures— the actual and the ideal—contribute to our understanding of Pauline Christianity in its practical expression, and we learn much of what Paul thought right from what the Corinthians got wrong. In the Corinthian epistles Paul deals with an exceptionally large number of practical problems, always on the basis of a theological grasp of the situation, so that there is in fact no more important source for Paul's conception of the Christian way of life.

It is also true that 1 and 2 Corinthians provide the most valuable information we have about early non-Pauline Christianity. There is no epistle (apart from Philemon) in which Paul does not deal with some deviation from or perversion of the Christian faith, but nowhere else is so great a variety of deviations and perversions so fully displayed; and their advocates were able to develop their views and consolidate their adherents to such an extent as almost to disintegrate the originally Pauline Church.

1. T. W. Manson, *Studies in the Gospels and Epistles* (Manchester, 1962), 'The Corinthian Correspondence', pp. 190–224.

Full as the Corinthian letters are of valuable raw material it is no easy task to win from them a clear account of what was going on in the Corinthian Church of the fifties of the first century. The difficulties that stand in the way of historical reconstruction are well known. First stands the fact, which we shall encounter from time to time, that among the verses of crucial importance there is scarcely one of which the interpretation is not disputed. This difficulty is one that often presents itself in the form of a vicious circle: a certain and unambiguous interpretation of a particular verse would give one a clear insight into part at least of the Corinthian history; yet only if one has a clear picture of history is it possible to interpret the verse with confidence. There is a trap here, evident enough, yet one that has snared a number of students. How easy to make a hurried inference from a text of one of the epistles to historical circumstances, and then to use the supposedly known historical circumstances to confirm the interpretation of the text!

The outstanding literary problem involved in the Corinthian letters is that of their integrity, and this, as can easily be seen, has important consequences for precisely the kind of historical question that is to be dealt with in this lecture. The view of the matter perhaps most commonly held in this country may be briefly set out as follows:[2]

Paul wrote four letters to Corinth.

The *first* has been lost, unless a part of it is preserved in 2 Cor 6.14—7.1.

The *second* consists of what we call 1 Corinthians.

The *third* has been partially preserved in 2 Cor 10–13.

The *fourth* is contained in 2 Cor 1–9 (omitting perhaps 6.14—7.1).

This hypothetical reconstruction has the effect of knitting the two epistles (as contained in our Bibles) very closely together; in particular, 2 Cor 10–13 stands next in time to 1 Corinthians. The more elaborate reconstructions,[3] in which 1 Corinthians also is partitioned, 2 Cor 2.14—7.5 attached to 2 Cor 10–13, and 2 Cor 8, 9 separated from each other, have the effect of dovetailing the two letters even more completely. If, however, the unity of 2 Corinthians is maintained or if, as is perhaps more probable, 2 Cor 10–13 is detached from the rest of the epistle but regarded as subsequent to it,[4] the two documents preserved to us stand further apart; in particular, it becomes less likely that the disturbances of 2 Cor 10–13 should be regarded as a simple continuation of the divisions of

2. See, e.g., T. W. Manson, op. cit., pp. 190f.

3. See, e.g., J. Weiss, *The History of Primitive Christianity* (ET, London, 1937), 356f.; G. Bornkamm, 'Die Vorgeschichte des sogenannten Zweiten Korintherbriefes', in *Sitzungsberichte der Heidelberger Akademie der Wissenschaften*, Philosophisch-historische Klasse, Jahrgang 1961:2 (Heidelberg, 1961) 16–23.

4. See, e.g., J. Munck, *Paulus und die Heilsgeschichte*, Asrsskrift for Aarhus Universitet, XXVI, 1, Teologisk Serie 6 (Aarhus-Copenhagen, 1954) 162–66.

1 Cor 1.12, and more likely that the Corinthian troubles had by this time taken a new turn.

Corinth was a place in which a rich development of Christian forms of thought, worship, and life was to be expected. Not that it was a centre of intellectual activity; it has no such reputation. But it was a commercial centre in which men of many races, and of many faiths, met, and were in constant contact. New Corinth was not a Greek city. The old πόλις had lain in desolation for a hundred years when the new foundation of Laus Julia Corinthus was made by the Romans in 44 B.C.[5] The town that commanded the Isthmus was bound to become a busy entrepôt; and so it was. Roman colonists, more or less local Greeks, and levantine traders, among them a community of Jews large and wealthy enough to have their own synagogue building,[6] probably made up the greater part of the population. It is probable that, before the Christian Gospel reached Corinth, Isis from Egypt, the Great Mother from Phrygia, Dionysus from Thrace and elsewhere, and the strange nameless deity from Judaea, had already met there, and added the spice of speculation and of ecstasy to the more formal, and politically inspired, worship that came from the west.

Moreover, we have in the epistles themselves the plainest evidence that Christian propagandists, other than, and some of them very different from, Paul, had been at work in the city: Apollos certainly; Peter, with very great probability, and if not Peter himself disciples of his who made free with his name.[7] These may have been embarrassing but comparatively harmless; there were others, and a different Gospel, another Jesus, and another Spirit were preached. Alexandrian Judaism, Jewish Christianity, Hellenism, all seem to have played upon the already inflammatory material assembled at Corinth. It is no wonder there was a blaze; no wonder the city could add to its trade fairs as fine an exhibition of Christian deviations as was to be seen anywhere in the world. There will be all too little time in this lecture to discuss them.

At this point we cannot do otherwise than turn to 1 Cor 1.12. Surely it is only by a *tour de force* that Johannes Munck can, in the heading of a chapter in his *Paulus und die Heilsgeschichte*,[8] describe Corinth as 'Die Gemeinde ohne Parteien'. True, he has done well to remind us that, when 1 Corinthians was written, the Church remained united: Paul could address all its members with a comprehensive 'you', and expect that all would read or hear what he had to say. The ἔριδες of 1.11 do not refer to separate, schismatic bodies, and the αἱρέσεις of 11.19 become manifest συνερχομένων ὑμῶν ἐν ἐκκλησίᾳ (11.18); they are not such as to prevent all from meeting in one place. Dr. Munck has also very

---

5. See PWSup, IV, 991–1036; VI, 182–99, 1350f. There is slight uncertainty about the date, and a few other forms of the name appear to have been in use.

6. A. Deissmann, *Light from the Ancient East* (London, 1927) 16.

7. T. W. Manson. op. cit., pp. 194–207; also C. K. Barrett, 'Cephas and Corinth', in *Abraham unser Vater, Juden und Christen im Gespräch über die Bibel. Festschrift für Otto Michel* (ed. O. Betz, M. Hengel, and P. Schmidt; Leiden-Cologne, 1963) 1–12.

8. See above n. 4.

properly reminded us how little we know about these groups.[9] Yet divided loyalties, and ecclesiastical preferences, were certainly visible, and caused Paul deep anxiety, and the unity of the Church, so far as it continued to exist, must have been an uneasy unity.

'I am of Paul', said some, doubtless a reactionary group. As long as no influence but Paul's was felt in Corinth such a slogan would have been meaningless. Other influences were now at work, into which we must shortly look, and in opposition some fell back on the old and familiar. How far the Paulinists understood Paul, and how far he approved of their tenets, are questions to which we may be able to give brief attention.

'I am of Apollos': here there is a familiar and almost certainly correct explanation. According to Acts 18:27f. Apollos formed and carried out the intention of visiting Achaea; the probability that such a journey would include Corinth is immediately confirmed by 19.1. That Apollos was a Jew (18.24) need not be disputed; that he was Ἀλεξανδρεὺς τῷ γένει is probably significant, for there is no ground for supposing that every Alexandrian Jew was a potential Philo (though some writers seem to think so); that he was ἀνὴρ λόγιος[10] would account for his acquiring a following of his own. Many no doubt found him a refreshing change after an apostle who could be dismissed as ἰδιώτης τῷ λόγῳ (2 Cor 11.6). Paul had no quarrel with him; they may well be right who see in Apollos's disinclination to visit Corinth again (1 Cor 16.12) a delicacy of sentiment that made him unwilling to appear even unintentionally in the character of a rival. It is nevertheless probable that Apollos contributed to the Corinthian development of thought about γνῶσις, λόγος, and σοφία.

'I am of Cephas' probably implies the presence of Peter himself in Corinth. T. W. Manson's argument[11] that the group that made use of Peter's name is to be detected (for example) in the way in which Paul handles such questions as litigation, the eating of sacrificial foods, and the Lord's Supper, is convincing. It adopted a Jewish Christian 'nomistic' attitude, not extreme enough actually to divide the Church (as a demand for circumcision would have done), or to disfranchise Paul from the apostolic body, but awkward enough to raise difficulties, and to cast a certain amount of doubt on Paul's status.[12]

'I am of Christ': here's the rub. Who said these words? According to some,[13] a copyist, who inserted in the margin of his New Testament the pious comment: These Corinthians had their various party leaders—ἐγὼ δὲ Χριστοῦ. It is sometimes replied that there is no textual evidence in support of this view; but this is not strictly true. There is no manuscript evidence; but it could be urged that the earliest textual authority for 1 Cor 1.12 is *1 Clem.* 47.3, where Clement says of

9. Op. cit., pp. 134, 141.
10. Eloquent probably, rather than learned, though it is a fault of the ancient world that it often confused the two.
11. Op. cit. pp. 197–206.
12. And perhaps to provide a foundation for more severe trouble at a later time.
13. Notably J. Weiss, ad loc.; also *Einleitung*, pp. XXXVIff.

Paul that ἐπ' ἀληθείας πνευματικῶς ἐπέστειλεν ὑμιν περὶ αὐτοῦ τε καὶ Κηφᾶ τε καὶ Ἀπολλῶ, διὰ τὸ καὶ τότε προσκλίσεις ὑμᾶς πεποιῆσθαι. In this context there is no reference to Christ, or to οἱ Χριστοῦ. It is at least possible to maintain that Clement did not read ἐγὼ δὲ Χριστοῦ in 1 Cor 1.12. There are, however, other possible explanations of Clement's silence. Lightfoot[14] thinks that Clement made no reference to the Christ-group because to refer to it would have 'complicated his argument', and adds that the exact theological position of this group was probably not known to him.[15] A further possibility is that Clement, who did not always verify his references, was thinking of, or was confused by, 1 Cor 3.22, where only Paul, Apollos, and Cephas are mentioned. It would be rash to conclude that ἐγὼ δὲ Χριστοῦ did not stand in Paul's own copy of 1 Corinthians.

We must still ask, however, Who said these words? Are they another party cry, parallel with and analogous to the other three? Or are they Paul's own comment? The latter is an attractive view,[16] for there is at least a superficial difficulty in supposing that the name Christ could be taken as in any sense on the same level as those of Paul, Apollos, and Cephas, and it could be argued that Clement, if the words ἐγὼ δὲ Χριστοῦ did stand in his text, understood them as a comment and not as referring to a fourth party. Moreover, the words seem—superficially again—to be an apt rejoinder to a Church making too much of its human leaders. Against this is the strict parallelism of the four clauses, and the complete lack of indication that in the fourth Paul has ceased to quote. The awkwardness, often remarked on, of the following words is perhaps to be explained by the fact that it was an embarrassment to Paul that one group had adopted as a party cry what should have been the watchword of all.

Perhaps the strongest argument for regarding the words ἐγὼ δὲ Χριστοῦ as indicating the existence of a fourth group is that when we have eliminated from 1 Corinthians everything that can reasonably be ascribed to a Paul-group, an Apollos-group, and a Cephas-group, there remains a well-defined body of opinion distinct from the views of the first three groups, consistent with itself and explicable in the context of events in Corinth The mere existence of such a body of opinion does not prove the existence of a fourth distinct section of the Church, still less that ἐγὼ δὲ Χριστοῦ was the slogan of this group, but it seems to weight the balance of probability in this direction.

14. *The Apostolic Fathers: Part I. Clement of Rome*, 2 (London, 1890) 143.
15. R. Knopf, in *Handbuch zum Neuen Testament, Ergänzungsband* (Tübingen, 1920) 123, mentioning this view, adds that the Christ-group may have been enigmatic to Clement 'wie sie es der neueren Auslegung ist'.
16. It finds some support in 3.22. See J. Héring *ad loc.*, with a reference to H. von Dobschütz, *Die urchristlichen Gemeinden* (Leipzig, 1902) 58 (*Christian Life in the Primitive Church* [London, 1904] 72).

Chapter 5

Paul and the Church at Corinth[*]

Nils A. Dahl

INTRODUCTION

In this essay, first published in 1967, Nils Dahl added his voice to an established consensus *against* Baur's reconstruction of Corinthian Christianity. He was unconvinced, however, with the alternatives that had been proposed in its place. While he agreed with Munck that there was no evidence in 1 Corinthians for Jewish-Christian opposition to Paul in Corinth, he disputed Munck's contention that what the apostle was confronting was merely internal bickering. In Dahl's view, this interpretation fails to take into account Baur's correct observation (see p. 57 above) that 1 Cor 1–4 functions as an *apology* for Paul's apostolic ministry. Dahl's essay, which is still widely cited, argues from a close reading of 1 Cor 1–4 that there was considerable opposition to Paul in Corinth. He contends that the

*Extracted from Nils Dahl, 'Paul and the Church at Corinth according to 1 Corinthians 1:10–4:21', in *Christian History and Interpretation: Studies Presented to John Knox* (ed. W. R. Farmer, C. F. D. Moule, and R. R. Niebuhr; Cambridge: Cambridge University Press, 1967) 313–35. Reprinted in N. A. Dahl, *Studies in Paul: Theology for the Early Christian Mission* (Minneapolis: Augsburg, 1977) 4–61; here pp. 44–55. Reprinted by permission of Cambridge University Press, The Edinburgh Building, Shaftesbury Road, Cambridge.

85

strife intimated in 1.10–12 was connected to this antagonism. Those who said 'I am of Paul' were loyal to Paul. The other slogans are not to be understood as avowals of allegiance to other leaders but 'as declarations of independence from Paul'. Before Paul could address any other pastoral matters in the letter, he had to fend off the Corinthian hostility toward him: he had 'to re-establish his apostolic authority as the founder and spiritual father of the whole church at Corinth'. The extracted section constitutes the main part of Dahl's argument. In the rest of the essay, Dahl examines the function of 1 Cor 5–6 within the letter, considers whether there was a theological dimension to the dispute between Paul and the Corinthians (concluding that there was and that it focused on the Corinthians' 'over-realised eschatology') and shows how his interpretation of the situation addressed in 1 Cor 1–4 fits well with the events reflected in 2 Corinthians (esp. chs. 10–13).

There is widespread agreement that even at the time of writing 1 Corinthians, Paul was facing a degree of opposition at Corinth and that already his authority was being challenged, at least by some within the church. Dahl's contention that the majority of the Corinthian church (all except Stephanas and his household) was hostile toward Paul has been taken up by Gordon Fee in his reconstruction of the situation at Corinth in his commentary on 1 Corinthians. Most recent interpreters have, however, tended to see the opposition to Paul as coming from a smaller section of the congregation (cf. 1 Cor 4.18–19), albeit a particularly powerful and influential one.

Further Reading

E. Best, 'Paul's Apostolic Authority—?' *JSNT* 27 (1986) 3–25.
E. A. Castelli, *Imitating Paul: A Discourse of Power* (Louisville: Westminster John Knox, 1991).
Clarke, *Secular and Christian Leadership.*
Fee, *First Epistle,* 7–10.
B. Holmberg, *Paul and Power: The Structure of Authority in the Primitive Church as Reflected in the Pauline Epistles* (Coniectanea biblica, no. 11, New Testament Series; Lund: Gleerup, 1978).
J. H. Schütz, *Paul and the Anatomy of Apostolic Authority* (SNTSMS 26; Cambridge: Cambridge University Press, 1975).
Theissen, *Social Setting.*

In the following pages it will be argued that while Baur was wrong in taking Paul's opponents in 1 Cor 1–4 to be Judaizers, he was fully right in speaking of these chapters as an 'apologetic section' in which Paul justifies his apostolic ministry. It is a main failure of theories like those of Munck and Hurd that they do not really take this into account.

An attempt to reach beyond the present impasse in the interpretation of 1 Cor 1–4 must be performed according to a strict method if the result is not going to add to a chaos which is already bad enough. I would suggest the following principles:

(1) The controversy must be studied as such. Due account must be taken of the perspective under which Paul envisages the situation at Corinth. But as far as possible, we must also try to understand the Corinthian reaction to Paul.

(2) While 1 Cor 1–4 must be understood against the historical background, any reconstruction of that background must mainly be based on information contained within the section itself. Relatively clear and objective statements concerning the situation at Corinth must serve as a basis. Evaluations, polemical and ironic allusions, warnings and exhortations may next be used to fill out the picture. Only when these possibilities have been exhausted, and with great caution, should Paul's own teaching be used as a source of information concerning views held by the Corinthians; Paul may have adapted his language to theirs, but this assumption remains highly conjectural.

(3) The integrity of 1 Corinthians may be assumed as a working hypothesis which is confirmed if it proves possible to understand 1 Cor 1.10—4.21 as an introductory section with a definite purpose within the letter as a whole. Materials from 1 Cor 5–16 should therefore be used for the sake of comparison. Special attention should be paid to chapters 5 and 6 which in the present context stand at the transition from 1–4 to those sections of the epistle in which Paul handles questions raised by the letter from Corinth.

(4) In so far as they do not directly serve the purpose of philological exegesis, but provide materials for a more general historical and theological understanding, information from other Pauline epistles, Acts, and other early Christian, Jewish, Greek, or Gnostic documents should not be brought in until the epistolary situation has been clarified as far as possible on the basis of internal evidence. Points of similarity, especially with 2 Corinthians, should be noted, but not used in such a way that the results of contextual exegesis are pre-judged.

(5) Any reconstruction of the historical background will at best be a reasonable hypothesis. A hypothesis will recommend itself to the degree to which it is able to account for the total argument and all details within 1 Cor 1–4 with a minimal dependence upon hypothetical inferences derived from extraneous sources. The results achieved will gain in probability if they can without difficulty be integrated into a comprehensive picture of the history of primitive Christianity in its contemporary setting.[1]

The basic information contained in 1 Cor 1.10—4.21 is what was reported by Chloe's people: there was quarrelling (*erides*) among the Christians at Corinth, each one of them saying, 'I belong to Paul', or 'I to Apollos', or 'I to Christ'. In 3.3–4, where only the names of Paul and Apollos are mentioned, Paul speaks about 'jealousy and strife' (*zēlos kai eris*). As the implication of the slogans is controversial, only the fact of the quarrels is unambiguous. Another piece of evidence is, however, added at the end of the section: 'Some are arrogant (*ephysiōthēsan*,

---

1. The statement of methodological principles will make it clear why I discuss the theories of Munck and Hurd rather than those of Schmithals and Wilckens. This does not reduce the value of the immense amount of material gathered, especially by Wilckens.

lit. have been puffed up) as though I were not coming to you' (4.18). That the persons in question were 'arrogant' (RSV), or 'filled with self-importance' (NEB), is Paul's evaluation. But we do get the information that some assumed that Paul would not come back to Corinth. It seems likely that they expressed their view openly. In view of this statement, the idea that Paul always deals with the congregation as a whole needs some modification; there are certain persons whom he regards as 'arrogant'. As often, he uses the indefinite pronoun *tines* to refer to definite persons whose names he does not want to mention.[2] This indicates that Paul is aware of the existence of some center of opposition to him within the church at Corinth.

The results of this search for objective information may seem to be very meager. But if combined the pieces of information disclose that the quarrels and the slogans at Corinth were related to the assumption that the apostle would not return. The general context supports this combination.

The whole section begins with Paul's appeal to his brethren in Corinth that they should agree and avoid divisions (1.10). It ends with an equally urgent appeal that they should be imitators of Paul: to that purpose he sends Timothy who will remind them of his instructions (4.16–17). Both in 1.10 and 4.16 we find periods headed by the verb *parakalō* ('I appeal', 'beseech', or 'urge'), a formal pattern which Paul uses when he sets forth what is a main purpose of his letters, expressing what he wants the addressees to do.[3] The *parakalō*-periods are distinguished from strict imperatives in that they call for a voluntary response. But Paul makes it quite clear that as the Corinthians' only father in Christ he does have authority to command, even if he does not do so. He hopes that he will not have to use his rod when he comes to Corinth which he plans to do if that is the will of the Lord (4.14–15, 19–21). At the beginning Paul asks for the mutual concord of the brethren; at the end of the section if not before, the reader understands that Paul at the same time asks his children to concur in harmony with their father in Christ. This is well brought out by John Knox, who has written, with reference to 1 Cor 1–4: 'He wants his converts to stand firm, not only in the Lord, but also in their loyalty to him.'[4]

The general content of the section adds further confirmation to this. It deals with four main themes:

(1) Unity in Christ and the quarrels at Corinth (1.10–13). This initial theme is taken up again in 3.3–4 and 21–23.

(2) Wisdom and foolishness, the power and wisdom of God over against the wisdom of men. Various aspects of this main theme are handled in 1.17—3.2, and taken up again in 3.18–21 and 4.7–10.

2. Cf. Rom 3.8; 1 Cor 15.12, 34; 2 Cor 3.1; 10.2, 12; Gal 1.7; Phil 1.15; 2 Thess 3.11 (1 Tim1.6, 19; 4.1; 6.10, 21). Sometimes even *tis* or *ei tis* is used in a similar way.

3. The clearest example of this epistolary use of *parakalō* is found in Phlm 8ff. Cf. John Knox, *Philemon among the Letters of Paul* (1935; 2nd ed.; New York: Abingdon, 1959) 22f.

4. *Chapters in a Life of Paul,* 95.

(3) The function of the apostles and Christian leaders, and the esteem in which they should be held (3.5—4.6, cf. 4.9–13).

(4) Paul's relations to the church at Corinth. This theme is implicit throughout the whole section from 1.13 onwards and comes into the foreground at the end (4.14–21).

It is clear how the first and the third theme are related to one another. The Corinthians are quarrelling because they 'boast of men', i.e., of one of the teachers, and are 'puffed up in favor of one (of them) against the other' (3.21; 4.6). It is somewhat less evident why the wisdom theme is given such a prominent place. However, Paul takes the Corinthians' boasting of the teachers to imply boasting of their own wisdom (cf. 3.18–21; 4.7–10). At the same time, he sees the quarrelling as clear evidence that the Corinthians are not as wise and spiritual as they imagine themselves to be (3.3–4). But in order to understand the structure of the total argument we have to realize that the fourth theme, the apostle and his relations to the church at Corinth, comes in at all important points of transition.

The initial appeal for unity immediately leads to Paul's activity at Corinth and to his commission as a messenger of the gospel (1.13–17). In 2.1–5 and 3.1–2 Paul returns to his own first preaching at Corinth, so that this provides the framework within which he deals with the word of the cross and with the way in which the Corinthian brethren were called (1.18–25, 26–31) as well as with the wisdom which is reserved for the mature (2.6–16).

From his first preaching at Corinth Paul returns to the present situation (3.2c–4; cf. 1.11–12). Even when he deals with the questions, 'What then is Apollos? What is Paul?' he not only makes statements of principle, but points to the special ministry assigned to him (3.10–11), and asserts that no human court, but only the Lord, is to pass judgment upon him (4.3–4). Even when he contrasts the predicaments of the apostles with the riches of the wise Corinthians, Paul has first of all his own ministry and sufferings in mind (4.8–13). Thus the whole argument quite naturally leads to the conclusion, 'For though you have countless guides in Christ, you do not have many fathers. For I became your father (*hymas egennēsa*) in Christ Jesus through the Gospel'. It would be unfair to say that preparation for this statement is the main function of everything that has been said; yet, one aim of what Paul has to say about the strife at Corinth about wisdom and foolishness, and about the function of Christian leaders, is to re-establish his authority as apostle and spiritual father of the church at Corinth.[5]

From the statement, 'With me it is a very small thing that I should be judged by you or by any human court' (4.3), we may safely infer that some kind of criticism of Paul has been voiced at Corinth. And it is not difficult to find out what

---

5. On several occasions the point that is most directly relevant to the actual situation comes towards the end of a section or an epistle, cf. 1 Cor 10.23—11.1; 11.33–34; Rom 15.30–33; Gal 6.11–17; Phil 4.10–18; 2 Thess 3.6–15. Thus there are good analogies for the assumption that the issue involved in 1 Cor 1–4 is most clearly to be seen in 4.14–21.

the main content of this criticism must have been. That becomes evident in phrases like, 'Not with eloquent wisdom' (*ouk en sophia logou*, 1.17), 'Not in lofty words of wisdom' (*ou kath' hyperochēn logou ē sophias*, 2.1), 'Not in persuasiveness of wisdom' (*ouk en peithoi sophias*, 2.4),[6] 'Milk, not solid food' (*gala . . . ou brōma*, 3.2). To what extent the phrases, and not merely their content, allude to what was reported to have been said, is immaterial. Since the Corinthians evidently understood themselves as wise because they thought themselves inspired, pneumatic persons (cf. 3.1), we must conclude that Paul was not merely held to lack the oratorical ability of a Greek rhetor, but also the gift of pneumatic wisdom. In 4.10 the apostles are not only said to be 'fools for Christ's sake', but also 'weak', and 'in disrepute'.[7]

In addition to Paul's alleged lack of wisdom, Paul's critics may have mentioned other failings. He had not baptized many (cf. 1.14). The catalog of sufferings in 4.11–13 deserves close attention. Hunger, thirst, and nakedness are common features in descriptions of persons in need (cf. e.g. Matt 25.35–36). That he is 'roughly handled' (NEB, *kolaphizometha*) refers in a more specific way to afflictions suffered during the apostolic ministry (cf. 2 Cor 11.23–25). The lack of stability (*astatoumen*) is characteristic of the apostle who is 'homeless' (RSV) and has to 'wander from place to place' (NEB); but the choice of the term may very well allude to what was said at Corinth about the unstable apostle who was not likely ever to come back (4.18; cf. 2 Cor 1.15ff). An unambiguous reference to a practice of Paul which is known to have caused objections at Corinth is contained in the clause 'We labor, working with our own hands' (cf. 1 Cor 9.3–18; 2 Cor 11.7–11; 12.13). Paul goes on: 'When reviled, we bless; when persecuted, we endure'. This is what a follower of Christ should do (cf. Lk 6.27–29; Rom 12.14). But adding, 'When slandered, we make our appeal' (*parakaloumen*, in RSV: 'we try to conciliate'), he once more alludes to the actual situation; at Corinth he is slandered and responds, not with harsh words, but by making his friendly—though not exactly 'humble' (NEB)—appeal.

Since the entire section contains an apology for Paul, and since the strife at Corinth was linked up with opposition against him, it becomes possible to interpret the slogans reported in 1.12. Those who said 'I belong to Paul' were proud of him and held that his excellence surpassed that of Apollos or Cephas. The other slogans are all to be understood as declarations of independence from Paul. Apollos is mentioned as the most outstanding Christian teacher who had visited

6. I am inclined to take this as the original text which by an early error was misspelled as *ouk en peithois sophias*. The other variant readings can all be understood as attempts to improve this. The problem has no material importance.

7. Adducing very interesting evidence, Munck demonstrates that Greek rhetors and sophists could be regarded as wise/powerful, and honoured: *Paul and the Salvation of Mankind*, 158f. and 162f., with notes. But he does himself see that the Corinthians thought of their power as participation in the kingdom of God (p. 165). The Greek analogies, therefore, do not suffice. At this date there were hardly any distinctions between philosophers, sophists, rhetors, hierophants and mystagogues. For Jewish analogies cf. D. Georgi, *Die Gegner des Paulus im 2. Korintherbrief* (WMANT 11; Neukirchen: Neukirchener Verlag, 1964).

Corinth after Paul. Cephas is the famous pillar, the first witness to the resurrection, an apostle before Paul. The slogan 'I belong to Christ' is not the motto of a specific Christ-party but simply means 'I myself belong to Christ—and am independent of Paul'. Understood in this way, all the slogans have a clear meaning in the context and in the situation. Paul had no reason to deal in detail with the various groups, and it becomes quite natural that he should concentrate his presentation on the relationship between himself and Apollos.

It may be added that on the interpretation proposed, the analogy between 1 Cor 1.12f and 2 Cor 10.7 becomes clear. In 2 Cor 10.7 there is no trace of a specific Christ-party: the wandering apostles simply attacked Paul and claimed to belong to Christ as his servants (cf. 11.23). Paul's answer is that he too belongs to Christ, and, more than they, he is distinguished as a servant of Christ by his sufferings. Here and there Paul finds it an anomaly that someone at the same time can claim to belong to Christ and yet oppose his apostle and faithful servant.

There is no reason to think that either Apollos or Cephas was in any way responsible for the use that was made of his name by people at Corinth who claimed to be independent of Paul.[8] Paul himself stresses their solidarity and dependence upon God's work (3.5–9, 22; 4.6; 15.11; 16.12). But what then was the occasion for the strife and the opposition to Paul? One fact, especially, needs explanation. The church at Corinth had sent Stephanas, Fortunatus and Achaicus as a kind of official delegation to Paul. In all probability, the Corinthians had commissioned these delegates to bring a letter from the congregation to Paul, asking for his opinion on a number of questions. In this letter it was stated that the Corinthians remembered Paul in everything and maintained the traditions he had delivered to them.[9] Thus, the official attitude of the congregation seems to have been one of loyalty to the apostle. Yet, Chloe's people could orally report that there was strife in Corinth and that there was some opposition to Paul. This tension between the written document and the oral report requires some explanation.

We do not know anything either about Chloe or about her people. From what Paul writes we do, however, learn one thing, namely that it was not Stephanas and the other members of the delegation who reported the quarrels at Corinth. It may mean that the quarrels had started after the departure of the delegation or it may mean that the delegates had not gossiped. In any case, Paul had his information about the quarrels and the opposition from some other source, and this may have been important both to him and to the recipients of his letter. The name of Stephanas is mentioned at the beginning of our section, in a very curious fashion. Paul first states that he baptized none of the Corinthians except

---

8. The Corinthians may well have derived their knowledge of Cephas from what Paul had told them; at least Peter may have been a great authority far away, in spite of the renewal by C. K. Barrett of the theory that he had visited Corinth: 'Cephas and Corinth', *Abraham unser Vater: Festschrift O. Michel* (Arbeiten zur Geschichte de Spätjudentums und des Urchristentums, 5; Leiden: Brill, 1963) 1–12.

9. 1 Cor 11.2. It is fairly generally agreed that Paul here alludes to what was said in the letter from Corinth. Cf. Hurd, *Origin,* 52 and 90f.

Crispus and Gaius. But he has to correct himself and add that he also baptized the household of Stephanas. This lapse of memory may simply reflect that at the moment Stephanas was with Paul and not at Corinth. But even without much depth psychology one might suspect that Paul first forgot to mention the household of Stephanas because he did not wish to involve Stephanas in his discussion of the divisions at Corinth.

Much more important is the way Paul mentions Stephanas at the end of the letter. First Paul recommends Stephanas and his household; they were the first-fruits, i.e. the first converts of Achaia, and have devoted themselves to the service of the saints, which may mean that they have taken an active part in the collection for Jerusalem.[10] With remarkable emphasis Paul urges the congregation to be subject to such men and to every fellow worker (16.15–16). After 1.10 and 4.16 this is the third *parakalō*-period of the letter! Next Paul speaks about his joy at the presence of the delegation, adding a new injunction: 'Give your recognition to such men' (16.17–18). It is risky to draw conclusions from such injunctions as to the state of affairs which they presuppose. But the double emphasis gives some reason to suspect that not everybody in Corinth was inclined to give due recognition to Stephanas, his household, and his fellow delegates. The evidence is so far inconclusive, but a hypothesis may be ventured: the quarrelling Corinthians were opposing Stephanas as much as they were opposing Paul. As Stephanas was the head of the delegation, he was quite likely also its initiator, and a chief advocate of writing a letter to Paul to ask for his opinion on controversial questions.[11]

The advantage of my conjecture is that it makes it possible to explain in a simple, perhaps somewhat trivial way, the data contained in 1 Cor 1.10—4.21. The delegation and the letter it carried were themselves the cause of the quarrels. I can imagine myself hearing the objections, and I put them in my own language:

> Why write to Paul? He has left us and is not likely to come back. He lacks eloquence and wisdom. He supported himself by his own work; either he does not have the full rights of an apostle, or he did not esteem us to be worthy of supporting him. Why not rather write to Apollos, who is a wise teacher? I am his man! Or, if we do turn to anybody, why not write to Cephas, who is the foremost of the twelve. I am for Cephas! But, why ask anyone for counsel? Should we not rather say: I myself belong to Christ? As spiritual men we ought to be wise enough to decide for ourselves.

The details of this picture are of course pure imagination. But they may help us visualize the delicate situation Paul was facing when he set out to write his

---

10. R. Asting mentions this possibility, but is more inclined to think that Paul refers to service rendered to Christian preachers, including himself. *Die Heiligkeit im Urchristentum* (FRLANT 46, nF 29; Göttingen: Vandenhoeck & Ruprecht, 1930) 151 and 182–83.

11. Hurd argues that the Corinthians' questions were veiled objections (*Origin*, 113 and ch. 5, 114–209). In that case, the role of Stephanas may have been that of a mediator who succeeded in persuading the brethren that the objections should be presented to Paul in the form of a polite letter.

answer to the Corinthians. He had to answer a polite, official letter that asked for his advice. But he had also received an oral report stating that some brethren at Corinth had objected to the idea of asking Paul for instructions. Quite likely, latent objections had become more open and had caused a good deal of quarrelling after the departure of the delegation. As a consequence, Paul had to envisage the possibility that his letter containing his reply might easily make a bad situation worse. Quarrel and strife might develop into real divisions of the church, if his recommendations were enthusiastically received by one group and rejected by others.[12]

If the situation was anything like what I imagine, Paul could not possibly go right ahead and answer the questions raised in the letter from the Corinthians. He had first of all to make it clear that he did not speak as the champion of one group but as the apostle of Christ, as the founder and spiritual father of the whole congregation. The first section, chapters 1–4, is therefore a necessary part of the total structure of the letter and has a preparatory function. This also explains the somewhat unusual pattern that a short thanksgiving (1.4ff) is immediately followed by the first *parakalō*-period.[13] Paul had first of all to urge the Corinthians to agree, to be of one mind. Only on the presupposition that they did so, and that no divisions arose, would whatever else the apostle had to write be of any help.

Answering his critics, Paul is very careful to avoid giving the impression that he favors any one group in Corinth. There is no competition between himself and Apollos or Cephas, and still less between Christ and himself. Therefore even the slogan 'I belong to Christ' is fittingly countered by the questions, 'Is Christ divided? Was Paul crucified for you? Or were you baptized in the name of Paul?'. There is only one Christ, and therefore no distinction between the Christ to whom the Corinthians belong and the Christ preached by Paul. Paul is Christ's delegate and in no sense his rival. At Corinth he laid the foundation, and it is impossible to belong to Christ without building upon this foundation, which is Jesus Christ himself (cf. 3.10–11, 21–23).

That Paul did not baptize many is for him a reason for thanksgiving. There is no risk that anyone will say that he was baptized in Paul's name and has been made his man. The task of the apostle was not to baptize but to proclaim the gospel (1.14–17). That he did not preach with eloquent wisdom was to the benefit of the Corinthians, and in accordance both with his own commission and with the nature of the gospel, which is the word of the cross. What may appear as sheer folly is God's saving power and wisdom (1.18–25). The Corinthians ought to know this from their own experience (1.26–31). When Paul in Corinth concentrated on preaching Jesus Christ as the crucified one, this was due to a conscious decision. He renounced all the effects of rhetoric and human wisdom,

---

12. While Munck rightly argues that the term *schismata* used in 1 Cor 1.10 (cf. 11.18 and 12.25) does not prove that there were 'parties' or 'factions', he has a tendency to play down the serious danger of divisions within the church: *Paul and the Salvation of Mankind*, 136–39.

13. The closest analogy is the period introduced by the equivalent *erōtōmen* in 2 Thess 2.1.

in order that the faith of the converts might rest in the power of God alone (2.1–5). But when he did not in Corinth elaborate the secret wisdom of God's way of acting, it was not because Paul lacked the pneumatic gift of wise speech, but because the Corinthians were immature (2.6—3.2).

My one-sided and incomplete summary of 1.14—3.2 may be sufficient for the purpose to show that everything Paul here says was relevant to the situation he faced. From 3.3 onwards he turns more directly to the present state of affairs. Using himself and Apollos as examples, he stresses their solidarity as servants and fellow workers for God. Those who make comparisons and are proud of the excellencies of their favourite fail to realize their own dignity as God's field, building, and temple (3.5–17). All things, including Paul, Apollos, and Cephas, belong to those who themselves belong to Christ (3.21–23). Yet it is also stressed that Paul had a special task of his own. He was the one who planted and laid the foundation, and this he did as a skilled master builder (*hōs sophos architektōn*). Certainly he did not lack wisdom (3.6, 10). While Paul has no authority of his own, all others have to build on the foundation laid by him. They have to take care, lest they build with materials that will perish, or even destroy the temple of God (3.10–17). The context suggests that those who vaunt their wisdom might easily be guilty of these offences.[14] When speaking about faithfulness as the one duty required of stewards, Paul once more immediately turns to the relations between the Corinthians and himself (4.2–5).

Even the riddle of the enigmatic statement in 1 Cor 4.6 may possibly find a solution. The phrase *mē hyper ha gegraptai* ('not beyond what is written') is widely assumed to be the quotation of a slogan used in Corinth. I would suggest that even this slogan was part of the discussions and quarrels connected with the delegation and the letter to Paul. The point would then be: 'We need no instructions beyond what is written. As spiritual men we can interpret the Scriptures for ourselves. Why ask Paul?' Paul picks the slogan up and returns it. There is no contrast between the apostle and 'What is written', but there might be one between the scriptures, Paul and Apollos on the one side and the assertive and quarrelling Corinthians on the other. By the example of Paul and Apollos they should learn not to go beyond what is written, viz., not to be puffed up, but faithfully to perform the appointed service, knowing that everything is a gift of God. In the context the slogan gets its content from the preceding citations from and allusions to what is written concerning the wisdom of God in contrast to the wisdom of men (cf. 1.19f; 1.31; 2.9; 3.19f).

Paul does not, as his adherents are likely to have done, deny the facts which his opponents alleged against him. But what they meant as objections Paul interprets as indications of the faithfulness with which he has carried out his commission. Lack of wisdom, power, and honor is part of the lot that God has assigned to the suffering apostles of the crucified Christ (4.9–13). In order to

---

14. I see no reason for making 3:18 the beginning of a new section.

forestall the possibility that quarrels could lead to divisions, Paul the whole time deals with the church at Corinth as a unity. Only at the end does he single out some persons and flatly deny what they have asserted (4.18f.), that he will not return to Corinth, and, therefore, that he no longer cares for the brethren there; it is simply not true. They are his dear children, and certainly he will come very soon, if the Lord wills. This assertion is repeated at the end of the epistle (16.5–7, cf. also 16.24).

We can now draw some conclusions:

(1) The section 1 Cor 1.10—4.21 is correctly, even if not exhaustively, to be characterized as an apology for Paul's apostolic ministry.

(2) The quarrels at Corinth were mainly due to the opposition against Paul.

(3) Probably, the quarrels were occasioned or at least brought into the open by the letter and the delegation which were sent to Paul.

(4) The section has a clear and important function within the total structure of 1 Corinthians; before Paul could answer the questions raised, he had to overcome both false appraisals and false objections, and to reestablish his apostolic authority as the founder and spiritual father of the whole church at Corinth.[15]

15. As to Paul's authority, cf. 1 Cor 5.3–4; 7.40b; 9; 11.16, 34b; 14.37–38; 15.1–2, and 2 Corinthians, *passim*.

Chapter 6

Social Stratification in the Corinthian Community: A Contribution to the Sociology of Early Hellenistic Christianity[*]

Gerd Theissen

INTRODUCTION

In a series of essays published in the 1970s, Gerd Theissen brought the socio-logical study of early Christianity to a new prominence. In the essay from which this extract is taken, Theissen examines the evidence concerning the social level of the Corinthian Christians, taking as his starting point the contrasting views of Adolf Deissmann and Edwin Judge. Looking both at information concerning the congregation as a whole and at statements concerning named individuals, Theis-sen argues that the Corinthian church was marked by internal social stratifica-tion: a few (prominent) members from the upper stratum, the majority from the lower strata. He uses various criteria—mention of offices, houses, services ren-dered, and travel—to ascertain whether certain individuals may belong to the

*Extracted from G. Theissen, 'Social Stratification in the Corinthian Community: A Contribu-tion to the Sociology of Early Hellenistic Christianity', in *The Social Setting of Pauline Christianity* (Edinburgh: T. & T. Clark; Philadelphia: Fortress, 1982) 69–119; here pp. 69–75, 83, 94–96, copy-right © 1982 Fortress Press (www.fortresspress.com). Used by permission of Augsburg Fortress. Orig-inally published as 'Soziale Schichtung in der korinthischen Gemeinde: Ein Beitrag zur Soziologie des hellenistischen Urchristentums', *ZNW* 65 (1974) 232–72.

upper stratum. Theissen's essay has been very influential, setting the basis on which the 'new consensus' on the social level of the early Christians stands. This new consensus—that the early Christians came from all social levels, high and low—stands in contrast to what is termed the 'old consensus', that the early Christians, as Deissmann suggested, came from among the poor. Although the new consensus, with varied emphases, is well established, it has not gone unquestioned, notably in the recent work of Justin Meggitt.

Further Reading

See also chapter 17.

G. A. Deissmann, *Light from the Ancient East* (London: Hodder & Stoughton, 1927).

B. Holmberg, *Sociology and the New Testament* (Minneapolis: Fortress, 1990) 21–76.

Horrell, *Social Ethos,* 63–198, esp. 91–101.

E. A. Judge, *The Social Pattern of Christian Groups in the First Century* (London: Tyndale, 1960).

D. B. Martin, 'Review Essay: Justin J. Meggitt, *Paul, Poverty and Survival'*, *JSNT* 84 (2001) 51–64.

Meggitt, *Paul, Poverty.*

J. J. Meggitt, 'Response to Martin and Theissen', *JSNT* 84 (2001) 85–94.

Theissen, *Social Setting.*

G. Theissen, 'The Social Structure of Pauline Communities: Some Critical Remarks on J. J. Meggitt, *Paul, Poverty and Survival'*, *JSNT* 84 (2001) 65–84.

G. Theissen, 'Social Conflicts in the Corinthian Community: Further Remarks on J. J. Meggitt, *Paul, Poverty and Survival'*, *JSNT* 25 (2003) 371–91.

To which social strata did the Christians of the Hellenistic congregations outside Palestine belong? Various opinions have been expressed on this problem. According to A. Deissmann, primitive Christianity was a movement within the lower strata. 'The New Testament was not a product of the colourless refinement of an upper class. . . . On the contrary, it was, humanly speaking, a product of the force that came, unimpaired and strengthened by the Divine Presence, from the lower class (Matt 11:25ff; 1 Cor 1.26–31). This reason alone enabled it to become the Book of all mankind.'[1] E. A. Judge has expressed the opposite view: 'Far from being a socially depressed group, then, if the Corinthians are at all typical, the Christians were dominated by a socially pretentious section of the population of the big cities.'[2] Both judgments appeal to the makeup of the Corinthian congregation and both can be confirmed by means of a sociological analysis of all the information about this congregation. Both opinions are probably correct, because—and this is the thesis to be argued here—the Corinthian congregation is marked by internal stratification. The majority of the members, who come from the lower classes, stand in contrast to a few influential members who come

---

1. A. Deissmann, *Light from the Ancient Near East* (London, 1927) 144.

2. E. A. Judge, *The Social Pattern of Early Christian Groups in the First Century* (London, 1960) 60. Judge stresses, to be sure, that members of the lower strata also joined the Christian community as part of the retinue of those from the higher classes.

from the upper classes. This internal stratification is not accidental but the result of structural causes. The social makeup of the Corinthian congregation may, therefore, be characteristic of the Hellenistic congregations as such.

To prove this thesis requires a systematic analysis of everything said about the Corinthian community, specifically, (1) statements about the whole congregation, (2) statements about individual members, and (3) statements about groups within the congregation. These results must then be interpreted, in the second part of this essay, by inquiring into the structural elements which render plausible the internal stratification of the Corinthian congregation, whether these are to be found in the social structure of the city of Corinth itself or arise from the structure of the Pauline mission. Finally, we will briefly discuss the significance of social stratification for the history and self-understanding of primitive Christianity and sketch some working hypotheses for further investigations in the sociology of religion.

THE SOCIOLOGICAL EVALUATION OF EVIDENCE FOR THE CORINTHIAN CONGREGATION

Statements about the Community as a Whole

Paul himself describes the social makeup of the Corinthian congregation: 'For consider your call, brethren; not many of you were wise according to worldly standards, not many were powerful, not many were of noble birth; but God chose what is foolish in the world to shame the wise, God chose what is weak in the world to shame the strong, God chose what is low and despised in the world, even things that are not, to bring to nothing things that are, so that no human being might boast in the presence of God' (1 Cor 1.26–29).

At first glance such a passage would seem to confirm the romantic idea of a proletarian Christian community, a religious movement of the lower classes. On closer analysis, however, we find that Paul mentions three categories of people: those who are wise, those who are powerful, and those of noble birth. The terms 'wise' and 'powerful' are linked to previously stated ideas about wisdom and foolishness, power and weakness. But noble birth (εὐγενεῖς) brings into play something entirely new, a specific sociological category which Paul especially emphasizes. When repeating the idea in vv. 27–28 he not only contrasts 'noble birth' with 'lower born', but sharpens the contrast between εὐγενεῖς and ἀγενῆ by two further designations: τὰ ἐξουθενημένα ('despised') and τὰ μὴ ὄντα ('things that are not'). Although it is true that by means of these designations social relationships are seen in a theological light,[3] the sociological implications

---

3. Without question, Paul is here applying the idea of creation from nothing to a social situation. On creation *ex nihilo* cf. 2 Macc 7:28; Philo, *Opif.* 81; *Spec.* 4, 187; *2 Baruch* 21.4f; Hermas *Mand.* I.1; Herm. *Vis.* 1.1.6; *2 Clem.* 1.8. The distinction between μή and μηδέν is not very relevant; cf. 1 Cor 11.22 with 2 Cor 6.10.

of the concepts cannot be denied.[4] Among other things, 'nothingness,' οὐδενία, is a *topos* derived from the realm of philosophical ridicule.[5] The truly wise Socrates qualifies as 'nothing' (Plato, *Phaedr.* 234e; *Theat.* 176c). Epictetus follows in these footsteps when he anticipates others' opinions that he amounts to nothing: οὐδὲν ἦν ὁ Ἐπίκτητος (Epictetus, *Diss.* 3.9.14; cf. 4.8.25; *Ench.* 24.1). Thus when Paul writes that those whom society and the world (κόσμος, 1 Cor 1.28) regard as nothing are in reality representatives of that true wisdom which is contained in Christ, his Greek diction reveals how others perceive the social status of those whom he is addressing. This becomes even clearer with the supplementary, appositive τὰ μὴ ὄντα. In Euripides, Hecuba complains about the divine actions which humble the exalted and exalt the humble: ὁρῶ τὰ τῶν θεῶν, ὡς τὰ μὲν πυργοῦς ἄνω τὰ μηδὲν ὄντα, τὰ δε δοκοῦντ' ἀπώλε-σαν ('I see the Gods' work/who exalt on high/that which was naught/ and bring the proud names low'). Andromache confirms this in her answer: . . . τὸ δ' εὐγενὲς εἰς δοῦλον ἥκει, μεταβολὰς τοιάσδε ἔχον ('high birth hath come to bondage—ah, the change, the change'; *Trojan Women* 612ff). This contrast between μηδὲν ὤν and εὐγενές is also found in Sophocles (*Ajax* 1094–97): οὐκ ἄν . . . θαυμάσαιμ' ἔτι, ὅς μηδὲν ὤν γοναῖσιν εἶθ' ἁμαρτάνει, ὅθ' οἱ δοκοῦντες εὐγενεῖς πεφυκέναι ('I shall never marvel after this if any base-born fellow gives offense when those who pride themselves on their lineage [offend thus by their perverted utterances]'). Since this same idiomatic use of μηδέν to express an opinion about social rank is attested in Hellenistic Judaism (Philo, *Virt.* 173–74), we can assume that for Paul, too, the phrase τὰ μὴ ὄντα has a sociological significance, especially since it stands in contrast to εὐγενεῖς; thus the last of the three categories mentioned (wise, powerful, of noble birth) is of unmistakable sociological significance. Because this particular term in the series goes beyond the catchwords of the preceding context, it can be assumed that in the new paragraph (1 Cor 1.26ff) Paul has a social fact in mind and probably intends the first two categories to be understood sociologically as well. The 'powerful' would be influential people; the 'wise', those who belong to the educated classes (that is, 'wise according to worldly standards') for whom wisdom is also a sign of social status. Unless Paul had also been thinking in these instances of sociological criteria he could scarcely have combined the three terms and, taking them collectively, contrasted to them the election of those who are not, the μὴ ὤν. Philo also combines references to the strong, powerful, and understanding in a similar way when he writes (*Somn.* 1.155), 'Are not private citizens continually becoming officials, and officials private citizens, rich men becoming poor men and poor men of ample means, nobodies becoming celebrated, obscure people becoming distinguished, weak men (ἀσθενεῖς) strong (ἰσχυροί),

---

4. Cf. J. Bohatec, 'Inhalt und Reihenfolge der "Schlagworte der Erlösungreligion" in I Kor 1 26–31', *TZ* (1948) 252–71.

5. For detailed discussion of this *topos* see H. D. Betz, *Der Apostle Paulus und die sokratische Tradition*, BHT 45 (Tübingen, 1972) 123–30.

insignificant men powerful (δυνατοί), foolish men wise men of understanding (συνετοί), witless men sound reasoners?' In my opinion there can be no doubt about the sociological implications of the language of 1 Cor 1.26–29.

If Paul says that there were not many in the Corinthian congregation who were wise, powerful, and wellborn, then this much is certain: there were some. As early as Origen this passage was cited as an objection to Celsus's opinion that in Christian gatherings one would find only the lower classes.[6] If the actual number of such people was small, their influence must be accorded all the more import. Were that not the case, Paul would scarcely think it necessary to devote a substantial portion of his letter to an exchange with their 'wisdom'. Nor could he identify these people with the whole congregation when writing, 'We are fools for Christ's sake, but you are wise in Christ. We are weak, but you are strong. You are held in honor, but we in disrepute' (1 Cor 4.10). Here again we find the same three categories—the wise, the powerful, the esteemed—even if the terminology has been modified. Moreover, here again these terms have a sociological significance, for Paul contrasts his circumstances with those of the Corinthians in terms bearing indisputable sociological implications. For example, Paul works with his hands, experiences hunger, has no permanent home, and is persecuted. He is 'the refuse of the world, the offscouring of all things' (1 Cor 4.11–13).[7] Paul puts himself at the bottom of the scale of social prestige but sees the Corinthians as occupying the top: *You* are clever, strong, honored. In doing so he addresses the entire congregation, although earlier he had said that there were 'not many' who were wise, powerful, and of noble birth. It can only be concluded that the phrase 'not many' doesn't mean very much. In 1 Cor 1.26ff Paul does not wish to contest the significance of those congregational members from the upper classes but simply objects to their all-too-well-developed consciousness of their own status. Naturally, he is right. These representatives of the upper classes were a minority within the congregation, but apparently a dominant minority. At the very least, several members of the Corinthian congregation who appear to be very active may be counted in their group.

Statements about Individual Members of the Congregation

We should be cautious in evaluating statements about individuals. Apocryphal legends may always want to know more about New Testament figures than the New Testament tells, but modern exegesis ought not to further this tendency. Instead, it should subordinate its (perfectly proper) curiosity to methodical criteria. In what follows, statements about holding office, about 'houses', about assistance rendered to the congregation, and about travel can all serve as criteria

---

6. Origen, *Cels.* 3.48.

7. Περικαθάρματα should be understood in a sociological sense, as is κάθαρμα in Philo, *Virt.* 174. The meaning 'propitiatory sacrifice' is attested only in later sources. Cf. Conzelmann, *1 Corinthians,* 90 n. 49.

for elevated social status. The first two of these have to do with position, the last two with activities. Each of the criteria raises specific problems.

References to Offices

From Acts 18.8 we learn that Crispus, one of the first Christians, was a synagogue ruler. His conversion to Christianity was probably of great significance for the founding of the community, setting off a small wave of conversions ('and many of the Corinthians, when they heard of it [RSV 'hearing Paul'] believed and had themselves baptized' [RSV 'were baptized']) (Acts 18.8). Paul mentions Crispus in 1 Cor 1.14 at the head of that short list of congregational members whom he has baptized but says nothing about his former position in the synagogue.

A synagogue ruler[8] was leader of the Jewish worship service, not head of the community as such. He controlled the reading of Scripture and the homilies (cf. Acts 13.15 where, however, several synagogue rulers are found). For our purposes it is particularly important to note that he had to assume responsibility for the synagogue building.[9] Since upkeep of the synagogue required money, there was reason to entrust this office to a wealthy man who would be in a position, should the occasion arise, to supplement the community's funds with his own contribution. This is confirmed by a number of inscriptions in which synagogue rulers have memorialized their expenditures for these Jewish houses of worship. In Aegina (that is, not far from Corinth) a certain Theodores completely rebuilt a synagogue over a period of four years, admittedly with money provided by collections and synagogue possessions, as he expressly states (Frey no. 722 = *CIG* 9894; *IG* [Berlin, 1873ff], IV, 190). But in Porto (Frey no. 548) and Acmonia (Frey no. 766) synagogue rulers also undertook repairs ἐκ τῶν ἰδίων, that is, using their own resources. An inscription at Side (Frey no. 781) is probably to be interpreted this way: A φροντιστὴς τῆς ἁγιωτάτης πρώτης συναγωγῆς ('superintendent of the most sacred premiere synagogue') has provided repairs. Certainly the best known is an inscription of Theodotus in Jerusalem (Frey no. 1404; cf. Deissmann, *Light*, pp. 439–41):

> Theodotus the son of Vettenus, priest and ruler of the synagogue, son of a ruler of the synagogue, son's son of a ruler of the synagogue, built the synagogue for reading of the law and for teaching of the commandments, also the strangers' lodging and the chambers and the conveniences of waters for

8. On the office of the ruler of the synagogue cf. E. Schürer, *Geschichte des jüdischen Volkes* (Leipzig, 1907) 2:509–12, ET *The History of the Jewish People in the Age of Jesus Christ (175 B.C.–A.D.135)* (Edinburgh, 1886–90) 2:433–36, rev. and ed. G. Vermes and F. Millar (Edinburgh, 1973–1979), and J. B. Frey, *Corpus Inscriptionum Iudaicarum* I (Rome, 1936) xcvii–xcix. It is noteworthy that Sosthenes, as the ruler of the synagogue, represents the case of the Jewish community before the procurator Gallio (Acts 18.17), since that was usually the task of the ἄρχοντες. Perhaps he held both offices.

9. That there was a synagogue in Corinth is shown by an inscription (cf. B. D. Merritt, *Greek Inscriptions, 1896–1927: Corinth, Results of Excavations conducted by the American School of Classical Studies at Athens VIII, 1* [Cambridge, 1931], no. 111). The style of the inscription, however, points to a later time (cf. 79).

an inn for them that need it from abroad, of which (synagogue) his father and the elders and Simonides did lay the foundation.

That these synagogue rulers were esteemed men—even beyond the boundaries of the Jewish community itself—can be deduced from a funerary inscription of one Staphylus of Rome (Frey no. 265 = E. Diehl, *Inscriptiones latinae christianae veteres* [Berlin, 1925–31], no. 4886): *Staff(y)lo arc(h)onti et archisynagogo honoribus omnibus fu(n)ctus restituta coniux benmerenti fecit.* Ἐν εἰρήνη ἡ κοίμησις σου. The phrase *omnibus honoribus functus* is often found in funerary inscriptions and indicates that the deceased held high offices in the *municipium*, the colony, the polis, or an association.[10] A majority of those inscriptions preserved from synagogue rulers emphasize that those who held these offices rendered a service to the Jewish congregation through their initiative and generosity. They were certainly not the poorest members of the community. So we may assume in the case of the synagogue ruler Crispus that he possessed high social status, which would explain why his conversion had great influence on others.[11]

The status of Erastus, described at the conclusion of Romans as 'the city treasurer' (οἰκονόμος τῆς πόλεως, 16.23), is more controversial. Did he hold a high municipal office to which he had been elected, or was he a less significant person employed in financial administration, possibly even a slave to be regarded as the city's property, an *arcarius rei publicae* ('public treasurer'; the Vulgate reads *arcarius civitatis*)?[12] The problem must be discussed at three levels. First, all New Testament statements must be evaluated, then the parallels outside the New Testament. Finally, and most important, is the analysis of inscriptional evidence pertaining to Corinthian offices.

[Theissen's discussion of the three levels of evidence pertaining to the Erastus inscription on pp. 75–83 is here omitted; we pick up at his conclusion on p. 83.]

Thus Erastus, later to be chosen aedile, could have occupied the office of οἰκονόμος τῆς πόλεως (perhaps that of quaestor) in the year in which Romans was written, an office which did not yet signify the pinnacle of a public career. I can see no compelling argument against this identification of the Christian Erastus. The name is not otherwise attested for Corinth, by inscriptions or literature, making a confusion of two persons less likely in this instance than with some other names. We can assume that Erastus belonged to the οὐ πολλοὶ δυνατοί. To have been chosen aedile he must have been a full citizen—and in a Roman colony that would mean Roman citizenship. His spending for the public indicates that he could claim a certain amount of private wealth. It is quite possible

---

10. Cf. Frey, *Inscriptionum*, 188.
11. Cf. E. Haenchen, *The Acts of the Apostles* (Philadelphia, 1971) 535.
12. H. J. Cadbury, 'Erastus of Corinth', *JBL* 50 (1931) 42–58, argues for the latter possibility. The genitive τῆς πόλεως would in this case probably be taken as a possessive genitive.

that he was a freedman as the inscription does not mention his father. Add to this the fact that he has a Greek name, and we may perhaps imagine him a successful man who has risen into the ranks of the local notables, most of whom are of Latin origin.

[Theissen next discusses 'References to Houses', 'References to Services Rendered' and 'References to Travel' (pp. 83–94). We pick up at the conclusion of his discussion of individual members of the community, on p. 94.]

We can now give a summary of what we know about those Corinthian Christians known to us by name. Apart from Chloe's people we have (at a maximum) sixteen names. However, it is not always certain that those names come from Corinth. Lucius (Rom 16.21) is frequently identified with Luke, Luke being a familiar form of Lucius. Similarly, it has been assumed that Sosipater (Rom 16.21) is the Sopater of Beroea mentioned in Acts 20.4. Sosthenes, who is mentioned alongside Paul in the prescript of the first letter to Corinth, could only be regarded as a Corinthian if identified with Sosthenes the synagogue ruler in Acts 18.17, which is by no means certain.

Achaicus:	1 Cor 16.17; companion of Stephanas.
Aquila:	Rom 16.3; Acts 18.2, 18, 26; 1 Cor 16.19; house-congregation; small business establishment; travel; support of apostles.
Erastus:	Rom 16.23; financial official of the city; probably later chosen aedile and, in consequence, made a public gift; travel.
Fortunatus:	1 Cor 16.17; companion of Stephanas.
Gaius:	Rom 16.23; 1 Cor 1.14; his house served the entire church and Paul. Connections with Erastus?
Jason:	Rom 16.1.
Crispus:	1 Cor 1.14; Acts 18.8; synagogue ruler; manager of a 'house'; his conversion to Christianity influenced others.
Lucius:	Rom 16.21.
Priscilla:	See Aquila.
Phoebe:	Rom 16.1–2; services rendered to Paul and the church; travel.
Quartus:	Rom 16.23.
Sosipater:	Rom 16.21.
Sosthenes:	1 Cor 1.1; Acts 18.17 (?); synagogue ruler; travel.
Stephanas:	1 Cor 1.16; 16.15; manager of a house; services rendered to the church; travel.
Titius Justus:	Acts 18.7; lodging for Paul.
Tertius:	Rom 16.22; scribe.
Chloe's people:	1 Cor 1.11.

Of the seventeen persons (including one group) listed, nine belong to the upper classes according to the criteria discussed above. In three instances, three of the criteria apply: houses, services rendered, and travel for Aquila, Priscilla, and Stephanas. In four cases, two criteria apply: offices and travel for Erastus and Sosthenes; office and 'house' for Crispus; services rendered and travel for Phoebe. In two cases, one criterion fits: services rendered for Gaius and Titius Justus, on the basis of whose character, however, a certain position in life seems a perfectly reasonable conclusion. Of these nine, Sosthenes possibly was not a Corinthian. In contrast to these there is only a small group of people of probably inferior social status, Chloe's people. This also may be true of Achaicus, Fortunatus, and Tertius, but is by no means certain. The social standing of Jason, Lucius, and Sosipater remains an open question, and we are not even certain if the last two belonged to the Corinthian community.

The result is clear. The great majority of the Corinthians known to us by name probably enjoyed high social status. We need not for that reason cast doubt on Paul's statement that 'not many' Corinthians belonged to the upper strata (1 Cor 1.26). In the letters it is understandably the most important people who are most likely to be mentioned by name, who keep in touch with Paul (that is, were free to travel), and who exercise influence within the congregation. Thus we may conclude that in all probability the most active and important members of the congregation belong to the οὐ πολλοὶ, σοφοί, δυνατοί, and εὐγενεῖς. Those of the lower strata scarcely appear as individuals in the Corinthian correspondence.

Chapter 7

Realized Eschatology
at Corinth[*]
Anthony C. Thiselton

INTRODUCTION

Before the publication of this extract, various scholars, including C. K. Barrett, Nils Dahl, and F. F. Bruce, had expressed the view that the Corinthians held to an overrealised eschatology, stressing the 'already' of salvation to the detriment of the 'not yet'. With this important and influential essay, published in 1978, Anthony Thiselton argued the case more thoroughly than had been attempted before, contending that an imbalance in the area of eschatology leading to hyper-spirituality provides a comprehensive explanation for all the difficulties with which Paul deals in 1 Corinthians. In his article, Thiselton seeks to address the criticism, made by E. E. Ellis among others, that apart from 1 Cor 15, which in any case offers doubtful support for the theory, the thesis of overrealised eschatology depends on a single verse, 1 Cor 4.8. In the extract printed here, which constitutes the bulk of the essay, Thiselton works through chapters 1–14 of the

*Extracted from A. C. Thiselton, 'Realized Eschatology at Corinth', *NTS* 24 (1978) 510–26; here pp. 513–23. Reprinted by permission of Cambridge University Press, The Edinburgh Building, Shaftesbury Road, Cambridge.

letter and tries to show that a defective eschatology provides a sufficient cause for each individual problem. He also endeavours to demonstrate that the Corinthians' realised eschatological outlook was linked to their enthusiastic theology of the Spirit. The remaining part of the essay (not printed here) concentrates on 1 Cor 15: Thiselton concedes that 15.12 ('How can some of you say, "There is no resurrection of the dead?"') does not in itself imply an overrealised eschatology, but he maintains that the argument of the chapter as a whole indicates that the Corinthians made too little of the future of salvation.

The essay is important as the 'definitive' argument for the influence of realised eschatology at Corinth, and for its attempt to show that all the key issues at Corinth stem from this doctrinal error. Enthusiasm for the view that the Corinthians developed an imbalanced eschatology has cooled somewhat in recent study, as more and more scholars have attempted to relate the problems at Corinth to the Greco-Roman context of the church. Those critical of the realised eschatology hypothesis have included John Barclay, Duane Litfin, and Dale Martin. Barclay points out that to describe the Corinthians' theology as an overrealised eschatology implies that they held to an eschatological time frame; that they did so is by no means evident. Barclay suggests that their framework may simply have been noneschatological. In his recent commentary, Thiselton himself has suggested that his earlier position should be combined with the more recent emphasis on the influence of the wider secular context: he now thinks that the problems in Corinth arose from the combination of eschatological misperceptions and secular attitudes (p. 40).

Further Reading

J. M. G. Barclay, 'Thessalonica and Corinth' (ch. 14 below).
E. E. Ellis, 'Christ Crucified', in *Reconciliation and Hope: New Testament Essays in Atonement and Eschatology Presented to L. L. Morris* (ed. R. Banks; Exeter: Paternoster, 1974) 69–75.
Litfin, *St. Paul's Theology*.
Martin, *Corinthian Body*.
A. C. Thiselton, *The First Epistle to the Corinthians* (NIGTC; Grand Rapids: Eerdmans, 2000).

The main issue in 1 Cor 1–4 turns not in the first instance on questions about wisdom as such, but upon the Corinthians' attitudes towards ministry. Questions about the communication of wisdom and about divisions which revolve around chosen personalities are discussed within this framework. In the view of the eschatological radicals, if the last days had already arrived, was it not part of the Christian message that the Spirit was poured out upon all believers indiscriminately? The notion that certain special men were marked out by the Spirit for particular leadership belonged to the era before the last days. Now that the last days had arrived one 'spiritual man' was as good as another. Once again, Paul seems to concede that there is a half-truth in this. This is why he himself can appear to endorse

what must be a quotation from the Corinthians' own theology: ὁ δὲ πνευ-
ματικὸς ἀνακρίνει μὲν πάντα, αὐτὸς δὲ ὑπ' οὐδενὸς ἀνακρίνεται
(2.15). Although these are apparently Paul's words, J. Weiss describes them as the
confessions of a spiritual mystic which are uncharacteristic of Paul, and Wilckens and Reitzenstein find parallel material in Hellenistic religious literature.[1] In
fact Paul quotes the words in order to give them a new twist which he achieves
in 2.16—3.4: 'I could not address you as spiritual men' (3.1). Thus B. A. Pearson rightly concludes that whilst 2.13b–16 'is Paul's own statement, yet it must
be regarded as incorporating the terminology of the opponents, albeit in a manner which Paul can use in his argumentation'.[2] The Corinthians insisted, firstly,
that they could all 'discern' which particular teacher could best meet their own
needs; and secondly, that if need be they could do without teachers altogether,
since each could discern spiritual truths for himself. The individual Christian, on
the other hand, possessed secret depths which others could not plumb (αὐτὸς
δὲ ὑπ' οὐδενὸς ἀνακρίνεται).

There is admittedly one difficulty to this interpretation. Paul seems to be
attacking a tendency to *over*value certain ministers, rather than to undervalue
them. Thus he asks: τί (neuter) οὖν ἐστιν Ἀπολλῶς; τί δέ ἐστιν Παῦλος;
διάκονοι . . . ἑκάστῳ ὡς ὁ κύριος ἔδωκεν (3.5). Let no one, he urges, glory
in men (3.21). In practice, however, Paul attacks both the tendency to overvalue
certain individual personalities (including himself), and also the danger of under-
valuing the ministry as a whole. He censures the Corinthians, for example, for
cheating themselves (μηδεὶς ἑαυτὸν ἐξαπατάτω) out of the fullness of their
inheritance in Christ: 'For all things are yours, whether Paul or Apollos or Cephas
or the world . . . and you are Christ's . . .' (3.18–23).

The most consistent group at Corinth were those whose slogan was ἐγὼ δὲ
Χριστοῦ. There is no adequate reason why we should take these words to be a
gloss, as Weiss and others have suggested, nor are they the reaction of exponents
of a radically Jewish Christianity. They represent the slogan of hyper-spiritual
enthusiasts who see no need for any human leader.[3] To adopt this interpretation
is not to make a supposed 'Christ-party' the basis of a reconstruction for the entire
situation at Corinth, but it would well harmonize with the situation we are
already describing.[4] Schmithals is right when he maintains that the self-styled
spiritual men at Corinth complained, 'How could you appeal to men instead of
to Christ? That is what the σαρκικοί do.'[5] But he is wrong when he argues that

---

1. U. Wilckens, *Weisheit und Torheit*, pp. 56–60; R. Reitzenstein, *Die hellenistischen Mysterienre-
ligionen nach ihren Grundgedanken und Wirkungen* (Berlin-Leipzig, 1927) 338–39; and J. Weiss, *Earliest Christianity* (ET New York, 1969) II, 513. Cf. Hans Lietzmann, *An die Korinther* 1–2 (Tübingen,
1949) 14.
2. B. A. Pearson, *The Pneumatikos-Psychikos Terminology in 1 Corinthians* (SBLDS 12; Montana,
1973) 38.
3. Cf. F. F. Bruce. *1 and 2 Corinthians* (London, 1971) 33; J. Moffatt, *The First Epistle of Paul to
the Corinthians* (London, 1938) 10; H. Lietzmann, op. cit., 6–7; and W. Schmithals, *Gnosticism*, 204.
4. Cf. the warnings of J. C. Hurd, *Origin,* 105–6, chiefly in relation to Schmithals.
5. W. Schmithals, op. cit., 204.

all the other three groups represent a single 'apostolic' anti-gnostic outlook. For the other side of the coin is that if the spiritual man judges or discerns all things, he is in a position to select whichever spiritual director is most in line with his own preferences or spiritual values. Thus there is no contradiction in suggesting that a low view of the ministry as a whole may also lead to a superficially 'high' view of certain individual ministers.

This interpretation is confirmed by the fact that Paul unambiguously sets questions about the assessment of individual ministers firmly *in the context of a future eschatological perspective.* 'Therefore *do not pronounce judgement before the time,* before the Lord comes, who will bring to light the things now hidden in darkness and will disclose the purposes of the heart. Then ($\tau\acute{o}\tau\epsilon$) every man will receive his commendation from God' (4.5). Paul asserts precisely the fact that all is *not* yet revealed even to the spiritual man. At the present moment only God, and no one else, knows the particular value of each man's ministry: 'each man's work will become manifest, for the day will disclose it' (3.13a). The model or picture is that of a building, the materials of which will be shown to be combustible or otherwise only when there is a fire. 'The fire will test what sort of work each one has done' (3.13b). No one else knows what wages should be paid to each: each shall receive ($\lambda\acute{\eta}\mu\psi\epsilon\tau\alpha\iota$) his wages in due course (3.8). Meanwhile, far from 'judging all things' ($\acute{o}$ $\delta\grave{\epsilon}$ $\pi\nu\epsilon\upsilon\mu\alpha\tau\iota\kappa\grave{o}\varsigma$ $\acute{\alpha}\nu\alpha\kappa\rho\acute{\iota}\nu\epsilon\iota$ $\pi\acute{\alpha}\nu\tau\alpha$ 2.15), Paul himself does not even 'judge' ($o\grave{\upsilon}\delta\grave{\epsilon}$ ... $\acute{\alpha}\nu\alpha\kappa\rho\acute{\iota}\nu\omega$) his own worth (4.3): $\acute{o}$ $\delta\grave{\epsilon}$ $\acute{\alpha}\nu\alpha\kappa\rho\acute{\iota}\nu\omega\nu$ $\mu\epsilon$ $\kappa\acute{\upsilon}\rho\iota\acute{o}\varsigma$ $\acute{\epsilon}\sigma\tau\iota\nu$ (4.4). For the present, as well as being a time of revelation, is also a time of human ignorance and spiritual hiddenness.

As against the Corinthians' watchwords of power ($\delta\acute{\upsilon}\nu\alpha\mu\iota\varsigma$), discernment ($\acute{\alpha}\nu\alpha\kappa\rho\acute{\iota}\nu\omega$), and especially wisdom ($\sigma o\phi\acute{\iota}\alpha$, 1.18—2.16; 3.18–20; 4.10) and spirituality ($\pi\nu\epsilon\hat{\upsilon}\mu\alpha$, 2.10—3.4) Paul brings forward a less finished but more dynamic perspective of being on the way to salvation ($\sigma\omega\zeta o\mu\acute{\epsilon}\nu o\iota\varsigma$, 1.19); feeding with gradations of diet ($\gamma\acute{\alpha}\lambda\alpha$ ... $\beta\rho\hat{\omega}\mu\alpha$ ... $\acute{\alpha}\lambda\lambda$' $o\grave{\upsilon}\delta\grave{\epsilon}$ $\acute{\epsilon}\tau\iota$ $\nu\hat{\upsilon}\nu$ $\delta\acute{\upsilon}\nu\alpha\sigma\theta\epsilon$, 3.2); the watering and the steady growth of that which has been planted ($\alpha\grave{\upsilon}\xi\acute{\alpha}\nu\omega$, 3.6); and especially the long process of 'building up' which is later contrasted with the instant or 'realized' counterfeit of being merely 'puffed up' ($o\grave{\iota}\kappa o\delta o\mu\hat{\omega}$, 3.10–15, cf. 8.1).

The thrust of Paul's futurist perspective, then, is not only to qualify an over-realized eschatology at Corinth; it also represents an anti-enthusiastic stance. Paul's eschatology is realistic rather than charismatic or ecstatic, precisely because it retains its future-orientated perspective. Christians are those who 'wait for' the revealing of our Lord Jesus Christ (1.7), and who must judge nothing before the time (4.5). It is quite misleading to imply that in the first four chapters this perspective can be found only at 4.8.

The second main part of 1 Corinthians stretches from 5.1 to 11.1, and concerns firstly a radical re-interpretation of Pauline attitudes towards black-and-white issues of right and wrong (5.1—6.20); and secondly, more delicate and complex questions about voluntary restraints (7.1—11.1). The heart of the matter is the interpretation of the slogan $\pi\acute{\alpha}\nu\tau\alpha$ $\mu o\iota$ $\acute{\epsilon}\xi\epsilon\sigma\tau\iota\nu$ (6.12; 10.23), and also the related use of the comparable catchphrase πάντες γνῶσιν ἔχομεν (8.1). There can be no doubt that these constitute quotations from the theologizing of the Corinthians themselves, even if they in turn originally took them from Paul. Whether they are now being quoted at second hand or third hand cannot be decided with certainty. It is noteworthy, however, that in J. C. Hurd's useful table of scholarly opinion on the subject, twenty-two of the twenty-four writers whom he consults regard 6.12 as some kind of quotation, and all twenty-four understand 8.1 in this way.[6]

We may assume that the Corinthians either took up Paul's own words about freedom from law, or more probably that they felt drawn towards a more radical application of Paul's own eschatological dualism than he himself had seemed to allow. If the spiritual man has died with Christ, he has already passed beyond the realm of the law (cf. Rom 7.14). Why then can it not be said with utter consistency that 'everything is permitted'? Perhaps no modern writer has shown more pointedly than Albert Schweitzer the fundamental incompatibility of eschatology and law. Since according to Paul, Schweitzer argues, the believer belongs to the new creation, he is like a house that is sold for breaking up: repairs to it have become irrational.[7] This is not to deny that Schweitzer himself draws complicated sets of distinctions between different lines of thought within Paul's eschatology, and traces an inner logic which each line follows. But his work enables us to see by implication how easily the Corinthian radicals could insist on a more ruthlessly consistent application of Paul's eschatology than the apostle had seemed to have the boldness to carry through. The charge that Paul vacillated perhaps extended beyond the question of his travel plans (cf. 2 Cor 1.17–19).

The outstanding case in point was the man who was co-habiting with his father's wife (v. 1). I have examined this section in detail elsewhere, and underlined the importance of the point that Paul's censure relates not primarily to the man in question, but to the fact that the community seemed pleased with the situation.[8] 'You are arrogant (πεφυσιωμένοι ἐστέ). Ought you not rather to mourn?' (v. 2). The RSV rendering 'arrogant' is less satisfactory than the NEB's words 'And you can still be proud of yourselves!' The self-styled 'spiritual' men at Corinth (not perhaps without some mixture of motives) wished to parade their new-found freedom as a bold testimony to their eschatological status. Might not some of the 'strong' have regarded with something akin to awe a man who unashamedly displayed a 'freedom' which went beyond the ordinary man's wildest dreams? He would be neither the first nor the last of those spiritual enthusiasts who raised themselves above the mundane level of everyday questions about ethics.

This outlook may also serve to explain the Corinthians' way of interpreting the injunction in the previous letter not to associate with immoral men (vv.

---

6. J. C. Hurd, op. cit., 68.

7. A. Schweitzer, *The Mysticism of Paul the Apostle* (ET London, 1931) 177–204.

8. A. C. Thiselton, 'The Meaning of Σάρξ in I Corinthians 5.5: a fresh approach in the light of logical and semantic factors', *Scottish Journal of Theology* 26 (1973) 204–27.

9–13). How could they be so obtuse as to think that Paul intended them to with-draw from having dealings with immoral men in the outside world?[9] Incredu-lously Paul exclaims, ' . . . then you would need to go out of the world' (v. 10). This is not a solemn theological statement about the Church and the world, but an incredulous comment to the effect that life under those conditions would be impossible. The Corinthians' sheer lack of realism must have proceeded from the maxim that 'the immoral' could not mean Christians, since Christians were beyond the scope of the law. However, the 'natural' man remained condemned as one who still belonged to the pre-eschatological era of the law.

The same kind of attitude is reflected in the situation behind 6.12–20. Ques-tions about food (6.13) were seen to relate only to the passing order, and were irrelevant to the Corinthians' eschatological status. The usual interpretation of this verse sees their slogan about food and the stomach as a gnostic one. C. T. Craig, for example, writes, 'The Gnostic libertines had used . . . the fact that food did not raise a moral issue to support their contention that sexual con-duct also had no moral significance. Paul grants that both food and the stomach belong to the transient physical sphere. . . . But . . . the body is not something transient, but will be raised from the dead.'[10] However, it is pure speculation to suggest that questions about food were matters of indifference to the sloganizers merely because they concerned the physical realm as such in the context of a *gnos-tic* type of dualism. Paul's immediate allusion to the resurrection shows that it is much more likely that the dualism in question was an *eschatological* one. The stomach (ἡ κοιλία) belongs to the old order which is passing away.

We may question whether two of the main English versions, the RSV and the NEB, are correct in closing the quotation marks where they do: 'Food is meant for the stomach and the stomach for food'—and God will destroy both one and the other (13a, RSV). More probably the whole of v. 13a constitutes an eschato-logically orientated slogan current at Corinth, and Paul only begins his rejoinder with the words, 'The body (το σῶμα) is not meant for immorality' (13b). Two factors seem to confirm this. Firstly, the parallel expression of the idea in Mark 7.14–19 is more likely (to say the least) to have its setting in primitive Christian tradition rather than in gnosticism, and may well point to there being a wide-spread maxim of this kind at a very early date in various Christian communities. Secondly, on its own and without its eschatological application, the slogan 'Food is meant for the stomach and the stomach for food' is almost ludicrously unin-formative and trivial, even as a shorthand popular slogan. However, if we con-cede that the second half of the quotation comes from Corinth rather than from Paul, we have as good as admitted that the flavour of the argument at Corinth is that of an eschatological, rather than a gnostic, dualism.

9. A convincing reconstruction of Paul's comments in the previous letter is given by Nils A. Dahl, 'Paul and the Church of Corinth', 330.

10. C. T. Craig, 'Exegesis of 1 Corinthians' in *The Interpreter's Bible* 10 (New York, 1953) 73–74. Cf. F. F. Bruce, *op. cit.* 62–63; C. K. Barrett, *A Commentary on the First Epistle to the Corinthians* (Lon-don, 1968) 144–48; and H. Lietzmann, op. cit., 27.

Paul makes no attempt to deny the eschatological reality of the Christian's situation. But he immediately brings into play the thought of a future resurrection, just as earlier in the same chapter he called attention to the *future* judgment and to a future inheritance of the kingdom (6.2, 3, 9, 14). Although there are variant readings for ἐξεγερεῖ in v. 14 (the first hand of P[46] has the present tense, and the second corrector of P[46] has the aorist), C. K. Barrett rightly declares, 'Only the future provides the argument that Paul needs'.[11] The whole argument of chapters 5 and 6 depends not only on the notion of corporate solidarity with Christ, but also on the concept of eschatological *destiny*. Christians must strive to be now what they are to *become*.

This can be seen in Paul's language about newness in 1 Cor 5.7: 'Cleanse out the old leaven that you may be fresh dough, as you really are unleavened'. Paul does not deny that newness of life is a present reality for the Christian. But precisely because this is so, the appropriation of this newness is an ongoing process which calls forth an imperative of Christian response. In a detailed study of newness R. A. Harrisville rightly shows that it is not simply, at least for Paul, a finished achievement, but something more progressive and dynamic. 'The new asserts itself over against the old and actually crowds it out of existence. . . . The new possesses the power of renewal, in contrast to the old which has the tendency to remain as it is.'[12] Whilst not necessarily endorsing the generalizing conclusions of Harrisville's study for the whole New Testament, we may endorse his points with reference to I Corinthians, namely that an emphasis on the eschatological contrast between the new and the old in no way undermines the notion of newness as an ongoing process, which gives rise to a clear imperative, and leads on towards a finality yet to be arrived at.

The section of 1 Corinthians which extends from 7.1 to 11.1 depends no less on eschatological considerations. There are two key issues: firstly, the difference between theory and practice; and secondly the need for a continual 'building up' of the community in readiness for the final goal. The *theory* is put forward by the Corinthians, on the basis of a realized eschatology: 'It is well for a man not to touch a woman' (7.1). 'All of us possess knowledge. . . . An idol has no real existence. . . . There is no God but one' (8.1, 4). 'All things are lawful' (10.23). By contrast, the *practice* is put forward by Paul on the basis of the fact that the present world-order still continues, and the Christian has not yet reached his final goal: 'But because of the temptation to immorality, each man should have his own wife . . .' (7.2). '"Knowledge" puffs up, but love builds up. If anyone imagines that he knows something, he does not yet know as he ought to know. . . . Not all of us possess this knowledge' (8.1b, 2, 7). 'But not all things are helpful. . . . Not all things build up' (10.23).

Questions about the seventh chapter are complex, and it is admittedly difficult to be certain at what points Paul is quoting from the Corinthians

11. C. K. Barrett, op. cit., 148.
12. R. A. Harrisville, 'The Concept of Newness in the New Testament', *JBL* 74 (1955) 75–76.

themselves.[13] In three respects, however, J. C. Hurd's comments are convincing. Firstly, 1 Cor 7.1b is most likely to be a quotation from the Corinthians' letter. Secondly, Paul does not so much contradict their viewpoints as radically qualify them. In effect he is saying: the theory may be correct, but there are these practical difficulties (although this is not to say that we follow all of Hurd's final conclusions about Paul's own position in chapter 7). Thirdly, there are clear connections between the Corinthians' outlook in chapter 7 and that reflected in chapters 8–10. Hurd comments, 'The Corinthians' attitudes towards idol meat and towards marital intercourse are entirely consistent. In each case they have claimed that . . . they have chosen the superior, harder, and more dangerous course of action. Confident of their strength, they boasted that they were able to expose themselves safely to the temptation of idolatry and the lure of sexual immorality.'[14]

The reason for this confidence, however, was not, as Hurd suggests, because they were 'informed by their higher knowledge'. There is no reason to interpret γνῶσις (8.1, 7) in any technical sense. This is particularly so since it was the Corinthians who claimed that *all* had knowledge (8.1) whilst Paul insists that *not* all have this knowledge (8.7). This is the exact opposite of what we should expect if this were an esoteric or 'higher' knowledge. The Corinthians' position depended on two causally related axioms: firstly, that all had access to revealed knowledge because the last days had arrived; secondly, that an enthusiast, or spiritual man, is invulnerable to the pressures which bring about failure in the case of the ordinary man. The watchword of the spiritual man is boldness; the outcome is victory. Ernst Käsemann has pinpointed the difference between the two outlooks sharply. At Corinth, he points out, 'those who are endowed with *pneuma* are exempt from the laws of those who have nothing but *psyche*'. On the other hand, earlier Christian tradition acknowledges the reality of temptation and those pressures which mark earthly existence even for the eschatological people of God.[15]

In the seventh chapter Paul bases part of the discussion not on an eschatological event which has already happened, but on an eschatological event which is about to happen. This does not mean, however, as Albert Schweitzer argued, that the believer's 'natural existence and all the circumstances connected with it have become of no importance'.[16] Indeed the opposite is the case. He must take fully into account his situation in the world (7.5, 7, 13, 15, 21, 37), and take whatever course of action enables him to serve God with least distraction (7.5, 9, 15, 29–35), taking account of his special gifts from God (v. 7). Schweitzer's attempt to elevate v. 20 (everyone should remain in the state in which he was

13. In addition to other sources cited, cf. R. Scroggs, 'Paul and the Eschatological Woman', *JAAR* 40 (1972) 283–303; and the extensive literature cited in W. O. Walker, 'I Corinthians 11.2–16 and Paul's Views Regarding Women', *JBL* 94 (1975) 94 n. 1.

14. J. C. Hurd, op. cit., 164–65.

15. E. Käsemann, *New Testament Questions of Today* (ET London, 1969) 117 and 126.

16. A. Schweitzer, op. cit., 194.

called) into a universal principle fails to take account of the fact that Paul's entire concern in this chapter is to encourage the Corinthians to settle individual cases on their own merits, in the light of the practical situation of life as it really is, rather than as it is seen by the 'spiritual' theorists. The one practical consideration is 'how to please the Lord' (vv. 32–35) in a given situation. Thus celibacy would be preferable for all, Paul seems to say, if there were no such thing as human nature. To leave human nature out of account, however, arises *either* from gnostic ideas which might or might not be present at Corinth, *or* from the combination of a radically realized eschatology and an atmosphere of spiritual enthusiasm.

The relationship of eschatological questions to 8.1—11.1 is much clearer, and need not detain us long. The tendency at Corinth was to regard the prize as already won (9.24). Paul, however, insists that the present is less a time of victory than a time for self-control and sustained effort (9.24–27). The lesson from the story of Israel (10.1–13) is even sharper. All of the Israelites *began* the journey, but the vast majority never completed it. 'Therefore let any one who thinks that he stands take heed lest he fall' (10.12). Käsemann may well be correct in claiming that 'the dominant group in Corinth believed themselves to have reached the goal of salvation already—in the shape of baptism'.[17] If so, it is especially pointed that Paul begins: 'our fathers were *all* under the cloud, and *all* passed through the sea, and *all* were baptized into Moses in the cloud and in the sea, and *all* ate the same supernatural food, and *all* drank the same supernatural drink . . . the Rock was Christ. Nevertheless *with most of them* God was not pleased; for they were overthrown in the wilderness' (10.1–5).

Once again Paul calls in question a one-sided realized eschatology, by asserting that Christians have not yet reached their goal. It is this which provides the theological basis for the contrast between theory and practice in 8.1–13. 'Knowledge' says that an idol has no real existence. Hence, in theory, there can be no harm in eating food offered to idols. But in practice, 'some through being hitherto accustomed (τῇ συνηθείᾳ) to idols, eat food as really offered to an idol' (8.7). In theory 'we are no worse off if we do not eat, and no better off if we do' (v. 8). But in practice, some supposedly 'weaker' brothers have a conscience that is conditioned to give them pain under given circumstances, and freedom must be qualified by love.

Even knowledge, later in Paul's argument, comes under the perspective of a future eschatology: 'Our knowledge is imperfect. . . . Now I know in part' (13.9, 12). Love is an eschatological reality (13.8–13), but it is also active in the present in building up Christians towards the measure of their final goal: ἡ γνῶσις φυσιοῖ, ἡ δὲ ἀγάπη οἰκοδομεῖ (8.1). The summary of the argument comes at 10.23: '"All things are lawful"—but not all things build up'. The rejoinder is

---

17. E. Käsemann, op. cit., 125. On the premature claim to 'freedom' in relation to 10.23—11.1, see, further, C. Hinz, '"Bewahrung und Verkehrung der Freiheit in Christo": Versuch einer Transformation von I. Kor. 10.23—11.1(8.1—10.22)', in *Gnosis und Neues Testament* (ed. K.-W. Tröger; Gütersloh and Berlin, 1973) 405–22.

an attack on an over-realized eschatology, made from the standpoint of a more forward-looking open-ended perspective. But it is also an attack on the enthusiast's preoccupation with 'liberty', made from the standpoint of realism.

Can we say the same about the next main section of 1 Corinthians, on worship, the Lord's Supper, and spiritual gifts (11.2—14.40)? We must first try to take account of a very recent argument put forward by W. O. Walker to the effect that 11.2–16 constitutes a non-Pauline interpolation.[18] Two considerations are central to this argument. Firstly, Walker suggests, 'the most compelling reason . . . for regarding 1 Cor 11.2–16 as an interpolation is the fact that it so obviously breaks the continuity of the letter at this point'.[19] Secondly, 'the ideas which it expresses regarding the relationship between man and woman are not in agreement with what Paul appears to say in his authentic writings'.[20] Among other points Walker adds that nowhere else in the authentic Pauline material do we find the idea of 'being taught by nature', in v. 14 (ἡ φύσις αὐτὴ διδάσκει ὑμᾶς) . . . 'although it is common in Greek philosophy generally'.[21]

With regard to the first point, the connecting factor between chapters 8–10 and 11.17–33 is taken by Walker to be that of eating and drinking: 8–10 concerns eating food offered to idols; 11:17ff concerns eating the Lord's Supper. But from the point of view of what is *theologically* at issue, this is almost like making a bad pun. The fact that two quite distinct theological questions happen both to relate to acts of eating is purely incidental. In the first case the unifying theme behind 8.1—11.1 is that of forbearance in love towards the supposedly weaker brother; in 11.2—14.40 it is that of conduct in the context of the assembled worshipping community. The only reason, it seems, why Walker is unable to notice this connection is because he is attempting to make a decisive break at 11.34, rather than at 12.1 (i.e. he divides (1) 8.1—11.34; and (2) 12.1—14.40; rather than (1) 8.1—11.1; and (2) 12.2—14.40). But the majority of commentators see no problem at all in understanding that the main change of topic takes place at 11.1.

With regard to the second and third points, this is precisely what we should expect given the distinctiveness of the situation that Paul is addressing. The discussion about women turns precisely on the contrast between eschatological status and life lived amidst the continuing conditions of the world. In terms of realized eschatology 'there is neither male nor female' (Gal 3.28). But in 11.2–16 Paul is concerned with arguments which relate strictly to the order of 'nature' (ἡ φύσις, v. 14), to the empirical life of the churches (v. 16), to what might offend social or aesthetic taste (v. 6), and to the order of creation (represented by the angels, v. 10).[22]

18. W. O. Walker, 'I Corinthians 11.2–16 and Paul's Views Regarding Women', loc. cit., 94–110.
19. Ibid., p. 99.
20. Ibid., 104; cf. p. 106.
21. Ibid., 107.
22. On angels as guardians of the created order cf. G. B. Caird, *Principalities and Powers: A Study in Pauline Theology* (Oxford: Clarendon, 1956) 17–22. On the arguments as a whole cf. F. F. Bruce, *op. cit.* 103.

Some of those commentators who wish to defend Paul's methods of argument find these verses embarrassing, on the ground that they are entirely relative to highly time-bound considerations. But this is no accident. Paul is concerned to show that the eschatological status of the Christian does not raise him above everyday questions about particular times and particular places. The sense of propriety of a first-century Christian Jew, or the practice of the time embraced by other Christian congregations, remain relevant factors; for *as well as* being a new creation the believer still belongs to the natural order. Yet again this stands in tension with a thoroughgoing theology of enthusiasm, in which liberation and emancipation from the restraints of mere convention are regarded as more important. Paul, however, does not accept uncritically either the Corinthians' eschatology or their theology of the Spirit.

The section on the Lord's Supper (11.17–33) seems to suggest that those Corinthian Christians who were in a financial position to do so regarded it as an occasion for feasting and revelry (11.21, 22). The eating and drinking became a social occasion, and there was even drunkenness. But was this not 'sitting down in the Kingdom', and feasting at the eschatological banquet of the Messiah? Was this not the marriage-supper of the Lamb, the feast of the King, to which apocalyptic literature bears abundant witness? It would be inappropriate for those who celebrated God's final victory to stint themselves on such an occasion!

Paul reminds his readers, however, that the final victory has not yet been achieved. Indeed the Lord's Supper has a distinctly *interim* character, for it looks *forward* to the parousia (ἄχρι οὗ ἄν ἔλθῃ, v. 26). Indeed the Lord's Supper was instituted before even the death and resurrection of Christ, which was the first of the last events. Because Christians still sin and still live in the world, it is a time for self-examination (v. 28). It would be better, Paul suggests, to think less about attempting to anticipate the final resurrection and more about attempting to anticipate the final judgment (vv. 31–32). For there can be no resurrection without death and judgment. In fact it is the Lord's death, and the believer's share in it, which is central in the Lord's Supper (v. 26; cf. 1 Cor 1.18–31; and 2 Cor 1.9; 4.8–12).

In his discussion of 'spirituality' (12.1—14.40) Paul returns to the perspective which we noted in 8.1—11.1. The criterion of spirituality is that which 'helps' and 'builds' towards an eschatological goal which has not yet been fully realized. Thus Paul insists, 'To each is given the manifestation of the Spirit *for the common good*' (πρὸς τὸ συμφέρον, 12.7). 'Since you are eager for manifestations of the Spirit, strive to excel *in building up the Church*' (14.12). The evaluation of tongues depends on whether anyone is *edified* (οἰκοδομεῖται) thereby (14.17). 'Let all things be done for edification' (πρὸς οἰκοδομήν, 14.26). At least nine times in 1 Corinthians Paul expresses a concern about 'building', six times in the fourteenth chapter (3.10; 8.1; 10.23; 14.3, 4, 5, 12, 17, 26).

The thirteenth chapter, on love, is an integral part of Paul's argument. It has been argued that this hymn is too metrical and stylized to be the work of the author of the rest of the epistle. But every phrase seems to reflect the situation at Corinth. 'Love is not jealous or boastful' (13.4; cf. 3.3, 21). 'It is not arrogant or rude . . .

love does not insist on its own way' (13.5; cf. 6.7; 8.1). 'It does not rejoice at wrong'
(13.6; cf. 5.2). Moffatt rightly observes, 'This "Hymn of Love" was written out of
a close and trying experience. If it is a rhapsody, it is the rhapsody of a realist who
has come safely through contact with the disenchanting life of the churches.'[23]
This element of realism is reflected in Paul's insistence that love is manifested not
simply as an eschatological quality (although it is this, 13.8–13), but also as a
dynamic which draws the community towards its yet unattained goal. C. T. Craig
notes, 'After v. 1 not a single descriptive adjective is used in the Greek. Paul uses
verbs, for love is dynamic and active, not static.'[24] 'Love builds up' (8:1).

It is hardly necessary to show that chapters 12–14 point to charismatic or
enthusiastic theology of the Spirit among the Corinthians. It is more than possible that Schmithals is correct when he understands Paul's introduction περὶ δὲ
τῶν πνευματικῶν (12.1) to refer to 'the pneumatics', or 'the spiritual people',
rather than to spiritual gifts. Schmithals continues, 'There was in Corinth a group
of Christians who claimed for themselves the title of πνευματικός as a characteristic which distinguished them from other members of the community. Such
a self-understanding is unPauline. According to Paul, every believing Christian
has the Spirit.'[25] In itself this statement is probably correct, but we do not draw
the same implications as Schmithals. This passage does not depend on gnostic
ideas. The Corinthians themselves may have admitted that, in a basic sense, all
Christians possessed the Spirit; but that only those who showed ecstatic tendencies were 'spiritual' in a particular sense of the term. This is no more inconsistent
than Paul's own outlook in 3.1, when he insists, 'I could not address you as "spiritual men" but as men of the flesh'. For Paul is hardly suggesting that those whom
he addresses as 'brethren' in no way possess the Spirit. Almost certainly in 3.1
Paul is taking up their own use of the term 'spiritual'. On the basis of persuasive
definition, they had defined 'spiritual' in such a way as to accord with their own
inclinations as charismatic enthusiasts. However, Paul quite deliberately re-
defines the concept in terms of day-to-day conduct: 'where there is jealousy and
strife among you, are you not of the flesh . . . ?' (3.1–4).[26]

There are other indications, then, besides the overvaluing of tongues, which
point to the phenomenon of enthusiasm in chapters 12–14. We have now seen
that in every single section from the beginning of the epistle to 14.40 there occurs
evidence of *both* a realized eschatology *and* an enthusiastic theology of the Spirit
on the part of the Corinthians. That these phenomena are causally related can
hardly be doubted. The criticism made by Earle Ellis and others to the effect that
arguments about an over-realized eschatology depend on 4.8 and 1 Cor 15 cannot be sustained.

23. J. Moffatt, *Love in the New Testament* (London, 1929) 182.
24. C. T. Craig, loc. cit., 167.
25. W. Schmithals, op. cit., 172.
26. I have discussed the phenomenon of persuasive definition in relation to the Corinthians' use
of the term 'spiritual' in A. C. Thiselton, 'The Meaning of Σάρξ in 1 Cor 5.5', loc. cit., 217–18.

Chapter 8

Gnosis in Corinth: I Corinthians 8.1–6[*]

Richard A. Horsley

INTRODUCTION

In a series of essays published in the 1970s and early 1980s, Richard Horsley argued that the Corinthians' religious outlook, particularly their emphasis on wisdom (*sophia* and *gnosis*), could best be explained against a Jewish sapiential background. He was developing a thesis that had been put forward by others before him, including Birger Pearson in his study published in 1973. The idea that the Corinthians were to be seen against a 'Gnostic' background was beginning to find less favour among scholars (cf. ch. 3 above). Horsley was able to exploit the comparative potential of some of the Jewish sources that had been used to construct an alleged pre-Christian Gnosticism within what appeared to be a more plausible paradigm—that of Hellenistic Judaism. In this essay, of which the introduction and main section are reproduced here, Horsley looks specifically at 1 Cor 8.1–6. Verses 1 and 4 are generally recognised to be Corinthian slogans,

*Extracted from R. A. Horsley, 'Gnosis in Corinth: I Corinthians 8.1–6', *NTS* 27 (1981) 32–52; here pp. 32–40. Reprinted by permission of Cambridge University Press, The Edinburgh Building, Shaftesbury Road, Cambridge.

and Horsley highlights their significance as the basic principles of the Corinthian theological *gnosis*. He attempts to illuminate the alleged Corinthian claims by drawing comparisons with similar motifs in Hellenistic-Jewish literature, mainly in the writings of Philo. Horsley argues that the viewpoint expressed in 1 Cor 8.1 and 4 represents a distinctively Hellenistic-Jewish religious philosophy, focusing on the oneness of God and the nonreality of 'idols'. At the time of its publication, Horsley's work helped to marginalise the view that Corinthian theology is best understood when compared with Gnosticism. With the recent arrival of studies focusing on the Greco-Roman setting of Corinthian Christianity, concern to find a specifically Jewish background to issues in the church has receded dramatically. Horsley's most recent work on the church at Corinth and Paul's first letter to the Corinthians has emphasised the setting of the Corinthian community within Roman imperial society (see ch. 18 below).

Further Reading

See also chapter 18 below.

J. M. G. Barclay, 'Thessalonica and Corinth' (ch. 14 below).

J. A. Davis, *Wisdom and Spirit: An Investigation of 1 Corinthians 1.18—3.20 against the Background of Jewish Sapiential Traditions in the Greco-Roman Period* (Lanham, New York and London: University Press of America, 1984).

R. A. Horsley, 'Consciousness and Freedom among the Corinthians: 1 Corinthians 8–10', *CBQ* 40 (1978) 574–89.

R. A. Horsley, ' "How can some of you say there is no resurrection of the dead?" Spiritual Elitism in Corinth', *NovT* 20 (1978) 203–31.

R. A. Horsley, 'Pneumatikos vs. Psychikos: Distinctions of Spiritual Status among the Corinthians', *HTR* 69 (1976) 269–88.

R. A. Horsley, 'Wisdom of Word and Words of Wisdom in Corinth', *CBQ* 39 (1977) 224–39.

B. A. Pearson, *The Pneumatikos-Psychikos Terminology in 1 Corinthians* (SBLDS 12; Atlanta: Scholars Press, 1973).

Scholars are gradually relinquishing the belief that the Corinthians were Gnostics. As a noted student of Gnosticism concludes, we find in Corinth 'at most only the first tentative beginnings of what was later to develop into full-scale Gnosticism'.[1] In fact, a kind of agnosticism has emerged with regard to the early Christian community in Corinth. 'The position in Corinth cannot be reconstructed on the basis of the possibilities of the general history of religion.'[2] I suggest, however, that it is possible to determine with some degree of precision the nature and background of the 'proto-Gnosticism' in Corinth: Hellenistic Jewish religiosity focused on *sophia* and *gnosis*.

The use of one's *gnosis* was one of the principal points of contention between Paul and those in the Corinthian church who considered themselves strong and

---

1. R. McL. Wilson, 'How Gnostic were the Corinthians?', *NTS* 19 (1972–73) 65–74.
2. Conzelmann, *1 Corinthians*, 15.

wise. The statements in 1 Cor 8.1 and 4: 'we all have knowledge', 'no idol exists in the world', and 'there is no god but One', are now generally recognized as Corinthian slogans quoted by Paul.[3] First Cor 8.6 as well is thought by some scholars to reflect the viewpoint of the strong Corinthians;[4] but this is somewhat less obvious, and analysis of this issue must await clarification of the principles which are most certainly from the Corinthians. The two quotations in 8.4 are, in effect, particular principles of the Corinthians' *gnosis*. In the most substantive recent commentary on 1 Corinthians, Conzelmann suggests three possibilities for the nature of the Corinthians' *gnosis*: it can be understood as popular philosophical enlightenment on the nature of the gods, or as illumination of the pneumatic, or as a specifically Gnostic insight (into the depths of being).[5]

There is, however, a fourth possibility which fits far better with other aspects of the particular situation of conflict in the nascent Corinthian community which Paul had 'planted' and Apollos 'watered' (1 Cor 3.5). It is becoming increasingly clear that Hellenistic Jewish speculation about and devotion to Wisdom forms the background of the Corinthians' obsession with *sophia* which Paul addresses in 1 Cor 1–4.[6] Perhaps an investigation of the Hellenistic Jewish background of the Corinthians' principles cited in 1 Cor 8 can illuminate both the specific nature of the Corinthians' *gnosis* and its relationship to other aspects of the Corinthians' religiosity.

A philologically centred approach which searches primarily for comparable words and phrases and then brings these directly to bear on particular words and phrases in the biblical text sometimes fails to consider broader patterns of thought. Conzelmann, for example, in dealing with 1 Cor 8.4 and other passages, lists an abundance of comparative phrases and formulas.[7] But he apparently does not consider it important to investigate the possible interconnections, for example, between the various Stoic passages he lists or between the many Philo passages he cites. He thus does not discern that Philo in particular displays a whole pattern of language and thought which is relevant to the polemical situation in Corinth.[8] It is important to take such patterns and interconnections into consideration. In particular it would be well to keep in mind how Paul's argument in 1 Cor 8 may be related to what he said in 1 Cor 1–4, how the Corinthians' principles of *gnosis* in 1 Cor 8 may be related to their obsession with *sophia* as discerned through 1 Cor

3. Hurd, *Origin*, 67–68, has tabulated scholarly opinions; more briefly, Conzelmann, *1 Corinthians*, 7 n. 54; see esp. J. Jeremias, 'Zur Gedankenfuhrung in den Paulinischen Briefen: (3) Die Briefzitate in I. Kor. 8, 1–13', in *Abba* (Göttingen, 1966), 273f.

4. Conzelmann, *1 Corinthians*, 7.

5. Conzelmann, *1 Corinthians*, 140.

6. Helmut Koester, 'GNOMAI DIAPHOROI: The Sources of Diversification in Early Christainity', *HTR* 58 (1965) 310f.; Birger Pearson, *The PNEUMATIKOS-PSYCHIKOS Terminology in 1 Corinthians* (Missoula, 1973), ch. 2; R. G. Hamerton-Kelly, *Pre-existence, Wisdom, and the Son of Man* (Cambridge, 1973) 112–23; R. A. Horsley, 'Wisdom of Word and Words of Wisdom at Corinth', *CBQ* 39 (1977) 224–39; and, 'Pneumatikos vs. Psychikos: Distinctions of Spiritual Status among the Corinthians', *HTR* 69 (1976) 269–88.

7. Conzelmann, *1 Corinthians*, 140–45.

8. Pearson, op. cit.; Hamerton-Kelly, op. cit., 121–22; Horsley, 'Wisdom of Word' and 'Pneumatikos vs. Psychikos'.

1–4, and whether the same comparative material elucidates different aspects of the Corinthians' viewpoint and thus (indirectly) Paul's argument as well.

With this perspective in mind I will attempt to demonstrate that the principles of gnosis and general religious viewpoint of the 'strong' Corinthians can be found in that Hellenistic Jewish theology represented by Philo and the Wisdom of Solomon. This particular tradition of Hellenistic Jewish religion should thus illuminate Paul's conflict with the 'strong' and 'wise' Corinthians.

THE HELLENISTIC JEWISH *GNOSIS* BEHIND THE PRINCIPLES IN 1 COR 8.1, 4

(a) 'We all possess "gnosis"'

The insights of Bultmann's investigation of the term *gnosis* are still valid even though his organization of the material may no longer be entirely satisfactory. Relying primarily on Reitzenstein and Hermetic literature, and partly on Neoplatonic philosophy and Christian Gnostic literature, Bultmann constructed a synthetic picture of 'the Gnostic usage', which he then used to interpret the Corinthian *gnosis*.[9] However, nearly all of the principal generalizations which Bultmann makes regarding 'the Gnostic usage' also fit the understanding of *gnosis* found in the Septuagintal wisdom literature, especially Wisdom, and in the treatises of Philo. Bultmann himself noted in this Hellenistic Jewish literature 'a plain subjective element of profound religious knowledge in the mystical and Gnostic sense'.[10]

More particularly, already in this Hellenistic Jewish literature, *gnosis* (or its equivalents, such as *epistēmē*) connotes a content possessed as well as the act of knowing. It is used in the absolute sense (e.g. *Fug.* 164; *Mos.* 2.98; *Decal.* 1) or with a genitive of an object known. The latter is most frequently 'knowledge of God' (e.g. Wisd. 15.2–3; *Fug.* 165; *Deus* 143), but can also be 'knowledge of truth' (*Quod Omn.* 74), or 'knowledge of holy things' (Wisd. 10.10), or even the commonplace 'Stoic' definition of *sophia*.[11] If not explicitly described as a *charisma*, knowledge is clearly divine and is given by God or by his consort Sophia (Wisd. 7.17; 10.10; *Deus* 92; *Opif.* 70–71). The recipients thereby have a special religious status, as 'wise' or 'righteous' or 'perfect'.

Whatever cosmic or divine content is imparted serves the salvation of the individual soul. Knowledge is a soteriological goal or content which brings divine power or even immortality to the soul (Wisd. 15.2–3).[12] Although Philo,

9. R. Bultmann, art. γινώσκω, *TWNT* 1.692–96, 709.

10. Bultmann, *TWNT* 1.701.

11. γνῶσις θείων καὶ ἀνθρωπίνων πραγμάτων καὶ τῶν αἰτίων, 4 Macc. 1.16; Philo, *Congr.* 79; Aristobulus, in Eusebius, *Praep. ev.* 667c; cf. Cicero, *Off.* 2.2.5; Seneca, *Ep.* 89; Plurarch, *Plac. philos.* 1.2.

12. Aristobulus, in Eusebius, *Praep. ev.* 688a, says that after the soul's forgetfulness and vice have been abandoned on the true sabbath, i.e. reason, we receive γνῶσις ἀληθείας.

like Plotinus after him, avoids the term *gnosis* in reference to the ultimate vision of God,[13] he does refer to the goal of the perfect way leading to God, i.e. *sophia*, as γνῶσις καὶ ἐπιστήμη Θεοῦ (*Deus* 143), or as ἐπίγνωσις τοῦ ἑνός and γνῶσις καὶ ἐπιστήμη καὶ τιμὴ τοῦ ἑνός (*Leg. All.* 3.46–48, 126). Knowledge is thus an integral aspect of the personal mystical piety in both Wisdom and Philo. Goodenough, through his sensitive and penetrating interpretation of Philo's religious mentality, has provided us with a vivid sense of the 'subjective element of profound religious knowledge' in Philo's writings.[14] Similarly, in the book of Wisdom, the *hieros gamos* described in ch. 8 expresses a profound personal intimacy with the heavenly Sophia, one manifestation of which is *gnosis*. The Hellenistic Jewish religion represented in Wisdom and Philo had long since appropriated the language of the mysteries.[15] Thus, well before the genuine Christian Gnostics and mystical Neoplatonists, Hellenistic Jews such as Philo were enjoying a mystical *gnosis* with a clearly other-worldly orientation.

If we attempt to determine more precisely what 'knowledge' is for Philo and Wisdom, three significant aspects in particular emerge. First, knowledge is almost always directly or indirectly knowledge of God (e.g., Wisd. 15.2–3; *Virt.* 178f., 213–16; *Leg. All.* 3.46–48, 100, 126f.). This is the case even when 'knowledge' appears in the absolute sense (*Fug.* 164; *Mos.* 2.98). Second, knowledge is parallel or similar to *sophia* (Wisd. 9.10–11; 10.10; *Leg. All.* 3.95; *Deus* 143; *Fug.* 76; *Mos.* 2.98). Third and more precisely, knowledge is the particular religious and theological content of *sophia*, i.e. the ontological and especially soteriological knowledge of divine teaching supposedly derived from the Scripture (Wisd. 10.10; 4 Macc. 1.16–17; *Deus* 92; *Congr.* 79; *Spec.* 1.30, 50, 269).

These three aspects of Hellenistic Jewish 'knowledge' are all directly relevant to the Corinthian situation and may help us discern more precisely how the 'strong' Corinthians understood their *gnosis*. Judging from the other Corinthian principles cited by Paul in the immediate context, 1 Cor 8.4, their *gnosis* was theological, i.e. knowledge of God. Moreover, the close relation between *gnosis* and *sophia* in Philo and Wisdom enables us to determine, by analogy, how the Corinthians' *gnosis* may have been related to the *sophia* rejected by Paul in 1 Cor 1–4. Although this relation must be further elaborated below, it may suffice at this point to suggest that *gnosis* was not identical with *sophia* for the Corinthians. But it apparently was an expression of the *sophia* they possessed. 'Knowledge' probably referred to the particular religious content of *sophia* including such fundamental theological principles as 'there are no idols in the world' and ' there is no god but One'.

---

13. Bultmann, *TWNT* 1.702 n. 60.
14. E. R. Goodenough, *By Light, Light* (New Haven, 1935).
15. Goodenough, op. cit., chs. 1, 9–10; H. A. Wolfson, *Philo* (3rd printing, Cambridge, Mass., 1962) I, 36–54; C. Larcher, *Etudes sur le livre de la Sagesse* (Paris, 1969) 255–59; James M. Reese, *Hellenistic Influence on the Book of Wisdom* (Rome, 1970) 33–50.

(b) 'There is no god but One'

Henology was a problem with which the philosophers of antiquity were preoccupied since the pre-Socratics.[16] The word Θεός, and eventually the name Zeus, had come to mean 'divinity', the divine principle in which all gods found unity. In religious philosophy there developed, as it were, a kind of henological confessional form of two or more declarations of unity: e.g. Marcus Aurelius 7.9, an affirmation of the interconnectedness of all things in terms of one cosmos, one God, one essence, one law, one truth, and even one perfection. The principle repeated by Josephus in *Ant.* 4.20 (and not derived from Exod 20.25–26 or Deut 12.5), 'for God is one and the Hebrew race is one', is probably a similar declaration.[17] Even more clearly Eph 4.4–6 should be compared with this henological confessional form traditional in Hellenistic religious philosophy.

The Corinthians' slogan quoted in 1 Cor 8.4, however, is the basic Jewish confession that 'God is one'.[18] Its credal character appears in a variety of Hellenistic Jewish literature, such as Pseudo-Sophocles.[19] For Josephus, 'that God is One' is the teaching of the first principle of the Decalogue in his summary, *Ant.* 3.91 (cf. 8.343). For Philo, 'that God is One' is the lesson Moses continually teaches in the Laws (e.g. *Spec.* 1.30) and is the second major principle in a five-part summary of essential Jewish doctrine (*Opif.* 170–72; cf. *Conf.* 170–71).

This does not exhaust the central significance of this principle of knowledge for Philo's religion, however. For the knowledge or vision *of God*, as reached via the 'perfect way', i.e. *sophia*, is the goal of mystical contemplation, as in the γνῶσις καὶ ἐπιστήμη Θεοῦ of *Quod Deus* 143. Moreover God, for Philo, is essentially 'the One', 'the truly Existing One'. Thus the knowledge of God is repeatedly expressed as the vision or recognition of *the One*, as in *Leg. All.* 3.48, 126, cited already above.

Moving back, by analogy, to the Corinthians' *gnosis*, it becomes clear that it is inadequate to say with Conzelmann that the confession that 'there is one God' is 'the self-evident presupposition of their faith'. The principle is rather the central and essential content of their faith. This would be true even if all of those who had joined the 'Christian' community in Corinth were already (Hellenistic) Jews, whose conversion to the new religious movement was a repentance or return to the proper knowledge of the One (see *Virt.* 178–79). But especially in the mission context of early Christianity, in which Gentiles were being converted, i.e. becoming proselytes to this new movement (which must have appeared basi-

---

16. On Parmenides and Heraclitus, see Werner Jaeger, *The Theology of the Early Greek Philosophers* (Oxford, 1947), chs. 6, 7, and p. 174; on Hellenistic 'monotheism' see Martin P. Nilsson, *Geschichte der griechischen Religion* II (2nd ed. Munich, 1961) 427–29, 569–78.

17. Cf. Josephus, *Ag. Ap.* 2.193; Philo, *Spec.* 1.67; 2 *Bar.* 49.24.

18. General discussion by Samuel S. Cohen, 'The Unity of God: A Study in Hellenistic and Rabbinic Theology', *HUCA* 26 (1955) 425–79.

19. As quoted in Hecataeus, 'Histories', in Eusebius, *Praep. ev.* 690d: εἷς ταῖς ἀληθείαισιν εἷς ἐστιν θεός.

cally as a branch of Judaism), the confession that there is no god but the One would have been central. For the essence of one's conversion to the true faith would be the realization that God is one—and that other gods are non-existent.

(c) 'An idol is nothing in the world'

Conzelmann may be right that 'the Corinthians argue after the fashion of Greek enlightenment philosophy'.[20] It would be historically more adequate and precise, however, to view these Corinthian principles as arising out of a Hellenistic *Jewish religion* of enlightenment. For, as he himself points out, Hellenistic Judaism had long since incorporated certain Hellenistic philosophical arguments 'concerning the nature of the gods' into its own polemic against polytheism.[21] In fact, not only did writers such as Philo, Aristobulus, and the authors of Wisdom and the Epistle of Aristeas feel at home in much of the language of Hellenistic philosophy, they even assumed that the Greek 'enlightenment' had learned all its wisdom from Moses and the Jews.[22] Moreover, if the term εἴδωλον was included in the Corinthians' principle (and is not Paul's rewording) then it is not a question of 'Greek enlightenment philosophy' at all, but a matter of basic Hellenistic Jewish theology. For εἴδωλον as used here in the sense of a false god was the product of Hellenistic Jewish translation and development of the Jewish (biblical) critique of heathen gods, and has no meaning like this in pagan Greek.[23] That the Corinthian *gnosis* of the One God and the nothingness of idols arises from a Hellenistic Jewish religion of enlightenment can be made clearer by contrasting the critique of false gods in Wisdom and Philo (1) with the attitude toward images in contemporary philosophy, on the one side and (2) with another and very different Jewish critique of false gods, on the other side.

(1) Wisdom and especially Philo had, to be sure, assimilated some of their arguments against false gods from Hellenistic philosophy. It is not surprising that a reflective Hellenistic Jewish mentality which emphasized the transcendence of God found affinities with a revived, though thoroughly eclectic, Platonic philosophy and absorbed its ontology. Philo heavily criticized the Stoic ('Chaldean')

---

20. *1 Corinthians,* 142.

21. On Hellenistic Jewish critique of false gods and idols see H. Eising, 'Der Weisheitslehrer und die Götterbilder', *Biblica* 40 (1959) 373–408; G. Delling, 'Josephus und die heidnischen Religionen', *Klio* 43–45 (1965), 263–69; Paul Wendland, 'Die Therapeuten und die philosophische Schrift vom beschaulichen Leben', *Jahrbuch für klassische Philol.,* Sup 22 (1896) 693–772; and *Die hellenistische-römische Kultur in ihren Beziehungen zu Judentum und Christentum* (Tübingen, 1912) 106ff., 140ff.; Wolfson, *Philo* 1, 8–17, 27–34.

22. This was a standard contention of 'Jewish apologetics'; see generally M. Friedländer, *Geschichte der jüdischen Apologetik* (Zurich, 1903) 77 ff.; Johannes Geffcken, *Zwei griechische Apologeten* (Leipzig and Berlin, 1907), esp. the introduction; P. Dalbert, *Die Theologie der hellenistisch-jüdischen Missionsliteratur unter Ausschluß von Philo und Josephus* (Hamburg, 1954); more imaginative recent treatment by Dieter Georgi, *Die Gegner des Paulus im 2. Korintherbrief,* WMANT 11 (Neukirchen, 1964) 95ff.; and see the sensible comments by V. Tcherikover, 'Jewish Apologetic Literature Reconsidered', *Eos* 48 (1956) 169–93.

23. F. Buchsel, art. εἴδωλον, *TWNT* 2.377.

theology and ontology for its deification of the cosmos itself (e.g. *Migr.* 176–83; cf. *Congr.* 49; *Mut.* 16; *Abr.* 68–71). It is indicative of these affinities between Hellenistic Jewish theology, such as that in Wisdom and Philo, and a reviving Platonism that we find so many similarities to 'Jewish' polemics against false gods in the 'Academic' critique of 'Stoic' theology in Cicero, *Nat. d.* 3.[24]

This same eclectic Platonic philosophy, however, takes a very positive stance toward *images* as an aid for people who otherwise would not be able to conceive of the divine. The later middle-platonist rhetor Maximus of Tyre (2.3, 9–10, ed. Hobein) gives full expression to this positive evaluation of images, finding some beneficial function even in Egyptian honour of animals. This view of statues and pictures can be documented, however, at least as early as Varro (Augustine, *Civ.* 8.5). Although it is no longer fashionable to push ideas such as this back to Posidonius,[25] this attitude probably gained currency during the eclectic revival of Platonism following Posidonius and Antiochus of Ascalon,[26] i.e. at least by the time of Cicero and Philo. The positive view of images and statues must be fairly standard and widespread by the time of Dio Chrysostom's strong defence of the renowned sculptor Pheidias (*Or.* 12, esp. 57–59) and Plutarch's justification of the symbolism of Egyptian animal worship (*Is. Os.* 74–76). Thus, not only does Greek enlightenment philosophy of the period not use the terminology of 'idols' but, more importantly, the very philosophical tradition from which Hellenistic Judaism and early Christianity were most likely to borrow (eclectic Middle-Platonism) took a very positive view of images.

(2) Within Judaism itself there were two distinctive traditions of polemic against idols or false gods. Bousset pointed out some time ago that at least since the exilic times there had been two lines of judgment of paganism.[27] The one line, expressed prominently in Deutero-Isaiah, derided the heathen gods as nothings and their worship as foolishness, since the idol-gods are merely the lifeless products of human craftsmanship—in contrast to the one, true, living God, usually described in terms of his creative activity. This is the most frequently encountered tradition of idol-critique, and at least traces of it appear in nearly all types of Jewish literature of the Hellenistic-Roman period. It should be pointed out, however, that this tradition is far less prominent in apocalyptic literature such as *1 Enoch* and *Jubilees* than in the wisdom tradition and Hellenistic Jewish literature, in contrast to the impression given by Bousset. The other attitude toward paganism, exemplified in passages such as Deut 4.19; 29.25; Jer 16.19 or Mal 1.11, held that whereas God had chosen Israel for his own people, He had subjected the other peoples to the subordinate cosmic powers—hence heathen polytheism was more or less God-ordained.

24. Esp. 3.20–64; e.g. neither the world nor heavenly bodies are gods, 3.23, 40, 51; deification of animals and of men is mere superstition, 3.39–41, 47, 49–50.

25. As in Geffcken, 'Bilderstreit', 296f.

26. Georg Luck, *Der Akademiker Antiochus* (Berne, 1953), esp. pp. 32ff.

27. Wilhelm Bousset, *Die Religion des Judentum im späthellenistischen Zeitalter* (4th ed., ed. H. Gressmann, Tübingen, 1966) 304f.

Since Bousset wrote, especially since the discovery of the Dead Sea Scrolls, we have a far better appreciation of the distinctiveness and importance of apocalypticism in Palestinian Judaism. It is necessary now to sharpen the picture of the two distinct traditions of polemic against pagan deities as they appear in the Hellenistic-Roman period—somewhat changed from the exilic period.

The tradition which contrasts lifeless idols (along with the 'ignorance' in which idolatry is based) with the one, true, creating and redeeming God (along with 'knowledge' of Him) is continued especially in Hellenistic Jewish literature, such as Bel and the Dragon, as well as Wisdom and Philo. This tradition has been supplemented with other distinct arguments against false gods, such as a commonplace condemnation of Egyptian animal worship. Some of these additional arguments have been appropriated from Hellenistic philosophy, such as the already Judaized Euhemeristic argument[28] in the *Epistle of Aristeas* 135–37, 139 (and Wisd. 14.15–21; *Spec.* 1.28) and the critique of the deification of cosmic elements and heavenly bodies in Wisdom and Philo. The most elaborate development and sophisticated combination of these arguments against pagan idolatry and theology (as Bousset realized) is the same schematized three-part polemic appearing both in Wisd. 13–15 and in Philo, *Decal.* 52–82; and *Contempl.* 3–9. This schematic polemic argues successively against worship of (a) cosmic elements and heavenly bodies (Wisd. 13.1–9; *Decal.* 53–65; *Contempl.* 3–5); (b) impotent, manufactured idol-gods (Wisd. 13.10—15.13; *Decal.* 66, 76; *Contempl.* 7); and (c) Egyptian animal deities (Wisd. 15.14–19; *Decal.* 76–80; *Contempl.* 8–9), as increasing stages of ignorance, foolishness and offensiveness.

The other distinct traditional Jewish polemic against idol-gods appears prominently in apocalyptic literature such as *Jubilees* and *1 Enoch*. This other tradition, although it agreed that idols are 'nothings' and lifeless human products, saw in idolatry the service or the influence of demons (*Jub.* 2.4–6; 22.16–22; *1 En.* 19; 99.6–10; *T.Naph.* 3.3–4). Most interesting for the conflict between Paul and the Corinthian dissidents is the connection of this other polemical tradition with the motif of divine judgment. Biblical texts on which this tradition draws connect the critique of idolatry as the service of demons with a recitation of Israel's historical disobedience in, and punishment for, its sacrificing to idols (Deut 32.17–21; Ps 106 (105 LXX).28–40). Paul himself draws on this tradition in formulating his argument against the implications of the Corinthians' *gnosis* in 1 Cor 10.20–22 as well as in 10.1–13.[29]

Wisdom and Philo, on the other hand, focus their critique of false gods and idols around an absolute antithesis between *ignorance of God* and *knowledge of God*. Ignorance of God is synonymous with supposing that idols or heavenly bodies are gods. Knowledge of God means knowing that other gods do not exist, that

---

28. On Euhemerism, see Nilsson, op. cit., 2.286–89; Fritz Taeger, *Charisma* 1 (Stuttgart, 1957) 375f., 295f.; H. Dorrie, 'Der Königskult des Antiochus von Kommagene' *Abh. der Akad. Göttingen* 3, 60 (1964) 218–24.

29. For a 'Jewish' attitude toward idols and other gods which is midway between Paul's and that of these Corinthians, see Trypho's comments in Justin Martyr, *Dial.* 55.2.

idols are mere foolishness. Knowing God/the One, moreover, means righteousness and immortality (Wisd. 13.1; 14.22; 15.2–3; Philo, *Decal.* 7–8, etc.). It is this Hellenistic Jewish tradition expressed in Philo and Wisdom which most precisely parallels and most helpfully illuminates the Corinthians' *gnosis* that God is One and that idols are nothing.

It may be useful to make more explicit what is already implicit, that this Hellenistic Jewish tradition also elucidates the significance of the phrase 'in the world' (ἐν κόσμῳ) in the Corinthians' slogan. According to this Hellenistic Jewish critique, the mistake which polytheists and idol-worshippers have made is to believe that certain things in the world such as heavenly bodies or forces of nature are divine (Wisd. 13.2–3; *Contempl.* 3–5; *Decal.* 53, 58–59), whereas true piety, the Jewish faith, recognizes that all these things are merely part of the *creation,* and that the true, Existent One is the *Creator* of the whole cosmos. This is the significance of the frequency with which God is described as 'Begetter', 'Father', 'Maker' or 'Cause' in the several Philonic and Wisdom passages in which wisdom is discussed (Wisd. 13.1, 4–5; *Contempl.* 5; *Decal.* 53, 61, 64; *Spec.* 1.14, 20, 22, 30; *Ebr.* 107; *Virt.* 213–16). Indeed the purpose of Hellenistic Jewish polemics and proselytizing was to convert and convince Gentiles as well as Jews that there were no divine entities (gods or idols) in the world, which itself was the handiwork of the true God, its Creator.

Chapter 9

House-Churches
and the Eucharist[*]

Jerome Murphy-O'Connor

INTRODUCTION

In recent decades, with a renewed focus on the social setting of early Christianity, scholars of Christian origins have increasingly come to realise the importance of archaeology for providing information about the concrete social context in which the early Christians lived. In contrast to a focus on religious texts and parallels, in Gnosticism, mystery cults, and so on—a focus characteristic of the 'history of religions' approach—much recent work is concerned with constructing a picture of everyday life in the cities of the Roman Empire using a wide range of sources. In the book from which this extract is taken, first published in 1983 and now in its third edition, Jerome Murphy-O'Connor gathers together information from ancient texts and from archaeological discoveries that enables us to construct a picture of life in ancient Corinth, the setting in which the first Corinthian

*Extracted from J. Murphy-O'Connor, 'House-Churches and the Eucharist', in *St. Paul's Corinth: Texts and Archaeology* (3rd ed.; Collegeville, Minn.: Liturgical Press, 2002) 178–85. Originally published Wilmingon, Del.: M. Glazier, 1983. Reprinted by permission of The Liturgical Press, Collegeville, Minnesota.

Christians lived. In the extract below, Murphy-O'Connor shows how considering the physical layout of a Roman villa from Paul's time can help us to understand how and why the problems Paul discusses concerning the Eucharist at Corinth came about (1 Cor 11.17–34). Of course, the relevance of the evidence depends on the supposition that the early Christians may well have met, at least on occasion, in a similarly sumptuous villa belonging to a wealthy member of the congregation. While such a supposition fits well with the picture of the social stratification in the Corinthian congregation proposed by Gerd Theissen and others (see ch. 6 above), it may also be argued that this kind of housing is unlikely to have been the setting for the early Christian meetings, if the Christians themselves came from among the nonelite poor (see chs. 17 and 19).

Further Reading

Barton, 'Paul's Sense of Place'.

D. Engels, *Roman Corinth: An Alternative Model for the Classical City* (Chicago and London: University of Chicago Press, 1990).

D. G. Horrell, 'Domestic Space and Christian Meetings at Corinth: Imagining New Contexts and the Buildings East of the Theatre', *NTS* (forthcoming 2004).

D. Jongkind, 'Corinth in the First Century AD: The Search for Another Class', *TynBul* 52 (2001) 139–48.

P. Lampe, 'Das korinthische Herrenmahl im Schnittpunkt hellenistisch-römischer Mahlpraxis und paulinischer Theologia Crucis', *ZNW* 82 (1991) 183–213.

C. Osiek and D. Balch, *Families in the New Testament World* (Louisville: Westminster John Knox, 1997), esp. pp. 5–35.

R. E. Oster, 'Use, Misuse and Neglect of Archaeological Evidence in Some Modern Works on 1 Corinthians (1 Cor 7.1–5; 8.10; 11.2–16; 12.14–26)', *ZNW* 83 (1992) 52–73.

G. Theissen, 'Social Integration and Sacramental Activity: An Analysis of 1 Cor. 11:17–34', in *Social Setting*, 145–74.

J. Wisemann, 'Corinth and Rome I: 228 BC–AD 267', *ANRW* 2.7.1 (1979) 438–548.

Private dwellings were the first centers of church life. Christianity in the first century A.D., and for long afterward, did not have the status of a recognized religion, so there was no question of a public meeting place, such as the Jewish synagogue. Hence, use had to be made of the only facilities available, namely, the dwellings of families that had become Christian. Four houses of the Roman period have been brought to light at Corinth.[1] Of these only one can be attributed to the time of Paul, the villa at Anaploga (Figure 3, p. 137) [c. 750m west of central Corinth]. The magnificent mosaic floor of the triclinium (dining room) is dated to the late first century A.D., and broken pottery in the fill laid to provide a level bed comes from the period A.D. 50–75, but the building was already in existence when the mosaic was created.[2]

---

1. J. Wiseman, 'Corinth and Rome', *ANRW* 2.7.1 (1979) 528.
2. Cf. S. G. Miller, 'A Mosaic Floor from a Roman Villa at Anaploga', *Hesperia* 41 (1972) 332–54.

Given the social conditions of the time, it can be assumed that any gathering which involved more than very intimate friends of the family would be limited to the public parts of the house, namely, the entrance area, the atrium (courtyard), the triclinium (dining room), and the toilet. How much space did that make available?

A TYPICAL HOUSE

In the villa at Anaploga the triclinium measures 5.5 × 7.5 meters (18 × 24.6 feet), giving a floor area of 41.25 square meters (442.8 square feet). The atrium located just outside measures 5 × 6 meters (16.4 × 19.7 feet), but the floor area of 30 square meters (323 square feet) must be reduced also because at least one-ninth of the floor was taken up by the impluvium. This was a pool to collect the water that came through a hole of corresponding size in the roof; this was called the compluvium and was designed to light the atrium.

These dimensions were very typical, as can be seen from a number of comparisons. 'Another sumptuous villa of the 2nd century has been excavated in the vicinity of the old Sicyonian Gate'.[3] The adjective used should be noted, together with the formulation which indicates that it also applies to the villa at Anaploga. The five magnificent mosaic floors were published by Shear.[4] No plan is given, but the dimensions of the rooms are provided: atrium, 7.15 × 7.15 = 51.12 square meters (23.5 × 23.5 = 552.25 square feet) with a square impluvium in the center; triclinium off the atrium, 7.05 × 7.05 = 49.7 square meters (23.1 × 23.1 = 533.6 square feet). The excavator considers it probable that the mosaic floors were made before 146 B.C. and were simply incorporated when the villa was rebuilt in the second century A.D.

The equally well-to-do House of the Vettii at Pompeii (Figure 4, p. 138), destroyed by the eruption of A.D. 79, was of similar size: the atrium measured 7 × 6 = 42 square meters (23 × 19.7 = 453.1 square feet), and the triclinium 4 × 6.3 = 25.2 square meters (13.1 × 20.7 = 271.2 square feet). The consistency of such figures for upper-class houses can be seen from the dimensions of the fourth-century B.C. Villa of Good Fortune at Olynthus (southeast of Thessalonica on the coast): the triclinium was 5.8 × 5 = 29 square meters (19 × 16.4 = 311.6 square feet), and the atrium with its impluvium 10 × 10 = 100 square meters (32.8 × 32.8 = 1075.8 square feet; Figure 5, p. 138).

In Ephesus two dwelling complexes in use in the first century A.D. have been excavated on the slope of Bülbül Dag.[5] The ground floor of the eastern complex spread over 3,000 square meters (32,292 square feet), and was the house of a single, very wealthy family. Its spacious and numerous public rooms would have been a boon to the expanding Christian community, but such magnates were rarely, if ever, to be found among its members.

3. J. Wiseman, 'Corinth and Rome', 528.
4. T. L. Shear, 'Excavations at Corinth in 1925', *AJA* 29 (1925) 381–97; here pp. 391–97.
5. S. Erdemgil, *Les maisons du flanc à Ephese* (Istanbul: Hitit., 1988).

The western complex, on the other hand, is made up of seven two-story dwelling units, two of which are illustrated in Murphy-O'Connor.[6] The atrium of one house measured $12 \times 8 = 96$ square meters ($39.4 \times 26.2 = 1032.3$ square feet), which would be reduced by the impluvium ($4 \times 4 = 16$ square meters; $13.1 \times 13.1 = 171.6$ square feet), but increased by a large alcove ($6 \times 4 = 24$ square meters; $19.7 \times 13.1 = 258$ square feet). The triclinium was $6 \times 4 = 24$ square meters ($13.1 \times 19.7 = 258$ square feet). The second house was slightly larger. The atrium was $14 \times 9 = 126$ square meters ($45.9 \times 29.5 = 1354$ square feet), from which the impluvium ($5.5 \times 7 = 38.5$ square meters; $18 \times 23 = 414$ square feet) has to be deducted. The dimensions of the triclinium were $7 \times 5.5 = 38.5$ square meters ($23 \times 18 = 414$ square feet).

If we average out the floor areas for the six houses, the size of the atrium is 74 square meters (797 square feet) and that of the triclinium 37 square meters (398 square feet). Not all this area, however, was usable. The effective space in the triclinium was limited by the couches around the walls; the rooms surveyed would not have accommodated more than nine diners (the usual number),[7] who reclined as they ate. The impluvium in the center of the atrium would not only have diminished the space by one-ninth, but would also have restricted movement, since circulation was possible only around the outside of the area. Thus the maximum number that the atrium could hold was fifty, but this assumes that there were no decorative urns or anything of that nature to take up space, and that everyone stayed in one place; the true figure would probably be between thirty and forty.

Let us for a moment assume that this was the house of Gaius, a wealthy member of the Christian community at Corinth (Rom 16.23), and try to imagine the situation when he hosted 'the whole church' (1 Cor 14.23).

THE SIZE OF THE COMMUNITY AT CORINTH

We know more about the community at Corinth than about any other church that Paul founded. Not only are we informed that it had a minority of members from established families who were well-educated and influential (1 Cor 1.26), but we are given specific names, both by Luke and Paul.

In Acts 18 we hear of Prisca and Aquila (v. 2), Titius Justus (v. 7), Crispus (v. 8), and Sosthenes (v. 17). At the beginning of 1 Corinthians Paul mentions the people he baptized personally at Corinth, namely, Crispus, Gaius (1.14), and Stephanas (1.16). At the end of that letter, in addition to Apollos (16.12), he compliments the members of the delegation that brought the letter (7.1) from

6. J. Murphy-O'Connor, *Paul: A Critical Life* (Oxford: Clarendon, 1996) 170.

7. D. E. Smith, 'Social Obligation in the Context of Communal Meals: A Study of Christian Meals in 1 Corinthians in Comparison with Graeco-Roman Meals' (Th.D. dissertation, Harvard University, 1980) 28.

Corinth to Ephesus (16.8), namely, Stephanas, Fortunatus, and Achaicus (16.17). Romans was written from Corinth, so that those who send greetings in the last chapter were members of the church there, namely, Lucius, Jason, Sosipater, Tertius, Gaius, Erastus, and Quartus (16.21–24).

If we discount the overlaps between the different lists we end up with sixteen specific individuals. Prisca and Aquila we know were married, and we can safely assume that the other fourteen also had spouses. That brings us to a total of thirty, which is obviously a minimum figure. Neither Luke nor Paul intended to give a complete list; mentions of particular names were occasioned by specific circumstances. Moreover, we are told that the households of two members of the community, Crispus and Stephanas, were baptized with them. Thus, we have to add an indeterminate number of children, servants/slaves, and perhaps relations. It would be more realistic, therefore, to think in terms of between forty and fifty persons as a base figure for the Christian community at Corinth. Visitors from the church at Cenchreae headed by Phoebe (Rom 16.2) could increase the number of participants on certain occasions.

THE CONSEQUENCE OF SHORTAGE OF SPACE

This number could barely be accommodated in our average house of Gaius, but it would have meant extremely uncomfortable overcrowding in the villa at Anaploga. It would appear, therefore, that a meeting of 'the whole church' (Rom 16.23; 1 Cor 14.23) was the exception rather than the rule; it would simply have been too awkward. Moreover, as Banks[8] has pointed out, the adjective 'whole' is unnecessary if Corinthian Christians met only as a single group, and so must be understood to imply that other groups existed. This observation suggests that the formulae 'the whole church' and 'the church in the home of X' (Rom 16.5; 1 Cor 16.19; Col 4.15; Phlm 2) should not be equated, but contrasted. Note that here I have used 'home' rather than the conventional 'house.' This is to avoid the misleading impression that people like Prisca and Aquila owned houses. They are more likely to have rented.

'The church in the home of X', then, would be a subgroup of the larger community. If Prisca and Aquila acted as the center of such a subgroup in Ephesus (1 Cor 16.19) and in Rome (Rom 16.5), it is very probable that they did likewise in Corinth. Such subgroups would have been made up of the family, servants, and a few friends who lived in the vicinity.[9] While such subgroups would have tended to foster an intimate family-type atmosphere at the liturgical celebrations, they would also have tended to promote divisions within the wider city community. It seems likely that the various groups mentioned by Paul in 1 Cor 1.12 would regularly have met separately. Such relative isolation would have

8. R. Banks, *Paul's Idea of Community* (Exeter: Paternoster, 1980) 38.
9. Banks, *Paul's Idea*, 38–39.

meant that each group had a chance to develop its own theology, and virtually ensured that it took good root before being confronted by other opinions.

The difficulty of getting the whole church together regularly in one place goes a long way toward explaining the theological divisions within the Corinthian community (1 Cor 1–4), but the difficulties of the physical environment also generated other problems when all the believers assembled as a church.

The mere fact that all the believers could not be accommodated in the triclinium meant that there had to be an overflow into the atrium. It became imperative for the host to divide his guests into two categories: the first-class believers were invited into the triclinium while the rest stayed outside. Even a slight knowledge of human nature indicates the criterion used. The host must have been a wealthy member of the community, so he invited into the triclinium his closest friends among the believers, who would have been of the same social class and from whom he might expect the same courtesy on a future occasion. The rest could take their places in the atrium, where conditions were greatly inferior.

Those in the triclinium reclined, as was the custom (1 Cor 8.10) and as Jesus always did with his disciples,[10] whereas those in the atrium were forced to sit (1 Cor 14.30). Moreover, the triclinium could be heated, but the hole (compluvium) in the roof of the atrium exposed those sitting there to the cold air coming down from Mount Parnassos (2480 meters/8136 feet), which is snow-covered for nine months of the year.

The space available made such discrimination unavoidable, but this would not diminish the resentment of those provided with second-class facilities. Here we see one possible source of the tensions that appear in Paul's account of the eucharistic liturgy at Corinth (1 Cor 11.17–34). However, his statement that 'one is hungry while another is drunk' (v. 21) suggests that such tensions may have been exacerbated by another factor, namely, the type of food served.

DIFFERENT CLASSES OF GUESTS

Since the Corinth that Paul knew had been refounded as a Roman colony in 44 B.C., and since Latin was the dominant official language up to the end of the first century A.D., it is legitimate to assume that Roman customs enjoyed a certain vogue in the colony. One such custom was to serve different types of food to different categories of guests. Pliny the Younger recounts the following experience:

> I happened to be dining with a man, though no particular friend of his, whose elegant economy, as he called it, seemed to me a sort of stingy extravagance. The best dishes were set in front of himself and a select few, and cheap scraps of food before the rest of the company. He had even put the wine into tiny little flasks, divided into three categories, not with the idea

10. J. Jeremias, *The Eucharistic Words of Jesus* (New York: Scribner's, 1966) 48–49.

of giving his guests the opportunity of choosing, but to make it impossible for them to refuse what they were given. One lot was intended for himself and for us, another for his lesser friends (all his friends are graded), and the third for his and our freedmen (*Letters* 2.6).

This invidious custom naturally proved fair game for the Roman satirists of the first and second centuries A.D. The entire Fifth Satire of Juvenal is a vicious dissection of the sadism of the host who makes his inferior guests 'prisoners of the great smells of his kitchen' (line 162):

> See now that huge lobster being served to my lord, all garnished with asparagus. See how his lordly breast distinguishes the dish. With what a tail he looks down upon the company, borne aloft in the hands of that tall attendant! Before you is placed on a tiny plate a crab hemmed in by half an egg—a fit banquet for the dead. The host souses his fish in Venafran oil. The sickly greens offered to you, poor devil, will smell of the lamp, for the stuff contained in your cruets was brought up the Tiber in a sharp-prowed Numidian canoe—stuff which prevents anyone at Rome from sharing a bath with an African, and which will even protect you from the black serpent's bite (*Satires* 5.80–91).

With much greater brevity, but equal effectiveness, Martial makes the same point:

> Since I am asked to dinner, no longer, as before a purchased guest, why is not the same dinner served to me as to you? You take oysters fattened in the Lucrine lake, I suck a mussel through a hole in the shell. You get mushrooms, I take hog funguses. You tackle turbot, but I brill. Golden with fat, a turtledove gorges you with its bloated rump, but there is set before me a magpie that has died in its cage. Why do I dine without you, Ponticus, though I dine with you? The dole has gone: let us have the benefit of that; let us eat the same fare (*Epigrams* 3.60).

> We drink from glass, you from murrine, Ponticus. Why? That a transparent cup may not betray your two wines (*Epigrams* 4.85).

Only the wealthy are attracted by this method of saving, and it is entirely possible that a Corinthian believer, responsible for hosting the whole church, found it expedient to both demonstrate his sophistication and exercise financial prudence by serving different types of food to the two groups of believers—a distinction imposed on him by the physical arrangement of his house. Since the host's friends were of the leisured class they could arrive early and feast on larger portions of superior food while awaiting the arrival of lower-class believers who were not as free to dispose of their time. The condition of those reclining gorged in the triclinium could hardly be disguised from those who had to sit in the atrium. In the house at Anaploga food from the kitchen destined for the triclinium had to be carried through the atrium.

The reconstruction is hypothetical, but no scenario has been suggested which so well explains the details of 1 Cor 11.17–34. The admonition 'wait for one another' (v. 34) means that *prolambanō* in verse 21 necessarily has a temporal connotation; some began to eat before others. Since these were households with plenty to eat and drink (vv. 22, 34), they came from the wealthy section of the community and might have made a contribution in kind to the community meal. This, they felt, gave them the right to think of it as 'their meal' (*to idion deipnon*). Reinforced by the Roman custom, they would then have considered it their due to appropriate the best portions for themselves. Such selfishness would necessarily include a tendency to take just a little more, so that it might easily happen that nothing was left for the have-nots (v. 22), who in their hunger had to be content with the bread and wine provided for the Eucharist. However, as Paul is at pains to point out, under such conditions no Eucharist is possible (v. 20).

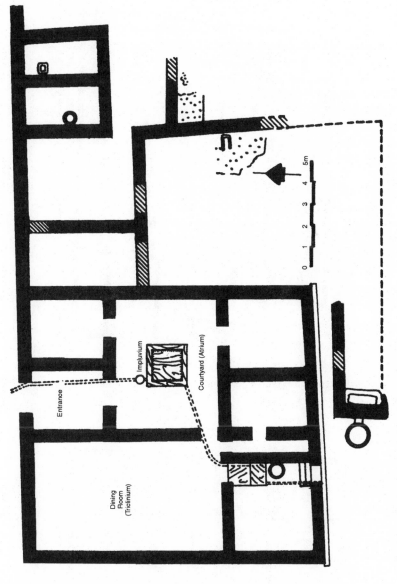

Figure 3.   The Roman Villa at Anaploga
(Reproduced with permission from The Liturgical Press)

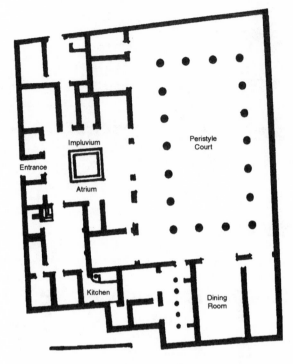

Figure 4.   The House of the Vettii at Pompeii
(Reproduced with permission from The Liturgical Press)

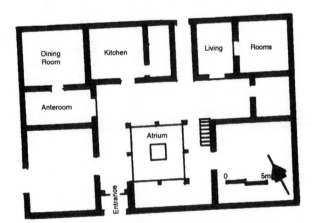

Figure 5.   The Villa of Good Fortune at Olynthus
(Reproduced with permission from The Liturgical Press)

Chapter 10

Discord in Corinth: First Corinthians 1–4 and Ancient Politics[*]

Laurence L. Welborn

INTRODUCTION

From F. C. Baur onward, many writers on 1 Corinthians have sought to explain the divisions and conflicts among the Corinthian Christians by considering the theological differences between two or more of the so-called parties (1 Cor 1.12). Paul's opponents may be identified as followers of a more judaizing Christianity linked with Peter and Jerusalem, or as Gnostics, 'enthusiasts', 'libertines', and so on. On such readings the crucial 'background' for understanding the Corinthians is taken to be various aspects of religious history: Gnosticism, mystery religions, and so on. Welborn argues that these explanations are largely misguided, and that there is a much more obvious background for the kind of language Paul uses to describe and confront the divisions and trouble at Corinth: the language of ancient politics. Paul's text gives little indication as to any doctrinal issues that

*L. L. Welborn, 'On the Discord in Corinth', *JBL* 106 (1987) 85–111. Reprinted with modifications in L. L. Welborn, *Politics and Rhetoric in the Corinthian Epistles* (Macon, Ga.: Mercer University Press, 1997), 1–42. This extract is taken from the latter, pp. 2–8. Reprinted with the permission of the author.

separate the parties; rather what he criticises is the way in which the Corinthians rally around certain leaders, competing for power and influence within the community. Welborn explores the close parallels between the slogans 'I am of Paul', and so on, and the expressions of allegiance recorded from the context of politics. Later in the same essay he considers the role of social and economic inequality in political division and strife, and the political background to Paul's talk of wisdom and knowledge, and his appeals for concord. Welborn's essay thus exemplifies a widespread trend in recent studies of the Corinthian church, away from the exploration of the religious or theological 'background' and toward a focus on the sociopolitical practices and customs that the Corinthians knew as citizens of a Roman colony. The introductory section of the essay is reproduced here.

Further Reading

See also chapters 1, 4, 5, 13.
Clarke, *Secular and Christian Leadership*.
R. M. Grant, *Paul in the Roman World: Conflict at Corinth* (Louisville: Westminster John Knox, 2001).
C. K. Robertson, *Conflict in Corinth: Redefining the System* (New York: Lang, 2001).
L. L. Welborn, *Politics and Rhetoric in the Corinthian Epistles* (Macon, Ga.: Mercer University Press, 1997).
Winter, *After Paul Left Corinth*.

One suspects that the tendency to look away from political aspects of life in the church has exercised a subterranean influence on modern interpreters of the factions in Corinth as well. F. C. Baur's reduction of the parties involved in the strife from the four attested by the slogans echoed in 1 Cor 1.12 to two, the adherents of Paul and those of Peter, allows him to assert that early Christian history was not a meaningless rivalry between factions, but a rational, dialectical process, the realization of the spirit in the synthesis of Hellenistic and Judaistic Christianity.[1] Part of the perennial attraction of the theory that the opponents of Paul (again reduced to a single group, the 'Christ party') are to be identified as spiritual enthusiasts or gnostics must be that it allows for the explanation of the controversy in religious terms, without reference to politics.[2] The strife between the Corinthian parties is thus transposed into the realm of Hellenistic mystery religions and syncretistic gnosis.[3] In the period since World War II, it has proven necessary for some to deny the existence of factions in the Corinthian church.[4]

---

1. Baur, 'Die Christuspartei'; idem, *Paul* (London: Williams & Norgate, 1875).

2. For the opponents of Paul as spiritual enthusiasts, see Lütgert, *Freiheitspredigt*; A. Schlatter, *Die korinthische Theologie*, BFCT 18/2 (Gütersloh: Bertelsmann, 1914). For the opponents of Paul as gnostics, see W. Schmithals, *Gnosticism;* U. Wilckens, *Weisheit und Torheit: Eine exegetisch-religionsgeschichtliche Untersuchung zu 1. Kor. 1 und 2*, BHT 26 (Tübingen: Mohr-Siebeck, 1959); most recently, G. Sellin, 'Das "Geheimnis" der Weisheit und das Ratsel der "Christuspartei" (zu 1 Kor 1–4)', *ZNW* 73 (1982) 69–96.

3. Richard Reitzenstein, *Hellenistic Mystery Religions* (Pittsburgh: Pickwick, 1978) 426–500.

4. J. Munck, 'Menigheden uden Partier', *DTT* 15 (1952) 251–53, incorporated as the fifth chapter of *Paul and the Salvation of Mankind* (Richmond: John Knox, 1959) 135–67.

Yet, however strong the aversion may be to the presence of political elements in the Corinthian epistles, it is impossible to resist the impression that Paul describes the situation in the church in terms like those used to characterize conflicts within city-states by Greco-Roman historians. Paul speaks first of σχίσματα (1.10). A σχίσμα is a rift, a tear, as in a garment; it is used metaphorically of a cleft in political consciousness (e.g., Herodotus 7.219; *PLond* 2710.13).[5] The verb from which the abstract noun derives is used by Diodorus to describe the civil strife at Megara: 'the multitude was divided (σχιζόμενος) according to party' (12.66.2). The clearest indication of the meaning of σχίσμα in 1 Cor 1.10 is provided by the author of 1 Clement. Applying the example of Paul and the parties to the 'abominable and unholy στάσις' in the church of his own day, he asks, 'Why are there quarrels and anger and dissension and divisions (σχίσματα) and war among you?' (46.5). The terms with which σχίσμα is associated make it clear that it is neither a religious heresy nor a harmless clique that the author has in mind, but factions engaged in a struggle for power.[6]

Chloe's people bring news of ἔριδες in the Corinthian church (1.11). Ἔρις is hot dispute, the emotional flame that ignites whenever rivalry becomes intolerable. It invariably appears in accounts of ancient political life the moment the pressure of circumstances, that is, the approach of an enemy army or the election of mutually hostile consuls, draws the citizens into confused knots.[7] A single example will suffice. Plutarch (*Caes.* 33) describes the state into which Rome was thrown by the news that Caesar had crossed the Rubicon. The tempest swept the inhabitants of the country into the city, while the senators, seizing whatever possessions came to hand, abandoned Rome. Conflicting emotions prevailed everywhere, and throughout the city violent disturbances erupted. As was inevitable in such a large city, those who were pleased at Caesar's coming encountered those who were in fear and distress, and both giving voice to their opinions, 'they began to quarrel with one another' (δι᾽ ἐρίδων ἦν).

In 1 Cor 3.3 Paul combines ἔρις with ζῆλος to describe the source of the Corinthians' divisive behavior. This ζῆλος is the gnawing, unquiet root of civil strife—the real, psychological cause of war, according to Lysias (2.48), not the minor infractions both parties allege. The Alexandrian mob that began the civil war against their Jewish fellow residents was driven by 'jealousy' in Philo's judgment;

[margin note: zeal/jealousy]

5. Herodotus (7.219) uses σχίζω to describe the 'division' in the Greek army before Thermopulae. At dawn the watchers came running from the mountains with news of the Persians' approach. Thereupon the Greeks held a council, Herodotus tells us, καὶ σφεων ἐσχίζοντο αἱ γνῶμαι. On the prohibition of the creation of σχίσματα in the νόμος of the gild of Zeus Hypsistos, see below.

6. Cf. *Catalogus Codicum Astrologorum Graecorum* 11.2, ed. H. Lambertin (Brussels, 1898) 122.24: '. . . πολέμους, φόνους, μάχας, σχίσματα.'

7. Of the many examples that could be given: Thucydides 6.35: τῶν δὲ Συρακοσίων ὁ δῆμος ἐν πολλῇ πρὸς ἀλλήλους ἔριδι ἦσαν, 2.21: while the Peloponnesian army ravages the countryside, the Athenian people κατὰ ξυστάσεις τε γιγνόμενοι ἐν πολλῇ ἔριδι ἦσαν οἱ μὲν κελεύοντες ἐπεξιέναι, οἱ δὲ τινες οὐκ ἐῶτες, Appian, *Bell. civ.* 2.2.6: the Senate elects Bibulus as Caesar's colleague in the consulship in order to hold him in check, καὶ εὐθὺς αὐτῶν ἦσαν ἔριδές τε καὶ ὅπλων ἐπ᾽ ἀλλήλους ἰδίᾳ παρασκευαί. See also Appian, *Bell. civ.* 3.86.357; Josephus, *Ant.* 14.16.1 §470.

enraged at the sight of the Jewish prince Agrippa, they seized a poor lunatic named 'Carabas', dressed him in the robes of a king, and hailed him as 'Marin' (Philo, *Flacc.* 41).[8] In 1 Cor 1.13 Paul asks rhetorically, μεμέρισται ὁ Χριστός, alluding by synecdoche to the notion of the church as the σῶμα Χριστοῦ. The translations fail to capture the political connotation that the verb undoubtedly had for its first readers. The customary term for 'party' in Greek is μερίς, corresponding to Latin *pars*. In the proem to his account of the civil wars, Appian relates that the senate and the plebs 'were split into parties' (ἐμερίζετο, *Bell. civ.* 1.1; cf. Polybius 8.21.9) over the appointment of magistrates, the former supporting the consuls, the latter the tribune of the plebs, each seeking to prevail over the other by increasing the power of its own magistrate. We may gain in clarity if we translate Paul's question: 'Has the body of Christ been split into parties?'[9]

Another explicitly political term, διχοστασία, appears in the earliest witness to the Pauline epistles, P[46] (ca. 200 C.E.), a number of important uncial manuscripts, and the majority text as characteristic of the situation in the church at Corinth (3.3).[10] It was such 'hardened difference of opinion', 'bitter irresolve', that, according to Dionysius of Halicarnassus, paralyzed the Roman assembly *(Ant. rom.* 8.72.1, 4).[11] It is this 'dissension' that Paul now identifies as the bane of the Corinthian church. What threatened the survival of the community of chosen people was not seductive gnostic theology or infectious Judaistic propaganda, but the possibility that its adherents might 'behave like ordinary men' (3.3).

There is one last phrase that Paul uses to describe the demeanor of the Corinthian Christians: each is 'puffed up on behalf of one against another' (4.6). It is symptomatic that this vivid image should prove so 'difficult to fathom.'[12] It is all too familiar to the student of political history as the caricature of the political windbag, the orator inflated at his own success (Ps.-Plato, *Alcibiades* 2.145e; Plutarch, *Cic.* 887b; Epictetus, *Diss.* 2.16.10), the young aristocrat, the aspiring tyrant, filled with a sense of his own power (Alcibiades and Critias in Xenophon, *Mem.* 1.2.25; Gaius in Philo, *Legat.* 86, 154; Pausanias in Demosthenes 59.97;

---

8. See also Plutarch, *Lyc.* 4.2–3; 1 Macc. 8:16; Cicero, *Tusc.* 4.8.17. In 2 Cor 12:20 and Gal 5:20 Paul again combines ζῆλος with ἔρις in the sense of 'rivalry' or 'jealous strife'.

9. G. Heinrici rightly designates *1 Clem.* 46:7 a 'commentary' on μεμέρισται *(Der erste Brief an die Korinther* [Göttingen: Vandenhoeck & Ruprecht, 1896] 61).

10. P[46] D F G M a b it sy; Marcion, Cyp., Ir[gr], Thdrt., cf. C. Tischendorf, *Novum Testamentum Graece 2* (Leipzig: Giesecke & Devrient, 1872) on 1 Cor 3:3. There is much to suggest that the word was originally present in the text, contra B. Metzger (*A Textual Commentary on the Greek New Testament* [New York: United Bible Societies, 1975] 548), who suspects the intrusion of a 'Western gloss', though P[46] is closer to the Alexandrian type of text. The term is an established part of Paul's vocabulary: Gal 5:20; Rom 16:17 (in a warning that immediately precedes mention of his friends and supporters in Corinth). Its appearance in *1 Clem.* 46:5 along with ἔρις and σχίσματα, in a passage that refers to 'the epistle of the blessed Paul', is also suggestive.

11. Cf. Diodorus 35.25.1: When Gracchus forms parties in support of his plan to abolish aristocratic rule, he is accused of securing power for himself διὰ τῆς πάντων διχοστασίας. See further, Herodotus 5.75; 1 Macc 3:29; Plutarch, *Mor.* 478e-479a; Solon 3.37–38; Dionysius of Halicarnassus, *Ant. rom.* 5.66.4.

12. Conzelmann, *1 Corinthians,* 86.

see also Thucydides 1.132.1–3; Dio Chrysostom 30.19; 58.5), the supercilious office holder (Demosthenes 19.314; Philo *Legat.* 69, 255). With savage irony Paul imprints the familiar image of self-conceit which gives rise to partisanship upon the surface of the text, the way a flash transfixes an image on film.

It is no longer necessary to argue against the position that the conflict that evoked 1 Corinthians was essentially theological in character. The attempt to identify the parties with views and practices condemned elsewhere in the epistle, as if the parties represented different positions in a dogmatic controversy, has collapsed under its own weight. Johannes Weiss already saw the flaw in this approach: Paul's strategy in dealing with the parties makes it impossible to differentiate between them.[13] Paul refuses to analyze the opinions of the various factions, but speaks to the community as a whole, as though all the parties had coalesced in his mind into 'one perverse, insubordinate, arrogant, and hostile group'.[14] No one doubts that doctrinal differences existed, or that the claim to possess divine wisdom and knowledge played an important role in the controversy. But a number of scholars are now returning to the view of John Calvin: that the real problem being addressed in 1 Cor 1–4 is one of partisanship.[15] As Calvin observed, Paul deals in a different manner with false teaching in Galatians and Philippians. There he engages in polemic; but 1 Cor 1–4 is deliberative in character.[16] Paul does not seek to refute a 'different gospel' (as in 2 Cor 11.4), but exhorts the quarreling Corinthians 'to agree completely, . . . to be united in the same mind and the same judgment' (1.10).

It is a power struggle, not a theological controversy, that motivates the writing of 1 Cor 1–4. So much Weiss and Lietzmann were ready to accept.[17] But interpreters have been slow to grasp the implications of this insight. It has not yet been realized how closely the situation in the church at Corinth resembles the

13. J. Weiss, *Der erste Korintherbrief* (Göttingen: Vandenhoeck & Ruprecht, 1910) xxx–xxxi. Even the sophistical conceit customarily associated with the adherents of Apollos, owing to his Alexandrian background and reputed eloquence (Acts 18.24), is rebuked in connection with the Cephas party in 3.18–23! Some have seen in 3.10–17 veiled polemic against the Cephas party: P. Vielhauer, 'Paulus und die Kephaspartei in Korinth', *NTS* 21 (1975) 341–52. G. Lüdemann (*Paulus, der Heidenapostel II: Antipaulinismus im frühen Christentum* [Göttingen: Vandenhoeck & Ruprecht, 1983] 118–23) argues from the literary structure of 3.6–17; this is a possibility, though θεμέλιος need not refer to Cephas specifically, since the building metaphor occurs frequently in writings on concord, e.g., Plutarch, *Mor.* 807c; Dio Chrysostom, *Or.* 38.15; Aelius Aristides, *Or.* 23.31; 24.8; 24.32–33.

14. J. Weiss, *The History of Primitive Christianity* (New York: Scribner's, 1937) 1:339; similarly, D. Patte, *Paul's Faith and the Power of the Gospel* (Philadelphia: Fortress, 1983) 302.

15. See, e.g., J. Héring, *The First Epistle of Saint Paul to the Corinthians* (London: Epworth, 1962) 44; H. Koester, *Introduction to the New Testament II: History and Literature of Early Christianity* (Philadelphia: Fortress, 1982) 121; Horrell, *Social Ethos.*

16. John Calvin, *The First Epistle of Paul the Apostle to the Corinthians* (repr. Grand Rapids: Eerdmans, 1959) 8. On 1 Corinthians as deliberative rhetoric, see H. D. Betz, 'The Problem of Rhetoric and Theology according to the Apostle Paul', in *L 'Apôtre Paul: Personalité, Style, et Conception du ministère* (ed. A. Vanhoye; BETL 73; Leuven: Peeters, 1986) 16–48.

17. See also A. A. T. Ehrhardt, *Politische Metaphysik von Solon bis Augustin,* vol. 2 (Tübingen: Mohr-Siebeck, 1959) 10–12.

conflicts within city-states described by Greek and Roman historians.[18] Nor has it been recognized how much Paul's advice in 1 Cor 1–4 has in common with speeches on concord (περὶ ὁμονοίας) by ancient politicians and rhetoricians, such as Dio Chrysostom and Aelius Aristides.[19] It is our contention that Paul's goal in 1 Cor 1–4 is not the refutation of heresy, but what Plutarch (Mor. 824C-E) describes as the object of the art of politics—the prevention of στάσις.[20] If this is so, then much light should be thrown upon Paul's admonitions by an investigation of these chapters in the context of ancient politics.

18. J. Weiss (Der erste Korintherbrief, on 1.10) and H. Lietzmann (Die Briefe des Paulus: An die Korinther I, HNT [Tübingen: Mohr-Siebeck, 1910] on 1.10) provided parallels to Paul's exhortation from Greek historians, Thucydides, Polybius, and Dionysius of Halicarnassus; but their insights were not pursued.

19. See Thrasymachus περί πολιτείας; Antiphon περὶ ὁμονοίας; Isocrates, Or. 4; Ep. 3, 8, 9; Plato, Ep. 7; Socratic Ep. 30; Ps.-Sallust Ep. 2; Dio Chrysostom, Or. 38–41; Aelius Aristides, Or. 23–24; (Herodes Atticus) περὶ πολιτείας, among others.

20. There is no satisfactory treatment of στάσις, although the subject is treated briefly by D. Loenen, Stasis (Amsterdam: Noord-Hollandische Uitg. Mij., 1953) and A. Lintott, Violence, Civil Strife and Revolution in the Classical City (Baltimore: Johns Hopkins University Press, 1982).

Chapter 11

Rhetorical Situation and Historical Reconstruction in 1 Corinthians*

Elisabeth Schüssler Fiorenza

INTRODUCTION

In this pioneering and influential essay, Elisabeth Schüssler Fiorenza attempts to use rhetorical criticism 'to read a historical text in such a way that we move from the "world of the text" of Paul to the actual world of the Corinthian community' (p. 146). She focuses attention on the 'rhetorical situation' of 1 Corinthians. Rhetorical discourse, she claims, is generated by a specific situation. That situation controls the rhetorical response. By analysing carefully the rhetorical organisation and dynamics of the text, one may assess the concrete situation in which the text was intended to function. As well as rhetorical criticism, Fiorenza draws on literary criticism and hermeneutical theory. She points out that interpreters usually take Paul's critique of the Corinthians at face value and reconstruct the community situation along the very lines he inscribes it. She proposes instead a four-step strategy to move from Paul's portrait of the Corinthians to the common

*Extracted from E. Schüssler Fiorenza, 'Rhetorical Situation and Historical Reconstruction in 1 Corinthians', *NTS* 33 (1987) 386–403, here pp. 388–400. Reprinted by permission of Cambridge University Press, The Edinburgh Building, Shaftesbury Road, Cambridge.

historical situation of writer and recipients. The first step is to identify the interests of contemporary interpretation. The second is to analyse the rhetorical structure of the text. The next step is to establish the rhetorical occasion to which the letter can be understood as an appropriate response. The fourth step is to evaluate Paul's rhetoric ethically, calling into question rather than accepting at face value the social values that he promotes. The article makes a significant methodological contribution to discussions of Corinthian Christianity: it commends a new approach to historical reconstruction, that of rhetorical criticism; and it challenges interpreters to read 1 Corinthians 'against the grain', or, in effect, against Paul, in order to restore the other, textually suppressed, voices in the original dialogue.

Antoinette Wire's *Corinthian Women Prophets* remains the most thoroughgoing attempt to reconstruct the situation in Corinth through a critical analysis of Paul's rhetoric in the letter, along the lines advocated by Fiorenza. Wire focuses specifically on the women in the Christian community. While Fiorenza here makes the distinction between the situation constructed by Paul and the actual historical situation at Corinth so that the latter may be more carefully delineated and investigated, Dennis Stamps, in his development of Fiorenza's approach, proposes that the rhetorical situation itself should be the object of study, given the problems involved in moving from analysis of a literary text to speaking of historical reality.

Further Reading

C. Briggs Kittredge, 'Corinthian Women Prophets and Paul's Argumentation in 1 Corinthians', in *Paul and Politics: Ekklesia, Israel, Imperium, Interpretation* (ed. R. A. Horsley; Harrisburg: Trinity Press International, 2000) 103–9.

S. M. Pogoloff, *Logos and Sophia: The Rhetorical Situation of 1 Corinthians* (SBLDS 134; Atlanta: Scholars Press, 1992).

D. Stamps, 'Rethinking the Rhetorical Situation: The Entextualization of the Situation in New Testament Epistles', in *Rhetoric and the New Testament: Essays from the 1992 Heidelberg Conference* (ed. S. E. Porter and T. H. Olbricht; JSNTSup 90; Sheffield: JSOT Press, 1993) 193–209.

Wire, *Corinthian Women Prophets*.

How can we utilize rhetorical criticism in order to read a historical text in such a way that we move from the 'world of the text' of Paul to the actual world of the Corinthian community?[1] In order to do so I would argue that rhetorical criticism needs to distinguish not only between poetic and rhetorical texts, but also between at least three levels of communication. Rhetorical criticism must distinguish between the historical argumentative situation, the implied or inscribed

---

1. For a discussion of this problem cf. B. C. Lategan and W. S. Vorstet, *Text and Reality: Aspects of Reference in Biblical Texts* (Semeia Studies; Philadelphia: Fortress Press, 1985); N. R. Petersen, *Rediscovering Paul: Philemon and the Sociology of Paul's Narrative World* (Philadelphia: Fortress Press, 1985) and W. A. Meeks, 'Understanding Early Christian Ethics', *JBL* 105 (1986) 3–11.

rhetorical situation as well as the rhetorical situation of contemporary interpretations which works with the canonical collection and reception of Paul's letters.

I therefore propose that a rhetorical critical analysis has to move through four stages: It begins—as I have sketched above—by identifying the rhetorical interests and models of contemporary interpretation, then moves to delineate the rhetorical arrangement, interests, and modifications introduced by the author in order to elucidate and establish in a third step the rhetorical situation of the letter. Finally, it seeks to reconstruct the common historical situation and symbolic universe of the writer/speaker and the recipients/audience. True, such a rhetorical reconstruction of the social-historical situation is still narrative-laden and can only be constituted as a 'sub-text' to Paul's text. Yet this 'sub-text' is not simply the story of Paul; it is, rather, the story of the Corinthian church to which Paul's rhetoric is to be understood as an active response.[2] Therefore, it becomes necessary to assess critically Paul's theological rhetoric in terms of its function for early Christian self-understanding and community. The nature of rhetoric as political discourse necessitates critical assessment and theological evaluation.[3]

In the following I would like to utilize these four levels of rhetorical critical analysis for the interpretation of I Corinthians:

First, reader-response criticism distinguishes between the actual writer/reader and the implied writer/reader. The implied writer/reader encompasses the contemporary interpreter who in the process of reading constructs the inscribed author and reader. Reader-response criticism has developed the notion of implied author and implied reader that can help us to elucidate Paul's rhetorical intention as it is constructed in the act of reading/interpretation today (reception hermeneutics[4]).

Second, the rhetorical arrangement or disposition of 1 Corinthians not only embodies the rhetorical strategies which Paul employs for persuading the Corinthian community to act according to his instructions, but also indicates the intended or implicit audience of the letter.

Third, the 'rhetorical situation' is constituted by the rhetorical occasion or exigency to which 1 Corinthians can be understood as a 'fitting' response as well as by the rhetorical problem Paul had to overcome. Attention to both can help us to avoid reconstructing the historical situation of the Corinthian community simply as the story of Paul.

Fourth, since rhetoric also can be used negatively as propaganda or crafty calculation, ethical evaluation of the speaker and moral judgment of the rhetorical

2. F. R. Jameson, 'The Symbolic Inference', in *Representing Kenneth Burke* (ed. Hayden White and M. Brose; Baltimore: Johns Hopkins University Press, 1982) 68–91.

3. W. C. Booth, 'Freedom of Interpretation: Baktin and the Challenge of Feminist Criticism', *Critical Inquiry* 9 (1982) 45–76, has called for a revived ethical and political criticism in literary criticism. Cf. also G. Greene and C. Kahn, eds., *Making a Difference: Feminist Literary Criticism* (New York: Methuen, 1985); J. Newton and D. Rosenfelt, eds., *Feminist Criticism and Social Change* (New York: Methuen, 1985); and especially E. A. Meese, *Crossing the Double-Cross: The Practice of Feminist Criticism* (Chapel Hill: Univ. of North Carolina Press, 1986) 133–50.

4. For an overview see R. C. Holub, *Reception Theory. A Critical Introduction* (London: Methuen, 1984).

discourse in a concrete political situation is an essential part of philosophical discussions in ancient rhetoric. New Testament rhetorical criticism, therefore, cannot limit itself to a formalistic analysis of 1 Corinthians, nor to an elucidation of its historical-social context; rather it must develop a responsible ethical and evaluative theological criticism.

FIRST: CONTEMPORARY INTERPRETATIONS

In *The Rhetoric of Fiction,* W. Booth has distinguished between the actual author/reader and the implied author/reader. The implied author is not the real author, but rather the image or picture which the reader will construct gradually in the process of reading the work. 'The actual reader is involved in apprehending and building up the picture of the implied author (and implied reader); but in doing this the reader is assuming the role dictated by the author.'[5] In other words, in the process of reading 1 Corinthians the interpreter follows the directives of the implied author, who is not identical with the 'real' Paul, as to how to understand the community of Corinth. That interpreters follow the directives of the implied author to understand the Corinthian Christians as 'other' of Paul or as 'opponents' becomes obvious in all those interpretations that characterize the Corinthians as foolish, immature, arrogant, divisive, individualistic, unrealistic illusionists, libertine enthusiasts, or boasting spiritualists who misunderstood the preaching of Paul in terms of 'realized eschatology'.

Since many things are presupposed, left out, or unexplained in a speech/letter, the audience must in the process of reading 'supply' the missing information in line with the rhetorical directives of the speaker/writer. Historical critical scholars seek to 'supply' such information generally in terms of the history of religions, including Judaism, while preachers and bible-readers usually do so in terms of contemporary values, life, and psychology. Scholarship on 1 Corinthians tends to 'supply' such information about Paul's 'opponents'[6] either with reference to the symbolic universe of contemporary Judaism, of pagan religion, especially the mystery cults, philosophical schools, Hellenistic Judaism, or developing Gnosticism. The studies of the social setting or 'social world' of Pauline Christianity in turn, do not utilize ideological, doctrinal models of interpretation, but supply the

---

5. E. V. McKnight, *The Bible and the Reader: An Introduction to Literary Criticism* (Philadelphia: Fortress Press, 1985) 102; see, however, the incisive critique of the de-politicising tendencies in reader-response criticism which do not take power-relationships into account: M. L. Pratt. 'Interpretative Strategies/Strategic Interpretations: On Anglo-American Reader Response Criticism', in *Postmodernism and Politics* (ed. J. Arac; Theory and History of Literature 28; Minneapolis: Univ. of Minnesota Press, 1986) 26–54.

6. For a discussion of this problem cf. E. E. Ellis, 'Paul and His Opponents. Trends in Research', in *Christianity, Judaism, and Other Greco-Roman Cults.* Vol. I (ed. J. Neusner; Leiden: Brill, 1975) 264–98; and especially K. Berger, 'Die implizíten Gegner. Zur Methode der Erschliessung von Gegnern in neutestamentlichen Texten', in *Kirche* (ed. D. Lührmann and G. Strecker; Tübingen: Mohr, 1980) 373–400.

missing information in terms of 'social data' gleaned from the Pauline corpus, Acts, and other ancient sources, which in turn, are organized in terms of sociological or anthropological models.

As diverse as these interpretations and their implications for the understanding of the community in Corinth are, they all follow Paul's dualistic rhetorical strategy without questioning or evaluating it. In short, a cursory look at scholarship on 1 Corinthians indicates that Paul is a skilled rhetorician, who, throughout the centuries, has reached his goal of persuading his audience that he is right and the 'others' are wrong. The difference in interpretations is more a difference in degree than a difference in interpretational model. It depends on which directions encoded in the letter exegetes choose to amplify historically and theologically. Moreover, insofar as New Testament scholars read 1 Corinthians as a 'canonical text', we often uncritically accept the implied author's claims to apostolic authority as historically valid and effective. However, we must ask whether the interpretation of 1 Corinthians would have developed different heuristic models if, for example, Paul was believed to be a Valentinian gnostic or a Jewish rabbi writing against Christians.[7] In other words, does Paul's power of persuasion rest on his presumed authority or did it have the same effect in the historical situation in which such canonical authority can not be presupposed?[8]

SECOND: THE RHETORICAL ARRANGEMENT OF 1 CORINTHIANS

At first glance, the rhetorical strategies and situation of 1 Corinthians seem to be obvious. The Corinthians had written to Paul about certain issues and 1 Corinthians is a response to their inquiries or declarations. The letter form is a 'fitting response' to the Corinthian correspondence. If that is the case, however, it must be explained why Paul's first reference to their correspondence is in chapter 7 and not in the beginning of the letter. If this ordering is an intended part of the rhetorical *dispositio,* then one must ask whether this indicates a different argumentative situation, since the rhetorical problem is usually articulated in the beginning of the discourse? In order to explore this question it becomes necessary to discuss the rhetorical genre of 1 Corinthians.

Ancient rhetoric distinguishes between 'three types of oratory, the deliberative, the forensic, and the epideictic, which . . . corresponded respectively to an audience engaged in deliberating, an audience engaged in judging, an audience that is merely enjoying the orator's unfolding argument without having to reach

7. V. Hasler, 'Das Evangelium des Paulus in Korinth. Erwagungen zur Hermeneutik', *NTS* 30 (1984) 109–29, points out that exegetes often succumb to the temptation to identify with Paul and to take over uncritically his theological interpretation.

8. For discussion and literature see G. Lüdemann, *Paulus,* vol. 2: *Antipaulinismus im frühen Christentum* (FRLANT 130; Göttingen: Vandenhoeck & Ruprecht, 1983).

a conclusion on the matter in question'.[9] Forensic or judicial rhetoric has its 'Sitz im Leben' in the courtroom. It seeks to accuse or to defend and to persuade the audience as the judge of its own assessment of the past. Deliberative rhetoric is at home in the *forum* and it seeks to convince and move the audience to make the right decision for the future, whereas *epideictic* or demonstrative rhetoric is exercised in the marketplace or amphitheatre, where the audience as spectators judge the oratory of the speaker in order to award praise or blame.

An exploration of rhetorical genre and its function can thus contribute to an understanding of the rhetorical situation insofar as arrangement and style reveal the speaker's perception of the audience and the ways chosen to influence it. Thus the audience is a construction of the speaker, but in a real life situation, as in the case of 1 Corinthians, care must be taken to form a concept of the audience as close as possible to reality if the speaker/writer wants to have any effect or influence on the actions of the hearers/readers.

1. In his article on 'Greek Rhetoric and Pauline Argumentation', W. Wuellner has argued that 1 Corinthians represents *epideictic* or demonstrative discourse.[10] He thereby relies on the work of Perelman, *The New Rhetoric,* that seeks to redefine the *genus demonstrativum* or *epideictic* genre. In antiquity, according to Lausberg, demonstrative rhetoric was, in distinction to forensic and deliberative rhetoric, not so much concerned with the content or topic of the discourse, as with the art of presentation or the rhetorical skills and eloquence which speakers exhibited at festivals and in the amphitheatre. Its primary function was the praise in celebration of a person, community, or action.[11] Perelman seeks to redefine the *genus demonstrativum* not so much with reference to the speaker's performance, but rather with respect to the audience and its values.[12] *Epideictic* discourse, he argues, 'sets out to increase the intensity of the audience's adherence to certain values which might not be contested when considered on their own but may nevertheless not prevail against other values that might come into conflict with them. In epideictic oratory the speaker turns educator.'[13] Such discourse is less directed toward changing or modifying beliefs than toward strengthening the adherence to what is already accepted. It seeks to reinforce the sense of *communio* between the speaker and the audience by utilizing every means available to the orator.

Wuellner examines the phenomenon of Pauline digressions in 1 Corinthians in order to show that they are not careless style but rather examples of Paul's rhetorical skill for, in classical rhetoric, digressions are introduced for the purpose

---

9. Ch. Perelman and L. Olbrechts-Tyteca, *The New Rhetoric. A Treatise on Argumentation* (Notre Dame: Univ. of Notre Dame Press, 1969) 21.

10. In *Early Christian Literature and the Classical Intellectual Tradition. In Honorem Robert Grant* (ed. W. R. Schoedel and R. Wilken; Théologie historique 53; Paris: Editions Beauchesne, 1979) 177–88.

11. H. Lausberg, *Handbuch der literarischen Rhetorik. Eine Grundlegung der Literaturwissenschaft* (2nd rev. ed.; München: Max Huber, 1973) 55.

12. Perelman/Olbrechts-Tyteca, *The New Rhetoric,* 48f.

13. Op. cit., 51.

of elucidating the issue at hand. He identifies three major digressions: 1.19—3.21; 9.1—10.13; and 13.1–13. These digressions function *affectively* to intensify adherence. They belong to three argumentative units: 1.1—6.11; 6.12—11.1; and 11.2—14.40. He concludes: 'The appeals to the audience to imitate the speaker . . . are an example, a paradigm, of the values lauded, with Paul seeking adherence to these values on the one hand, and on the other hand to strengthen disposition toward action'.[14] He therefore rejects the thesis of Nils Dahl, who on the basis of a contentual but not formal analysis had argued that chapters 1–4 are best understood as an *apologia* because in these chapters Paul seeks to 'reestablish his apostolic authority as the founder and spiritual father of the whole church in Corinth'.[15]

2. However, Dahl's rhetorical understanding of chs. 1–4 as Pauline apology has received support from recent formal studies of Paul's rhetoric. In his dissertation, *Briefformular und rhetorische Disposition im 1. Korintherbrief*, Michael Bünker has analyzed 1 Cor 1.10—4.21 and 1 Cor 15 in terms of epistolary form and rhetorical arrangement. He shows that both sections have the rhetorical structure of forensic or judicial discourse. Although Paul claims that he did not speak in Corinth with 'lofty words of wisdom', his distinction between ἐν πειθοῖ σοφίας and ἐν ἀποδείξει πνεύματος indicates that he knew the rhetorical distinction between oratory as mere persuasion and speech as a process of forming one's opinion on the basis of arguments and proofs.[16]

Moreover, Bünker argues that, according to rhetorical conventions, Paul's arrangement and disposition is artful and well planned, but not obvious. This is the case especially in those sections in which Paul could not count on the agreement of the audience but rather expected attacks and counter arguments. Bünker, therefore, concludes that while Paul formally addresses the whole community in Corinth, in reality he is arguing with those few Corinthian Christians who are well educated and of high status. His rhetorical location of the implicit or intended reader thus confirms Theissen's social identification of the troublemakers in Corinth who have caused divisions and conflicts by competing with each other for the approval of different apostolic authorities.[17] Bünker's results, however, speak against Wuellner's thesis that Paul did not choose the *epideictic* genre in order to change the beliefs of the audience but rather in order to strengthen the Corinthians' adherence to values and beliefs which, although already accepted by many, were still contested by some.

In my opinion, Bünker's argument, however, also has several weaknesses: He discusses the rhetorical disposition of chapters 1–4 and 15 only and not the

14. W. Wuellner, 'Greek Rhetoric and Pauline Argumentation', 184.

15. N. A. Dahl, *Studies in Paul: Theology for the Early Christian Mission* (Minneapolis: Augsburg Publishing House, 1977) 329; cf. also J. Bradley Chance, 'Paul's Apology to the Corinthians', *Perspectives in Religious Studies* 9 (1982) 144–55.

16. M. Bünker, *Briefformular und rhetorische Disposition im I. Korintherbrief* (Göttinger theologische Arbeiten 28; Göttingen: Vandenhoeck & Ruprecht, 1983) 48–76.

17. M. Bünker, *Briefformular,* 17 and 52f.; cf. also Theissen, *Social Setting,* 56f.

rhetorical genre of the whole letter. Furthermore, his delineation of the intended or implicit audience is derived from considerations of general rhetorical practices which can be used in all kinds of rhetorical discourse. Finally, the ending of 1 Corinthians, where Paul appeals to the Corinthians to acknowledge and accept the leadership of Stephanas and his co-workers, speaks against an identification of the intended audience whom Paul wishes to compel to act with those who cause the difficulties in the community. Since Stephanas is clearly one of the better situated and educated members of the community, and since he belongs to those who are loyal to Paul, we have to conclude, to the contrary, that Paul relies on such persons for implementing his directives. Consequently, if Paul does not argue against, but rather appeals to, the social status group of Stephanas as the intended or the implicit readers, the overall genre of 1 Corinthians is not judicial or forensic. Rather, it appears that the genre of 1 Corinthians is best understood as 'largely deliberative although it contains some judicial passages. . .'.[18]

3. The disposition or arrangement of deliberative rhetoric is closely related to that of the forensic genre. It consists basically of three sections: The *exordium* intends to secure the goodwill of the audience and states the desired goal of the speech. In the main body or proofs the argument is advanced with reference to what is honourable, useful, and possible by appeal to *ethos* as a reflection of one's own good character (Paul's example), to *pathos* as a stirring appeal to the heart and the emotions, and to *logos,* that is, to reasoned argument. The *peroration* restates with all possible force factors that are alluded to in the exordium and adduced or developed in the proofs.[19]

The major goal of deliberative rhetoric is to persuade the audience to take action for the future and that this action is in its best interest. This goal is expressed in 1 Cor 1.10 where Paul appeals to the Corinthians that they should all agree without dissensions and be united in the same mind and the same opinion.[20] It is also articulated in the *peroration* 16.15–18, where Paul urges the Corinthians to subject themselves and to give recognition to such persons as Stephanas and every co-worker.[21] Bünker is thus correct in his suggestion that the inscribed or intended audience which is asked to decide the issues under discussion is composed of those who have either social or missionary status or both. The major issues which need to be settled are discussed in the main body of the letter: marriage and sexuality (chapters 5–7);[22] meat sacrificed to idols (8.1—

18. G. Kennedy, *New Testament Interpretation Through Rhetorical Criticism* (Chapel Hill: North Carolina Univ. Press, 1984) 87.

19. See the literature cited by F. Forrester Church, 'Rhetorical Structure and Design in Paul's Letter to Philemon', *HTR* 71 (1978) 17–31.

20. H. Conzelmann's classification of this passage as 'paraenetic' is too general; cf. *1 Corinthians*, 31.

21. The emphatic expression παρακαλῶ ὑμας serves as rhetorical marker in 1.10; 4.16; and 16.15. For 4.16 see B. Sanders, 'Imitating Paul: 1 Cor 4:16', *HTR* 74 (1981) 353–63 but with a different emphasis in interpretation.

22. It is debated where the first part of 1 Corinthians ends and the second section begins. The traditional outline is chapters 1–6 (subjects raised with Paul orally) and 7–16 (subjects about which the Corinthians have written) cf. W. F. Orr and J. A. Walter, *I Corinthians* (AB 32; Garden City, N.Y.:

11.1);[23] worship (11.2—14.40);[24] resurrection (15.12–37);[25] and the collection for the saints (16.1–4). In order to show that this delineation of 1 Corinthians as deliberative rhetoric is plausible, we have to see whether it can be construed as a 'fitting' response to the rhetorical situation.

THIRD: RHETORICAL SITUATION

At first glance the rhetorical situation of 1 Corinthians seems to support the understanding of the letter as epideictic rhetoric. The Corinthians had written to Paul about certain issues and 1 Corinthians is a response to their request for advice and answers. If that were the case, however, it must be explained why Paul does not in the beginning but only in chapter 7 refer to the Corinthian letter. This observation suggests a different argumentative genre and situation. As we have seen, the 'rhetorical situation' is constituted by the rhetorical occasion or exigency to which 1 Corinthians can be understood as a 'fitting' response as well as by the rhetorical problem Paul had to overcome. Attention to both can help us to avoid reconstructing the historical situation of the Corinthian community simply as the story of Paul. Therefore it is necessary to define the argumentative situation in terms of the exigence and rhetorical problem articulated in the beginning of 1 Corinthians.

The basic issue of the case is usually discussed in the beginning of the discourse, but it needs to be restated also during the discourse. This seems to be the case in chapters 1.11—4.21; 9; 15.1–12; and 16.5–12. In 1 Corinthians *stasis* seems to be understood best as *status translationis* that is given when the speaker's/writer's *auctoritas* or jurisdiction to address or settle the issue at hand is in doubt and needs to be established.[26]

'Those of Chloe' in 1.11 function as interlocutors who articulate such doubt as to the qualifications of Paul to settle the issues about which the Corinthians have written. It is generally assumed that Stephanas delivered the formal written questions or statements of the community,[27] whereas 'those of Chloe' supplied

---

Doubleday, 1976), 120–22; K. E. Bailey, 'The Structure of 1 Corinthians and Paul's Theological Method with Special Reference to 4:17', *NovT* 25 (1983) 152–81, argues that 4.17–21 are an introduction to chapters 5–7; the semiotic analysis of G. Claudel, '1 Kor 6,12—7,40 neu gelesen', *Trierer theologische Zeitschrift* 94 (1985) 20–36, argues for the unity of this section.

23. For bibliography cf. W. L. Willis, *Idol Meat in Corinth. The Pauline Argument in 1 Corinthians 8 and 10* (SBLDS 68; Chico: Scholars Press, 1981); idem, 'An Apostolic Apologia? The Form and Function of 1 Corinthians 9', *JSNT* 24 (1985) 33–48, argues that here Paul is not defending his conduct but that he argues on the basis of it.

24. Cf. H. Wendland, *Die Briefe an die Korinther* (NTD 7; Göttingen; Vandenhoeck & Ruprecht, 1965) 80; cf. also E. Schüssler Fiorenza, 'Women in the Pre-Pauline and Pauline Churches', *Union Seminary Quarterly Review* 33 (1978) 153–66.

25. Cf. the careful structural analysis of W. Stenger, 'Beobachtungen zur Argumentationsstruktur von 1 Cor 15', *Linguistica Biblica* 45 (1979) 71–128.

26. H. Lausberg, *Handbuch der literarischen Rhetorik*, 128f.

27. H. Lausberg, *Handbuch der literarischen Rhetorik*, 128f.

the oral information, hearsay, and gossip to which Paul refers. Scholars such as J. Hurd, N. Dahl, or G. Theissen who seek to reconstruct the social-historical situation in Corinth from the information of the letter and not through outside influence also make this distinction. For example, Dahl assumes that the official delegation of the church in Corinth headed by Stephanas 'had not gossiped'[28] whereas the people of Chloe had supplied the oral information referred to by Paul in 1.10—5.8; 5.13b—6.11; and 11.17–34.[29] G. Theissen, on the other hand, argues that the 'people of Chloe' who provided the information on party-strife were slaves who looked at the problems in Corinth from 'below' whereas the letter which did not mention that problem was probably written by people who possessed some degree of culture and, therefore, by some of the more prominent members of the community.[30] He concludes from this that Paul adopts the view 'from below' and argues against the upper-class members who were responsible for the divisions in the church. However, we have no indication that Stephanas was the carrier of the letter sent by the Corinthians. It appears that he arrived later and gave Paul a more positive view of the situation at Corinth so that Paul could rely on him to present his response to the community and to see to it that his instructions were followed, for the community is told to subordinate itself to Stephanas and his co-workers.

'Those of Chloe' are usually understood to be either slaves or family members of the household of Chloe, a woman who might or might not have been a Christian. This prevalent interpretation overlooks, however, that here the Greek grammatical form (article with *genitivus possessivus*) is the same as the expression used for characterizing the followers of Paul, Apollos, Cephas, and Christ. It also overlooks that Paul uses a different grammatical expression (τοὺς ἐκ τῶν with *gen. poss.*), for instance, in Rom 16.10 and 11, where he greets the members of the households of Aristobulos and of Narkissos.[31] It seems likely that the expression 'those of Chloe' means 'the people or followers of Chloe' in Corinth; therefore, I would suggest they were the official messengers of the community. They not only supplied Paul with oral background information but they also presented the written communication of the community to him. Chloe's status in the community of Corinth was probably similar to that of Stephanas even though she and her followers did not belong to the converts of Paul because they obviously were not baptized by him. However, her social status and that of her followers is not clear.[32]

28. N. A. Dahl, *Studies in Paul,* 50.

29. Ibid., 93.

30. Theissen, *Social Setting,* 57.

31. Cf. E. Schüssler Fiorenza, 'Missionaries, Apostles, Coworkers: Rom 16 and the Reconstruction of Women's Early Christian History', *Word and World* 6 (1986) 420–33.

32. It is debated whether Chloe's followers live in Corinth or have returned from Corinth to their residence in Ephesus. Meeks, *First Urban Christians,* 59 argues that Chloe lived in Corinth because Paul expects that her name is recognized. However, he considers the people of Chloe to be her slaves or freedmen.

If the delegation travelled under the name of a woman, women must have had influence and leadership in the Corinthian church not only in worship meetings but also in everyday life and the decision-making processes of the community. Against this assumption one cannot argue that Paul uses only 'brothers' to address the members of the community, for androcentric language functioned in antiquity just as today as generic, inclusive language.[33] Furthermore, this reading would explain the crucial place women are given in the discussion of marriage in chapter 7,[34] and especially, in the ring-composition of chapters 11.2—14.40, a section beginning and ending with a discussion of women's role.[35]

In this section persuasive argument breaks down and is replaced with strong appeals to authority. After a *captatio benevolentiae* in 11.2 that the Corinthians have observed the traditions which Paul preached to them, Paul in v. 3 emphatically ('but I want you to know') introduces a peculiar theological patriarchal chain: God-Christ-man-woman [the head or source of every man is Christ, the head of woman is man and the head of Christ is God] which is restated in v. 7 as 'man is the image and glory of God but woman is the glory of man'. The argument in 11.2–16 is so convoluted that we can no longer say with certainty what kind of custom or style Paul advocates for women prophets and liturgists. It is clear, however, that he does so because he wants them to know that the head or source of woman is man just as the head or source of Christ is God.[36]

Just as 11.2–16 ends with an authoritative assertion of the will of Paul, so does the argumentation in chapter 14 which demands silence, order, and subordination from speakers in tongues, interpreters of pneumatic speech, and prophets as well as from women or wives who participated in public discourse. 'What, did the word of God originate with you. . . . If anyone believes that he or she is a prophet, or spiritual, he or she should acknowledge that what I am writing to you is a command of the Lord. If anyone does not recognize this, he or she is not recognized.'[37] Did Paul fear that some of the Corinthian women prophets would not acknowledge what he is writing? Why does he need to appeal to a command of the Lord which is not known from anywhere else? Finally, it is interesting to

33. See my book *In Memory of Her: A Feminist Theological Reconstruction of Christian Origins* (New York: Crossroad Press, 1983) 41–67.

34. See *In Memory of Her*, 220–26.

35. 1 Cor 11.2–16 and 14.33b–36 are both considered to be post-Pauline 'pastoral' insertions by W. Munro, *Authority in Paul and Peter: The Identification of a Pastoral Stratum in the Pauline Corpus and 1 Peter* (SNTSMS 45; Cambridge: Univ. Press, 1983) 67–82; I consider not only 1 Cor 11.2–16 but also 1 Cor 14.33b–36 as authentically Pauline since these verses cohere with the overall argument in chapter 14; cf. also the structural analysis of W. A. Grudem, *The Gift of Prophecy in 1 Corinthians* (Lanham: Univ. Press of America, 1982) 231–55, however with a different interpretational emphasis.

36. For discussion of the literature and interpretation see *In Memory of Her*, 226–30.

37. D. W. Odell-Scott. 'Let the Women Speak in Church: An Egalitarian Interpretation of 1 Cor 14:33b–36', *BTB* 13 (1983) 90–93 has argued that 1 Cor 14.33b–36 represent a slogan of the Corinthian males against whom Paul argues. Cf. also C. H. Talbert, 'Paul's Understanding of the Holy Spirit', in C. H. Talbert (ed.), *Perspectives on the New Testament. Festschrift Stagg* (Macon, Ga.: Mercer University Press, 1985) 95–108. However, in light of Paul's argument in 1 Cor 11.3f. such an interpretation is not convincing.

note that in the final greetings of Corinthians only is Prisca mentioned after Aquila, a change which corresponds to patriarchal custom.

If, as I have argued, a reconstruction of the argumentative situation cannot assume without discussion that only oral information was communicated by Chloe and, conversely, can also not demonstrate that the written information was entrusted to Stephanas as the head of the 'official delegation', then the question must be raised anew: What was the rhetorical situation to which Paul's letter can be construed as a 'fitting response'? Although the literature extensively debates whether there were four, three, or only two factions in Corinth,[38] it usually overlooks that the information of Chloe's followers about ἔριδες (Pl.) that is, that debates, discussions, or competing claims among them are reinterpreted by Paul (λέγω δὲ τοῦτο) as party-strife. It is Paul, and not the Corinthians, who understands their debates as party or school divisions.

Whereas Hurd has insisted that the Corinthians have not challenged Paul's authority as an apostle,[39] Dahl has argued that Paul had to establish himself as the apostle of the whole church. He construes the following situation: The quarrels in Corinth were the result of the Corinthians' debate about whom to consult for answers to some of their questions. Some might have suggested Cephas, because he was the foremost among the twelve, whereas Paul's credentials were questionable; others might have voted for Apollos who, in contrast to Paul, was a wise and powerful teacher; many might have argued that they did not need to consult anyone since as a spirit-filled people, they were mature and competent enough to decide for themselves. Since the letter was sent to Paul, those like Stephanas who thought that Paul was their best choice must have won out. While the official delegates, Dahl argues, represented the Corinthians as loyal to Paul, the people of Chloe informed him of the quarrels and latent objections which broke into the open after the delegation had left. 'As a consequence, Paul had to envisage the possibility that his letter containing his reply might easily make a bad situation worse. Quarrel and strife might develop into real divisions of the church, if his recommendations were enthusiastically received by one group and rejected by others.'[40]

However, Paul's rhetoric of biting irony, and his attempt to shame, belittle, and undermine the Corinthian self-understanding, is hardly designed to lessen tensions and to prevent divisions. Rather, just as in chapter 15, so also here the combative style of this section introduces dualistic categories and antagonistic alternatives.[41] Moreover, Hurd has observed that Paul's attitude towards the Corinthian community 'contained a substantial measure of veiled hostility'.[42]

---

38. Cf. Ph. Vielhauer, 'Paulus und die Kephaspartei in Korinth', *NTS* 21 (1975) 341–52; F. Lang, 'Die Gruppen in Korinth nach 1. Korinther 1–4', *Theologische Beiträge* 14 (1983) 68–79; and especially the overview by Hurd, *Origin*, 95–107; Conzelmann, *I Corinthians*, 33–34 (Excursus: The Parties); and H.-J. Klauck, *I. Korintherbrief* (Würzburg: Echter Verlag, 1984) 21–23.

39. Hurd, *Origin*, 111.

40. N. A. Dahl, *Studies in Paul*, 49ff.

41. W. Stenger, 'Beobachtungen zur Argumentationsstruktur', 85f.

42. Hurd, *Origin*, 113.

While I agree with Dahl that the rhetoric of 1 Corinthians clearly intends to *establish* 'the authority of Paul *as* the founder and father of the entire church at Corinth', I would argue that it does not reestablish, but introduces such unique authority claims. In other words, Paul does not defend his authority as an apostle among other apostles but rather, argues for his authority as the *sole* founder and father of the Corinthian community.

Paul establishes a line of authority: God, Christ, Paul, Apollos, Timothy, Stephanas, and other local co-workers to which the Corinthians should subordinate themselves because they are 'Christ's'. Paul understands himself not only as Christ's steward and administrator, but he can also say that 'in Christ he has begotten them through the gospel' (4.15). Moreover, the Corinthians do not only owe their Christian existence to Paul's generative action but they also are seen as passive objects (field, temple) of his missionary activity that establishes his unique authority. This hierarchy of authority which extends from God down to the community seems to be paralleled by the one established in 11.2: God-Christ-man-woman. Just as the community is admonished to 'subordinate' itself, so women/wives are not allowed to speak in the *ekklesia* but must subordinate themselves. In 1 Corinthians Paul introduces the vertical line of patriarchal subordination not only into the social relationships of the *ekklesia,* but into its symbolic universe as well by arrogating the authority of God, the 'father', for himself. He does so in order to claim for his interpretation of divine power the authority of the singular father and founder of the community. He thereby seeks to change the understanding of persuasive-consensual authority based on pneumatic competence accessible to all into that of compulsory authority based on the symbolization of ultimate patriarchal power. It is Paul who introduces into the early Christian special missionary movement 'Christian patriarchalism which receives its coloration from the warmth of the ideal of love'.[43]

FOURTH: HISTORICAL RECONSTRUCTION AND THEOLOGICAL ASSESSMENT

The rhetorical situation to which 1 Corinthians can be understood as a 'fitting' response might then be conceived as follows: The Corinthians had debates and discussions as to how their new self-understanding expressed in the pre-Pauline baptismal formula in Gal 3.28 could and should be realized in the midst of a society rooted in the patriarchal status divisions between Greeks and Jews, slave and free, men and women, rich and poor, wise and uneducated. Especially, the notion 'no longer male and female', that is, patriarchal marriage is no longer constitutive for the new creation in the Spirit, presented difficult practical problems in everyday life and might have raised questions such as: Did baptism abolish all

---

43. E. Troeltsch, *The Social Teaching of the Christian Churches* (New York, 1931) 1:78; cf. Theissen, *Social Setting,* 107.

previous marriage relationships; could one, especially a woman, remain marriage-free even though this was against the law; if one remained married to a pagan, what about the children; did it mean that one could live together without being married; did it imply that one should live as a celibate and abstain from all sexual intercourse; was marriage only a legal, but not also a religious affair; did women just like men have control over their own body and life?

In this situation of competing interpretations and practices of what it meant to realize the 'new life' in Christ the Corinthian community decided to write to different missionaries for their advice since some of their differing interpretations most likely originated in different theological emphases of these missionaries and their preaching. Thus, the Corinthians and not Paul understood God's power of salvation in the sense that John Schütz has described as Paul's own understanding of power. 'Power is not a personal attribute because power is essentially an historical force. The central role of the gospel as an interpretation of this power stems from the fact that all Christians have access to power through the gospel. The apostle may preach the gospel, he may thereby make power available but he does not himself provide it or control it.'[44]

Given this understanding, the consultation of missionaries did not mean that the community would accept and obey such advice without critical evaluation and judgment in terms of their own pneumatic self-understanding. Moreover, among those asked, Paul could have appeared—at least to some—as the least qualified in terms of pneumatic competence: he preaches on the elementary level and, as for actual pastoral experience, he hasn't shown up for a long time and does not live a lifestyle appropriate to an apostle. Paul must somehow have learned that some of the Corinthians held his pneumatic as well as his practical competence in low esteem. In order to secure their acceptance of this interpretation he had to argue why they should follow his instructions and not those of others if these turned out to be different from his own.

If Paul had only to assert that he shared access to divine power for building up the community with the Corinthians and other apostles we could understand 1 Cor 1–4 as an apology for his apostleship and spirit-filled status. Yet, Paul asserts more than this when he presents himself not only as the father of the community who in analogy to God, the Father, has begotten or brought forth the community in Christ through the gospel, but also as the one who has the power to command and to punish,[45] although he ostentatively chooses persuasion and

---

44. J. H. Schütz, *Paul and the Anatomy of Apostolic Authority* (London: Cambridge Univ. Press, 1975) 285.

45. Cf. C. Forbes, 'Comparison, Self-Praise and Irony: Paul's Boasting and the Conventions of Hellenistic Rhetoric', *NTS* 32 (1986) 14, who suggests two alternative models: 'those of a parent with children whose position is guaranteed by his paternity and of an ambassador, whose position is guaranteed by his sender'. For a different understanding cf., however, B. Holmberg, *Paul and Power. The Structure of Authority in the Primitive Church as Reflected in the Pauline Epistles* (Philadelphia: Fortress Press, 1980) 188f.; for the function of the father-title in Paul's symbolic universe cf. N. R. Peterson, *Rediscovering Paul*, 104–50.

love. Therefore, whenever, as in 1 Cor 11.1–16 or 1 Cor 14.33b–40, appeals and arguments break down, he resorts to commands and claims the authority of Christ and that of other churches. His rhetoric does not aim at fostering independence, freedom, and consensus, but stresses dependence on his model, order and decency,[46] as well as subordination and silence. His theological reasoning and skilful rhetorical argument demonstrate, however, that the rhetorical situation required persuasion but did not admit of explicitly coercive authority.[47] Whom did Paul seek to persuade to accept his interpretation as 'authoritative'? Following the lead of Theissen, Bünker has argued, as we have seen, on grounds of a formal rhetorical analysis that the intended or inscribed audience against whom Paul argues are the few members of the community of high social status and considerable education who have caused the party-strife in Corinth. However, this claim that the intended readers are those who have caused the problems in Corinth can be maintained only if 1 Corinthians is classified as forensic or judicial discourse. In deliberative discourse the author does not seek to pass judgment but to appeal to the audience so that they will make the right decision for the future just as an orator appeals to the *ekklesia,* i.e. the voting assembly of freeborn men, to make the right political decisions for the common good of the *polis.* If my assessment of 1 Corinthians as deliberative discourse is correct, then Paul appeals to those who, like himself, were of higher social and educational status. They should make the ecclesial decisions which are, in his opinion, necessary in Corinth. His emphatic recommendation of Stephanas speaks for this understanding. His 'veiled hostility' and appeal to authority in the so-called women's passages indicates, however, that he does not include women of high social and educational status in this appeal.

One could object to my thesis that Paul appeals to the well-to-do and knowledgeable male members of the community by pointing to 1 Cor 1.26–29, where he reminds the Corinthian community that not many of them—when called— were wise, powerful, and highborn according to worldly standards. Rather, God has chosen what is foolish, weak, low, despised, even what is nothing in the world.[48] This objection is not valid, however, because Paul does not say here that God has chosen the foolish, low, weak and despised in order to make them wise, powerful, strong, and esteemed, a theology which the baptismal self-understanding of the Christians in Corinth seems to have asserted. Paul himself confirms this theological self-understanding of the Corinthian community in the *proem* in which he gives thanks that in Christ Jesus the Corinthians were made

---

46. Cf. also S. Barton, 'Paul and the Cross: A Sociological Approach', *Theology* 85 (1982) 13–19. 18: 'Paul augments his authority by focusing attention on how he himself interprets "Christ crucified", thereby increasing dependence on himself as leader'.

47. For different understandings of authority in antiquity and today cf. Th. Eschenburg, *Über Autorität* (Frankfurt: Suhrkamp, 1976); R. Sennett, *Authority* (New York: Vintage Books, 1980); D. H. Wrong, *Power: Its Forms. Bases, and Abuses* (New York: Harper & Row, 1979).

48. Cf. L. Schottroff, 'Nicht viele Machtige. Annäherungen an eine Soziologie des Urchristentums', *Bibel und Kirche* 40 (1985) 2–8.

rich in everything, in all speech and in all knowledge, lacking in nothing. The whole letter documents this baptismal self-understanding of the many who were nothing in the eyes of the world before their call, but who now have freedom, knowledge, wisdom, riches, and power over their own bodies and life in their new kinship-community.

This pattern of reversal—the old life is contrasted with the new, weakness with power, foolishness with wisdom—also shapes Paul's own theological pattern of cross and resurrection. But he asserts it over against the baptismal self-understanding of the Corinthians for whom being in Christ, that is, in the church, meant living the 'new creation' here and now. Paul also contrasts his former life with his new life in Christ, but he sees this new life as suffering, hardships, and cross, the marks of his apostleship for which he will be recompensed in the future. This different emphasis in theological interpretation must be rooted in Paul's own experience. If, as Hock and Bünker have argued, Paul himself was of relatively high social and educational status,[49] then his experience of becoming a follower of Jesus Christ was quite different from that of the majority of the Corinthians. While for them their call meant freedom and new possibilities not open to them as poor, slave and even freeborn women in 'the eyes of the world', for Paul and those of equal social status, their call implied relinquishment of authority and status; it entailed hardship, powerlessness, and foolishness 'in the eyes of the world'.

---

49. R. Hock, 'Paul's Tentmaking and the Problem of His Social Class', *JBL* 97 (1978) 555–64; M. Bünker. *Briefformular*, 75; C. Forbes, 'Comparison, Self-Praise and Irony', 24.

Chapter 12

Women Holy in Body and Spirit: The Social Setting of 1 Corinthians 7*

Margaret Y. MacDonald

INTRODUCTION

Margaret MacDonald, who two years earlier had published her groundbreaking work, *The Pauline Churches* (Cambridge: Cambridge University Press, 1988), highlights in this essay the prominent role that women played in the Corinthian church. Through a gender-sensitive reading of 1 Cor 7, MacDonald concludes that women were also the main proponents of the radical sexual asceticism about which Paul here feels so uneasy. She argues that their behaviour was inspired by the ideal that 'there is neither male nor female' (Gal 3.28) and that they were seeking to transcend sexual differentiation (as expressed in marriage and the rearing of children). The printed extract forms the first section of the essay, entitled 'Paul's Opponents: Worshipping Women'. The second section examines Paul's response, arguing that Paul resisted the liberated behaviour of the women out of

*Extracted from M. Y. MacDonald, 'Women Holy in Body and Spirit: The Social Setting of 1 Corinthians 7', *NTS* 36 (1990) 161–81; here pp. 162–73. Reprinted by permission of Cambridge University Press, The Edinburgh Building, Shaftesbury Road, Cambridge.

a concern for order within the community and for social respectability within the wider world.

This essay draws attention to gender issues in Paul's text (gender signals are frequent in 1 Cor 7) and shows how a heightened awareness of those issues can enable a fuller reconstruction of the community addressed. MacDonald's essay was published in the same year as Antoinette Wire's *Corinthian Women Prophets*. Wire too connects the women worshipers referred to in ch. 11 with the sexual ascetics of ch. 7, but goes further than MacDonald in maintaining that these women were involved in all the other problems and issues Paul addresses in the course of the letter, and are in fact Paul's opponents throughout.

While there remain questions as to how fully the actual situation Paul addresses can be reconstructed, through the studies of MacDonald, Wire, and others—including of course the groundbreaking feminist work of Elisabeth Schüssler Fiorenza—scholars have been made much more aware of the need to account for the prominence and role of women in Corinthian Christianity. Feminist studies have also raised important questions about the interests and (gendered) location of contemporary interpreters, exposing some of the reasons why the Corinthian women have often been marginalised or ignored (see further chs 11, 21).

Further Reading

W. Deming, *Paul on Marriage and Celibacy: The Hellenistic Background of 1 Corinthians 7* (SNTSMS 83; Cambridge: Cambridge University Press, 1995).

E. Schüssler Fiorenza, *In Memory of Her: A Feminist Theological Reconstruction of Christian Origins* (2d ed.; London: SCM, 1995), esp. ch. 6.

J. M. Gundry-Volf, 'Controlling the Bodies: A Theological Profile of the Corinthian Sexual Ascetics (1 Cor 7)', in *The Corinthian Correspondence* (ed. R. Bieringer; Leuven: Leuven University Press, 1996) 519–41.

C. Briggs Kittredge, 'Corinthian Women Prophets and Paul's Argumentation in 1 Corinthians', in *Paul and Politics: Ekklesia, Israel, Imperium, Interpretation* (ed. R. A. Horsley; Harrisburg: Trinity Press International, 2000) 103–9.

Wire, *Corinthian Women Prophets*.

When we speak about the Corinthian community as a whole, attitudes towards sexuality seem contradictory. The matter is complicated by the contrast between the asceticism reflected in 1 Cor 7 and the libertine attitude visible in 1 Cor 5–6.[1] On the one hand, the incest case described in 1 Cor 5, and the warning against taking the members of Christ and making them members of a prostitute in 1 Cor 6.15–20, indicate that, in light of the Corinthians' newfound freedom in Christ (cf. 1 Cor 4.8; 15.12), all things were permissible with respect to sex. On the

---

1. Scholars are divided with respect to the exact nature of the problems in Corinth. For example, compare the hypothesis of W. Schmithals who believes the main problem involves a libertine attitude (*Gnosticism in Corinth*, 234) with that of O. L. Yarbrough who believes that 'ascetic' elitism was the main issue (*Not Like the Gentiles: Marriage Rules in the Letters of Paul* (SBLDS 80; Atlanta: Scholars Press, 1985] 124–25).

other hand, some Corinthians saw their transcendence of the material world reflected in complete abstinence from sex—abstinence that would apparently result in both the avoidance of intercourse within marriage and the rejection of marriage altogether (1 Cor 7.1–9).[2] These were the Corinthians who would champion the slogan, 'It is well for a man not to touch a woman' (1 Cor 7.1).[3]

The polarization of attitudes towards sexual morality in Corinth ironically triggers the same response within Paul: fear of the dreaded disease 'immorality' (πορνεία). It is a report of incest (possibly made by Chloe's people—1 Cor 5.1; cf. 1 Cor 1.11) which leads to Paul's impassioned argument about the importance of the community ridding itself of all immorality. It is because of the temptation of immorality that marriage should take place among those who do not possess the gift of celibacy and that physical union must remain an integral part of the life of the couple (1 Cor 7.1–7, 9).[4] The modern reader is often disheartened by Paul's failure to develop a theology of marriage in more positive terms. But Paul's interest was less in exposing the significance of abstinence or marriage in the Lord, than in protecting a community where immorality threatened. Moreover, while a modern reader might be inclined to see marriage and celibacy as the predominant points of contrast in 1 Cor 7—a contrast which continues to have significant meaning in our own time—for Paul, the more important opposition seems to have been between celibacy/marriage and immorality. Celibacy might allow for a more perfect representation of the freedom of the eschaton, but marriage is also good, and for some, because of the temptation to immorality, it is the only desirable choice.

In 1 Cor 7 Paul explicitly links marriage (which must include physical union) with the avoidance of sexual immorality: 'But because of sexual immorality, each man should have his own wife and each woman her own husband' (1 Cor 7.2). It is possible that the Apostle's words came as somewhat of a shock to those Corinthians who perhaps were convinced that their abstinence from sex was by far the best precaution against any immorality. What better sign of separation from the outside world than continence?[5] Ironically, Paul feared that the Corinthians' scrupulous attitude could lead to disaster—precisely the kind of immoral behaviour he sought to avoid. He provides no specific case of abstinence leading to indulgence in 1 Cor 7, but 1 Cor 5 assures us that he had been reminded of the dangers of immorality looming over Corinth by the report of the incest case (1 Cor 5.1). In Corinth, defiling the holy community and perhaps

2. See Hurd, *Origin,* 155–57.

3. See D. R. MacDonald, *There Is No Male and Female: The Fate of a Dominical Saying in Paul and Gnosticism* (Philadelphia: Fortress, 1987) 69–72, esp. p. 70. Note that 'to touch a woman' is a euphemism for sexual intercourse; see Hurd, *Origin,* 158. Whether 1 Cor 7.1b is a slogan or a straightforward statement of Paul's position is a matter of debate. See for example discussion in R. Scroggs, 'Paul and the Eschatological Woman', *JAAR* 40 (1972) 295–96.

4. 1 Cor 7.36–37 might be added to this list if it refers to an engaged couple and not to a father's duty towards his unmarried daughter.

5. O. L. Yarbrough, 'Elitist Sexual Ethics in Corinth' (paper presented at the annual meeting of the SBL, December 1987) 13.

also incurring the disrespect of outsiders was, in Paul's estimation, a very grave threat.[6] With his eye on the outside world, Paul announces with disgust: 'Such immorality is not even found among the Gentiles' (1 Cor 5.1).

In contrast to Paul's general warnings in 1 Cor 7, a specific case of enthusiastic celibate efforts leading to immoral action is mentioned by the author of the Pastoral Epistles. Without losing sight of the distance between Paul and the author of the Pastorals, the instructions concerning widows in 1 Tim 5 may prove useful in an attempt to describe the social setting of 1 Cor 7.[7] The efforts on the part of the author of the Pastorals to limit the membership of enrolled widows to older women probably indicates that the office, with its celibacy requirement, was a popular one (1 Tim 5.9–11). Yet, the reference to violation of the celibacy pledge and straying after Satan implies that immorality and apostasy were taking place (1 Tim 5.11–15). Widows, who are also instructed in 1 Cor 7.39–40 (without reference to male counterparts), had become a source of serious concern for the author of the Pastorals. The activity of these women seems to have resulted in the slander of the good repute of the community (1 Tim 5.14). They had apparently become attracted to false teaching (2 Tim 3.6)—teaching which included a command to abstain from marriage (1 Tim 4.3). Moreover, as in the Corinthian letter, we find evidence that ascetic tendencies may have been related to the belief that one had already transcended the boundaries of the material world; the false teachers proclaimed that the resurrection had already happened (2 Tim 2.18; cf. 1 Cor 4.8; 1 Cor 15.12).[8]

Unfortunately, a straightforward correlation between the situation in Corinth and the situation in the community of the Pastorals cannot be drawn. Nevertheless, the fact that a strong pro-celibacy teaching seems to have caused problems in both communities leads one to ask whether the activity of the young widows of 1 Tim 5 had a forerunner in Corinth. Were women especially drawn to the strongly ascetic teaching? Had some who so fervently sought to live purely lapsed into some kind of immoral behaviour? Having separated from their husbands, had some entered into questionable liaisons with other males, as is perhaps suggested by 1 Cor 7.10–11? Was the activity of women especially visible to critical onlookers who were to be treated cautiously as outsiders, but with respect as potential converts? First-century Corinth is indeed renowned among New Testament scholars not only for a variety of attitudes towards sexual morality, but also for housing problematic women.

6. That Paul's instructions on marriage and sexual morality reveal an interest in the relationship between church communities and the outside world is suggested by 1 Thess 4.3b–5. O. L. Yarbrough has noted the similarity between Paul's language and Jewish paraenesis which served to distinguish the community of the Diaspora from the outside world. See *Not Like the Gentiles*, 86–87.

7. On the relation between the authentic epistles and the deutero-Pauline writings see M. Y. MacDonald, *The Pauline Churches: A Socio-historical Study of Institutionalization in the Pauline and Deutero-Pauline writings* (SNTSMS 60; Cambridge: Cambridge University Press, 1988).

8. For detailed arguments to support this description of the social setting of 1 Tim 5 see M. Y. MacDonald, *The Pauline Churches*, 167–68, 176–89.

Investigations of such passages as 1 Cor 11.2–16 and 1 Cor 14.33–36 have led to numerous conclusions about the nature of the problems with women in the Corinthian community. Moreover, it is commonly observed that in contrast to Gal 3.28, Paul omitted the male/female pair when he spoke of unity in Christ with reference to Gentiles/Jews and slaves/free in 1 Cor 12.13. This may have been deliberate on the Apostle's part, given his knowledge of the situation in the community. Perhaps Paul had previously told the Corinthians that in Christ 'there is neither male nor female' and they had sought to put the gospel of freedom into practice by eliminating the distinction between the sexes.[9] A second link with Gal 3.28 is suggested by the fact that in 1 Cor 7.17–28 Paul follows a discussion of the social divisions of circumcision/uncircumcision (17–19) and slave/free (21–23) with consideration of the desirability of marriage (25–28).[10] Although it is impossible to arrive at any certainty about the relationship between Gal 3.28 and the activity of females in Corinth, it is most often to this relationship that scholars turn when discussing the origin of the theology which inspired the Corinthian women.[11] A recent study of the background of Gal 3.26–28 and its significance for understanding 1 Corinthians, *There is No Male and Female* by D. R. MacDonald, is especially relevant to the present discussion of the social setting of 1 Cor 7.[12]

MacDonald argues that Gal 3.27–28 originated in the Dominical Saying recorded in the Gospel of the Egyptians: 'When you tread upon the garment of shame and when the two are one and the male with the female neither male nor female' (Clement of Alexandria *Strom.* 3.13.92) and found in similar versions in *2 Clement* and the *Gospel of Thomas* (*2 Clem.* 12.2; *Gos. Thom.* 37, 21a, 22b).[13] After a careful study of the occurrences of the saying, MacDonald proposes the following hypothesis about its meaning: 'When you tread upon the garment of shame' points to the necessity of trampling on the body in order that the believer might achieve perfection. 'When the two are one' refers to the reunification of the sexes, the return to the perfection of the androgyne. Finally 'the male with the female neither male nor female' is the consequence of the reunification—abstinence from sexual relations.[14] A study of the circles he identifies with the Dominical Saying, Valentinian Gnosticism and early Syrian Christianity,

---

9. See J. P. Meier, 'On the Veiling of Hermeneutics (1 Cor 11.2–16)', *CBQ* 40 (1978) 217.

10. On the relationship between Gal 3.28 and 1 Cor 7.17–28 see S. S. Bartchy, *Mallon Chresai: First-Century Slavery and the Interpretation of 1 Cor 7. 21* (SBLDS 11; Missoula; Scholars Press, 1973) 174.

11. For a summary of the literature linking the situation in Corinth with Gal 3.28 see MacDonald, *No Male and Female,* 87–88, n. 75.

12. See especially ibid., 65–111.

13. See ibid., 17–21. Note that the Gospel of the Egyptians here should not be confused with its namesake from Nag Hammadi. Note also that MacDonald argues that the relationship between these versions is oral not literary; see p. 21. See also MacDonald's arguments in favour of the Dominical Saying being more primitive than Gal 3.27–28, pp. 114–26.

14. Ibid., 50; MacDonald traces the long history of the images of putting off garments and of making the two one in anthropological discussions among Greek philosophers. He argues: 'It is within the context of this philosophical tradition and its religious permutations in hellenized Judaism and Gnosticism that we should interpret the imagery of the Dominical Saying' (p. 25).

leads MacDonald to conclude that baptism constituted the Saying's performative setting.[15]

Both the Gospel of the Egyptians and Gal 3.27–28 contain garment imagery ('putting on Christ'—Gal 3.27), speak of unification, and mention the pair of opposites male/female. If, as MacDonald argues, Paul was aware of the Saying that later became recorded in the Gospel of the Egyptians or a very similar saying, it seems that the Apostle disagreed with the anthropology and soteriology it presupposed.[16] For Paul, the putting on of Christ at baptism did not mean release from the body and return to androgyny. As is implied by the use of the spatial term 'in Christ' throughout Gal 3.26–28, 'there is neither male nor female' referred to the ideal of social unification—membership in Christ's body where antagonisms were eliminated. The church was a new creation where alienated social groups—Jews/Greek, slaves/free, and men/women—could come together.[17]

The possible relationship between the proclamation 'there is neither male nor female' recorded by Paul in Galatians and the activity of Corinthian women leads one to consider whether a theology similar to that implied by the Dominical Saying inspired Paul's pneumatic opponents in Corinth. It is likely that the problem underlying 1 Cor 11.2–16 involves the activity of pneumatic Corinthian women who, during ecstatic worship, believed that they had transcended sexual differentiation.[18] These women symbolized their status by becoming like men; they removed their veils—symbols of the inferiority and subordination which characterized their day-to-day living.[19] According to MacDonald, the activity of the Corinthian women is to be understood as one of many examples from antiquity of women imitating the male appearance in an effort to become androgynous.[20] Paul responded to this quest for liberation (which seems to have included some devaluation of what is particularly female) by speaking of the indispensability of women as women (1 Cor 11.11–12), but also by legitimating the subordinate status of women in the community on the basis of his understanding of Genesis.[21]

If indeed the theology of the Dominical Saying inspired the pneumatic Corinthian women, the fact that some sought to avoid sexual relations at all costs should come as no surprise. The link between the notion of salvation as a return to androgynous perfection and abstinence from sexual relations implied by the Dominical Saying is reinforced by other passages in the sources where it is cited. For example, the Gospel of the Egyptians contains the following question and

15. See ibid., 50–63. On the relation between baptism and asceticism in the early church see A. Vööbus, *Celibacy, A Requirement for Admission to Baptism in the Early Syrian Church* (Stockholm: Papers of the Estonian Theological Society in Exile, 1951); and R. Murray, 'The Exhortation to Candidates for Ascetic Vows at Baptism in the Ancient Syriac Church', *NTS* 21 (1974) 59–80.

16. MacDonald, *No Male and Female*, 113–26.

17. Ibid., 119–26, esp. pp. 121, 126.

18. The exact nature of the problem addressed in this passage has long been debated. See the discussion of the various possibilities in MacDonald, *No Male and Female*, 81–91.

19. Ibid., 72–98; see pp. 108–9.

20. Ibid., 98–102.

21. Ibid., 108–10.

answer: 'Salome said, "How long will people die?" Jesus answered, "As long as women bear children"' (Clement of Alexandria *Strom.* 3.9.64). Similarly, this passage might be interpreted as a plea for sexual asceticism: 'Jesus said, "I have come to destroy the works of the female"' (Clement of Alexandria *Strom.* 3.9.63).[22]

Of course we shall never know whether or not the Dominical Saying was actually known by the Corinthians, but the remarkable interest in the sayings of Jesus with respect to sexuality in 1 Cor 7 implies that they were using such sayings to support their position (1 Cor 7.10, 12, 25).[23] In fact, we need only look so far as the synoptic tradition to find sayings that might justify a radically ascetic attitude (e.g. Luke 14.26; 17.26–27; 18.29–30; 20.34–35).

It seems that women who removed their veils mentioned in 1 Cor 11 may also be of primary concern in 1 Cor 7.[24] But if this is so, why does not Paul himself link celibacy with women baring their heads? The contrast between Paul's qualified approval of celibacy and determined rejection of women removing their veils is probably related to the difficulty of his own position. He was convinced of the need to break the link between a theology with which he fundamentally disagreed and the gift of celibacy which he cherished if it were exercised by the truly gifted. He sought to do this by rooting his discussion of marriage in his own theology— a theology suited to a world which was on the verge of transformation, but which was still very much capable of inducing troubles in community life.

The possible relationship between women removing their veils while the community gathers for prayer and prophecy (1 Cor 11.4–5) and ascetic tendencies in the community suggests a link between continence and a ritual context. Studies of ritual by social scientists have alerted us to the fact that ritual is extremely important for the development of a religious worldview. Clifford Geertz, for example, notes that for the participant in a religious performance the ritual becomes the realization of a particular religious perspective—both a model of what is believed and a model for believing it.[25] In a manner that recalled the momentous event of their baptism, the women in Corinth who removed their veils during ecstatic worship were probably simultaneously experiencing and

22. Ibid., 30–31. See also *Gos. Thom.* 37, 49, 75, 79, 104, 112, 114; *2 Clem.* 12.5. On sexual asceticism in the *Gospel of Thomas* see for example the discussion of the contrast between logion 79 and Luke 11.27–28; 23.29 in J. É. Ménard, *L'Évangile Selon Thomas* (NHS V; Leiden: E. J. Brill, 1975) 180–81. On the similarities between the Gospel of the Egyptians and the *Gospel of Thomas* see MacDonald, *No Male and Female*, 49 n. 105. On asceticism in *2 Clement* see MacDonald, *No Male and Female*, 41–43.

23. For an excellent treatment of the relationship between 1 Cor 7 and the sayings of Jesus congenial to asceticism in the Synoptics see D. L. Balch, 'Backgrounds of I Cor VII: Sayings of the Lord in Q; Moses as an Ascetic ΘΕΙΟΣ ΑΝΗΡ in II Cor III', *NTS* 18 (1972) 351–58.

24. MacDonald's hypothesis that the theology of the Dominical Saying inspired the Corinthian 'pneumatics' allows for a direct connection to be made between Paul's response to the problems involving women in 1 Cor 11 and his comments against obligatory celibacy in 1 Cor 7. In fact, MacDonald identifies such a connection, but does not discuss it in detail; see *No Male and Female*, esp. pp. 69–72, 110.

25. See C. Geertz, 'Religion as a Cultural System', in *Anthropological Approaches to the Study of Religion* (ed. M. Banton; London: Tavistock, 1966) 1–46, esp. p. 29.

expressing their connection with the Divine, their rebirth as a new perfect creation.[26] Of course, like all rituals, this one would have come to an end and they would have needed to deal with the everyday world once more. They may have been willing to put on their veils once again, but they nevertheless had been profoundly changed.[27] Their new status was visible to themselves and to outsiders as it was reflected in their continence.

Horsley has observed that the connection between celibacy and ecstatic experiences of worship in Paul's world is made especially clear by Philo's description of the ascetic sect, the Therapeutae.[28] The devotion of the Therapeutae has as its goal the vision of the Divine (*Contempl.* 12). Philo describes their 'sacred vigil' which involves the fusion of a male choir with a female choir. The lively worship of the Corinthians comes to mind:

> . . . they sing hymns to God composed of many measures and set to many melodies, sometimes chanting together, sometimes taking up the harmony antiphonally, hands and feet keeping time in accompaniment, and rapt with enthusiasm reproduce sometimes the lyrics of the procession, sometimes of the halt and of the wheeling and counter-wheeling of a choric dance. Then when each choir has separately done its own part in the feast, having drunk as in the Bacchic rites of the strong wine of God's love they mix and both together become a single choir, a copy of the choir set up of old beside the Red Sea in honour of the wonders there wrought (*Contempl.* 84–85).

The group that mixes together as a single unified choir follows a strict ascetic way of life which is in keeping with a dualistic vision of the world (*Contempl.* 34–37). Their contemplative identity means that homes and, at times, even spouses must be left behind (*Contempl.* 13, 18). With respect to their suitability as celibates, Philo shares none of Paul's worry about the danger of some lacking the required self-control. It is suggestive for the present discussion that when Philo speaks of sexual asceticism, his attention turns especially to the admirable behaviour of women:

> The feast is shared by women also, most of them aged virgins, who have their chastity not under compulsion, like some of the Greek priestesses, but of their own free will in their ardent yearning for wisdom. Eager to have her for their life mate they have spurned the pleasures of the body and desire no mortal offspring but those immortal children which only the soul that is dear to God can bring to the birth unaided because the Father has sown in her spiritual rays enabling her to behold the verities of wisdom (*Contempl.* 68).

26. On the relationship between baptism and 'pneumatic' activities in Corinth see MacDonald, *No Male and Female*, 67–69.

27. See Geertz, 'Religion', 38.

28. See R. A Horsley, 'Spiritual Marriage with Sophia', *VC* 33 (1979) 40–43; see Philo, *De Vita Contemplativa* (trans. F. H. Colson; 10 vols.; LCL; Cambridge: Harvard University Press, 1929–1962). A connection between asceticism and spiritual experiences is also discussed by Horsley in relation to Philo's description of Moses (*Mos.* 2.66–70), the Wisdom of Solomon, and devotion to Isis; see pp. 33–34, 38–40, 43–46.

While it is perhaps inappropriate to describe the Corinthian 'pneumatics' as either Philo-like mystics or as being akin to the gnostics of the second and third centuries, Hellenistic Judaism and Christian Gnosticism provide much valuable material for understanding the religious mentality of Paul's opponents.[29] It is likely that as in the case of the Therapeutae, the asceticism of the Corinthians was related to their ecstatic experiences in the midst of worship. However, both their sexual ethics and their ritual behaviour were shaped by, and indeed helped to shape, a theology which may well have included the Dominical Saying recorded in later gnostic writings.[30] Paul's opponents seem to have believed that they had transcended the material world (1 Cor 4.8; 15.12). They may have understood their rising with Christ at baptism as a return to primordial perfection (1 Cor 1.21—2.16; 3.18–23) which included a new sexless state (1 Cor 11.2–16). As they worshipped, women were inspired to symbolize their new status by removing their veils. With the ritual ended, the fact that the male was with the female meant that they should avoid sex altogether.[31]

At this point, an obvious question begs attention: Does 1 Cor 7 make any reference to women being the main proponents of ascetic teaching? A quick reading of 1 Cor 7 reveals a number of almost monotonously parallel statements about the obligations, respectively, of men and women—parallel statements that call to mind Paul's approach in 1 Cor 11. Yet a closer reading may indicate that the parallelism of 1 Cor 7 conceals a major concern with women. Divorcées, widows, and virgins are three groups of women that Paul is especially careful to exhort.

In 1 Cor 7.10–11 Paul applies the command from the Lord on divorce equally to believing men and believing women.[32] Yet the fact that the exhortation to females is longer and precedes the corresponding instruction to males (cf. 7.12–13) suggests that women were the main instigators of the separations.[33] If women were especially attracted to the false teaching, they may have sought to dissolve unions with their believing husbands on the basis of the fact that sex desecrated their holiness. Abstinence from sex within marriage would not be enough if the husband was less enthusiastic about celibacy than his wife and found the temptation of living with her too great.

---

29. See MacDonald, *No Male and Female*, 65–66.

30. On the relationship between human thought and the social context in which it arises see the valuable treatise on the sociology of knowledge by P. L. Berger and T. Luckmann, *The Social Construction of Reality* (Garden City, N.Y.: Doubleday, 1967).

31. See MacDonald, *No Male and Female*, 60. But note that spiritual transcendence for some in Corinth seems to have meant freedom to perform any sexual act (1 Cor 5.2; 6.12). See pp. 69–70.

32. Note that Paul is using the terms 'to separate' (χωρίζειν) and 'to divorce' (ἀφιέναι) interchangeably in 1 Cor 7.10–16; see the discussion in Jerome Murphy-O'Connor, 'The Divorced Woman in 1 Cor 7.10–11', *JBL* 100 (1981) 605.

33. Murphy-O'Connor notes that the structure of Paul's argument indicates that the Apostle may have had a particular case in mind. But Murphy-O'Connor believes that men were the main instigators of divorce here, arguing that, contrary to the usual reading, 1 Cor 7.10b should be translated as 'the wife should not allow herself to be separated from her husband'; see 'The Divorced Woman', 601–3. See the response to Murphy-O'Connor's hypothesis in Yarbrough, *Not Like the Gentiles*, 111 n. 67.

Paul's teaching in 1 Cor 7 closes with an instruction to widows without reference to male counterparts (1 Cor 7.39–40; cf. 1 Cor 7.8).[34] The fact that these women could possess a relatively large amount of autonomy in society at large, especially if they were financially independent, meant that they were in a position to make a substantial contribution to the leadership of early church communities as single women (cf. 1 Tim 5.13–14).[35] An interesting testimony to the resolve of these women is the impression Paul gives that he expects to be contradicted on the basis of some claim to spiritual authority. Widows may have understood their determination to remain unmarried as an extension of their experiences of the Spirit in the midst of worship. Perhaps they sought to impose their understanding on widows who found celibate life unattractive or financially difficult. Paul can agree that a widow is happier if she remains as she is, but acknowledges that this may not always be possible. With considerable irony, he states: 'I think that I, too, have the Spirit of God' (1 Cor 7.40; cf. 7.25).[36]

Paul's use of the term 'παρθένος' throughout 1 Cor 7.25–38 suggests that the virginity of women was considered to be extremely important by the ascetical party. Although there is nothing to indicate gender in the first instance (1 Cor 7.25), the three other uses of 'παρθένος' (1 Cor 7.28, 34, 36) in the passage refer to women.[37] Certainly Paul seeks to embrace the efforts of both men and women who remain unmarried within his eschatological perspective (1 Cor 7.26–34), but the special use of 'παρθένος' in 1 Cor 7.34 and 7.36 implies that the virginity of women was of central significance in Corinth and was causing considerable concern for Paul.

Paul speaks of the unmarried man (ὁ ἄγαμος) in 1 Cor 7.32–33, but of both the unmarried woman and the virgin (ἡ γυνὴ ἄγαμος καὶ ἡ παρθένος) in 1 Cor 7.34. It seems impossible to be clear about what Paul means by these two categories. If he were trying to distinguish virgins from other unmarried women such as widows, it is difficult to understand why he did not use more specific terminology.[38] Perhaps the best explanation is that Paul was clarifying the term 'unmarried' to be sure that the audience was well aware that he was addressing a specific problem in their community. It is as if Paul was saying: 'By "unmarried", yes I mean the virgins, those who strive to be holy in body and spirit' (1 Cor 7.34).[39]

---

34. C. K. Barrett argues that Paul probably addressed the circumstances of wives because he was thinking of a specific case; see *A Commentary on the First Epistle to the Corinthians* (London: Adam and Charles Black, 1968) 185.

35. Note that Augustan legislation encouraged widows and divorced women to remarry. But the legislation does not seem to have hampered the activity of wealthy widows who chose to remain in control of their affairs and were in fact praised for remaining faithful to the memory of their dead husbands; see Pomeroy, *Goddesses, Whores, Wives and Slaves: Women in Classical Antiquity* (New York: Schocken, 1975) 149–50, 158, 161; J. P. V. D. Balsdon, *Roman Women: Their History and Habits* (London: Bodley Head, 1962) 76–77, 89–90, 220–22; MacDonald, *Pauline Churches,* 185–87.

36. Barrett, *I Corinthians,* 186.

37. Ibid., see discussion pp. 173–85.

38. Ibid., 180–81 for consideration of possible meanings.

39. Ibid., 180.

That the heading 'virgin' was popular in Corinth and was causing the Apostle concern is also implied by the odd usage to refer to an engaged woman or daughter in 7.36.[40] Favouring the former interpretation, Barrett makes the following suggestion about the convictions of Paul's ascetic opponents: ' . . . perhaps it is significant of their point of view that a fiancée should be described as a virgin—the implication being that this is the important thing about her and that she would do well to remain as she is'.[41]

That Paul harbours a special concern for women in 1 Cor 7 comes as somewhat of a surprise since the impression one gains from the Corinthian slogan quoted at the beginning of his discussion is one of male initiative: 'It is well for a man not to touch a woman' (1 Cor 7.1). Moreover, falling prey to one's passions seems to have been a danger for both unmarried men and women (1 Cor 7.8–9). This, however, does not preclude the fact that the impulse for celibacy came mainly from women, since the celibate efforts of these traditionally subordinate members would most likely require the blessing of males if the community was to continue as a mixed group.[42] Indeed, male members of the community may have understood their own holiness as related to the preservation of the sexual purity of females.[43] For example, if the engaged couple translation of 1 Cor 7.36–38 is preferred, Paul is perhaps referring to a man's hesitancy to take as his wife a woman who is reminding him that she is doing far more for his sanctity by remaining his virgin than by becoming his bride. The fear that an engaged man might act inappropriately towards his virgin (violate her virtue) leads Paul to instruct that the man might do as he wishes and to reassure him that he is not sinning: the engaged couple may go on to marriage (1 Cor 7.36). If a man is to be joined to a woman at all, she is undoubtedly to be the pure vessel of 1 Thess 4.4—the wife taken in holiness and honour, not in the passion of lust like the pagans who do not know God.

The belief system of Paul's opponents in 1 Corinthians has frequently been described as one of 'realized eschatology'.[44] As Mercia Eliade has pointed out in his study of the doctrine of the androgyne, symbols depicting the abolition of

40. Ibid., 183–84. Note that some scholars have argued that the problem here involves 'spiritual marriages': couples living together without physical union. As Barrett points out, against this interpretation is the fact that we have no other evidence of 'spiritual marriages' from this early period and the difficulty of harmonizing Paul's apparent approval of the practice with 1 Cor 7.2–5. On this notoriously difficult passage see also the discussion by Conzelmann, *1 Corinthians*, 134–36; Hurd, *Origin*, 169–75; J. D. M. Derrett, 'The Disposal of Virgins', *Studies in the New Testament* (vol. 1; Leiden: E. J. Brill, 1977) 184–91.

41. Barrett, *I Corinthians*, 185.

42. From 1 Cor 7.28 and 7.36 it is clear that Paul acknowledges the authority of the male in marriage arrangements. Ibid., 176.

43. See the anthropological discussion by J. Pitt-Rivers, 'Honour and Social Status', in *Honour and Shame: The Values of Mediterranean Society* (ed. J. G. Peristiany; London: Weidenfeld and Nicholson, 1965) 45; see also the discussion in B. Malina, *New Testament World* (London: SCM, 1983) 42–48.

44. See for example Meeks, 'The Image of Androgyne: Some Uses of a Symbol in Earliest Christianity', *HR* 13 (1974) 202–3.

opposites and conflicts are eschatological symbols par excellence. They denote '. . . that the "profane" Universe has been mysteriously replaced . . . by a World purely spiritual in nature'.[45] The reunification of opposites could indeed serve as an appropriate way for Paul to legitimate the new pattern of relating between Gentiles and Jews in this new age (Gal 3.28). As the eschatological language of 1 Cor 7 indicates, the Apostle was convinced that the world was on the brink of transformation and that the celibacy of men and women was a sign of the transformation. But Paul could not agree with these opponents that the old universe had already been replaced by a world purely spiritual in nature, nor that celibacy was vital to the spiritual perfection of the entire community. It was simply that for Paul the conditions of the old world were still binding to a certain extent— the kingdom was not as yet perfectly realized. Immorality threatened and community members could still lose control.

45. M. Eliade, *Mephistopheles and the Androgyne* (New York: Sheed and Ward, 1965) 121.

Chapter 13

Σοφία in 1 Corinthians*

Michael D. Goulder

INTRODUCTION

In a series of essays and books, Michael Goulder has sought to revive an interpretation of early Christianity most famously associated with F. C. Baur (see ch. 1 above). According to this view the basic division in the early Christian movement was between a Pauline wing and a Petrine wing. Baur, and before him J. E. C. Schmidt, suggested that this major fault line in early Christianity was reflected in the divisions at Corinth (1 Cor 1.12), which were essentially between two groups, one following Paul, the other Peter. However, for a range of reasons—represented in a number of the essays in this book—this view of Corinthian Christianity has been widely rejected. In this essay, Goulder sets out his own reasons for supporting the view of a twofold division between Paul and Peter at Corinth. In particular, he focuses on the meaning of σοφία, 'wisdom', which is clearly a topic of especial concern for Paul in 1 Cor 1–3. Goulder's

*Extracted from Michael D. Goulder, 'Σοφία in 1 Corinthians', *NTS* 37 (1991) 516–34; here pp. 516–23. Reprinted by permission of Cambridge University Press, The Edinburgh Building, Shaftesbury Road, Cambridge.

proposal is that σοφία here refers not to some form of Greek sophistry but to the *Torah*, the Jewish law, and its interpretation. It is this tradition of 'words of wisdom' that Peter's followers at Corinth are promoting, and it is this against which Paul polemicises. Other aspects of Paul's writing in 1 and 2 Corinthians are also seen by Goulder as reflecting the same basic argument. Goulder's proposal has been subjected to criticism, notably by Christopher Tuckett, and goes against the grain of much recent study of the Corinthian correspondence, which rejects the Baur/Tübingen view of the Corinthian situation and focuses more on the Corinthian Christians in their Greco-Roman setting.

Further Reading

See also chapter 1.

M. D. Goulder, *Paul and the Competing Mission in Corinth* (Peabody, Mass.: Hendrickson, 2001).

M. D. Goulder, *A Tale of Two Missions* (London: SCM, 1994).

M. D. Goulder, 'The Unity of the Corinthian Correspondence', *Journal of Higher Criticism* 5 (1998) 220–37.

C. M. Tuckett, 'Jewish Christian Wisdom in 1 Corinthians', in *Crossing the Boundaries: Essays in Biblical Interpretation in Honour of Michael D. Goulder* (ed. S. E. Porter, P. Joyce, and D. E. Orton; Leiden: Brill, 1994) 201–19.

First Corinthians presents many problems,[1] whose difficulty consists in large measure in their interrelatedness; but the major problem of the first four chapters is the nature of the σοφία against which Paul polemicizes. This is especially mysterious because the apostle treats it with unquestionable seriousness, and yet it does not apparently recur in any other letter, not even in 2 Corinthians. As it is so closely linked in the text with the σχίσματα which are the topic of 1.12–17, 3.1–17 and 3.22–23, if not other verses, it is necessary to begin with a brief discussion of that question.

Paul ends 1.12–17 by saying that Christ sent him to evangelize 'not ἐν σοφία λόγου', and 3.18–23 begins, 'Let no one deceive himself: if any among you thinks he is σοφός, in this age . . .'; so the σχίσματα question and the σοφία question are intertwined. In 1.12–13 Paul speaks of four groups, under the names of Paul, Apollos, Cephas and Christ; and the same option is open at 3.22, 'whether Paul or Apollos or Cephas . . . all are yours, and you are Christ's, and Christ is God's.' However, there have been many doubts over the 'Christ' group,[2] leading to suggestions that there were only three groups; and from the beginnings of modern scholarship it has been argued that there were only two groups. In 1797 J. E. C. Schmidt suggested that the converts of Paul and Apollos were effectively one group, and that the second group regarded Peter as leader but expressed

---

1. Cf. G. Sellin, 'Hauptprobleme des Ersten Korintherbriefes', *ANRW* 11.25.4 (1988) 2940–3044.

2. These are listed in many commentaries: cf. recently E. Fascher, *Der erste Brief des Paulus an die Korinther*, 1. Teil (3. Aufl.; Berlin, 1984) 90–92.

their ultimate allegiance as Χριστοῦ.[3] This hypothesis was developed and made famous by F. C. Baur in the nineteenth century,[4] but has fallen on evil days in modern times because of the apparent absence of 'Judaizers' in 1 Corinthians.[5] But viewed on its own, Schmidt's hypothesis has much to be said for it.

(i) The reproaches over the σχίσματα run straight on into the σοφία discussion from 1.17, and in that there appears to be a polarization: the Pauline λόγος of the cross is set against the σοφία λόγου / λόγοι σοφίας, without the suggestion of some third 'gospel'.

(ii) When Paul draws the analogy of his mission with the building of a house, he speaks of the opposition in the singular: 'I laid a foundation and another (ἄλλος) builds on it. . . . If someone (τις) builds on the foundation . . .' (3.10ff.). We might have had ἄλλοι / τινες.

(iii) Paul sums the discussion up at 4.6. He has 'transferred' these things to himself and Apollos for two reasons (ἵνα-clauses), of which the second is, 'that none of you be puffed up for the one against the other (ὑπὲρ τοῦ ἑνὸς κατὰ τοῦ ἑτέρου)'. RSV's translation, 'in favour of one against another' is inaccurate: the opposition seems to be between *two* leaderships.

(iv) Those who were puffed up in 4.6 'judged' Paul in 4.3: 'But to me it is a very small thing that I should be judged (ἀνακριθῶ) by you or by human judgment: no, I do not even judge (ἀνακρίνω) myself.' Paul returns to this theme at 9.3, 'My reply to those who judge me (ἀνακρίνουσιν) is this'; and here the context is an attack on his apostleship. It is not easy to see how anyone could have drawn a distinction in apostolic authority between Paul and Apollos to the latter's advantage, while it is only too easy to see that such a distinction could have been drawn between Paul and Cephas. Indeed, this could well account for the critics being puffed up in ch. 4: they said to the Paulines, 'Our leader is an apostle, yours is not.' It is also easy to read 9.4–5, 12 as a sour comment on Peter: 'Have we not the right to eat and drink? Have we not the right to take round a Christian wife, like the other apostles, and Cephas? . . . If others share in this right over you, do not we more?' The unnecessary 'and Cephas' sounds like the bitter reflection of many 'judgments' on Paul. The argument implies that only apostles had the right to free hospitality, and suggests that it has been exercised by an apostle other than Paul, and perhaps his wife. Perhaps people said, 'Cephas was a true apostle, and the church paid for him, and his wife too.' Such a reading is strengthened by the presence of a passage of similarly sour, anti-Petrine tone in Gal 2. But

---

3. *Bibliothek für Kritik und Exegese* (1797) I, 91.

4. Baur cites Schmidt in 'Die Christuspartei in der korinthischen Gemeinde', *Tübinger Zeitschrift für Theologie* 4 (1831) 76 [cf. above p. 55].

5. Variations of it are defended by C. K. Barrett, 'Cephas and Corinth', in *Abraham unser Vater. Festschrift für Otto Michel* (Leiden, 1963) 1–12, and P. Vielhauer, 'Paulus und die Kephaspartei in Korinth', *NTS* 21 (1974/5) 341–52. But N. A. Dahl says of it: 'there is wide negative agreement that in 1 Corinthians Paul is not opposing Judaizers' ('Paul and the Church at Corinth according to 1 Corinthians 1:10—4:21', in *Christian History and Interpretation. Studies Presented to John Knox* [Cambridge, 1967] 315).

of course Paul wants any support he can have from Peter and James, and gladly cites their resurrection-appearances in 15.5ff. to help his case.

(v) On the other side, it is not at all likely that there was any real tension between Paul and Apollos. Paul mentions him in 16.12, in the same paragraph as Timothy, and has 'strongly urged him to visit you with the brethren', which he would hardly have done if he had not trusted him. The following clause, 'οὐκ ἦν θέλημα that he should come now', should surely be translated 'It was not God's will . . .'.[6] θέλημα is never used on its own of human will in the NT, but cf. Rom 2.18, γινώσκετε τὸ θέλημα, 'you know the will (of God)'; Matt 18.14, 'οὐκ ἔστιν θέλημα before my Father in heaven'. θέλημα is a direct rendering of the rabbinic *raṣon*. Furthermore, we have an account of Apollos in Acts 18 from Luke who was a Pauline Christian with the benefit of hindsight, and he is clearly presented there as an asset to the Pauline movement. So Schmidt's Paul-Apollos axis looks quite plausible.

(vi) The problematic genitive Χριστοῦ recurs twice in the NT. At 2 Cor 10.7 Paul says, 'If anyone trusts to himself that he is Χριστοῦ . . .', and the context is strikingly similar to 1 Cor 1: 'boasting' and ἐξουσία (10.8); judging (συγκρῖναι, 10.12); the same quotation from Jer 9.22–23, 'He that boasts, let him boast in the Lord' (10.17). But this time those involved are said to be Hebrews, Israelites, the seed of Abraham (11.22), and to think that Paul is inferior to τῶν ὑπερλίαν ἀποστόλων (11.5; 12.11); so it is open to us to think that both passages are concerned with Jewish Christians with a loyalty to the Jerusalem apostolate.[7] As they preach 'a different Jesus whom we did not preach' and a different gospel, there may be a Christological issue behind the term Χριστοῦ; but there is not sufficient evidence to make this clear. Similarly the Marcan logion, 'If anyone gives you a cup of cold water to drink in the name that you are Χριστοῦ . . .', has been associated with the old Jerusalem mission,[8] with the missionary making himself totally dependent on his hearers: Pauline missionaries earned their living. So such evidence as we have tends to support Schmidt's association of the Cephas and Χριστοῦ groups: they were 'Jewish Christians' in the sense of having a primary loyalty to Peter, John and James, whether or not they were Jewish by birth, and they may have had a non-Pauline Christology.

(vii) 1 Cor 4.6 is a cardinal text for understanding the Letter, because, having wrapped up his meaning for three chapters, Paul now kindly tells us what he has been doing, and why. The apparent meaning is this: 'I have represented the situation, brethren, as being about myself and Apollos for your sake, so that by us

---

6. Standard Jewish use omitted the divine name, *yᵉhi raṣon (lᵉpaneika)*, G. Schrenk, *TDNT* 3, θέλημα, 54; cf. E. Käsemann, *Commentary on Romans* (ET London, 1980 = Tübingen, 1973) 70, ad 2.18, 'As in I Cor. 16.12, θέλημα in the absolute denotes in good rabbinic fashion the divine will.'

7. Baur took it in this sense, 99; as does Dahl, art. cit, 323. But the meaning is much disputed, cf. Barrett, *The Second Epistle to the Corinthians* (London, 1973) 256–57.

8. Theissen, *Social Setting*, 67, 'The slogan ("I am of Christ") does not arise from local Christians but (at least originally) from itinerant missionaries (cf. Mark 9.41).'

you may learn the principle, The Bible and nothing but the Bible (τὸ μὴ ὑπὲρ ἃ γέγραπται) so that you may not be puffed up for one leadership (Cephas') against the other (ours).' Μετασχηματίζειν means to transform, as when Satan transforms himself into an angel of light (2 Cor 11.13ff.), or God will transform the body of our humiliation (Phil 3.21). So Paul says he is transforming 'these things' on to himself and Apollos—that is, the real issue was between the two of them and Cephas, but he has changed it to be as between himself and Apollos, for pastoral reasons (δι' ὑμᾶς).[9] He did a closely parallel thing at 1.13, 'Was Paul crucified for you?', taking the sting out of the discussion by limiting it to the unexceptionable instance of himself. So here he has spoken as if it were only his converts and Apollos' that were involved, with friendly images about planting and watering, so that the Corinthians may grasp the principle by them, i.e. by their complementary teaching (ἐν ἡμῖν). In this way they will not be seduced by the vacuous issue of Cephas' status (φυσιοῦσθε): but Cephas is carefully left anonymous throughout—he is τοῦ ἑνός here as he was ἄλλος at 3.10 and τις at 3.12–17. So the apparent meaning makes good sense. We are still left with the surprising τὸ μὴ ὑπὲρ ἃ γέγραπται, which I consider below. It is the key to understanding the Letter.

(viii) In 3.10 Paul contrasts his laying a foundation for the Corinthian church with the work of the ἄλλος who builds on it: 'for no one can lay another foundation than that which is fixed, which is Jesus Christ' (3.11). It has been thought[10] that there may be a polemical contrast here with claims that Cephas, as his name implies, was the true rock of the Church, with or without the support of Matt 16.18. While this proposal would hardly constitute an argument on its own, it is an attractive suggestion in the light of the preceding points.

(ix) But if Schmidt is right (albeit on rather different grounds from those he advanced himself), we have a final question to resolve. If there really were two parties, why does Paul so complicate the situation, representing it that there were four? He does it, as my old Theological College Principal used to say, from holy guile: he is trying to avoid a confrontation (μετεσχημάτισα . . . δι' ὑμᾶς). We may see him doing the same thing in 12–14. Ch. 14 makes it clear what the issue was: how was the precious time of church worship to be used? There were two principal competing activities: prophecy, that is edifying and inspired addresses; and tongues, that is incomprehensible ecstatic utterance. Paul is strongly in favour of the former, but he knows better than to say so directly. 'Now about spiritual gifts', he begins: there are a lot of different gifts, but the Spirit gives them all—wisdom, knowledge, faith, healing, miracles, prophecy, discernment of spirits, tongues, interpretation of tongues. Then we hear a long piece of sweet-reasonableness

9. So Barrett, *A Commentary on the First Epistle to the Corinthians* (2nd ed.; London, 1971) 105–6. M. D. Hooker, '"Beyond the Things Which Are Written": An Examination of 1 Cor. iv.6', *NTS* 10 (1963/64), 127–32, among others, takes the clause to refer to the images of gardening and building in ch. 3: but these are ten verses back, and there is no parallel for μετασχηματίζειν to mean 'express in metaphors'.

10. So Barrett, *First Corinthians*, 87–88.

about every part of the body needing every other part. Then the gifts are put in Paul's order, with a rider to desire the higher gifts: first apostles, second prophets, third teachers, then miracles, healers, helpers, administrators, and (last and least of all, though not of course said to be) tongues. As Paul is the only apostle around the place, and prophecy is second and tongues bottom, it is quite clear what Paul feels about the issue. But before he comes to discuss it in 14, he hives off to consider a still more excellent way. Thus the wise apostle has won the battle before he comes to fight it. He has complicated the issue and divided the enemy; and he has used exactly the same tactic at 1.12 with the σχίσματα.

For these reasons it seems to me that if we limit the discussion to the σχίσματα, Schmidt's hypothesis is soundly based. We have an alignment rather reminiscent of Galatians: Paul, Barnabas and Titus there, Paul, Apollos (at a different time) and Timothy here; Cephas and the other pillars there, Cephas and the other apostles here (9.5). But of course we cannot limit the discussion to the σχίσματα.

As is notorious, σοφία has a number of meanings in the first century, but a central meaning for Greek-speaking Jews was in association with *torah*. Σοφία had always been a practical wisdom, and the Stoics made it increasingly an ethical concept, with indeed a theological component: ἐπιστήμη θείων τε καὶ ἀνθρωπείων πραγμάτων.[11] *Hokmah* was a similar compound of the pragmatic and the religious in the Bible. Judaism had its own understanding of divine and human affairs, which led likewise to a pattern of life that was both ethical and a recipe for success: even in the later Biblical books there is a tendency to praise Wisdom as providing a way of living based on the fear of the Lord, and leading to riches and honour. By Ben Sira's time Wisdom was felt to be embodied in the Torah:

> In the beloved city likewise he gave me (Wisdom) rest;
> And in Jerusalem was my authority . . .
> All these things (Wisdom's blessings) are the book of the
>   Covenant of the Most High God,
> Even the law which Moses commanded us for a heritage
>   unto the Assemblies of Jacob.
>
> (Sir 24.11, 23)

Baruch 3.9—4.3 is a commendation of *torah* as Wisdom comparable to Ecclus 24, and beginning, 'Hear, O Israel, the commandments of life: give ear to understand wisdom': wisdom and the commandments are virtually identical. In time[12] the pre-existent Wisdom of Prov 8 was taken by some in this way to be the pre-

---

11. Aëtius, *Placita* 1.2; Sextus Empiricus, *Math.* 9.13; cf. G. Fohrer, *TDNT* 8, σοφία, 473. The phrase is a tag, and reappears in 4 Macc 1.16, and in Latin in Cicero, *Tusc.* 4.25.37.

12. M. Hengel, *Judaism and Hellenism* (ET London, 1974 = 2nd German ed. 1973) I, 161. Hengel cites J. Fichtner: 'Over against Hellenism and its wisdom, a wisdom in Judaism could only assert itself if it approximated to *the* factor which played the decisive role in this struggle on the side of the Jews: *the law*' (*Die altorientalische Weisheit in ihrer israelitisch-jüdischer Ausprägung* [Giessen, 1933] 127).

existent Torah, but the relationship is perhaps better expressed in 4 Macc 1.16, 'This wisdom, I assume, is *the culture* which we acquire from the Law.'

Martin Hengel saw the development of *ḥokmah* in Judaism as a defence against Hellenization; but it is possible to read the same evidence as a sign of Jewish outreach. Judaism sounded more attractive in Greek ears when presented as a σοφία, a wise way of life, based on revealed truth about God, honourable and leading to honour, rather than as νόμος, a set of divine rules with severe penalties attached. My proposal is that σοφία carries this meaning in 1 Cor 1–3, a way of life in accord with *torah*. We are encouraged to try this hypothesis by the probability (just discussed) that the σχίσμα by which Paul was distressed was that of Cephas, i.e. the Jewish Christians; for we should then have an explanation for the similar atmosphere of sourness with Cephas in Gal 2, which is also about the Law. It was indeed inevitable that there should be tension everywhere between Paul and Jerusalem about the Law, and sourness too. It is there in Galatians and Romans and Philippians, and soon after in Colossians and Ephesians and the Pastorals: it even comes in that uncomfortable text, 1 Cor 15.56, 'The power of sin is the law'.[13] It is really not conceivable that any mixed church of Gentiles and Jews could have evaded this central issue, especially once there was contact with the Jerusalem apostles. The difference in Corinth was one of vocabulary, and probably turned on the numerical balance of Jews in the community. Where there were many Jews, as in Antioch, or Asia Minor, or Rome, *torah* was naturally thought of as law: in other European cities like Corinth there were fewer Jews, and in discussion with Gentiles, as in the church, it was presented as σοφία.

Keeping *torah* does not mean observing 613 Biblical commandments from scratch. How would one know what they implied, what to do? It means knowing, and following, the interpretation of the Biblical Torah given by the Jewish community. Moses was believed to have received both written law and interpretation on Sinai,[14] and the latter came to be the core of the Oral Law in time, *torah šibe ʿal-peh*. The point is well put in the discussion in *b. Qidd* 49b: 'What is meant by Torah? The exegesis *(midraš)* of the Torah'. There follows a comment on who is competent to make this exegesis, and the answer is given, 'One who can be asked a matter of wisdom *(debar ḥokmah)* in any place, and he can answer it'. One needs to know these rulings, these points of law, these *dibre ḥokmah;* and the Greek for *dibre ḥokmah* is λόγοι / ῥήματα σοφίας'. Ben Sira already says of the scribe that 'he shall pour forth his ῥήματα σοφίας (39.6), and the context shows that these arise from his learning in the law and tradition,[15] and are his rulings. *1 Enoch* 99.10 says, 'Blessed are all those who accept the words of wisdom and understand them (Gk: learn them), and follow the paths of the Most

---

13. Fee, *First Epistle,* 806, is not untypical in calling it 'this theological aside'—like Cato the Censor perhaps, who was said to have ended every speech, 'Ceterum censeo delendam esse Karthaginem'.

14. *M. 'Abot* 1.1. G. F. Moore renders, 'Moses received the Law (written and unwritten) from Sinai', *Judaism* (Cambridge, Mass., 1927) I, 255–56.

15. Cf. J. A. Davies, *Wisdom and Spirit* (Lanham, Md., 1984) 18ff.

High': the words of wisdom show the way of God. The term used in the Mishnah for currently mooted halakhic interpretations is the similar *dibre ḥ^akamin,* the Words of the Wise.[16]

In 1 Cor 1–3, σοφία and σοφός are frequent on their own in the paradoxical theology passages, where Paul gives his own view of Christ as God's wisdom, or of God's wisdom hidden in a mystery: but in the directly controversial passages, where he indicates the opposition's position by prefixing the word 'not', σοφία tends to be associated with λόγος:

> ... not to baptize but to evangelize, not ἐν σοφίᾳ λόγου (1.17)
>
> I came not καθ' ὑπεροχὴν λόγου ἢ σοφίας proclaiming to you (2.1)
>
> my word and my preaching were not ἐν πειθοῖς σοφίας λόγοις (2.4)[17]
>
> that your faith should not be ἐν σοφίᾳ ἀνθρώπων (2.5)
>
> which also we speak, not ἐν διδακτοῖς ἀνθρωπίνης σοφίας λόγοις (2.13).

The five 'not's show clearly that in these verses Paul is countering a different teaching; and the σοφία-λόγος combination is not likely to be an accident because it recurs as the first of the gifts of the Spirit at 12.8, where Paul is doing his best to be conciliatory:

> For to one is given by the Spirit λόγος σοφίας.

Σοφία is not mentioned in Paul's equally tactful thanksgiving (1.4–9), but he opens the list there also with λόγος:

> that in everything you were enriched ἐν παντὶ λόγῳ (1.5).

The combined suggestion of these passages is evident. The Petrine Christian leaders were delivering halakha as under inspiration of the Spirit, 'words of wisdom' interpreted from the Bible. In the tactful, pastoral, unitive passages, the thanksgiving and ch. 12, Paul is prepared to go along with this (cf. 2 Cor 8.7); after all, he did it himself (1 Cor 7.40). But in fact he abominated such enrichment, and withers it with sarcasm in 4.8. They have supplanted his magisterial

---

16. *M. Neg.* 9.3; 11.7. E. Schürer, *The History of the Jewish People in the Age of Jesus Christ* (ed. G. Vermes et al.; rev. ed.; Edinburgh, 1979–87) 2, 342.

17. The long text is printed in NA[26] with brackets and a D vote—B. M. Metzger, *A Textual Commentary on the Greek New Testament* (UBS, 1971) 546. But it is stronger than this. πειθοῖ is an Atticism (dat. of the neuter Attic noun πειθώ), while the adj. πειθός is a hapax in all Greek writing. But it is formed from the verb like Matthew's φάγος, and Paul himself writes many such nouns/adjectives, λοίδορος, μέθυσος, μοιχός, πόρνος; no Greek father demurs at πειθοῖς.

evangel with 'the wisdom of a ruling' (1.17), with 'the superiority of a ruling or of wisdom' (2.1), with 'argued (πειθοῖς) words of wisdom' (2.4), with 'the wisdom of men' (2.5). The clearest phrasing is at 2.13, 'taught words of human wisdom'. It has nothing whatever to do with eloquence.[18] It is the delivery of *dibre ḥokmah,* which are not (Paul says) divine law at all, but mere human cleverness, taught in the Church as the Tannaim taught them in Judaism.

18. R. A. Horsley has argued for σοφία = eloquence in his 'Wisdom of Word and Words of Wisdom at Corinth', *CBQ* 39 (1977) 224–39. He bases the case on Philo, the basis of many cases: but the 'taught words of human wisdom' do not read naturally as eloquence.

Chapter 14

Thessalonica and Corinth: Social Contrasts in Pauline Christianity[*]

John M. G. Barclay

INTRODUCTION

Recent decades have seen an increased interest in the social aspects of the Pauline churches, and John Barclay's essay reflects this interest while exploring a neglected dimension of it: the social relations between Christians and non-Christians. The essay as a whole explores the contrasts between the two Pauline communities in Corinth and Thessalonica; only the section on Corinth is reproduced here. Barclay argues that the Christians at Thessalonica experienced conflict, suffering, and hostility in their relations with outsiders, a social experience linked with, and rendered meaningful by, their apocalyptic faith, with its stark contrasts between light and dark, those inside and those outside, and the expectation of an imminent end. By contrast, the Christians at Corinth seem to experience no conflict, no social dislocation. If the Thessalonians sense a rather stark boundary between church and world, the Corinthians seem to have little sense of such a boundary,

*Extracted from John M. G. Barclay, 'Thessalonica and Corinth: Social Contrasts in Pauline Christianity', *JSNT* 47 (1992) 49–74; here pp. 57–72. Reprinted by permission of The Continuum International Publishing Group.

at least in terms of their ongoing social interaction. Barclay suggests various reasons for this social experience on the part of the Corinthian Christians, relating it again to their particular perceptions of the Christian faith. The essay is important in two respects, both of which have been developed by others in further research: first, in drawing attention to the contrasts between the various Pauline churches—we should not assume that Corinth is a 'typical' example, or that all the Pauline churches were similar—and second, in highlighting the importance of Christian interaction with outsiders in shaping the social character and symbolic world of the Christian communities.

Further Reading

E. Adams, *Constructing the World: A Study in Paul's Cosmological Language* (SNTW; Edinburgh: T. & T. Clark, 2000) 85–103.

G. Schöllgen, 'Was wissen wir über die Sozialstruktur der paulinischen Gemeinden?', *NTS* 34 (1988) 71–82.

T. D. Still, *Conflict at Thessalonica: A Pauline Church and Its Neighbours* (JSNTSup 183; Sheffield: Sheffield Academic Press, 1999).

C. S. de Vos, *Church and Community Conflicts: The Relationships of the Thessalonian, Corinthian, and Philippian Churches with Their Wider Civic Communities* (SBLDS 168; Atlanta: Scholars Press, 1999).

SOCIAL HARMONY IN CORINTH

One of the most significant, but least noticed, features of Corinthian church life is the absence of conflict in the relationship between Christians and 'outsiders'. In contrast to the Thessalonian church, the believers in Corinth appear neither to feel hostility towards, nor to experience hostility from, non-Christians. In writing to the Corinthians, Paul certainly refers to the rejection and harassment which *he himself* experiences. He fought with 'wild beasts' in Ephesus, and claims to be in peril every day (1 Cor 15.30–32); he is hungry and thirsty, ill-clad, homeless and abused, a public spectacle, like a convict sentenced to die in the arena (4.9–13). But precisely in this passage, where he gives his own catalogue of suffering, Paul notes (with some bitterness) the painless experience of the Corinthians: 'We are fools for Christ's sake, but you are wise in Christ. We are weak but you are strong. You are held in honour, but we in disrepute' (4.10). In the light of Paul's usage of similar terms in 1.26–28, we might be inclined to think that he is referring here only to the minority of Corinthians with relatively high social status. But the ironic rebuke is directed at the whole church and may reflect a consciousness among the Corinthians that, whatever their social origins, their status had been enhanced by their adoption of Christianity.[1] It is particularly sig-

---

1. The terms in 4.10 do not, then, refer to the original social status of Paul's converts (*pace* Theissen, *Social Setting.* 72–73). But neither is it necessary to interpret them as indicating only the Corinthians' spiritual illusions (so Fee, *First Epistle,* 176–77; and W. Schrage, *Der erste Brief an die*

nificant that Paul refers to them as ἔνδοξοι (in contrast to the apostles who are ἄτιμοι) since the context shows that these terms concern their public reputation. Clearly, whatever individual exceptions there may be, Paul does not regard social alienation as the characteristic state of the Corinthian church.[2]

In fact there are plenty of signs suggesting the social acceptability of the Corinthian Christians. That some of them (presumably the wealthier) take their disputes to the civic law-courts (6.1–6) signals their confidence in the legal system; they do not anticipate that believers will receive prejudicial treatment at the hands of non-Christians. Corinthian Christians are invited to meals in the houses of non-believers (10.27) and, conversely, non-believing friends or neighbours might well drop in to the house where the Christian meeting is taking place (14.24–25). Most significant, however, is the fact that some of the leaders of the Corinthian church (whose examples others are likely to follow) are to be found as participants in parties and feasts in the dining rooms of the temples (8.10). As Theissen has shown, these people must be not only of some social status, but also sufficiently integrated into Corinthian society to be strongly disinclined to raise any objections on the grounds of religious scruple;[3] it was important for them to retain the social contacts which such temple-dinners provided. Of the individuals named in 1 Corinthians, leaders like Gaius and Stephanas might well have acquired their wealth through that trading and 'dealing with the world' which Paul lists as the occupation of some Corinthian Christians (7.30–31); and, of course, Erastus, as the οἰκονόμος τῆς πόλεως (Rom 16.23), whether or not he subsequently became aedile, must have sought some tolerable *modus vivendi* with his non-Christian associates at work.[4]

It is clear that Paul is somewhat uneasy about the degree of integration which the Corinthian Christians enjoy. To be sure, contacts with 'outsiders' are to be expected, and indeed welcomed, as opportunities for witness (9.19–23; 10.32–33; 7.16?). Paul is concerned that his converts should be able to buy freely in the meat-market and share non-cultic meals with unbelievers (10.25–27). He is careful to show that those married to non-Christians are not thereby polluted (7.12–16) and he recognizes as a general principle that complete separation from

---

Korinther [EKKNT 7.1; Zürich: Benzinger Verlag; Neukirchen-Vluyn: Neukirchener Verlag, 1991] 343). Paul's ironic contrast between the Corinthians and the apostles depends on the fact that the Corinthians have good grounds for considering themselves 'wise, strong and honoured', just as Paul has grounds for describing himself as the opposite.

2. While there are many opponents in Ephesus (ἀντικείμενοι πολλοί, 16.9) there is no hint of any such opposition in Corinth. The illness and death referred to in 11.30 is divine punishment, and the suffering of individual members in 12.26 is non-specific; there is no indication in either case of the agency of hostile parties. In 7.26 Paul refers in general terms to the 'present distress' (ἐνεστῶσα ἀνάγκη); this may refer to eschatological woes (cf. 7.28–29; Luke 21.23) or to difficult physical conditions in general (cf. 2 Cor 6.4; 12.10); there is nothing to indicate an experience of persecution.

3. Theissen, *Social Setting*, 121–43.

4. Theissen, *Social Setting*, 69–119. At 7.18 Paul appears to counter the desire of some of the Jewish converts to cover up the marks of circumcision. This indicates a concern to avoid dishonour, but it appears that opprobrium would attach to them not as Christians but as Jews!

the world is impossible (5.9–10). Nonetheless, he has a much more sectarian and separatist expectation of the social standing of the church than the Corinthians. He attacks their recourse to the law-courts not just for pragmatic reasons but on ideological grounds: it is absurd for Christians to submit to the judgment of the ἄδικοι and ἄπιστοι whom they will soon themselves judge, along with the rest of 'the world' (6.1–3).[5] In fact, 'this world' and 'the present age' are spoken of in consistently derogatory terms throughout the letter, for they, together with their rulers, are doomed to imminent destruction (1.18—2.8; 3.18–20; 7.31). In the Corinthians' easy dealings with the world Paul detects a failure to comprehend the counter-cultural impact of the message of the cross (1.18—2.5); the wisdom of the world to which they are so attracted is, he insists, a dangerous enemy of the gospel. Such a consistent stress on the church's distinction from the world would hardly have been necessary in Thessalonica! But in Corinth such things needed to be said, and with heavy emphasis. The Corinthians must be warned against the corrupting influence of 'bad company' (15.33). As the holy temple (3.16), they are a distinct body of 'saints', washed and purified through their baptism (6.11). Their dealings with the world must be controlled by the ὡς μή principle which recognizes its imminent collapse (7.29–31).

In fact there is good evidence to suggest that the Corinthian Christians were quite conscious of their difference from Paul on this matter. Paul's remarks about his earlier letter (5.9–13) indicate that the relationship between believers and nonbelievers had already been a contentious issue between them. It is possible that the strange outburst in 2 Cor 6.14—7.1 is a fragment of that earlier letter, with its clarion call to separate from unbelievers.[6] But even if it is not, and if, as Paul now claims (5.10), his earlier letter urged only separation from wayward Christians, that would still represent an attempt to establish boundaries quite different from those the Corinthians are willing to accept. While allowing a degree of social contact with 'outsiders', Paul still paints the starkest contrast between the church and the world. He understands the church as a community whose rules govern all departments of life and he expects the members to find in it their primary and dominant relationships: their ties to their fellow ἀδελφοί and ἀδελφαί are to be more significant than any others.[7] The Corinthians, however,

5. What concerns Paul is not the embarrassment caused by the public display of dirty linen, nor the corruption endemic in Corinthian civil courts (so B. Winter, 'Civil Litigation in Secular Corinth and the Church: The Forensic Background to 1 Corinthians 6.1–8', *NTS* 37 [1991] 559–72). It is the fact that the Corinthian judges are 'unbelievers' and representatives of 'the world' which makes them inappropriate adjudicators of the affairs of believers. If, as appears likely, Paul refers to them as οἱ ἐξουθενημένοι ἐν τῇ ἐκκλησίᾳ (6.4), the apocalyptic venom is unmistakeable.

6. See the discussion by V. P. Furnish, *II Corinthians* (AB 32A; Garden City, N.Y.: Doubleday, 1984) 375–83. If, as most concede, this passage does not belong in its present context, it is much more likely that it has been interpolated from another part of Paul's correspondence with Corinth than from some other Pauline (or non-Pauline) source. The usual objection against the identification with the 'earlier letter' is that it urges separation from unbelievers; but this is precisely how the Corinthians have understood it, and Paul's claim in 1 Cor 5.10 that he meant otherwise is supported by a suspiciously ambiguous πάντως.

7. Hence the rule on excommunication in 5.1–13; it is assumed that contact with 'a brother' will corrupt the church in a way that contact with 'outsiders' will not.

seem to understand the social standing of the church quite differently. They see no reason to view the world through Paul's dark apocalyptic spectacles and are no doubt happy to enjoy friendly relations with their families and acquaintances.[8] Their reluctance to excommunicate even such a flagrant moral offender as the man discussed in ch. 5 may suggest that they do not see the church as a moral arbiter at all; they may have considered that it had no claim on their lives outside the worship gatherings. The behaviour of the wealthier members at the Lord's Supper and the legal disputes between members are eloquent testimony to the lack of close affective ties within the church; and it is clear, from their continued participation in temple-dinners, that those who are socially well-placed set much more store on the opinions of their non-Christian friends than on the feelings of their 'weaker' Christian ἀδελφοί. Paul's vision is of a church community, where members are open to the world but nonetheless forever conscious of the difference between 'insiders' and 'outsiders', and where the intense relationships among members of the family make belonging to the church the core of their existence. The Corinthian Christians apparently do not see themselves in this light; and their different self-perception is surely not unconnected to the harmony they enjoy in their relationships with non-Christians.[9]

THE CORINTHIAN INTERPRETATION OF CHRISTIAN FAITH

The title of this section is of course over-simplistic. There is no single interpretation of the Christian faith operative in the Corinthian church, but many different perspectives existing alongside or in competition with one another. There are libertines and ascetics, rich and poor, weak and strong—not to mention the four parties whose slogans Paul ridicules in 1 Cor 1–4. In contrast to the Thessalonian church, where no major differences of opinion are detectable, the Corinthian church contains a complex tangle of varying interests and opinions.

Yet it is still possible to talk of a dominant ethos in the Corinthian church, a consistent theological pattern which is the recognizable target of Paul's critical comments in most sections of the letter.[10] Judging from Paul's citations of the Corinthian letter in ch. 8, the leading Christians in Corinth are proud of their knowledge (γνῶσις); and this, it seems, is what Paul has in view in his discussion

---

8. N. Walter rightly notes the oddity for Gentiles of the notion that religion could be the cause of suffering, in 'Christusglaube und heidnische Religiosität in paulinischen Gemeinden', *NTS* 25 (1979) 422–42.

9. On 'boundaries' in general, see Meeks, *First Urban Christians*, 84–110; cf. M. Y. MacDonald, *The Pauline Churches* (Cambridge: Cambridge University Press, 1988) 32–45. However, in both cases their description of the boundary-rules of 'Pauline Christians' are generalizations over-dependent on statements made by Paul himself, while MacDonald adopts uncritically Wilson's model of a 'conversionist sect'. The different views and different circumstances of Paul's churches are not adequately explored.

10. The problems in reconstructing Corinthian theology are fully laid out by Schrage, *Der erste Brief an die Korinther*, 39–47; but he rightly does not despair of the task altogether.

of wisdom (σοφία) in 1.18—3.23.[11] In his concern to disparage 'the wisdom of the world' and to relativize knowledge (1.18—2.5; 3.18–23; 13.8–12), Paul does not clearly describe what content the Corinthians gave to it; but we know that it concerns the understanding of mysteries (13.1–2) and it seems to include some conviction of the oneness of God and the insignificance (or non-existence) of εἴδωλα (8.4–6).

What is sufficiently clear is that the special insight the Corinthians enjoyed was a product of their much vaunted possession of the Spirit. We can legitimately deduce from Paul's ironical remarks in 2.6—3.3 that these Corinthians considered themselves πνευματικοί and τέλειοι in a way which set them apart from the ordinary mass of ψυχικοί.[12] When Paul claims that he too possesses the Spirit of God (7.40), we can be sure that we are picking up echoes of Corinthian claims; indeed Paul directly describes them as ζηλωταὶ πνευμάτων (14.12; cf. 14.1, 37). They had first drunk deeply of the Spirit at baptism (12.13) and they continued to be nourished at the Lord's Supper with the πνευματικὸν βρῶμα and πνευματικὸν πόμα (10.3–4). It was in such gatherings for worship that their possession of the Spirit was vividly displayed—first of all in glossolalia (polemically relegated to the end of the list by Paul), but also in prophecy and inspired speech of every kind. First Cor 11–14 provides a fascinating glimpse of the electric atmosphere of such gatherings; the sparks of the Spirit, in the shape of prophecy, tongues and knowledge (13.8), flew indiscriminately between male and female πνευματικοί (11.4–5).

The confidence provided by this surge of spiritual energy is evident in the slogan of authorization, πάντα ἔξεστιν. The primary context for its use seems to have been in matters of food (6.12–13; 10.23), and, in particular, the consumption of meat imbued with cultic associations. How far this principle of ἐξουσία was extended, it is difficult to know: perhaps as far as the conscious rejection of sexual taboos (5.1–2). The 'knowledge' provided by the Spirit was evidently a versatile commodity; it also provided a sense of immunity and of indifference to apostolic warnings.

Some features of Corinthian practice and belief are not so easily explained. It is unclear, for instance, what motivated the sexual asceticism which prompted a major section of the Corinthians' letter to Paul. Sexual abstinence, in varying degrees, was advocated for so many reasons in early Christianity that the pursuit of parallels could lead us in many different directions.[13] Perhaps the most plau-

---

11. It is possible that Paul deliberately changes the terminology in this passage. While he can only be positive about the possession of γνῶσις, apart from the danger of arrogance (1.5; 8.1–3; 1 Thess 4.5; Gal 4.8–9), it is easier to rubbish an attachment to σοφία, whose connotations are more ambiguous. 'The wisdom of the world' can denote mere sophistry and 'the wisdom of words' mere rhetorical ingenuity; it would have been a lot harder to build pejorative associations into a discussion of 'knowledge'.

12. It is generally recognized that Paul here polemically reuses Corinthian vocabulary (cf. 15.44–46); such terms are not used similarly in other letters. See B. A. Pearson, *The Pneumatikos-Psychikos Terminology in 1 Corinthians* (SBLDS 12; Missoula, Mont.: SBL, 1973).

13. See especially P. Brown, *The Body and Society: Men, Women and Sexual Renunciation in Early Christianity* (London: Faber & Faber, 1989).

sible explanation is the one most closely tied to the Corinthians' passion for πνευματικά. Both in Judaism and in Graeco-Roman religion it was recognized that receptivity to the divine was greatly improved where there was no interference from sexual activity. Perhaps, like Philo's Moses, the πνευματικοί in Corinth wished to hold themselves 'continually in readiness to receive prophetic oracles' and to that end 'disdained sexual intercourse'.[14] Even Paul considers prayer a good reason to abstain from sex (7.5) and it is not unreasonable to surmise that the women who aimed to keep themselves holy in body and spirit (7.34) were those who most desired to act as channels of the Holy Spirit in their prayer and prophecy (11.5).[15]

It is also not entirely clear why some of the Corinthians said there was no resurrection of the dead (15.12). Paul uses such a variety of counter-arguments in ch. 15 that it is not easy to identify his target, and it remains possible that he partially misrepresents or misunderstands the Corinthian position.[16] However, if the extensive argument about σῶμα in 15.35–58 is not wholly irrelevant, it would appear that it was the notion of bodily resurrection in particular (rather than continuance beyond death in general) which the Corinthians could not accept. And this again can best be explained in the light of the Corinthians' fascination with πνευματικά. The human person was generally regarded, according to their cultural koine, as a hierarchical dualism of soul and body; few could imagine, or wish for, a bodily existence beyond death. But the gift of the πνεῦμα, with the extraordinary and special powers which it brought, would serve to sharpen this dualism and to throw the body further into the shade of inferiority. In their ecstatic experiences they rose high above the tawdry concerns of the body—indeed, even above the realm of the mind (14.19); in moments of ecstasy it was unclear whether they remained within the body at all.[17] From this perspective the body would obviously seem a hindrance one could well do without (6.13); the notion of a bodily resurrection would be particularly unpalatable to such πνευματικοί.

It has become the scholarly fashion to refer to Corinthian theology as an example of 'realized' or 'over-realized' eschatology. While some dispute continues about the relevance of 2 Tim 2.18 (those who claim 'the resurrection is past already'), it is widely held, on the basis of 4.8 and Paul's continual references to the future, that the Corinthians considered themselves to have arrived already in the sphere of heavenly glory. But it is important to be aware how Paul's perspective on the Corinthian church tends to control our description of them. *In Paul's view* the freedom, knowledge and spiritual ecstasy enjoyed by the Corinthians

14. *Mos.* 2.68–69; see Brown, *The Body and Society,* 65–82; and, for Judaism, G. Vermes, *Jesus the Jew* (London: SCM Press, 1973), pp. 99–102. Compare the decades of celibacy practised by Anna (Lk. 2.36–37) which established her credentials as a reliable prophetess.

15. M. Y. MacDonald, 'Women Holy'.

16. The continuing debate on such matters is most recently reviewed in A. J. M. Wedderburn, *Baptism and Resurrection* (WUNT 44; Tübingen: Mohr, 1987) 6–37.

17. Cf. Paul's uncertainty in his competitive account in 2 Cor 12.1–10. On the possible understandings of ecstasy in the Graeco-Roman world, see Wedderburn, *Baptism and Resurrection,* 249–68.

constituted a falsely claimed pre-emption of eschatological glory: 'Already you are filled! Already you have become rich! Without us you have come into your kingdom!', he sarcastically remarks (4.8). But did the *Corinthians* see their experience as related to an eschatological time-frame like this? Did they consider that they had already entered the future, or did they simply not operate with Paul's typical contrasts between present and future? Paul downplays present Christian knowledge as partial and imperfect (13.8–12) because he holds an apocalyptic worldview in which the future will be radically new and glorious in contrast to the present (15.42–44): 'if for this life only we have hoped in Christ, we are of all people most to be pitied' (15.19). But the Corinthians apparently see nothing pitiable about the present, because their non-apocalyptic perspective anticipates no radical disjunctions in the future. Their Spirit-filled lives are not an early experience of the future; they simply consider themselves to have reached the heights of human potential. If Paul had read Philo's descriptions of the soul's ascent above the concerns of the world to the pure vision of reality or of the wise man's ecstatic and joyous contemplation of divine truths, 'borne aloft into the heights with a soul possessed by some God-sent inspiration', he would no doubt have scribbled in the margin, 'Already you are filled!'[18] It would be misleading to describe Philo's theology as '(over-)realized eschatology'; his theological framework is simply non-eschatological. Perhaps this is also true of the Corinthian Christians.[19]

Unlike the Thessalonians, the Corinthians did not regard their Christian experience as an eager anticipation of a glory ready to be revealed at the coming of Christ. Rather, their initiation in baptism and their receipt of the Spirit had

18. *Spec.* 3.1–2; cf. *Opif.* 70–71; *Deus* 148–51; *Gig.* 31, 53, 60–61; *Somn.* 2.234–36.

19. This parallel with Philo is not meant to suggest that Corinthian theology is derived from 'Hellenistic Judaism', as has been argued by Pearson (*The Pneumatikos-Psychikos Terminology*) and by R. A. Horsley (in a number of articles, including 'Pneumatikos vs. Psychikos; Distinctions of Spiritual Status among the Corinthians', *HTR* 69 [1976] 269–88 and '"How can some of you say that there is no resurrection of the dead?": Spiritual Elitism in Corinth', *NovT* 20 [1978] 203–31). Their (and other similar) attempts to pinpoint the 'background' to the Corinthians' theology in 'analogies' and 'parallels' from Philo and Wisdom of Solomon are problematic on several counts.

a. They fail to explain what is different and new in Corinth, in particular the heavy emphasis on πνεῦμα (and its associated adjective πνευματικός). In their concern to deny that the Corinthians have adopted a 'Gnostic' package of terms and ideas, they have simply substituted a package from 'Hellenistic Judaism'. The extent to which the Corinthians may be forging new language under the influence of Christian teaching and their experience of the Spirit is not explored.

b. Their thesis puts some weight on the role of Apollos as the mediator of such 'Hellenistic Jewish wisdom speculation'. But one can hardly imagine Paul urging Apollos to return to Corinth (1 Cor 16.12) if he was responsible for an interpretation of Christianity which so greatly threatened Paul's gospel. In any case, many of the Jewish features of this theology (the oneness of God and nothingness of 'idols', the emphasis on πνεῦμα and its connection with knowledge) could have been as easily derived from Paul and from the LXX as from Apollos!

c. Many of the purported parallels from Philo are from passages where Philo strives to interpret the biblical text in terms drawn from Stoic or Platonic philosophy. It is quite possible that the Corinthians, without any Platonic influence, were engaged in a similar process, combining their Hellenistic theological culture with Jewish terms and traditions taught by Paul. They were forging a form of Judaized Hellenism, parallel to (in the strict sense, not dependent on) Philo's Hellenized Judaism. This would account for the fact that Paul associates their 'wisdom' with the interests of Greeks, not Jews (1.22).

signified the grant of a superior insight into divine truths. The regular infusion of the Spirit in the Lord's Supper gave them privileged access to knowledge, and the display of spiritual powers in worship confirmed the superior status which they had attained. They did not daily look up to heaven to await the coming of the Son who would rescue them from the wrath to come, nor did they eagerly search for signs of their impending vindication. Their Christian enlightenment, through the agency of the divine Spirit, was their salvation, and their prophetic, glossolalic and miraculous powers were the proof of its effectiveness.[20]

FACTORS INFLUENCING THE CORINTHIAN INTERPRETATION OF FAITH

We come now to the most difficult stage of this investigation. In the case of the Thessalonian church we saw an obvious correlation between their apocalyptic understanding of Christianity and the social alienation which they experienced from the very beginning. I have now set out the evidence for the notable absence of hostility in the Corinthians' social relations and have sketched in outline their interpretation of Christian faith, with its distinctive emphasis on Spirit and knowledge. The question thus arises: can we posit in this case, too, some correlation between the structure of their symbolic world and the character of their social experience?

We must consider first what other factors might have been at work in shaping the Corinthian hermeneutics.

a. By the time Paul writes 1 Corinthians, there have been other Christian teachers active in Corinth and some would attribute the particular ethos in Corinth to such figures. Attention has focused especially on Apollos, whose name continually recurs through 1 Cor 1–4.[21] Now, it would be rash to deny that Apollos may have had some influence in this connection, but he can hardly bear the sole, or even the chief, responsibility for the theological stance of the Corinthians. In 1 Corinthians Paul nowhere suggests (as he does to the Galatians) that his converts started off running well, but have been misled by subsequent instruction.

---

20. I have resisted referring to this interpretation of Christianity as 'gnostic'. New Testament interpreters this century (notably Schmithals, *Gnosticism*, and U. Wilckens, *Weisheit und Torheit* [Tübingen: Mohr, 1959]) have so muddied the waters with their loose combination of sources that this term is still liable to mislead (even if one adopts the distinction between *gnosis* and Gnosticism). There are in fact some important similarities between Corinthian theology and that which became popular in educated 'Gnostic' circles in later generations, some of whom found parts of the Corinthian letters extremely congenial. But if 1 Cor 8.4–6 reflects Corinthian views at all, it is incompatible with that radical pessimism about the material world which is one of the hallmarks of Gnosticism.

21. See, e.g., C. K. Barrett, 'Christianity at Corinth', in *Essays on Paul* (London: SPCK, 1982) 1–27; cf. the views of Pearson and Horsley discussed above in n. 19. The reference to the Cephas party in 1.12 has led some to posit the influence of conservative (Palestinian) Jewish voices; so, most recently, Goulder, 'Σοφία'. His thesis founders on the distinction he is forced to create between the advocates of σοφία in 1 Cor 1–4 and of γνῶσις in 1 Cor 8–10.

The burden of the blame lies on the Corinthians themselves, not on Apollos. As far as we know, in the first formative period of the church's life it was Paul alone who had the dominant influence, and there is no clear indication that the Corinthian church has undergone a radical shift since Paul left the scene.

b. That leads us to ask whether Paul himself preached the gospel in Corinth in different terms from those he had used in Thessalonica. Did he abandon apocalyptic language on his way south from Macedonia? We are hampered here by our lack of information about the way Paul first preached in Corinth. Apart from the creed in 15.3–5, the tradition about the Lord's Supper (11.23–26) and his exaggerated claim that he knew nothing among them except Christ crucified (2.1–2), we have no direct evidence to go on.[22] However, I think there are strong reasons to doubt that there was any significant change in Paul's message between Thessalonica and Corinth. When he writes 1 Corinthians Paul has just as much an apocalyptic understanding of the gospel (6.1–3; 7.25–31; 15.20–28) and just as sectarian a view of the church (see above) as in his initial preaching and subsequent letter to the Thessalonians. It is unlikely that Paul has done a double about-turn, first abandoning apocalyptic then taking it up again. Moreover, it is highly probable that Paul wrote 1 Thessalonians precisely while he was on his initial visit to Corinth. The apostle could be all things to all men, but it is doubtful that even he could present such an apocalyptic face in his letter to one church but effectively veil it in his preaching to another!

In fact, one can well imagine how the apocalyptic emphases in Paul's preaching could give rise to a concentration on knowledge as the focus of salvation. An essential element in many forms of apocalyptic thought, including Paul's, is the announcement of secret truths to a select coterie. In Paul's ministry this elite group is defined by initiation through baptism and by receipt of the divine Spirit. It was natural for the Corinthians to conclude that they had been given access in the Spirit to mysteries hidden from others. In other words, the *mode* of revelation was the all-important fact for the Corinthians (not least because it was re-enacted in miraculous ways at each gathering); the *content* of the message could be either ignored or reinterpreted. The possibility of variant interpretations of similar language can be well illustrated from 1 Cor 2.6–16. Here Paul probably adopts a number of the Corinthians' terms, which emphasized their sense of privilege in the knowledge and communication of 'deep truths'. Paul is able to rework this language, and to fill it with apocalyptic content, by stressing the eschatolog-

22. Hurd's reconstruction of Paul's original preaching in Corinth is subject to criticism on a number of counts. It posits the unlikely influence of the 'Apostolic Decree' on Paul in causing him to undergo a fundamental volte-face in his theology (only to revert towards its original form in 1 Corinthians!). He follows Knox in abandoning the chronology of Acts and thus creates a crucial interval between the mission to Corinth and the composition of 1 Thessalonians. This reordered Pauline chronology has rightly failed to gain wide support. Despite this, I am in general agreement with Hurd's thesis that the Corinthians' theology arises from Paul's own preaching; but instead of Hurd's suggestion of radical changes in Paul's thought, it is only necessary to imagine a particular socially- and culturally-related Corinthian hermeneutic.

ical nature of the truths revealed (2.7, 9). One can imagine, then, a reverse process in which an apocalyptic message is interpreted by the Corinthians in non-apocalyptic terms: the eschatological message could be lost under the impact of its revelatory medium.

c. It seems, then, that the Corinthians' style of faith is not entirely the responsibility of Paul nor wholly the result of later Christian instruction. We need to investigate also the responsibility of the Corinthian Christians themselves. The fact that most were of Gentile origin (12.2) is not a sufficient explanation: so were the Thessalonian believers. Would we come closer to an answer if we focused on their social status? G. Theissen's well-known social investigations of the Corinthian church have certainly demonstrated the importance of the few leading members of relatively high social status; and one would be inclined to think that higher social standing and greater exposure to Hellenistic education might play a significant role in the interpretation of the Christian faith. Those deeply enmeshed in the social networks of Corinthian life at a higher level would certainly have a lot to lose if they adopted too sectarian a mentality; and their Hellenistic training would give them an established mental framework within which to understand Paul's message.

The social status of the dominant minority in the Corinthian church is certainly a factor of some significance. But it would be a mistake to build everything on this foundation alone. In discussing Thessalonica I suggested that there was no necessary correlation between economic deprivation and an apocalyptic world-view; similarly, in Corinth, wealth and its associated social status are not necessarily wedded to a non-apocalyptic and non-sectarian perspective. It is possible for those of high status to undergo major social dislocation and significant resocialization, under the influence of a newly adopted ideology or as a result of social denigration by others. Thus, we cannot rule out the possibility that some of the 'weak' in Corinth—those who had scruples about eating food offered to idols—could have been among the wealthier members of the church; indeed, if they were present at the same dinner parties as the strong (10.27–30) we would have to assume that they were of the same social class.[23] Their unease about such food was, in that case, the product of a strong theological conviction about the dangers of 'idols' which overrode their social convenience. But even if such social dislocation is not self-imposed, it can be imposed by others. The Corinthians' retention of their social status was only possible so long as others did not reject them as 'impious' or 'atheist'. In other words, continuing social interaction with 'outsiders' is at least as significant in determining the Corinthian outlook as initial social status.

---

23. It is crucial to Theissen's argument (*Social Setting*, 121–43) that the 'weak' are socially inferior and that the informant in 10.28 is not a Christian, However, see the contrary opinion on 10.28 in C. K. Barrett, *A Commentary on the First Epistle to the Corinthians* (London: A. & C. Black, 2nd ed., 1971) 239–40; cf. earlier, J. Weiss, *Der erste Korintherbrief* (Göttingen: Vandenhoeck & Ruprecht, 1910) 264–65.

When the Corinthian church was founded it did not, apparently, suffer the social ostracism experienced by its sister church in Thessalonica. It is possible that this was because the leading converts deliberately played down the potential offensiveness of their faith, and this may be not unconnected to their social status. But it is intriguing to note that even Paul did not run into trouble in Corinth the way that he did in Thessalonica. Although he lists his woes in 1 Cor 4.9–13 and 15.30–32, he does not locate any of them in Corinth itself. Indeed, it is striking that the account in Acts 18 has him staying in Corinth more or less peacefully for 18 months. The narrator seems to have felt the need to give some explanation of this unusual phenomenon; he records a specific vision of the Lord which reassures Paul: 'I am with you and no-one shall attack you to harm you; for I have many people in this city' (Acts 18.10). The only opposition comes from some Jews, and their attempt to arraign Paul before Gallio is abortive (Acts 18.6, 12–17). Even after this incident Paul is under no compulsion to leave the city.

The correlation between the harmony of the Corinthians' social context and their particular theology is evident at a number of levels.

a. In the first place, the Corinthian focus on knowledge and possession of the Spirit creates a distinction from the mass of ordinary people, but a *distinction without a sense of hostility.* As πνευματικοί, they are certainly of a superior status, but the rest, the ψυχικοί, are not thereby classed as evil or threatening, merely inferior and unprivileged. The Corinthian symbolic world is structured by contrasts, to be sure, but not such contrasts as represent struggle or conflict. There is no 'present evil age' to be redeemed from, no cosmic warfare against Satan and his powers, no destructive wrath due to fall on all non-believers. That apocalyptic and tension-laden perspective is not characteristic of the Corinthians; their own symbolic world gives them a sufficient sense of superiority to make their conversion worthwhile, without fostering a sense of hostility towards (or the expectation of hostility from) non-Christians.

b. Secondly, Corinthian theology correlates well with the practice of *differentiation without exclusivity.* The infusion of the divine πνεῦμα at baptism, and its dramatic presence in their midst in worship, were clearly prized features of their Christian existence. They presumably felt that this was in some respects a deeper or richer experience of divine power than they had known before in Graeco-Roman religion (12.2). Yet this did not necessarily annul the claims of others—prophets, poets, seers and philosophers—to similar experiences of ecstasy or inspiration.[24] Their knowledge of the 'oneness' of God was not unlike the monotheistic convictions of those educated in Hellenistic theology. Since others did not define their Christian convictions as alien, there was no reason why they could not accept a kind of theological pluralism, which distinguished their views without discounting all others. This is a theology which both reflects and fosters harmonious relationships.

---

24. See Wedderburn, *Baptism and Resurrection*, 249–68.

c. Finally, their religious ethos permits an *involvement in the church which does not entail significant social and moral realignment.* It is important to note the limited context in which the identity of the πνευματικός is displayed: in the worship meetings of the church where the practice of knowledgeable speech, tongues and prophecy fulfils the initiate's calling. Outside these semi-private gatherings in the house of Gaius, the Corinthian Christians might consider their faith of only limited significance. If the church's ecstatic celebrations were the peak of its experience, they could also become its sole focus of interest. Beyond that socially (and temporally) confined context, the πνευματικοί had authority to behave as they wished. They were not bound by a moral tradition which tied them to a distinctive communal lifestyle; indeed, the authority of each individual πνευματικός could not be challenged (2.14). If behaviour is, then, not a matter of ethics but of 'consciousness' and self-understanding, the Christian is not committed in advance to any group norms which might have awkward social implications.[25] The church is not a cohesive community but a club, whose meetings provide important moments of spiritual insight and exaltation, but do not have global implications of moral or social change. The Corinthians could gladly participate in this church as one segment of their lives. But the segment, however important, is not the whole and not the centre. Their perception of their church and of the significance of their faith could correlate well with a life-style which remained fully integrated in Corinthian society.

Once again, then, we have an example of the mutual reinforcement of social experience and theological perspective, which this time involves a major realignment of Paul's apocalyptic symbols. When the first Corinthians became Christians, they did not experience hostility, nor was their apostle hounded out of town. And the more firmly the church got established in conditions of social harmony, the more implausible the apocalyptic content of Paul's message became, with its strong implications of social dislocation. In the face of continuing close and friendly relations with 'significant others' it was hard to sustain an atmosphere of beleaguered hostility. And the more the Corinthians understood their faith as a special endowment of knowledge and a special acquisition of spiritual skills, the less they would expect or embrace hostility: any intimations of conflict would be resolved or minimized. To posit this is not to succumb to some sociological determinism, but simply to note the complex interplay between beliefs and social experience. We must remember how successful the Corinthian church appears to have been, both in its numerical strength and in the intensity of its spiritual experience. The apocalyptic notes in Paul's theology which harmonized so well with the Thessalonians' experience simply failed to resonate with the Corinthians. It is possible that some of them would have felt distinctly

25. On the individualism of the Corinthians, expressed through their term συνείδησις, see R. A. Horsley, 'Consciousness and Freedom among the Corinthians: 1 Corinthians 8–10', *CBQ* 40 (1978) 574–89. He rightly suggests that 'for the Corinthians . . . the eating of idol-meat and other matters were issues only in an internal personal sense, for one's own individual consciousness, and not in a truly ethical, i.e. relational, sense' (p. 589).

uncomfortable in the Thessalonian church and would not indeed have joined, or remained members of, the church in Corinth if it had developed the same ethos as its Thessalonian sibling.

CONCLUSION

This study of the divergent development of these two Pauline churches has shown how misleading it is to generalize about 'Pauline Christians'. It is ironic that it was the church in Corinth which diverged most from Paul's own point of view although he apparently spent much more time there than in Thessalonica! That may be a salutary lesson to us, as it was to Paul, that he had less control than he imagined over the ways his converts interpreted their own conversion.

Chapter 15

The Rich Patron*

John K. Chow

INTRODUCTION

A number of recent studies of Corinthian Christianity, following the lead of Gerd
Theissen (see ch. 6 above), have focused on the presence of certain socially prominent individuals in the congregation. John Chow, in his monograph *Patronage
and Power*, takes Theissen's claims a step further and argues that certain wealthy
and powerful figures (such as Chloe, 1 Cor 1.11) acted as patrons or benefactors
of the church. Chow endeavours to show that patronage was part and parcel of
the wider society within which Paul and the Corinthians operated, and that it had
a significant bearing on relations within the Corinthian Christian community. In
a chapter entitled 'The Power of the Patrons', from which the extract here is taken,
he argues that a number of the problems dealt with in 1 Corinthians can be related
to the dynamics of patronage. In this section, Chow deals specifically with the
problem addressed in 1 Cor 5. Here Paul relates a situation in which a member of

*Extracted from John K. Chow, *Patronage and Power: A Study of Social Networks in Corinth*
(JSNTSup 75; Sheffield: Sheffield Academic Press, 1992) 130–40. Reprinted by permission of The
Continuum International Publishing Group.

the church is living with his father's wife without incurring the condemnation of the congregation. A standard explanation for the church's toleration of the man's action is that they saw his behaviour as an expression of their spiritual liberty in Christ, enabling them to flout social conventions of the day. Chow, however, argues that the man was a rich protector of the church who had entered into the domestic arrangement for financial reasons and whose action was condoned by the other members of the church because of the patronage ties that obligated them to him. A similar argument was independently made by Andrew Clarke.

This interpretation of 1 Cor 5, and the wider social reconstruction on which it is based, has been challenged by Justin Meggitt (see chs. 6, 17, 19 herein). Meggitt doubts that the evidence allows the man in question to be identified as rich and powerful. He also questions whether the conventions of patronage were so rigid as to prevent clients from criticising their patrons in extreme matters like this. More generally, Meggitt is critical of the recent trend in the interpretation of Corinthian Christianity which places certain members of the believing community among the elite of Corinthian society.

Further Reading

See also chapters 6, 17.
Clarke, *Secular and Christian Leadership*.
P. Marshall, *Enmity in Corinth: Social Conventions in Paul's Relations with the Corinthians* (WUNT 2.23; Tübingen: Mohr Siebeck, 1987).
Meggitt, *Paul, Poverty*, esp. pp. 149–53.
R. P. Saller, *Personal Patronage under the Early Empire* (Cambridge: Cambridge University Press, 1982).
B. W. Winter, *Seek the Welfare of the City* (Grand Rapids: Eerdmans, 1994).

In 1 Cor 5.1–13 a case of gross immorality which Paul heard of is disclosed. A man, a member in the church, cohabited with his step-mother[1] who apparently is not a member of the church (1 Cor 5.1). In the eyes of Paul such a relationship is not acceptable even in a pagan world,[2] and certainly not to himself. Paul is therefore of the opinion that the community should exclude the man from their midst (1 Cor 5.3–5, 7, 13). However, it seems to have surprised Paul that the church not only accepted the man, but appears to be proud of the man (1 Cor 5.2, 6).

That there was such a case of immorality in the church and that it was approved by the church certainly arouses interest. Could this case of immorality, like the case of litigation, be concerned with material benefits? What do we know about the man? Could he be one of the 'strong' people? How could the church be proud of the man if it was so clear-cut to Paul that the man should be excluded from the community?

---

1. On γυνὴ πατρός as a reference to stepmother, see Lev 18.8 (LXX).
2. C. Talbert has marshalled some helpful parallel materials from Jewish and Graeco-Roman sources showing the unacceptability of this kind of relationship (*Reading Corinthians: A Literary and Theological Commentary on 1 and 2 Corinthians* [New York: Crossroad, 1987] 12–14).

The answer to the last question lies partly in the self-understanding of the Corinthians. They probably believed that the man's action was a valid expression of their newly found freedom in the Spirit.[3] To Schmithals, it is Gnostic *eleutheria*.[4] But Thiselton sees in this case a testimony to the over-realized eschatological outlook of the spiritual people at Corinth.[5] Horsley has not spent any time on this episode. While the nature of such freedom has been explained in different terms, its inner logic is probably coherent. The Corinthians might have believed that no physical action has any moral significance (1 Cor 6.13, 18b).[6] Because they had wisdom and knowledge (1 Cor 1.5; 3.18; 8.1–3) they were therefore free from moral law (1 Cor 6.12).[7] They might also have believed that they were protected by the baptism they had received (1 Cor 1.13–17).[8] Consequently they were proud (1 Cor 5.2; 4.6, 18) and boastful (1 Cor 5.6; 1.29; 3.21; 4.7). They were like kings (1 Cor 4.8) and could be judged by no one else (1 Cor 2.15–16a). Since the man was only exercising his freedom, the church not only could not judge him, but should actually have reasons to be proud of the man's courage.

The man's action could certainly be justified theologically in the name of freedom in the Spirit. But a theological explanation does not answer all the questions concerning the social reality of the man's relationship with his stepmother. From our study of the problem of litigation we have seen that freedom to seek justice before the pagan magistrate might in reality have been exercised by only a few powerful Corinthians and not necessarily by all, and that their freedom might also have been exercised for material gain. It leads one to wonder if a similar kind of situation lies behind this case of immorality. To enlarge our understanding of the situation some questions have to be examined. For example, could any person who experienced the freedom in the Spirit act in such a way, even though it meant a violation of both Jewish[9] and Roman law?[10] What kind of a son would the man be who sought apparently to maintain a kind of incestuous relationship with his stepmother? Why would the man choose to live with the stepmother? What was the nature of that relationship?

3. E.g. J. Moffatt, *The First Epistle of Paul to the Corinthians* (London: Hodder & Stoughton, 1938) 54; C. K. Barrett, *A Commentary on the First Epistle to the Corinthians* (London: A. & C. Black, 1968) 121–22.

4. Schmithals, *Gnosticism*, 236–37.

5. Thiselton, 'Realized Eschatology', 516.

6. Murphy-O'Connor, 'The First Letter to the Corinthians', in *New Jerome Biblical Commentary* (Engelwood Cliffs, N.J.: Prentice-Hall, 1990) 803.

7. Talbert, *Reading Corinthians*, 15.

8. L. E. Keck, *Paul and his Letters* (2nd ed.; Philadelphia: Fortress, 1988) 106–7.

9. Lev 18.8; Deut 22.30; 27.20; *Jub.* 33.10–13.

10. Gaius 1.63: 'I may not marry one who once was my stepmother. We say, who once was, since if the marriage producing that alliance were still continuing, I should be precluded from marrying her on another ground' (D. Daube, 'Pauline Contributions to Pluralistic Culture: Re-creation and Beyond', in *Jesus and Man's Hope* [ed. D. G. Miller and D. Y. Hadidian; Pittsburgh: Pittsburgh Theological Seminary, 1971] 241 n. 3). Cf. also T. C. Sandars, *The Institutes of Justinian* (London: Longmans, 1952) 35–36.

THE RELATIONSHIP

Regarding the relationship between the son and the stepmother, it would be safe to assume that it was a long-term one.[11] Beyond this, scholars differ in their assessment concerning the nature of their relationship. Conzelmann and Fiorenza[12] prefer to see it as cohabiting rather than marriage. Their judgment is based mainly on the assumption that a son is forbidden to marry a stepmother by both Jewish and Roman law. But Barrett, who builds his argument on Paul's use of ἔχειν, suggests that the relationship could have been one of either marriage or concubinage.[13]

As to the nature of the relationship, it should first be pointed out that it would be difficult to draw a clear line between marriage and living together in those days.[14] For the deciding factor lies basically with the intention of the couple, that is, whether they intended to live together as husband and wife.[15] Unfortunately, intention is something which is very difficult to assess from this distance in time. Having said that, on balance it still appears that the relationship is best seen as marriage or concubinage.[16]

In response to those, such as Fiorenza, who do not regard the relationship as marriage or concubinage because of legal prohibitions, two points can be made. First, as far as Jewish law is concerned, it should be noted (although not all rabbis would agree[17]) that it was possible for the man to argue that, because he was a proselyte, his former social relations were dissolved and that he could marry his stepmother.[18] It is, of course, questionable if the status as a proselyte could render the requirement of the Roman law ineffective. But then we should not forget the fact that Roman law, as seen from our previous discussion, could be manipulated by the strong and the powerful for their own ends. Secondly, whether the relationship was marriage or not, it is important to underscore the

11. The long-term nature of the relationship is suggested by Paul's use of ἔχειν (e.g., A. Robertson and A. Plummer, *A Critical and Exegetical Commentary on the First Epistle of St Paul to the Corinthians* (New York: Charles Scribner's Sons, 1911) 96; Barrett, *First Corinthians*, 122; Fee, *First Epistle*, 220.

12. Conzelmann, *I Corinthains*, 96; E. S. Fiorenza, '1 Corinthians', in *Harper's Bible Commentary* (New York: Harper and Row, 1988) 1174.

13. Barrett, *First Corinthians*, 122. According to Robertson and Plummer, Origen also sees the relationship as a marriage (*First Corinthians*, 96). Cf. 1 Cor 7.2.

14. Robertson and Plummer, *First Corinthians*, 96.

15. Sandars, *Institutes*, 31–32; Crook, *Law and Life of Rome* (London: Thames & Hudson, 1967) 101. For further discussion on marriage in the Roman world, see P. E. Corbett, *The Roman Law of Marriage* (Oxford: Clarendon Press, 1930) 47–51; J. F. Gardner, *Women in Roman Law and Society* (London: Croom Helm, 1986) 31–80; P. Garnsey and R. P. Saller, *The Roman Empire: Economy, Society, Culture* (London: Gerard Duckworth, 1987) 130–36.

16. So E. von Dobschütz draws the following conclusion: 'There is tolerable agreement among exegetes as to the nature of the case of incest concerned; it was marriage (not only an immoral relationship) with the stepmother (probably not belonging to the Church) after the father's death' (*Christian Life in the Primitive Church* [London: Williams & Norgate, 1904] 387).

17. Conzelmann, *I Corinthians*, 96 n. 29.

18. H. W. A. Meyer, *Critical and Exegetical Handbook to the Epistles to the Corinthians*, I (5th ed.; Edinburgh: T. & T. Clark, 1883) 140; Daube, 'Re-creation and Beyond', 223–24; Fiorenza, '1 Corinthians', 1174.

long-term nature of the relationship. In actual effect, a long-term cohabiting would perhaps be regarded as a marriage by a contemporary.

Furthermore, as Fiorenza has observed, Paul's discussion in 1 Corinthians 7 on marital problems could have been occasioned by Paul's earlier discussion of the relationship between the insiders and the outsiders in 1 Cor 5 and 6.[19] So if 1 Cor 5.1 is read in the light of 1 Cor 7, it can be inferred that the problem which involved the immoral man might be one related to the institution of marriage. Fiorenza seems to accept also the view that a fragment of Paul's previous letter to the Corinthians (1 Cor 5.9) might have been preserved in 2 Cor 6.14—7.1 where the problem of intermarriage with unbelievers is probably discussed. This connection is not assumed in our discussion. But if the above view is right, then we would have a perfect match between the situation in 1 Cor 5.1 and part of the situation presupposed in Paul's previous letter to the church.

To sum up, the relationship between the man and the woman is best seen as one of marriage or concubinage. This being so, can we know why the man took his stepmother and not another woman? Why especially did the man choose an outsider to the church rather than an insider? Would an insider be more understandable and natural? Granted that to associate with a stepmother could be a good way to express the freedom one enjoyed, the action itself is still difficult to understand. For there may be truth in the suggestion that, in most cases, there were tensions rather than affection between children of the former wife and the stepmother even in the Roman Empire.[20] Why then did the man marry the stepmother?

Could it be because she was still young and attractive? Could it be for sexual pleasure?[21] Because girls in the Roman Empire tended to marry early,[22] it is quite possible that the stepmother was still a young woman. We have no way of knowing if she was especially attractive. But if tensions in the relationship between a son and a stepmother were as common as suggested, that would speak against these two otherwise reasonable guesses. More importantly, it should be pointed out that to see sex as the main reason for a long-term relationship is to overestimate the role of sex in ancient marriage arrangements. For the idea that the aim of marriage is to enjoy sexual pleasure does not appear to have been a prevalent one in the early Empire. Philosophers such as Musonius Rufus taught that the aim of having sex in marriage was to have children, not pleasure.[23] The satirist

19. Fiorenza, '1 Corinthians', 1174. She sees 1 Cor 5–7 as a unity.

20. Plutarch, *Cat. Maj.* 24.4; *Comp. Arist. Cat.* 6.1. B. Rawson points also to 'the sinister nature of the stepmother's role in Tacitus's treatment of Livia and Agrippina junior' (*The Family in Ancient Rome* [London: Croom Helm, 1986] 36, 55 n. 112).

21. This is suggested especially by Moffatt, *First Corinthians*, 53–54; Murphy-O'Connor, *1 Corinthians* (Dublin: Veritas, 1979) 43.

22. Recent studies have shown that, on average, girls in the Roman Empire married between nine to twelve (e.g., Crook, *Law and Life*, 100), and usually to older men (Garnsey and Saller, *Roman Empire*, 131). Thus, it would not be difficult for women in the Roman Empire to marry for a second time.

23. Musonius Rufus: 'Men who are not wantons or immoral are bound to consider sexual intercourse justified only when it occurs in marriage and is indulged in for the purpose of begetting children, since that is lawful, but unjust and unlawful when it is mere pleasure-seeking, even in marriage' (Lutz, 'Musonius Rufus', 87).

also emphasized the non-affective relationship between husband and wife.[24] Furthermore, marriage as an institution among the well-to-do in Rome who could enjoy sex in other ways might not have been popular at all. Indeed some laws may have been passed by Augustus to encourage marriage and the procreation of children.[25] Actually, it was claimed by some of the Corinthians, probably those who were overtaken by enthusiasm,[26] that it was good for a man/a husband not to touch (or to have sexual relationship with) a woman/a wife (1 Cor 7.1).[27] Since the man could be one of those who were devoted to enthusiasm,[28] it is not impossible that he would hold such a view. Of course, it does not necessarily follow that the man could not have sexual relationships with other women (1 Cor 6.12–20). But it is reasonable to argue that sex might not be a very important factor in the relationship between the son and the stepmother.

If the son did not live with the stepmother because of physical attraction, what could be the reason behind his action? Again, Fiorenza's observation may provide us with a clue. As mentioned before, she suggests that the legal case in 1 Cor 6.1 could be about one of those problems related to marriage, like dowry, inheritance and so on.[29] In which case, just as the litigants were interested in material possessions, the man's association with the stepmother could also be related to material concerns.

This close relationship between marriage and wealth management in first-century Corinth is spotlighted in the marriage arrangement of two important personages known to the people in the colony. The first one concerned Lollia Paulina, a lady with immense wealth.[30] She was first the nominal wife of Memmius Regulus, the popular governor of Achaia from AD 35–44, but later became the bride of Caligula.[31] Part of the reason why Lollia Paulina was chosen by Caligula as his bride could have been because she was wealthy.[32] Another case involved a freedman and a woman from a rich family.[33] As a result of this marriage, the name of the freedman, Cleogenes, was included on an inscription of

---

24. Juvenal, *Sat.* 6. The study of J. P. Hallett has shown that women, especially elite women, in Roman society clung closer to their fathers and kin than to their husbands (*Fathers and Daughters in Roman Society: Women and the Elite Family* [Princeton: Princeton University Press, 1984] 219–43).

25. Tacitus, *Ann.* 3.25. See also R. I. Frank, 'Augustus' Legislation on Marriage and Children', *CSCA* 8 (1975) 41–52.

26. Thiselton, 'Realized Eschatology', 518; Talbert, *Reading Corinthians,* 38.

27. See, e.g., W. F. Orr and J. A. Walther, *I Corinthians* (Garden City, N.Y.: Doubleday, 1976) 206, 207–8; Barrett, *First Corinthians,* 154.

28. Thiselton, 'Realized Eschatology', 516.

29. Fiorenza, '1 Corinthians', 1175.

30. According to Pliny the Elder, she owed her wealth to her grandfather and was able to wear 40 million sesterces worth of jewellery at a party (*Nat.* 9.117–18). Cf. Tacitus, *Ann.* 12.22.

31. Suetonius, *Cal.* 25; Dio Cassius 59.12.

32. On wealth and the choice of an emperor's consort, see Tacitus, *Ann.* 12.1; cf. J. H. Oliver, 'Lollia Paulina, Memmius Regulus and Caligula', *Hesperia* 35 (1966) 150–53.

33. A. B. West, *Latin Inscriptions 1896–1926. Corinth Results,* VIII.2 (Cambridge, Mass.: Harvard University Press, 1931), nos. 124, 125; Kent, *The Inscriptions, 1926–1950. Corinth: Results* VIII.3 (Princeton: American Schools of Classical Studies at Athens, 1966), no. 321.

the Augustan age made to the family of Quintus Cornelius Secundus who probably built a meatmarket and a fishmarket at Corinth. Whether Cleogenes was
accepted because he was wealthy or became rich through the marriage is not clear,
but that material benefits might have been involved in the union of a man and
woman should not be difficult to see. Small wonder that, in his correspondence,
Pliny states clearly that, when arranging for a marriage, for the sake of the children, he would consider seriously the financial factor.[34]

Could a man gain from the taking of a wife and if so, how? A dowry,[35] of
course, was what the husband could immediately gain from a marriage. There
were, however, other material benefits to be gained from a marital relationship at
that time. According to the Augustan marriage laws[36] unmarried men and
women would be penalized by heavier taxes;[37] bachelors were forbidden to
receive inheritances or legacies; the childless married could only take half of any
bequest.[38] Besides, there was also the likelihood that a man could have access in
an informal way to the wife's inheritance and material possessions of the wife's
relatives.[39] If a man married a widow, his chance of gaining direct access to the
wife's inheritance was even higher, since it would be likely that her father was
already dead by then.[40] Apart from making material gains, one could also marry
for the preservation of family wealth. The following comment by J. F. Gardner
serves to sum up the phenomenon well:

34. Pliny, *Ep.* 1.14.9.

35. For a good discussion of dowry in the early Empire, see R. P. Saller, 'Roman Dowry and the
Devolution of Property in the Principate', *CQ* 34 (1984) 195–205; Gardner, *Women,* 97–116.
According to Saller, in Greek marriage the size of the dowry could be very substantial because it was
related to the daughter's share of the family's inheritance. It could amount to a quarter of the whole
estate ('Dowry', 195). In comparison, the size of the dowry in Roman marriage at the time of the
early Empire was smaller, but not too small. It varied from tens of thousands among the local aristocracy to millions among the wealthiest in the empire ('Dowry', 200–202). It may be worth noting
that the capital of a town councillor at Coraun was assessed to be 100,000 sesterces (Pliny, *Ep.* 1.19.2).

36. For detailed discussions of the Augustan marriage laws, see P. Csillag, *The Augustan Laws on
Family Relations* (Budapest: Akademiai Kiado, 1976). Cf. also P. A. Brunt, 'The Augustan Marriage
Laws', in *Italian Manpower: 225 BC–AD 14* (Oxford: Clarendon Press, 1971) 558–66; A. Wallace-
Hadrill, 'Family and Inheritance in the Augustan Marriage Laws,', *PCPhS* 27 (1981) 58–80;
J. A. Crook, 'Women in Roman Succession', in Rawson (ed.), *Family in Ancient Rome,* 58–82.

37. Tacitus, *Ann.* 3.25; Dio Cassius 54.16.1.

38. Gaius 2.286. See Sandars, *Institutes,* 228–29; Wallace-Hadrill, 'Family and Inheritance', 62;
Brunt, 'Augustan Marriage Laws', 564.

39. This possibility is reflected in an epitaph of the Augustan age (V. Ehrenberg and
A. H. M. Jones, *Documents Illustrating the Reigns of Augustus and Tiberius* [2nd ed.; Oxford: Clarendon Press, 1955], no. 357 = D. C. Braund, *Augustus to Nero: A Sourcebook on Roman History, 31
BC–AD 68* [London: Croom Helm, 1985], no. 520). In this eulogy of the wife, her courage to fight
for the right to keep her father's possessions and her willingness to share it with the husband is praised
highly by the latter. While such total sharing might not be common in those days (Gardner, *Women,*
p. 72), different degrees of sharing can perhaps be assumed with confidence. Even Pliny claims that
the property of the mother of his former wife is at his free disposal (*Ep.* 3.19; 1.4).

40. According to Saller's estimation, roughly one third of the brides would have lost their
fathers when they got married, and three out of four married girls would outlive their father ('Dowry',
197 n. 14).

In the senatorial class, the political aspects of such marriage alliances are too well attested to need comment; and both there and at lower levels of society a degree of endogamy could be a strategy, to restrict the dispersal of family property.[41]

From this discussion we may conclude that, in Paul's day, material interests, which might include money and power, rather than sex and affection, seem to have a bigger role to play in the establishment of a marital relationship. Indeed, for the sake of keeping wealth, men in those days could do some strange things. The satirists tell us that there were husbands who were willing to condone their wives' acts of adultery in return for the control of their dowries.[42] If we measure the immoral man's action against these husbands, his behaviour would appear less shocking and more understandable.

To see in the man's action, whatever his theological views, a way to preserve or to increase family wealth may well provide a better explanation of why the son chose to associate with the stepmother against all the odds. For on the one hand, through marriage, he would not have to pay higher taxes. On the other hand, he would immediately be able to have total control over his share of the inheritance from the father who probably was dead at that time.[43] Better still, through marrying his stepmother he might have been able to preserve in his house his stepmother's dowry to his father and might even have access to the possessions of his wife's family.

Although the above reconstruction of the situation behind 1 Cor 5.1 depends quite heavily on the assumption that the relationship involved was one of marriage, it nevertheless makes good sense and fits in well with the general context of 1 Cor 5–7. First, the material interests which might involve the immoral man could well have led to the kind of litigation in 1 Cor 6.1–11, as suggested by Fiorenza and further developed previously. Secondly, Paul's asking of the church

41. Gardner, *Women*, 35.

42. Juvenal, *Sat.* 6.135–41; cf. Andocides 4.13. This may be one of the reasons why Augustus made the husband's condoning the wife's adulterous act a crime (Crook, *Law and Life*, 106). At this point, it is worth explaining briefly the marriage custom in the Principate and its relationship to the management of the dowry. The more common form of marriage at this time is the so-called 'free-marriage' which allowed the wife to have independent control over the property she inherited from her father's family. Dowry was under the control of the husband until the marital relationship was dissolved by divorce or death (Saller, 'Dowry', 196–97; Corbett, *Law of Marriage*, 154–55, 181–82).

43. Although it is not immediately clear whether the association of the man with his father's wife took place while the father was still alive or after he was dead (Barrett, *First Corinthians*, 121), it looks more likely that the latter is the case. J. H. Bernard's attempt to sustain the thesis that the lawsuit in 1 Cor 6.1 was started by the father by assuming that the father was still alive is not necessary and not required by the text ('The Connexion between the Fifth and Sixth Chapters of 1 Corinthians', *Exp* 7:3 [1907] 437–38). On the contrary, given the fact that the father was given enormous power over the son in those days (W. K. Lacey, 'Patria Potesias', *Family in Ancient Rome*, 121–44; Garnsey and Saller, *Roman Empire*, 136–37), it is difficult to conceive that the son could have his way if the father was still alive. Moreover, recent studies have shown that, because of the late marriage age of men in the Roman Empire, usually in their late twenties, the average age difference between father and child was about 40 years. Hence, few fathers lived to see their sons' marriages (Garnsey and Saller, *Roman Empire*, 136–37).

not to associate with a person who bears the name of a brother, but is in fact a
πόρνος and a πλεονέκτης, could have been a reference to the immoral man
(1 Cor 5.11). In associating with his stepmother, he is certainly a πόρνος. If he
did so for material reasons he could also be seen as a πλεονέκτης, a person who
is eager to have more,[44] more money and even more power.[45] *6 Other 5:11 nouns...*

THE IMMORAL MAN

In 1 Cor 5.2, the community is accused by Paul of being 'puffed-up' because it
did not cast the immoral man from its midst. The 'puffed-up' people appear to
be Paul's opponents in the church (1 Cor 4.18).[46] In 1 Cor 1–4 they are behind
the divisions in the church (1 Cor 4.6). In 1 Cor 8.1 and 13.4 they are people
who have knowledge but no love. Hence it is very likely that in 1 Corinthians 5
Paul is still responding to the opponents in 1 Cor 1–4 and those in 1 Cor 8–10.[47]
It is therefore natural to identify the immoral man as one of those who were
puffed up and did not expect Paul to return (1 Cor 4.18). As seen from our previous discussion,[48] it looks likely that the opponents of Paul were the powerful
people in the church. This again points to the conclusion that the immoral man
was one of the powerful patrons in the church.

In the light of the above discussion, it may be inferred that the case of
immorality basically concerns a man with material possessions. In that case, the
problem in 1 Cor 5.1 was not a problem of the have-nots or of the slaves, but
one of a rich man who was rich enough to have concerns about preserving or
increasing wealth. If so, more was involved in the case of immorality than simply religious freedom. The immoral man, not unlike the litigants, while devoted
to the pursuit of freedom in the Spirit, was probably greatly interested in material matters. It may be further surmised that the man might be one of the patrons
in the church. We have seen how the Corinthians could have approved the man's
action by reference to their theology of freedom. If the spiritual and immoral man
was also a rich patron in the church, he would certainly have a better chance of
being approved by the church. For who would want to dishonour a powerful
patron who could provide protection and benefaction to the church? On the
contrary, as faithful clients, members in the Christian church should perhaps

44. BAGD, 667. See G. Delling, 'πλεονέκτης', *TDNT* 5:266–74; F. Selter, 'πλεονεξία',
NIDNTT, 1:137–39.

45. Πλεονεξία is also used to represent the immoral lust for power or ambitions on the part of
the politically powerful. See Ezek 22.27; Jer 22.17; 2 Macc 4.50 (LXX); Dio Chrysostom, *Or.* 17.

46. G. Forkman, *The Limits of the Religious Community: Expulsion from the Religious Community
within the Qumran Sect, within Rabbinic Judaism, and within Primitive Christianity* (Lund: Gleerup,
1972) 139.

47. Dahl, 'Church at Corinth', 331.

48. Chapter 2 of *Patronage and Power.*

support and honour such a patron. The church's boasting in the immoral man's action can, to a certain extent, also be seen against this background.

We may now look briefly at another problem. If it was illegal for a son to marry a stepmother, how did the man manage to survive without being prosecuted? In his attempt to understand why the church failed to take action against the immoral man, Moffatt surmises that the man could have been 'too important or wealthy' for the church to raise any objection.[49] I have shown that the man could have been a wealthy man. But it is difficult to tell if the man was in fact an important person. However, it looks probable that the church had some important persons in its midst. We have seen previously how the Roman law served the interests of the powerful and could be manipulated by the powerful for their own ends. If the immoral man was a man of influence and power, it is doubtful that any one would dare to challenge his action. This, I submit, would help partly to explain how the man could associate with the stepmother without being prosecuted.

49. Moffatt, *First Corinthians*, 53.

Chapter 16

Stoicism, ἐλευθερία and Community at Corinth[*]

Terence Paige

INTRODUCTION

Terence Paige's essay is one of a number of recent studies that have gone beyond
the general claim that Corinthian Christianity was deeply affected by the surrounding Greco-Roman culture and have sought to find a source for the various
problems and issues confronted by Paul in some specific school or branch of
Greco-Roman philosophy. The whole article is reproduced here. Paige argues that
Stoicism provides the most plausible background to various aspects of Corinthian
thought and practice criticised by Paul in the course of 1 Corinthians. He contends that Paul's frequent use of Stoic terminology and motifs in the letter indicates the prevalence of Stoic ideas within the Corinthian congregation and, more
particularly, among its most prominent members. Paige shows that Stoicism was
a popular philosophy of the day and argues that members of the Corinthian

*T. Paige, 'Stoicism, ἐλευθερία and Community at Corinth', in *Worship, Theology and Ministry
in the Early Church: Essays in Honor of Ralph P. Martin* (ed. M. J. Wilkins and T. Paige; JSNTSup 87;
Sheffield: Sheffield Academic Press, 1992) 180–93. Reprinted by permission of The Continuum
International Publishing Group.

church, especially those with some education, could easily have been acquainted with it. He then argues that the influence of Stoicism helps to shed light on specific Corinthian claims (such as the claims to be wise, to have knowledge, to be like kings) and actions (including eating meat sacrificed to idols). He concludes that Stoic influence helps to explain the emergence of an elite group of 'wise' within the church who advocated a style of 'freedom' (in matters judged to be *adiaphora,* inconsequentials), which was highly individualistic and self-serving and which was consequently affecting the unity of the community.

Various other scholars, such as Will Deming, have also looked to Stoicism as a background to what was going on in Corinth. But the influence of other philosophical traditions has been also been proposed in recent scholarship. This raises the important question as to whether the parallels between ideas expressed by Paul or the Corinthian Christians and various branches of Greco-Roman philosophy are such as to justify specific labels—some Corinthian Christians were Stoics, this idea of Paul's is Cynic, and so on—or whether they reflect a more general influence from the popular discussion of the day.

Further Reading

W. Deming, *Paul on Marriage and Celibacy: The Hellenistic Background of 1 Corinthians 7* (SNTSMS 83; Cambridge: Cambridge University Press, 1995).

F. G. Downing, *Cynics, Paul, and the Pauline Churches: Cynics and Christian Origins II* (London and New York: Routledge, 1998).

T. Engberg-Pedersen, *Paul and the Stoics* (Edinburg: T. & T. Clark, 2000).

A. J. Malherbe, 'Determinism and Free Will in Paul: The Argument of 1 Corinthians 8 and 9', in *Paul in His Hellenistic Context* (ed. T. Engberg-Pedersen; SNTW; Edinburgh: T. & T. Clark, 1994) 231–55.

Martin, *Corinthian Body.*

T. Paige, '1 Corinthians 12.2: A Pagan *Pompe?*' *JSNT* 44 (1991) 57–65.

G. Tomlin, 'Christians and Epicureans in 1 Corinthians', *JSNT* 68 (1997) 51–72.

What were the forces shaping the thoughts and actions of the church of God at Corinth, the forces which, in the relatively short time between Paul's founding the church and the writing of 1 Corinthians, led to the rise of behavior and teaching so at variance with what the apostle laid down? What I suggest here is that the influence of Stoicism or a Stoicizing source (perhaps with Cynic tendencies) may have been one very significant element affecting the Corinthian Christian leadership. The presence of Stoic thought would account for several problems at Corinth often attributed to Gnosticism[1] or Jewish Wisdom Theology, especially the apparent pursuit of a spirituality that was elitist and devoid of a community-oriented dimension. Other items that could be explained on the basis of a Stoicizing influence include the characterization of the Corinthians as kings and as rich; the assertion of absolute freedom for the Christian who is σοφός, together with the creed 'πάντα μοι ἔξεστιν'; the Corinthian argument that an idol is 'nothing'; and the

---

1. Including here 'gnosis' and 'proto-Gnosticism'.

highly individualistic approach to moral problems (e.g. ch. 8; 6.12–20; 11.17–22). In addition to evidence of the Corinthians' language and behavior, Paul's own answers or correctives sometimes use Stoic-sounding language: the apostles as a 'spectacle' (4.9);[2] the argument from conscience (8.7); his defense of his actions at Corinth as one who is ἐλεύθερος (9.1, 19); his advice to Christians to live as though not married, not possessing, unattached to ephemeral things so that they may be ἀμέριμνος, 'without care' (7.29–32); the description of the purpose of Spirit-endowments as πρὸς τὸ συμφέρον, 'for the purpose of profit' (12.7);[3] the use of 'body' imagery (ch. 12); and the argument from 'nature' (φύσις, 11.14).[4]

The similarity of Paul's language in many places to that of the Stoa, especially Seneca's, has been observed for some time. Sevenster chronicles the debate concerning the relationship between Paul and Seneca, which has lasted over a hundred and thirty years.[5] The debate whether Paul borrows from Seneca or vice versa seems to have ended in a general acceptance of the view carefully argued first by Lightfoot and later by Sevenster, that the similarities of expression in the writings of Paul and Seneca most often turn out to be purely formal. Paul is neither a Stoic nor is he expressing Stoicizing thoughts when he uses body[6] imagery, speaks of an indwelling Spirit, commends the imitation of God, or decries the sinfulness of man—all of which may be found in Seneca. The fundamental conceptions of deity and of the relationship between man and God are very different between the two. Sevenster showed that there is no ground to believe that the two ever met, or that Seneca borrowed language from Paul (which is the other way to explain the similarities).[7]

The question I wish to raise is *not* whether or not *Paul* thought in Stoic manner; rather, could it be that he is writing to people who themselves use such language, think in a Stoicizing manner, or are impressed with Stoic ideas? Otherwise why does he so frequently use language that appears Stoic, though he operates with different assumptions? After all, the manner of Paul's expression is not shaped solely by his Jewish background and Christian confession, but surely to some extent by the needs of his audience as well? Do not their problems, vocabulary, and level of understanding influence the manner of the apostle's communication with them?

2. J. N. Sevenster, *Paul and Seneca* (Leiden: Brill, 1961) 115f., and Fee, *First Epistle*, 174f. n. 50. Both point to the intent of Paul's expression as differing greatly from the sense found in Seneca of a proud display of the wise man's triumphant will before men and gods.

3. Diogenes Laertius (= D.L.) 7.93, 98f., 149. Compare Plutarch's attack on Stoic ἀπαθεία, of which he says ἔξω καὶ τοῦ δυνατοῦ καὶ τοῦ συμφέροντος οὖσαν (*Consolatio ad Apollonium* 102C): 'it is beyond what is possible and what is beneficial'.

4. Discussions of many of these may be found in Conzelmann or Fee, *ad loc.*

5. Sevenster, *Paul and Seneca*, esp. pp. 1–5; cf. also J. B. Lightfoot, 'St. Paul and Seneca', in *Dissertations on the Apostolic Age* (London: Macmillan and Co., 1892) 249–322 (originally part of Lightfoot's commentary on Philippians, 1890).

6. Though this is not to say he could not have adapted Stoic themes to suit his own purpose. See J. D. G. Dunn, 'The "Body of Christ" in Paul' in *Worship, Theology and Ministry in the Early Church*, 146–62.

7. Sevenster, *Paul and Seneca*, 6–25.

In order to better assess the viability of this proposal, I begin with a brief synopsis of Stoicism's influence in the era I BC—AD I, and then its view of the 'wise man' and its orientation in ethics.

Stoicism was a native Greek philosophy which had thrived for some three hundred and fifty years prior to Paul's arrival in Greece. By the beginning of our era, Sandbach believes Stoicism to be 'without doubt the predominant philosophy among the Romans'.[8] Stoic philosophers befriended and were in turn patronized by Roman aristocrats and senators beginning in the second century BC.[9] Several emperors also maintained Stoic philosophers, notably Augustus and Nero.[10] One Stoic supported by Augustus was Athenodorus of Tarsus, from Paul's home town. He was in his later years entrusted with a mission to straighten out the constitution and leadership of Tarsus, where he became its chief citizen.[11] Several other Stoic teachers hailed from Tarsus as well. It is only reasonable to expect that Stoicism would be known to Paul, and would be a lively intellectual current in the Corinth of the first century; what better ground could there be for a Greek philosophy popular with Romans than a major city of Greece refounded by Rome? A Stoicizing influence could easily have entered the church via its members who had received some education in their youth. Christians coming from citizen families, and especially families of wealth or social status, would have become familiar with rhetoric and philosophy if they had attended tertiary education; and even if they only made it through secondary education, some philosophy had entered the syllabus of general education (ἐγκύκλιος παιδεία) by this time; and the Ephebic colleges also included a smattering of rhetoric and philosophy.[12] Such training was believed to fit one for public service.[13] I use the term 'Stoicizing' influence, because I am not talking about people who are full-time philosophers or are necessarily acquainted with the system in great depth.[14]

For the Stoa there was a vast gulf between the 'wise man' (ὁ σοφός) and the common people (οἱ πολλοί). The σοφός (who is also described as σπουδαῖος, 'good',

---

8. Sevenster, *Paul and Seneca,* 16.

9. F. H. Sandbach, *The Stoics* (London: Chatto & Windus, 1975) 16f., 142–44.

10. Nero eventually forced Seneca to suicide and had other Stoics put to death, including a senator (Thrasea Paetus) and a governor of Asia Minor (Barea Soranus). These judgments, which did not occur until AD 65–66, were inspired by the assassination conspiracy and Nero's suspicious paranoia (Sandbach, *The Stoics,* p. 144). Hadrian, Antoninus Pius, and Marcus Aurelius also supported Stoics.

11. Sandbach, *The Stoics,* pp. 142f.; *OCD* s.v. 'Athenodorus' (of Tarsus): PWSup, V, pp. 47ff.

12. H. I. Marrou. *A History of Education in Antiquity* (trans. George Lamb; London: Sheed & Ward, 1956) 108, 210–11; Stanley F. Bonner, *Education in Ancient Rome* (London: Methuen & Co., 1977) 85–87, 110. Some of the wealthier families might hire a qualified private tutor to train their children at home. A famous example of this in pre-Roman Corinth was the household of Xeniades, who purchased the Cynic philosopher Diogenes in a slave auction to become his sons' tutor (D.L. 6.30–31).

13. R. L Fox, *Pagans and Christians* (New York: Alfred Knopf, 1987) 13–15, 18.

14. So Rist remarks 'many Stoics had merely read their Stoicism or talked to Stoicizing individuals, and then claimed to be Stoics or desiderant Stoics' ('Are You a Stoic? The Case of Marcus Aurelius', in *Jewish and Christian Self-Definition,* vol. 3: *Self-Definition in the Greco-Roman World* [ed. Ben Meyer and E. P. Sanders; London: SCM, 1982] 23).

and φρόνιμος, 'wise/prudent') is one who has made the goal of his existence the 'life in accord with nature' (κατα φύσιν ζῆν). This is intended to aid the pursuit of virtue, which is the only absolute 'good' recognized by the Stoa.[15] Only virtue is necessary to be happy (εὐδαίμων) and wise; all else is ἀδιάφορον ('indifferent').

However, one could pursue a life according to nature and yet not have achieved virtue and not be a Stoic wise man. For the Stoa consider no degrees of virtue or progress. One who is 'making progress' is still drowning and not yet safely ashore, still committing 'sins' and far from virtue. Either one is *perfect*, a σοφός, or one is still φαῦλος, a scoundrel who is lost.[16] Attaining the status of a σοφός could be described as a kind of enlightenment that put one in a class above all others, with instinctive insight into the world. From Plutarch's sarcastic description of the Stoic wise man we can still see this ideal of the enlightened sage who stands above the rest of humanity in regard to virtue:

> Among the Stoics the man who is most vicious in the morning, if so it chance to be, is in the afternoon most virtuous. Having fallen asleep demented and stupid and unjust and licentious and even, by heaven, a slave and a drudge and a pauper, he gets up the very same day changed into a blessed and opulent *king*, sober and just and steadfast and undeluded by fancies. He has not sprouted a beard or the token of puberty in a body young and soft, but in a soul that is feeble and soft and unmanly and unstable has got perfect intelligence, consummate prudence, a godlike disposition, *knowledge* free from fancy, and an unalterable habitude and this not from any previous abatement of his depravity, but by having changed instantaneously from the most vicious of wild beasts into what may almost be called a kind of hero or spirit [δαίμων] or god. For, if one has got virtue from the Stoa, it is possible to say 'Ask, if there's aught you wish; *all will be yours* [πάντα σοι γενήσεται]'. It brings *wealth* [πλοῦτον], it comprises *kingship* [βασιλείαν], it gives luck, it makes men prosperous *and free from all other wants* and self-sufficient [αὐτάρκεις], though they have not a single drachma of their own.[17]

The italicized words parallel descriptions of the Corinthians (by themselves or by Paul) in 1 Corinthians which are usually thought to arise from an over-realized eschatology. So 1 Cor 4.8, 'Already you are full, already you have become rich, without us you reign (as kings—ἐβασιλεύσατε). . . .' Yet the use of these terms could have arisen from a misplaced, Stoic-like ideal of themselves as wise. For according to the Stoa, only the wise man is truly happy, truly wealthy, truly fit to govern as king, truly free.[18] This is because he shares the world with the gods, and is enriched with the wisdom of the divine λόγος which governs nature.

15. Sandbach. *The Stoics,* 53f.; Terence Irwin, *A History of Western Philosophy,* vol. 1: *Classical Thought* (Oxford: Oxford University Press, 1989) 174. The living of a life according to nature may even be said to be equivalent to living virtuously (D.L. 7.87).

16. D. L. 7.120f.; Sandbach, *The Stoics,* 44; A. H. Armstrong, *An Introduction to Ancient Philosophy* (3d ed.; London: Methuen & Co., 1957; rpt. ed., 1968) 126.

17. Plutarch, *Stoic. abs.* 1058B-C (H. Cherniss' translation in the Loeb edition of the *Moralia,* vol. 13.2, pp. 615, 617).

18. Cf. also Plutarch, *Comm. not.* 1060B; 1062E; D.L. 7.122.

Besides the ideal of an enlightened sage, the Stoic understanding of virtue is closely tied to *knowledge*. The key is to know what is 'according to nature' and then what is virtuous—which is akin to nature, since for the Stoic God is in nature everywhere. God has shaped nature and Destiny or Fate as well, therefore virtue is in accord with the divine reason or λόγος as expressed in the formation of the universe. In fact, according to I. G. Kidd, the true Stoic wise man at the pinnacle of his moral progress leaves behind the study of ethics to concentrate on the *logos*-philosophy, since understanding the mind of Nature/God is the higher pursuit.[19] To achieve virtue, the student must begin his training by learning to *choose* rightly the things that are κατὰ φύσιν.[20] If one asks how the wise man is to know what is κατὰ φύσιν, the Stoa never give a clear answer. They seem to picture him as intuitively understanding both his own nature and that of the cosmos, and these are in harmony.[21]

This heavily rationalized view of virtue saw error or 'sin' accordingly as simply a bad judgment of the intellect, and denied the existence of any irrational forces in the soul.[22] The goal of the wise life then was aided by the extirpation of irrational 'passions', products of bad judgment of the mind. Those who were not wise were foolish, ruled by irrational passion, incapable of real friendship and therefore enemies of the wise.[23]

What most people held to be important and necessary for happiness the Stoics regarded as 'indifferent', dispensable. Such things included health, wealth, clothing, reputation, even death. Therefore, most people's pursuit of the normal things of life, and their sadness at the loss of such things, was treated by the Stoa as simply examples of irrational passion. These were things to be overcome, not something to sympathize with or to help along. Even the death of a spouse or children is classed as an 'indifferent', and to grieve over such things is irrational, the mark of one who does not yet think aright and is not perfect.[24] Such a philosophy could easily lead to a callous attitude towards one's fellow human beings.

The odd thing is that the Stoics did advocate involvement in political life.[25] And many Stoics are recorded in the Roman senate and high government offices

19. I. G. Kidd. 'Stoic Intermediates and the End for Man', in *Problems in Stoicism* (ed. A. A. Long; London: Athlone Press, 1971) 165–66.

20. Compare Paul's argument to the Corinthians at 1 Cor 11.14.

21. 'It has been argued in the preceding pages that to live consistently with nature was an aim accepted by all Stoics, that this nature was universal nature, with which man's fully-developed nature must always coincide, and which in great part allowed him to have what suited his own individual nature' (Sandbach, *The Stoics*, 59). Kidd argues that in the first stage of progress toward becoming wise, the Stoic-in-training was thought to look toward harmony with his own (human) nature, eventually leading him into harmony with the universal nature and world-logos which shaped him (Kidd, 'Stoic Intermediates', 165–67).

22. D. L. 7.111; Sandbach, *The Stoics*, 41f. Plato had postulated an irrational part of the soul that fought against the rational part, and was sealed in a different locus from it. Posidonius was the only Stoic to admit such an irrational 'force' in the soul (which he held to be a unified whole, in Stoic fashion).

23. D. L. 7.32–33.

24. Irwin, *A History of Western Philosophy*, 174–76.

25. Though none of the leaders of the school was in politics until after the time of Chrysippus in the mid II BC (cf. D.L. 7.121). When Chrysippus was asked why he did not enter politics, he replied 'Bad politics displeases the gods; good politics the citizens'.

from the late first century BC to the second century AD. Terence Irwin attempts to uphold the Stoic claim that they are truly unselfishly interested in others' welfare by their involvement in public life, yet in the end must concede 'Stoic ethics seems to be an unstable combination of self-sufficiency and concern for others'.[26] For the true Stoic sage neither wishes to nor can he extend any 'passionate sympathy' to others. Pity and compassion (ἐλεημοσύνη) are *vices*, not virtues.[27] They arise from a wrong judgment of things that are really indifferent.

Further, there is a strong drive in Stoicism, as noted by Irwin, to self-sufficiency. This they inherited from Cynicism, where the 'life according to nature' was usually interpreted to mean a way of life dependent on no one and nothing but the barest essentials, a kind of hyper-Socratic existence.[28] For Cynic and Stoic ethics, pursuit of virtue is a wrestling with oneself and the world; it is the individual seeking to embrace nature and his Fate, whatever is thrown at him. All that happens to one can be seen as opportunities for personal testing, advancement and victory over circumstances. You must test the appearances of things, says Epictetus, not accepting what they seem to be (good or evil), but judging them rationally in line with nature (φύσις; Epictetus *Diss.* 3.12.14f.). Even the encounter with another human being is reduced to an opportunity to 'test the appearances of things', to exercise oneself in judgment and in passionlessness (Epictetus *Diss.* 3.12.1–8, 10–12). It is not viewed as an opportunity to do good to the other, or to shun doing evil to the other. The only evil one can do is to oneself. The other is seen only in respect of the needs of oneself. There is no sense of community obligation, or of any community bond.

The Stoic can indeed say that Zeus is father of all, and this man is my brother;[29] but in reality it is only the σοφοί / σπουδαῖοι who can have true community. Only the perfect can be true friends and share all things with the gods. They have nothing in common with the masses, who are base and do not know how to love (D.L. 7.124; 7.32–33). This limits 'community' to the perfect few, though even here one wonders what kind of mutual empathy and society could exist. The wise man, it is said, is able to be content alone and solitary, like Zeus at the end of the world. He needs no one but himself to speak to (Epictetus *Diss.* 3.13.4, 6–8). The Stoic will neither give nor receive sympathy for any of the common pains and troubles of life.

Now as with most philosophies, and especially one as rigorous as Stoicism, few practised what they preached. But where the Stoics, their pupils and admirers tended to lapse was not in the direction of more love of neighbor and good community feelings than they ought to have. Rather, they tended to begin justifying the pursuit of so-called 'indifferents' (ἀδιάφορα), which everyone else called 'goods', such as health and wealth. So Aristo from Chios, a pupil of Zeno's who was denounced by his master, argued that none of the 'morally indifferent'

---

26. Irwin, *A History of Western Philosophy*, 182.
27. D. L. 7.115 lists pity along with envy and strife as a sickness of the soul.
28. Armstrong, *An Introduction to Ancient Philosophy*, 117 (Cynics); Epictetus, *Diss.* 3.13.
29. Epictetus, *Diss.* 1.3; 1.9.6–7.

things had advantage in or of itself, and so the wise man ought to be free to do whatever he chooses, whatever seems good to him 'without pain, desire, or fear'.[30] Seneca, while praising the poor and simple life according to nature and the brotherhood of men, was amassing one of the greatest fortunes of the empire, with the aid of hosts of slaves, and had complicity in several political murders, including that of the emperor Nero's mother.[31] Epictetus complained that most who professed to be Stoics lived like Epicureans (*Diss.* 2.19).

As said earlier, a Stoicizing influence on prominent Corinthian Christians (and through them, on the whole church) may help to explain many things in the letter. Thus the Corinthians can claim to be satisfied, rich and kings—not because the kingdom has already arrived, but because by the Spirit they have moved from being base to being σοφοί and τέλειοί. Compare D.L. 7.121–23:

> μόνον τ' [τὸν σοφὸν] ἐλεύθερον, τοὺς δὲ φαύλους δούλους· εἶναι γὰρ τὴν ἐλευθερίαν ἐξουσίαν αὐτοπραγίας . . . οὐ μόνον δ' ἐλευθέρους εἶναι τοὺς σοφούς, ἀλλὰ καὶ βασιλέας . . . ἔτι καὶ ἀναμαρτήτους, τῷ ἀπεριπτώτους εἶναι ἁμαρτήματι.

> [The wise man] alone is free, while the common people[32] are slaves; for freedom is the power of independent action . . . and not only are the wise free, but also kings . . . and further, they are also sinless, not being liable to sin.

These Stoicizing-Christian Corinthians see themselves as wise ones who share all with God and have true insight (γνῶσις) into the universe. They know that an idol—that is, an image—is 'nothing' in the cosmos, and that only one God exists (1 Cor 8.4; 10.19). It is interesting to compare this argument with Zeno's prohibition of building temples in the ideal city of his *Republic,* because no work of human builders is worth much, and consequently not sacred.[33] A similar argument against the divinity of images or temple precincts, but now bolstered with a more pure monotheism, is used by the 'strong' at Corinth to justify their attendance at temple feasts or their partaking of food that had been dedicated to pagan gods (8.1–13; 10.14–24). The reaction of the 'weak' to this new development is regarded by the 'strong' solely as the problem of the weak. It is a matter of choice—of how one regards the appearances of things—and of having knowledge or insight into the true nature of the universe. One can only be offended and stumble if his/her thinking is amiss. After all, does not even the Apostle himself agree that it is wrong to think of images as having any power or sacrificial meat as having any significance (1 Cor 10.19)? The problem, think the strong, surely lies in the sick passions and fears of the weak.

---

30. Cicero, *Fin.* 4.69, 43: Sandbach, *The Stoics,* 38f.

31. Sandbach. *The Stoics,* 155f.; *OCD* s.v. 'Seneca'. Seneca's *De Beata Vita* contains some self-justification in its defense of the wise man's guilt-free enjoyment of wealth (25.1–2).

32. Or perhaps 'bad people'.

33. D. L. 7.33; Plutarch, *Stoic. rep.* 1034B: 'it is a doctrine of Zeno's not to build temples of the gods, because a temple not worth much is also not sacred and no work of builders or mechanics is worth much'.

Some premises that Paul agrees with—and which he may have asserted himself in his preaching at Corinth[34]—were being made to serve a conclusion at variance with Paul's theology and, further, at odds with the new existence in Christ. For though the idol is 'nothing', yet to act in accord with those who serve idols is something. Though my conscience may not be harmed, yet to harm another's conscience, to act in a way that encourages another brother or sister to question his faith or return to idolatry is *not* an ἀδιάφορον, an indifferent thing. In Christ the existence of the other Christian is interlinked with my existence (1 Cor 8.12; 12.27). Hence a choice which may be rationalized on one level may affect one's Christian existence at another level because the believer has a union with the risen Lord and with other believers through the Holy Spirit. This union might be expressed as the 'fellowship in [God's] Son Jesus Christ' (1 Cor 1.9) or the 'fellowship of the Holy Spirit' (2 Cor 13.13). 'It is', says Ralph Martin, 'the common life shared by all believers on the ground that they all, by their calling as Christians, participate in Jesus Christ.'[35]

Just such a callousness of individuals toward others as we find at Corinth, such a disregard for the community dimension of their new existence, would likely be fostered by a Stoicizing influence, which would in fact exalt the individual σοφός at the expense of the community. And a Stoic could behave in this individualistic, community-destroying fashion at the same time that he believes he is pursuing a virtuous life according to nature and reason, asserting his divine right of freedom of choice (αὐτοπραγία). We could say Paul counters this by asserting that a Christian's 'interlinked-ness' with Christ limits independence of action for the true σοφός.[36]

Again in chapter 6 Paul warns that some actions corrupt the relationship we have with the indwelling Christ. So to be 'joined' to a prostitute, by an exegesis of Gen 2.24, is said to form a union which is intolerable for a member of the body of Christ. Mental choice and attitude are not the only determining factors in one's existence. Neither can one dismiss what is done with the body as an ἀδιάφορον. Paul reminds them that there is a question of ownership in the new existence. They belong to God; the Spirit of God they have is resident within them, but is not subject to their autonomous control.

---

34. E.g., most commentators agree that the principle of individual freedom (9.1; 10.29, 31; cf. Gal 2.4; 5.1, 13) originates with Paul, not the Corinthians.

35. R. P. Martin, *The Family and the Fellowship: New Testament Images of the Church* (Exeter: Paternoster, 1979) 37; idem, *2 Corinthians* (WBC; Waco: Word, 1986) 254–55, 504–5; 'The Spirit in 2 Corinthians in Light of the "Fellowship of the Holy Spirit" in 2 Corinthians 13:14', in *Eschatology and the New Testament* (ed. W. H. Gloer; Peabody, Mass.: Hendrickson, 1988) 113–38. See also A. R. George, *Communion with God in the New Testament* (London: Epworth, 1953); Jerome Murphy-O'Connor, 'Eucharist and Community in First Corinthians', *Worship* 50 (1976) 370–85; and idem, 'Eucharist and Community in First Corinthians', *Worship* 51 (1977) 56–69; esp. 50 (1976) 383–85; Josef Hainz, *KOINONIA: 'Kirche' als Gemeinschaft bei Paulus* (Regensburg: F. Pustet, 1982).

36. Cf. 1 Cor 10.15, 'I speak as to φρονίμοις' in his warning against taking part in events at pagan temples. φρόνιμος is a synonym for the σοφός in Stoic literature.

Or don't you know that your body is the temple of the Holy Spirit within you, which you possess *from God?* And that *you do not belong to yourselves?* You were purchased with a price: therefore glorify God in your bodies (6.19–20).

πάντα μοι ἔξεστιν, the defense of those whom Paul is correcting (6.12), is not only to be understood as a gnostic proclamation; it expresses very well the prerogative of the Stoic wise man who is good and perfect:

> οὐκοῦν οἱ φρόνιμοι ὅσα βούλονται πράττειν, ἔξεστιν αὐτοῖς· οἱ δὲ ἄφρονες ὅσα βούλονται οὐκ ἐξὸν ἐπιχειροῦσι πράττειν. ὥστε ἀνάγκη τοὺς μὲν φρονίμους ἐλευθέρους τε εἶναι καὶ ἐξεῖναι αὐτοῖς ποιεῖν ὡς ἐθέλουσι ... (*SVF* III:356).[37]

> Therefore whatever the wise wish to do is permitted, but whatever the foolish wish to do, though it is not permitted, they attempt to do. So of necessity the wise are free and it is permitted them to do as they wish ...

The wise man may do whatever he wishes, since he alone has right judgment. The case under consideration in 1 Cor 6.12–20 need not be a libertine whose fleshly actions make no difference. It is not inconceivable that a Stoic could have regarded this sort of sexual immorality (as we call it) an ἀδιάφορον. Though it is true the Stoics generally held up marriage as a good thing,[38] Zeno had advocated a radical communism of women (as had Plato), and a rather free attitude towards sexual matters characterized the school.[39] But more significant is that the specific immorality mentioned in 1 Corinthians chapter 6 is concourse with a prostitute (not sexual immorality in general). And this was usually not held to be in the same class at all as an affair with a married woman.[40]

It is also interesting that Paul begins the defence of his conduct at Corinth in chapter nine with the words, 'Am I not free?' Freedom is one of the most cher-

---

37. From Dio Chrysostom, *Or.* 14.17 (64.17 in von Arnim ed.); cf. Plutarch, *Stoic. abs.* 1058B-C, above.

38. So Antipater of Tarsus *(SVF* III:254f., ap. Stobaeus, *Flor.* 67.25); cf. Sandbach. *The Stoics,* 118; Marcia L. Colish, *The Stoic Tradition from Antiquity to the Early Middle Ages,* vol. 1: *Stoicism in Classical Latin Literature* (Leiden: Brill, 1985) 41.

39. Zeno had taken a radical view of marriage, advocating that the wise hold all women in common; however, his view was not maintained after Chrysippus (Sandbach, *The Stoics,* 25f.; Colish, *The Stoic Tradition,* 38).

40. Prostitution had been common in Greece for well over six centuries, Solon having introduced public brothels, and the Romans were relatively lenient on it as well (W. Krenkel, 'Prostitution', *Kleine Pauly* IV:1192–94). Though one would not usually bring a prostitute home, to frequent the brothels was regarded as a mere *peccadillo.* Antisthenes the Cynic is said to have commented, on seeing an adulterer fleeing the scene of his crime, 'ὦ δυστυχής, πηλίκον κίνδυνον ὀβολοῦ διαφυγεῖν ἴσχυες' (D.L. 6.4): 'Oh unfortunate man, what a great danger you could have escaped with the price of an obol'—referring to the price of a prostitute, whose company would not have brought down on the man's head a husband's wrath. Compare Plutarch's advice to the married wife to look the other way if her husband should share his drunken debauchery with a girl servant or prostitute (ἑταῖρα); she should consider it a sign of his respect for her that he does not behave so indecently with his lawful wife (*Conj. praec.* XVI/140B).

ished and exalted of attributes of the Stoic wise man: freedom from irrational passions; freedom to choose or reject those things which are in his power; freedom to live the life according to nature and to pursue virtue. But Paul overturns this self-centered perspective by his very life, which in its *imitatio Christi* makes a new definition of freedom: Ἐλεύθερος γὰρ ὢν ἐκ πάντων πᾶσιν ἐμαυτὸν ἐδούλωσα, ἵνα τοὺς πλείονας κερδήσω· (9.19). Bultmann vividly describes the Pauline concept thus: 'This freedom arises from the very fact that *the believer*, as one "ransomed", *no longer belongs to himself* (1 Cor 6.19). . . . He recognizes himself to be the property of God (or of the Lord) and lives for Him'.[41] And in another place, 'this basic freedom may at any moment take on the form of *renunciation*—seemingly a renunciation of freedom itself, but in reality it is a paradoxical exercise of that very freedom'.[42] The reason self-renunciation may be the order of the moment, and the reason freedom is not an absolute principle for Paul is the coterminous theological principle of κοινωνία, the community or fellowship which Christians have with God, Christ, and the Holy Spirit on the one hand and with one another on the other hand. This is not the *koinonia* which the Stoic wise man has with God whereby all things belong to him, for it is not individualistically oriented. It signifies a mutual and interconnected existence which has a reality established by God, and which is affirmed emotively by believers.

The same idea is signified in chapter twelve by the expression 'body of Christ' (12.12f., 27). As the parts of a body fit together and serve each other, so the Christians who form Christ's body must be aware of their interdependence, and of their collective dependence on Christ (12.12–27).[43] Such intimate interlinking of individual lives and such a call for emotive union would be unthinkable for the Stoa (despite their affirmation of political life). We know that community was breaking down in this church, for one member could say of another, 'I have no need of you' (12.21)—and yet this appalling sentiment is exactly the sort of proud boast that the σοφός of the Stoa would make, that he needs nothing but himself and nature to be happy and virtuous.

However, the 'parts' of Christ's 'body' must be concerned for each other (12.25). Christians who are truly wise and perfect regulate their 'freedom' in the light of the *koinonia* of believers and the example of their Lord. 'Everything is permitted' can no longer be understood in Stoic fashion, because 'not everything builds up' (10.23). The salvation which is from the Crucified One brings forth the demand, 'let no one seek his own good, but the good of others' (10.24). This is consistent with the 'message of the cross' which is the foundation of the community's new existence in Christ (1.18). It is not that Paul is unconcerned for the fate of the individual; rather, his care for individuals is most intimately linked

41. R. Bultmann. *Theology of the New Testament* (vol. 1; trans. Kendrick Grobel: London: SCM, 1952) 331.

42. Bultmann, *Theology of the New Testament*, 1:342.

43. Cf. R. P. Martin, *The Spirit and the Congregation: Studies in 1 Corinthians 12–15* (Grand Rapids: Eerdmans, 1984) 19–30.

with their participation in the community and the expression of community life—or danger to that life—that their individual lives represent.

Although the problems at the community's celebration of Eucharist (11.17–22) are not directly related to problems of ἐλευθερία and γνῶσις, the attitudes displayed by the wealthier members are attitudes that could easily be furthered by Stoicizing teaching.[44] The Stoic's belief that any apparent evil may be 'overcome' by a proper judgment (in this case, that the lack of the poor is not really an evil and cannot affect their virtue), coupled with his firm belief in a divine Fate which has determined everything rationally, could easily support a lack of concern for the poor.

Given the popularity of Stoicism in the first century, the mixed Greek and Roman character of Corinth, the presence of Stoicizing terminology in 1 Corinthians and the evidence of Corinthian attitudes just discussed, it is not unreasonable to suppose that part of the problem at Corinth may well have been a Stoicizing (or Cynic and Stoicizing) influence. Such an influence would not only explain the presence of Stoic-like terminology, but the development of an elite group of self-styled *sophoi* within the church who held a highly individualistic, self-centered ethics. This influence probably helped to foster a similarly self-centered spirituality. It advocated a concept of Christian 'freedom' which was at odds with community. This was leading to a breakdown of community, and Paul's answer was to display the fully dependent status of their existence in Christ. No one is autonomous (6.19–20; 12.12–27). And *koinonia*—with the Son Jesus Christ (1.9), with the Holy Spirit (2 Cor 13.13; cf. 1 Cor 3.16; 6.19), and with each other—has the status of a theological principle which also must co-determine ethics, spirituality, and worship.

44. These are also the members who could have afforded rhetorical and philosophical education in their youth. For recent analyses of 1 Corinthians pointing to evidence of sociological stratification and problems arising from the wealthier, more influential members at Corinth, see G. Theissen, *Studien zur Soziologie des Urchristentums* (WUNT, no. 9; Tübingen: J. C. B. Mohr, 1979) = ET *Social Setting*; Abraham J. Malherbe, *Social Aspects of Early Christianity* (2nd enlarged ed.; Philadelphia: Fortress, 1983) 30, 82–84; Meeks, *First Urban Christians*, 70–71, 118f.; Jerome Murphy-O'Connor, *St. Paul's Corinth: Texts and Archaeology* (Wilmington, Del.: Michael Glazier, 1983) 153–61.

Chapter 17

The Social Status
of Erastus (Rom. 16:23)[*]

Justin J. Meggitt

INTRODUCTION

Erastus, mentioned by Paul in Rom 16.23, features prominently in discussions of the social status of the Corinthian Christians. Proponents of what has come to be known as the 'new consensus' (see ch. 6 above) have generally promoted the view that the Erastus to whom Paul refers is the same person as the Erastus whose name features on a pavement inscription unearthed at Corinth (see photo 4, p. 47). The Erastus of the inscription was undoubtedly a wealthy man with a high position in Corinthian society—the inscription states that he laid the pavement at his own expense in return for being elected as one of Corinth's aediles (two were elected annually to serve in the city's administration). In this article Justin Meggitt challenges the strength of the evidence for identifying Paul's Erastus with the Erastus of the inscription and also questions other arguments put forward to support the view that the Christian Erastus was of high social status. Meggitt argues to the contrary, that 'Erastus' socio-economic situation was most

*J. J. Meggitt, 'The Social Status of Erastus (Rom. 16:23)', *NovT* 38 (1996) 218–23. Reprinted by permission of Brill Academic Publishers.

likely indistinguishable from that of his fellow believers' (p. 225). His arguments about Erastus form part of his wider case against the new consensus view of the socioeconomic status of the early Christians, a case he presents in his controversial book, *Paul, Poverty and Survival*. For Meggitt, it is much more likely, given the evidence that we have, that all of the early Christians shared in the poverty that was the lot of the vast majority of the inhabitants of the Roman empire. Dale Martin and Gerd Theissen, however, in recent responses to Meggitt's work, seek to show that some form of the 'new consensus' picture remains more plausible.

Further Reading

See chapters 6, 19.

H. J. Cadbury, 'Erastus of Corinth', *JBL* 50 (1931) 42–58.

Clarke, *Secular and Christian Leadership*, 46–56.

D. W. J. Gill, 'Erastus the Aedile', *TynBul* 40 (1989) 293–300.

D. B. Martin, 'Review Essay: Justin J. Meggitt, *Paul, Poverty and Survival*', *JSNT* 84 (2001) 51–64.

Meggitt, *Paul, Poverty*.

J. J. Meggitt, 'Response to Martin and Theissen', *JSNT* 84 (2001) 85–94.

Theissen, *Social Setting*, 75–83.

G. Theissen, 'The Social Structure of Pauline Communities: Some Critical Remarks on J. J. Meggitt, *Paul, Poverty and Survival*', *JSNT* 84 (2001) 65–84.

G. Theissen, 'Social Conflicts in the Corinthian Community: Further Remarks on J. J. Meggitt, *Paul, Poverty and Survival*', *JSNT* 25 (2003) 371–91.

B. W. Winter, *Seek the Welfare of the City: Christians as Benefactors and Citizens* (Grand Rapids: Eerdmans, 1994) 179–97.

For many New Testament scholars the Erastus mentioned by Paul in Rom 16.23 gives us some of the firmest evidence that we possess for the spread of Christianity, in its earliest phase, amongst the urban elite of the Roman Empire. Most notably, it provides the proponents of the so-called 'New Consensus'[1] (those who maintain that the new faith was characterised, from the outset, by a broad social as well as geographical dispersion) with one of the most tangible pieces of data in support of their thesis. But such an interpretation of Erastus does not, I believe, stand up to close scrutiny.

There are a number of reasons advanced for believing that Erastus came from the privileged circles of his day. Firstly, from the New Testament alone, the description of this individual as ὁ οἰκονόμος τῆς πόλεως (Rom 16.23) appears unequivocally to indicate this. Whilst the expression is, by itself, socially somewhat ambiguous (it could be used both for high ranking municipal officials and also for low ranking public slaves)[2] the fact that Rom 16.23 is the only occasion

---

1. A title coined by Abraham Malherbe, *Social Aspects of Early Christianity* (Baton Rouge: Louisiana State University Press, 1977) 31.

2. G. Theissen, 'Soziale Schichtung in der korinthischen Gemeinde: Ein Beitrag zur Soziologie des hellenistischen Urchristentums', *ZNW* 65 (1974) 239–241; Clarke, *Secular and Christian Leadership*, 49–54. For an example of the full title ὁ οἰκονόμος τῆς πόλεως being used during our period of a slave see Ἀρχαιολογικὸν Δελτίον 35 (1980) B369 (Thessalonika).

in which Paul mentions the secular status of a member of the congregation is often taken as evidence of its social significance.[3]

But such an argument is less than convincing. It presupposes that Paul would take special pride in having a powerful convert—yet the apostle, if anything, shows antipathy to the notion of secular prestige in his epistles.[4] The title, in fact, may be used by Paul to distinguish between the several Erastuses mentioned in the New Testament as associated with the Pauline mission (Rom 16.23; Acts 19.22; 2 Tim 4.2—if we assume, as many exegetes do, that they refer to more than one individual).[5] Or, perhaps (though somewhat more speculatively) it could be argued that this is not a reference to a secular title at all. Rather, the apostle might be referring to an office *within* the church: Erastus may be *the* steward or treasurer, overseeing, for example, the financial contributions towards the 'collection', a significant element of the life of the Pauline congregations (Rom 15.25–32; 1 Cor 16.1–4; 2 Cor 8 and 9; Gal 2.10). This is quite possible given the literary context of Rom 16.23,[6] and also the propensity for *collegia* (which have many parallels to the early communities)[7] to employ the terminology of civic government for their own offices.[8]

Secondly, in addition to the New Testament evidence there is also a famous piece of epigraphical data marshalled to support this reading. An inscription from Corinth refers to a figure called Erastus who held the important civic office of *aedilis,* and had the resources to pay for the paving of part of that city's marketplace.[9] If he is the same individual as that referred to in Rom 16.23 then evidently Paul's Erastus would have been amongst the most socially powerful of his day. Some scholars have been quite bold about making this identification,[10]

3. Theissen, 'Soziale Schichtung', 238. Followed by Clarke, *Secular and Christian Leadership,* 56.

4. For instance, 1 Cor 1.27–28; 1 Cor 6.1.

5. For example, C. Hemer, *The Book of Acts in the Setting of Hellenistic History* (Tübingen: J. C. B. Mohr, 1989) 235. It is surely not enough to protest, as Theissen does, that, 'Paul himself, however, never mentions any other Erastus' (Theissen, 'Soziale Schichtung', 238).

6. Rom 15.25ff. refers to the collection and the description of Erastus and follows immediately from that of Gaius, who, though not holding a specific office, clearly has a distinct role in the church, as its 'host'.

7. Superficially, of course, there were significant similarities between the Christian churches and these institutions, as we can see both from pagan and Christian commentators (see Pliny, *Ep.* 10.96; Origen, *Cels.* 1.1; 8.17.4–7; SHA, *Vita Alexander* 49; Tertullian, *Apol.* 38–39). See R. L. Wilken, 'Collegia, Philosophical Schools and Theology', in *Early Church History: The Roman Empire as the Setting of Primitive Christianity* (ed. S. Benko and J. O'Rourke; London: Oliphants, 1971) 268–91, and *The Christians as the Romans Saw Them* (New Haven: Yale University Press, 1984) 31–47.

8. J. P. Waltzing, *Étude historique sur les corporations professionelles chez les Romains depuis les origines jusqu'à la chute de l'Empire d'Occident* (Louvain: Charles Peeters, 1885) 4:323–430.

9. J. H. Kent, *Inscriptions 1926–1950: Corinth,* viii. *Part Three* (Princeton: The American School of Classical Studies at Athens, 1966) 99.

10. Otto F. A. Meinardus, *St. Paul in Greece* (6th ed.; Athens: Lycabettus Press, 1992) 75; D. Engels, *Roman Corinth: An Alternative Model for a Classical City* (Chicago: University of Chicago Press, 1990) 108; V. P. Furnish, 'Corinth in Paul's Time. What Can Archaeology Tell Us?', *Biblical Archaeology Review* 15 (1988) 20; Kent, *Corinth,* 99; O. Broneer, 'Corinth, Center of St. Paul's Missionary Work in Greece', *Biblical Archaeologist* 14 (1951) 94; T. L. Shear, 'Excavations in the Theatre District and Tombs of Corinth in 1929', *AJA* 33 (1929) 526; B. Winter, *Seek the Welfare of the City: Christians as Benefactors and Citizens* (Carlisle: Paternoster Press, 1994) 192.

whilst others have been somewhat more cautious,[11] but few, if any, resist assuming an association between the two characters.

There are a number of grounds posited for maintaining that the Erastus of Rom 16.23 and that of the inscription are one and the same: a) the dating of the inscription; b) the possibility that the expression ὁ οἰκονόμος τῆς πόλεως is synonymous or closely related with that of 'aedile'; c) the relative rarity of the name 'Erastus'. However, on closer inspection, it is evident that these arguments are much weaker than has hitherto been recognised.

a) *Dating*. The dating of the inscription to 'sometime near the middle of the first century after Christ',[12] by J. H. Kent (in the fullest excavation report yet produced) appears to support such an identification, given the likelihood that Paul wrote the last chapter of Romans from Corinth sometime in the early 50s.[13] However, Kent's claim is somewhat too precise. Palaeography alone can only give us the roughest approximation of a date.[14] When the crucial central slab was discovered in 1929[15] it was initially rather more vaguely dated to the second half of the first century[16] and some subsequent commentators have placed it even later.[17] A *terminus ad quem* is provided by the fact that the inscription seems to have been used in repair work to a pavement that was undertaken some time in the middle of the second century,[18] but as H. Cadbury noted, 'The original inscription is therefore older than that, but whether one generation older or more cannot be determined'.[19] The dating of the inscription is much more problematic than has often been assumed[20] and therefore the correlation between the date of its dedication and that of the composition of the apostle's words about Erastus in his letter to the Romans is considerably less impressive than is normally maintained.

b) ὁ οἰκονόμος τῆς πόλεως has also encouraged the association of the two Erastuses. Scholars have been somewhat divided upon the exact relation-

---

11. Clarke, *Secular and Christian Leadership*, 55; D. Gill, 'In Search of the Social Élite in the Corinthian Church', *TynBul* 44 (1993) 325.

12. Kent, *Corinth*, 99.

13. See for example C. K. Barrett, *First Epistle to the Corinthians: A Commentary* (2nd ed.; London: A. and C. Black, 1971) 5; and Fee, *First Epistle*, 15. Even Gerd Lüdemann's chronology does not differ substantially from this date (*Paul: Apostle to the Gentiles: Studies in Chronology* [London: SCM, 1984] 363).

14. Writing, ' . . . may be conjecturally datable within a century or two' (A. E. Gordon, *Illustrated Introduction to Latin Epigraphy* [Berkeley: University of California Press, 1983] 40).

15. Of the three pieces that make up the inscription as we have it, the central slab was found in 1929, almost intact, and the two pieces that constitute the somewhat less preserved right-hand slab, in 1928 and 1947 respectively.

16. F. J. Waele, 'Erastus, Oikonoom van Korinthe en Vriend van St. Paulus', *Mededelingen van het Nederlandsch Historisch Instituut te Rome* 9 (1929) 43.

17. According to Henry J. Cadbury's account of the history of relevant scholarship, 'Erastus of Corinth', *JBL* 50 (1931) 46.

18. R. Stillwell, *The Theatre: Corinth ii* (Princeton: The American School of Classical Studies at Athens, 1962) 4.

19. See note 17.

20. It certainly is not the case that, 'The dating of the inscription to the middle of the first century AD is not widely disputed' (Clarke, *Secular and Christian Leadership*, 49).

ship of this office to that of *aedilis* mentioned in the inscription. For some they are identical. As Kent remarked, 'Saint Paul's word οἰκονόμος describes with reasonable accuracy the function of a Corinthian aedile'.[21] For others, such as Theissen, the term indicates a position that, 'one held prior to the office of aedile'.[22] But whichever option is the most plausible, the link between the office referred to by Paul and that mentioned in the inscription appears compellingly close.

But whilst ὁ οἰκονόμος τῆς πόλεως may indeed be used to indicate a powerful civic functionary we should not forget, as we have observed above, that it does not necessarily do so at all; there are numerous examples of the phrase being used of individuals who held much more menial roles and possessed far less socioeconomic standing.[23] For example, Longeinos, the οἰκονόμος τῆς πόλεως of Thessalonika, who erected a simple epitaph to his wife, was unlikely to have been socially very exalted: the brevity of the inscription, cut into recycled stone, is hardly indicative of wealth or status. Indeed, the fact that he refers to himself with a single name, and one particularly common to the enslaved at that, confirms his modest status.[24]

c) *The relative rarity of the name.* The assumed relative rarity of the name Erastus has also invited this identification.[25] For example, V. P. Furnish asserts 'since the name itself is not common, it would appear that this Erastus is the same one whom Paul and the author of 2 Timothy mention.'[26] However, we have substantially more epigraphic attestations for the name than has hitherto been realised. I have discovered 55 examples of the use of the Latin cognomen Erastus[27] and 23 of the Greek Ἔραστος,[28] making it, in fact, a relatively common

21. Kent, *Corinth,* 99.

22. Theissen, 'Sociale Schichtung', 81. See also Chow, *Patronage and Power,* 93, 155.

23. Cadbury, 'Erastus of Corinth', 50. See also R. Lane Fox, *Pagans and Christians* (Harmondsworth: Penguin, 1986) 293.

James Dunn makes the pertinent point that we should not interpret the definite article as evidence that Erastus held high public office: 'The definite article does not necessarily indicate that there was only one oikonomos; it could just mean the oikonomos who was a Christian' (*Romans 9–16* [Waco: Word Books, 1988] 911).

24. The full inscription reads: ΛΟΝΓΕΙΝΟΣ ΟΙΚΟΝΟΜΟΣ ΤΗΣ ΠΟΛΕΩΣ ΑΡΤΕΜΙΔ-ΩΡΑ ΤΗ ΣΥΜΒΙΩ Μ(ΝΕΙ)ΑΣ ΧΑΡΙΝ. (AD 35 [1980] B369 [Thessalonika]). See also H. W. Picket's comments on SEG 38 (1988) 710.

25. Kent, *Corinth,* 100.

26. Furnish, 'Corinth in Paul's Time', 20.

27. *CIL* III 2840, 9052; IV 179, 4614, 4641, 5820; V 6821, 7232; VI 695, 1300, 1914 (379), 1934 (219), 5232, 5858, 7513, 8518 (twice), 8875, 9865 (12), 9759, 9915 (6), 11178, 13501, 14040, 14457, 15031, 15325, 15439, 15483, 15492, 15728, 17253, 24452, 24776, 24739, 27452, 33109, 33614, 36364; IX 3418; X 527, 1878, 2002, 2519, 6144; XI 227, 1620, 3613 (12), 6700 (320), 6712 (133); XII 128; XIV 1255, 4032, 4562 (4); XVI 33. AE 1984, 625.

28. AM 95 (1970) p. 212 nos. 149–150; SEG XI 622, 994; XXIV 194; XXV 194; XXVIII 1010; XXIX 301; XXXV 1259. *CIG* 1241; 1249; 6378. *IG* II²1945 (4), 1968 (7), 1973 (76), 1985 (3), 1990 (12, 22), 2030 (20), 2059 (93), 2067 (90), 2323 (221), 3762 (10); *IG* IV 1488 (39); P. Heid Bi7 (IIa). There are also a number of literary references—Plato, *Ep.* 6.322d, 323a; Diogenes Laertius 3.46; Strabo 13.608.

name for our period,[29] and the identification of the inscriptional Erastus with that in Rom. 16.23 therefore much less likely.[30]

Finally, we have another reason for doubting the relevance of the Corinthian inscription for determining the socio-economic status of Paul's Erastus. It might well be the case that the inscription was actually set up by an individual who was not called Erastus at all but rather *Eperastus*,[31] a widely attested, if somewhat less popular, cognomen.[32]

This is not quite as improbable as it might at first sight seem. The inscription that we have is not complete. A left hand section has yet to be recovered. What remains is broken on the E of ERASTUS and so, by itself, we have no reason to assume that ERASTUS is actually a complete word (except ignorance of the possible alternative EPERASTUS).

The chief objection to the name Eperastus being present in the inscription is the problem of space. Most scholars have followed Kent's assumption that line two (which appears to be complete) was placed symmetrically below the partially complete line one, allowing us to estimate that the number of letters from line one that were on the left hand missing section must have amounted to about seven[33]—enough room for an abbreviated praenomen and short nomen of five or six letters[34] but not for the two additional letters EP that the Eperastus option would require. However, it is quite possible that the inscription is, in fact, *not* symmetrical and more than seven letters might be missing. There are plenty of examples of even prestigious inscriptions being badly executed,[35] and difficulties in spacing were quite a regular occurrence. Indeed, the inscription belongs to a type that was particularly susceptible to error. Its long width and short height encouraged problems of spacing that were less common on, for example, narrower *stelae*. Certainly, the irregular gaps between the letters in the complete second line are hardly indicative of precision. It is therefore quite possible that there

29. The most recent study by Clarke has produced 11 attestations. See Clarke, *Secular and Christian Leadership*, 54–55, and also 'Another Corinthian Erastus Inscription', *TynBul* 42 (1991) 146–51.

30. Interestingly, as Clarke has pointed out, the assertion that no other Erastus is attested for Corinth, made by Kent *(Corinth,* 99) and Theissen ('Soziale Schichtung', 246) is, in fact, inaccurate. See Clarke, 'Another', 146–51.

31. H. van de Weerd, 'Een Nieuw Opschrift van Korinthe', *Revue Belge de Philologie et d'Histoire* 10 (1931) 91.

32. I have found 15 attestations of the Latin *Eperastus*: *CIL* III 14.195, 14.0; VI 1879, 7381, 12816, 16262, 16403, 17195, 21834, 22397, 24267a (twice); X 1403 (d, 1, 13); XI 982; 1. Ephesus 860; and 18 of the Greek Ἐπέραστος: *IG* II²1996 (21), 2086 (49, 120), 2094 (70), 2119 (27), 2123 (19), 2123 (25), 2191 (61), 11278, 11449; *IG* IV 1230; VII 2434; IX 1121 (3); Ag. xv 307, 6; SEG IX 917; XI 1274, XVIII 53; XXI 639, 2; XXVIII 166 (7).

33. Kent, *Corinth,* 100.

34. The treatments of both Clarke *(Secular and Christian,* 48) and D. Gill ('Erastus the Aedile', *TynBul* 40 [1989] 295 n. 4) follow Kent in assuming centring *(Corinth,* 100).

35. See G. C. Susini, *The Roman Stonecutter: An Introduction to Latin Epigraphy* (Oxford: Basil Blackwell, 1973) 39–49.

was room for these two letters. Certainly a margin of error of two letters is not in itself substantial.[36]

But this is only a possibility. Regardless of the veracity of the Eperastus option, it is still improbable that the Erastus of Rom 16.23 is identifiable with the figure mentioned in the Corinthian inscription.

We can conclude therefore that, despite the current fashion to the contrary, Erastus' socio-economic situation was most likely indistinguishable from that of his fellow believers. He cannot be used as evidence of the spread of the new faith amongst the socially powerful of the Principate. He is incapable of bearing the weight of the speculative reconstructions that have been placed upon his shoulders by 'New Consensus' scholars.

36. The available space on the original inscription, which can be estimated from the surviving fragments, would certainly allow room for these extra letters.

I should like to thank Tina Wilson for her invaluable assistance during the preparation of this article.

Chapter 18

1 Corinthians: A Case Study of Paul's Assembly as an Alternative Society[*]

Richard A. Horsley

INTRODUCTION

In the late 1970s and early 1980s Richard Horsley published a series of essays on aspects of the Corinthian correspondence, showing the parallels between the Corinthians' ideas on wisdom, knowledge, and so on, and those evident in Hellenistic Judaism, particularly as known through the writings of Philo (see ch. 8 above). In his more recent work Horsley has again turned his attention to 1 Corinthians, though from a quite different angle. Drawing on recent historical work on the imperial cult and other aspects of imperial ideology, Horsley seeks to show how Paul attempts a *political* task, to establish an 'alternative society' within the setting of the Roman Empire. In 1 Corinthians, Paul depicts the fate that awaits the rulers of the empire (2.6–8), thus showing his 'adamant opposition to Roman imperial society' (p. 229 below). Positively, he also 'articulates ways in which the assembly of saints is to constitute a community of a new society alternative to the

[*]R. A. Horsley, '1 Corinthians: A Case Study of Paul's Assembly as an Alternative Society', in *Paul and Empire: Religion and Power in Roman Imperial Society* (ed. R. A. Horsley; Harrisburg; Trinity Press International, 1997) 242–52. Reprinted by permission of Trinity Press International.

dominant imperial society' (p. 230 below). This exclusive, alternative society, Horsley argues, was formed in small assemblies, or ἐκκλησίαι, based in households, and—at least in Paul's view—required its members to live independently from and in contrast to 'the world', and to withdraw from participation in basic forms of external social relations.

One may question whether Paul's vision of the Christian community implies the degree of separation and opposition to the world that Horsley sees, and, indeed, whether the Corinthian ἐκκλησία was as 'alternative' as Horsley suggests. The picture of a community in which the practice of egalitarian solidarity stands in stark contrast to the dominant social order around, while convincing to some degree, may seem to reflect contemporary political values and aspirations as well as historical reality. Yet part of the challenge of Horsley's work lies precisely in its call for political interests and commitments, contemporary as well as historical, to be made conscious and explicit, rather than remaining veiled beneath a spurious claim to detached objectivity. Furthermore, Horsley's work is important not least in drawing attention to the integration of religion and politics in the ancient world and specifically in the Roman Empire and thus in forcing us to consider the ways in which early Christian faith and practice were intrinsically political as well as religious.

Further Reading

E. Adams, *Constructing the World: A Study in Paul's Cosmological Language* (SNTW; Edinburgh: T. & T. Clark, 2000) 105–49.

D. G. Horrell, 'Idol-Food, Idolatry and Ethics in Paul', in *Idolatry in the Bible, Early Judaism and Christianity* (ed. S. C. Barton and L. T. Stuckenbruck; London: T. & T. Clark, forthcoming).

R. A. Horsley, *1 Corinthians* (ANTC; Nashville: Abingdon, 1998).

R. A. Horsley, ed., *Paul and Empire: Religion and Power in Roman Imperial Society* (Harrisburg: Trinity Press International, 1997).

R. A. Horsley, ed., *Paul and Politics: Ekklesia, Israel, Imperium, Interpretation* (Harrisburg: Trinity Press International, 2000).

R. A. Horsley, 'Rhetoric and Empire—and 1 Corinthians', in *Paul and Politics,* 72–102.

P. Oakes, *Philippians: From People to Letter* (SNTSMS 110; Cambridge: Cambridge University Press, 2001) 129–74.

First Corinthians has traditionally been a generous source of proof texts that Christians have used as scriptural bases for theological doctrines such as the pre-existence of Christ and social institutions such as slavery. More recently it has been the focus of debates on the degree to which Paul subordinated women and urged slaves to remain in their servile status.[1] In the excitement of these debates,

---

1. Major recent treatments, with references to previous discussion, are Elisabeth Schüssler Fiorenza, *In Memory of Her: A Feminist Theological Reconstruction of Christian Origins* (New York: Crossroad, 1983); Wire, *Corinthian Women Prophets*; Amos Jones, Jr., *Paul's Message of Freedom: What Does It Mean to the Black Church?* (Valley Forge, Pa.: Judson, 1984); Neil Elliott, *Liberating Paul: The Justice of God and the Politics of the Apostle* (Maryknoll, N.Y.: Orbis Books, 1994). See also my *1 Corinthians,* (ANTC; Nashville: Abingdon, 1998); and the issue of *Semeia* (1998) devoted to 'Slavery in Text and History'.

however, little attention has been given to the wider horizon within which Paul understands the assembly's struggles, that is, to the fulfillment of history between the crucifixion and exaltation of Christ, in the immediate past and the *parousia* and general resurrection in the imminent future, and to Paul's adamant opposition to Roman imperial society. Since, among Paul's letters, it covers the greatest number of different facets of assembly life in relation to the dominant society, 1 Corinthians may provide a good case study of the ways in which Paul appears to be fostering an alternative society.[2]

The relations between Rome and Corinth exemplify the most extreme forms of Roman imperial practice and of the imperial society it produced. Having maneuvered Corinth and the Achaian league into war, in 146 B.C.E. the Romans ruthlessly sacked the city, killed its men, and enslaved its women and children. A century later Julius Caesar established a colony at Corinth to which were sent, along with some army veterans, large numbers of urban poor from Rome, over half of them freed slaves (Strabo 8.6.23). Ambitious freedmen and others of low social status thus set the tone in a hypercompetitive urban ethos (e.g., Apuleius, *Metam.* 10.19, 25). The elite, hungry for honor and office, cultivated the patronage of governors and emperors and sponsored construction of new civic and imperial temples in the city center and festivals such as the newly instituted Caesarean Games. Populated by the descendants of Roman riffraff and deracinated former slaves, Corinth was the epitome of urban society created by empire: a conglomeration of atomized individuals cut off from the supportive communities and particular cultural traditions that had formerly constituted their corporate identities and solidarities as Syrians, Judeans, Italians, or Greeks. As freedpeople and urban poor isolated from any horizontal supportive social network, they were either already part of or readily vulnerable for recruitment into the lower layers of patronage pyramids extending downwards into the social hierarchy as the power bases of those clambering for high honor and office expanded. Amidst all the luxuries provided by the increasingly munificent and honored elite, Corinthians had a reputation as uncultured and lacking in social graces, partly because the wealthy so grossly exploited the poor (Alciphron, *Letters* 15 and 24).

The letter as a whole is framed by discussion of the crucifixion of Christ in the opening of the first major argument (1.17–2.8) and the resurrection in the last major argument (ch. 15). In those arguments, moreover, Paul articulates his basic (Judean) apocalyptic orientation and perspective. The crucifixion and resurrection of Christ has become the turn of the ages, from 'this age' (1.20; 2.6, 8) to the next. Paul reminds the Corinthians about just this historical crisis throughout the letter, with references to the imminent judgment (3.12–15; 4.5; 5.5; 6.2–3), to the appointed time of fulfillment having been foreshortened so that the scheme of the present order is passing away (7.29, 31), to 'the ends of the

2. It is also the letter with which I am most familiar, from a series of programmatic articles in the late 1970s and a commentary (*1 Corinthians,* on the research for which much of the analysis and construction below is based).

ages' having come upon them (10.11), and to the Lord's coming anticipated in the very celebration of the Lord's death (11.26). Paul also mentions explicitly that the events of the crucifixion and resurrection are happening according to God's (now revealed) *mystery* or plan for the fulfillment of history (2.7; 15.51; cf. 'the wisdom of God' in 1.21, used parallel with the more technical Judean apocalyptic 'mystery', e.g., Dan 2.18–19, 27–28; 1QS 3.13—4.25; 1QpHab 7.1–5).

What we may not notice immediately, because of the assumption that we are reading about the formation of a religion, is just how politically Paul conceives of these events by which 'this age' is being terminated and the next inaugurated. To be sure, God has also turned the tables on pretentious aristocratic Hellenistic culture. The gospel of Christ crucified is indeed utter foolishness to the elite who benefit from Roman terrorization of subject peoples through crucifixion of rebellious provincials and intransigent slaves. But it is through the despicably crucified Christ and now his lowborn, weak, and despised followers, the Corinthian believers themselves, that God has shamed the pretentious elite questing after power, wealth, wisdom, noble birth, and honorific public office (1.21–23, 26–29; 4.8, 10). Those terms, of course, in their literal meaning, describe not simply a cultural elite but the provincial (Corinthian) political elite. The most important casualties of God's implementation of his plan (mystery), however, are the imperial 'rulers of this age' (2.6–8). Here as elsewhere in Paul (cf. Rom 13.3) and the New Testament, 'rulers' *(archontes)* refers to earthly political rulers.[3] While Paul probably does not have Pontius Pilate explicitly in mind, he is thinking of the Romans and their imperial system who, precisely in crucifying Christ in their unthinking practice of violence, have now been 'doomed to destruction.' In 15.24–28 Paul comes around to the completion of the eschatological events in which the imperial rulers will be destroyed, along with all other 'enemies': At 'the end' Christ will hand the kingdom to God the Father, 'after he has destroyed every rule and every (governing) authority and power'. *Dynamis* in this case may well point to 'powers' such as Death. But *archē* and *exousia,* parallel to 'the rulers of this age,' appear to be the rulers of the Roman imperial system (cf. 'governing authority' in Rom 13.1–3).[4] In 1 Corinthians Paul's gospel, mission, and the struggles of his assembly are part of God's fulfillment of history in the doom and destruction of Roman imperial rule.

In that context, then, we can perceive how at several points in 1 Corinthians Paul articulates ways in which the assembly of saints is to constitute a community of a new society alternative to the dominant imperial society.

First, 1 Corinthians and related references in other letters provide just enough information for us to discern the structure of the mission and the nascent assem-

3. With no real linguistic evidence indicating demonic powers; see Fee, *First Epistle,* esp. pp. 103–4; and Wesley Carr, 'The Rulers of this Age—1 Corinthians II.6–8', *NTS* 23 (1976–77) 20–35.

4. The Christian scholarly mystification of 'rule and governing authority' here and 'rulers of this age' in 2.6–8 into 'cosmic forces' is heavily influenced by their original spiritualization by Paul's 'disciples' in Colossians and Ephesians.

bly(ies) in Corinth and the surrounding area.[5] Paul was teamed with a number of coworkers, not simply Timothy and Silvanus, who had worked with him earlier (1 Thess 1.1; 2 Cor 1.19). He formed a special collaborative bond with Prisca and her husband, Aquila, perhaps because of their common 'trade' (cf. Acts 18.2–3). Contrary to the popular image of Paul preaching the gospel in public places, he and his coworkers almost certainly avoided the marketplace of religious competition (cf. 2 Cor 2.17) for the more intensive interaction of small groups in people's houses. From references to 'the assembly in the house of Prisca and Aquila' (1 Cor 16.19; Rom 16.5; cf. Phlm 2) it seems clear that the movement in Corinth (and again in Ephesus) took the form of a number of small 'assemblies' based in households. Paul's references to 'the whole assembly' coming together for certain purposes such as the Lord's Supper and discussion (1 Cor 14.23; cf. 10.20; Rom 16.23) indicate that at other times only a portion of the whole assembly functioned semi-separately in some way. This is the basis for surmising that households of figures such as Stephanas, Gaius, and possibly Crispus hosted house-based (sub-)assemblies (1 Cor 16.16–17; 1.14–16). The hosts of the latter then constituted leaders and, in effect, additional coworkers in the movement on whom Paul could rely for communication, coordination, and group discipline.[6] The assembly at Cenchreae in which Phoebe was the principal leader (Rom 16.1) illustrates how the network of smaller household-based communities spread out from Corinth into the satellite towns and villages. The picture that emerges from such observations is not one of a religious cult, but of a nascent social movement comprised of a network of cells based in Corinth but spreading more widely into the province of Achaia. That is surely indicated when Paul, writing later in coordination of the collection 'for the poor among the saints in Jerusalem', refers not to Corinth alone but to Achaia more generally, just as he refers not simply to the Thessalonians or Philippians but to 'the assemblies of Macedonia' in general (2 Cor 8.2; 9.2, 4).

Second, besides urging group solidarity, Paul insisted that the Corinthian assembly conduct its own affairs autonomously, in complete independence of 'the world', as he writes in no uncertain terms in 1 Cor 5–6. That did not mean completely shutting themselves off from the society in which they lived. The purpose of the mission, of course, was to bring people into the community. The believers should thus not cut off all contact with 'the immoral of this world, or the greedy and robbers' (5.10). The assembly, however, should not only (a) maintain ethical purity and group discipline in stark opposition to the injustice of the dominant society, but also (b) it should handle its own disputes in absolute independence of the established courts.

---

5. Meeks, *First Urban Christians,* ch. 3, topically organizes much useful information, but sacrifices a sense of the dynamics of a developing movement for analysis in terms of social 'Models from the Environment'.

6. Although structurally the 'house assemblies' also posed an obvious problem for integration and potential conflict, illustrated by the divisiveness to which Paul responds in 1 Corinthians (e.g., 1 Cor 1.11–13; 11.17–34).

The assembly stands diametrically opposed to 'the world' as a community of 'saints'. As often observed, in Paul holiness refers to social-ethical behavior and relations, the maintenance of justice. In these paragraphs Paul states rather bluntly that those who run the civil courts, as well as those 'in the world' outside the assembly generally, are 'unjust' (6.1). His list of unjust outsiders in 5.10 pointedly features the economic injustices of coveting and theft. That surely sets up his suggestion in 6.7–8 that the issue over which one member had taken another to civil court was economic (most likely the plaintiff defrauding the defendant precisely by that action).[7] Thus economic matters as well as matters of sexual morality were included in Paul's concern that the assembly embody just social relations within its autonomous community. By implication in both paragraphs, 5.1–13 and 6.1–11, the assembly of 'saints' should be exercising strict group discipline (cf. the stringent standards and discipline of the Qumran community in 1QS and of the [idealized!] early Jerusalem community of Jesus followers in Acts 2.44–45 and 5.1–6). For Paul, the assemblies at Corinth and elsewhere, as the eschatological people of God, were set over against 'the world' which stood under God's judgment. Indeed, as paralleled in Judean apocalyptic writings (e.g., 1QpHab 5.4; *1 En.* 1.9; 95.3; cf. Rev 20.4), at the judgment the 'saints will judge the world' (6.2).

The assembly's independence and autonomy, moreover, meant that members should work out any and all disputes within the community and have no relations with the dominant society, such as resorting to the established courts. The law and the courts in the Roman empire were instruments of social control, a vested interest of the wealthy and powerful elite which operated for their advantage over that of those of lesser status. Paul does indeed have just such a concern about economic relations in mind, hence his concern cannot be reduced to the later separation of 'church' and 'state' that tends to block recognition of the political-economic dimension of his statement here.[8] His concern, however, is not simply a parallel to that of diaspora Jewish communities to conduct their own internal community affairs semiautonomously insofar as possible by permission of the Roman authorities. Paul's insistence that the assembly run its own affairs was more of a complete declaration of independence and autonomy, as in apocalyptic literature, where Judean scribes advocate independence of Judea or their own circles from imperial governments or their local clients. Statements of self-government from Qumran and branches of the Jesus movement appear to parallel Paul's statement to the Corinthians (cf. 1QS 5.25—6.1; CD 9.2–8; Matt 18.15–17 || Luke 17.2–3; 12.57–59 || Matt 5.25–26).

Third, Paul's prohibition of the Corinthians' eating of 'food sacrificed to idols', despite their *gnosis* that 'no idol in the world really exists' and that 'there is no

---

7. See further the suggestive discussion of the issues in 1 Corinthians 5–6 in the context of the patronage system by Chow, *Patronage and Power*, 123–41. Cf. ch. 15 above.

8. Many commentators (e.g., Fee, *First Epistle*, 232; Conzelmann, *1 Corinthians*, 105), still projecting the 'church-state' separation back into the situation of Paul, claim that Paul was not rejecting the civil courts.

God but one', cut the Corinthians off from participation in the fundamental forms of social relations in the dominant society. Christian theological interpretation of 1 Corinthians has tended to forget that religion in the ancient Roman world did not consist primarily of personal belief and was often inseparable from political, economic, and other fundamental social forms. We have been reminded recently from outside the field that temples and shrines to the emperor, located in the very center of public space, and citywide festivals played an important role in constituting the cohesion of the Roman empire as well as the local society under the domination of the sponsoring local elite.[9] From within the field, moreover, we are reminded that sacrifice was integral to, indeed constitutive of, community life in Greco-Roman antiquity at every social level from extended families to guilds and associations to citywide celebrations, including imperial festivals.[10] With that in mind, it should be possible to realize that Paul's discussion in 1 Cor 8–10 is about far more than individual ethics.

Contrary to a prominent tradition of Pauline interpretation, Paul did not share the enlightened theology that informed the 'liberty' *(exousia)* of the Corinthians he was addressing in chs 8–10. In fact, he not only rejects its effects rather bluntly in 8.1–3, but he also contradicts their *gnosis* that 'no idol in the world really exists' and 'there is no God but one' in the awkward aside of 8.5b: 'in fact there are many gods and many lords' alive and functioning in the world. The issue addressed in 1 Cor 8–10, moreover, is not the dispute imagined by modern scholars between the 'weak' and the 'strong', that is, between Jews or Jewish Christians still obsessed with traditional Jewish food codes and enlightened Christians, including Paul. The term 'food offered to idols', which does not occur in Jewish texts prior to Paul, always refers to food eaten in a temple.[11] And that is clearly what Paul has in mind, as indicated both in 8.10 and 10.14–20. Thus the strongly Lutheran reading of 1 Cor 8–10 that found the main point in 10.23—11.1, with 10.1–13 and 14–22 as digressions, should be abandoned. Paul is addressing enlightened Corinthians who presume that they have the liberty to banquet in temples (since the gods supposedly honored there do not exist). His argument climaxes in 10.14–22 with the absolute prohibition of such banqueting, with 10.23—11.1 being a conciliatory afterthought and summary of his argument.[12]

If we come to the text with the assumptions of ancient Greco-Roman society instead of modern theological ones, then we can see precisely in the climax of Paul's argument, 10.14–22, not a 'sacramental' realism, but the societal or

---

9. See esp. S. R. F. Price, *Rituals and Power: The Roman Imperial Cult in Asia Minor* (Cambridge: Cambridge University Press, 1984).

10. Stanley K. Stowers, 'Greeks Who Sacrifice and Those Who Do Not: Toward an Anthropology of Greek Religion', in L. M. White and L. Yarbrough, eds., *The Social World of the First Christians: Essays in Honor of Wayne Meeks* (Minneapolis: Fortress, 1995) 293–333.

11. Ben Witherington III, 'Not So Idle Thoughts about *Eidolothuton*', *TynBul* 44 (1993) 237–54.

12. More fully explained in Fee, *First Epistle*; and Horsley, *1 Corinthians*, both of which contain documentation and explanation that supports the interpretation 1 Cor 8–10 which follows below.

:al' realism that Paul shared with both the nonenlightened majority of nt Greeks and Romans and the biblical traditions of nonenlightened ites/Judeans. In the preceding paragraph, 10.1–13, Paul insisted that biblical traditions not be taken as symbols of spiritual realities ('spiritual food/drink/rock'), but as histories of events that had happened to the Israelites who were en route in the wilderness from their liberation from Egyptian oppression to the land in which they would become a firmly implanted independent people. That many Israelites were struck down by God because of their idolatry served as warnings to the Corinthians to maintain their group discipline until, analogously, they reached their goal now 'at the ends of the ages'. In 10.14–22 Paul makes even more explicit the exclusivity of the assembly of believers. He starts with their own celebration of the Lord's Supper. The cup of blessing is 'a *sharing* or fellowship *(koinōnia)* in the blood of Christ' and the bread a 'sharing in the body of Christ'. As becomes clearer in ch. 12, 'body' was also a well-established political metaphor for the 'body politic', the citizen body of a city-state *(polis)*. With Israel also, those who ate the sacrifices were sharers in the altar. Similarly, those who eat food sacrificed to idols are sharers or partners with the demons (idols/gods) to whom they sacrifice, establishing social bonds of sharing. In contrast to the dominant society in which many overlapping social bonds were established in sacrifices to multiple gods, however, the assembly of sharers in the body of Christ was exclusive. It was simply impossible and forbidden therefore for members of the body politic established and perpetuated in the cup and table of the Lord to partake also in the cup and table of demons.

For Paul the sharing of 'food offered to idols' was not an issue of ethics, but of the integrity and survival of the Corinthians' assembly as an exclusive alternative community to the dominant society and its social networks. In his concern to 'build up' the assembly of saints over against the networks of power relations by which the imperial society was constituted, he could not allow those who had joined the assembly to participate in the sacrificial banquets by which those social relations were ritually established. In 10.14–22 Paul insists on political-religious solidarity over against the dominant society which was constituted precisely in such banquets or 'fellowship/sharing' with gods. For the members of the new alternative community that meant cutting themselves off from the very means by which their previously essential social-economic relations were maintained.

Fourth, at several points Paul indicates that his assembly(ies) should embody economic relations dramatically different from those in Roman imperial society. As noted above, in 1 Cor 5.10 and 6.7–8 he insinuated disapprovingly that the assembly member who was taking another to civil court was defrauding him economically. Economics play a more obvious and important role in 1 Cor 8–10. In the structure of his argument, Paul offers an autobiographically framed principle to guide behavior with regard to the Corinthians' 'liberty' *(exousia)* to eat 'food offered to idols' in 8.13, which he then proceeds to illustrate autobiographically, telling how he refrains from using his own apostolic 'right' *(exousia)* in ch. 9. His illustration, far more elaborate and 'defensive' than necessary to illustrate the principle, becomes an explicit defense (9.3) of his practice of not accepting economic support for his ministry, contrary to the standard practice among apostles of the movement. That had been his practice in Thessalonica (1 Thess 2.7, 8–9), and he apparently continued the practice in Corinth, judging from his repeated references to how he had not wanted to 'burden them' or 'sponge off of them' in his later Corinthian correspondence (2 Cor 11.9; 12.13, 16). His mention of Barnabas in this connection indicates that his peculiar practice of not accepting economic support dated from at least the time he was working with Barnabas in a mission based in Antioch. But why does he refuse support, contrary to the norm within the movement, and what point is he driving at here in his 'defense' in 1 Cor 9?

Prior to his 'calling' Paul presumably would have received support in the tributary system of the Jerusalem temple state whereby the high priestly rulers 'redistributed' revenues they took from Judean and other villagers (that is, if Paul had indeed been a Pharisee, Phil 3.5). By contrast with the tributary flow of goods upwards from peasant producers to their rulers, the early Jesus movement adapted the horizontal economic reciprocity of village communities following the traditional Mosaic covenantal ideal of maintaining the subsistence level of all community members (see, e.g., Lev 25). Households and village provided for the economic subsistence of apostles and prophets moving from place to place building the movement (Mark 6.8–10; Luke 10.2–9). Paul's distinctive refusal of such support may have been rooted in his distinctive background prior to becoming an apostle in the movement. The original apostles, themselves from the peasantry, were used to sharing in the poverty of village life. But Paul as a former scribal 'retainer' may have been sensitive about continuing to live off of poverty-stricken people once he identified with them in joining the movement. 'Paying his own way' by working with his own hands, despised as it was in aristocratic Hellenistic culture, may also have been another way he could identify with the humiliation of the crucified Christ (cf. 1 Cor 4.12).

The Corinthians who were 'examining' him on this matter must have been still attuned to the values of the patronage system that had permeated the provincial cities of Greece during the early empire. Perhaps one or more of the Corinthian householders who were able to contribute to Paul's and other apostles' support were eager to enhance their own prestige and honor by serving as patron(s). It seems that Apollos, Paul's rival in Corinth, had accepted such patronage (3.5–15; 4.3–5; 9.12). According to the protocol of the patronage system, Paul's refusal of such support would have been an offensive repudiation of the prospective patron's 'friendship.' His shameful working with his own hands would have constituted a further humiliation for their proud posture as potential patrons.[13] Paul's personal concern was surely to avoid becoming a 'house apostle' to some Corinthian patron. But his larger concern may have been to prevent the assembly he was

13. On such 'friendship' and 'enmity' in the patronage system, see Peter Marshall, *Enmity in Corinth: Social Convention in Paul's Relations with the Corinthians* (Tübingen: Mohr [Siebeck], 1987).

attempting to 'build up' from replicating the controlling and exploitative power relations of the dominant society.

It is conceivable, of course, that in warding off the unwanted patronage of some, he in effect began to build his own network of 'friends' in the assemblies of Achaia as he began to rely on Stephanas and his household as his own mediators with the Corinthians and Phoebe in relation with the assembly in Cenchreae (1 Cor 16.15–18; Rom 16.1–2). Paul did not come up with any vision of an alternative political economy for his alternative society—which would have been extraordinary for antiquity. In his explanation of why he did not accept support, he simply resorted to the imagery of household administration ('commission', 9.17), with the implied image of God as the divine estate owner and himself as the steward. Such imagery fits with similar controlling metaphors, such as God as a monarch, Christ as the alternative emperor, and himself as the Lord's 'servant' or 'slave'. He used his overall controlling vision of the 'kingdom' of God as a basis for rejecting the patronage system, but remained within that traditional biblical vision.

Fifth, at the close of 1 Corinthians Paul mentions briefly another economic aspect of the movement that is unprecedented and probably unique in antiquity: the collection for the poor among the saints in Jerusalem (16.1–4).[14] This project which Paul pushes so adamantly in the Corinthian correspondence (see further the two short letters contained in 2 Cor 8 and 9) was an outgrowth of an agreement with James, Peter, and John that Paul and Barnabas, then based in the Antioch assembly, could expand the movement among the nations, but that they should 'remember the poor' (Gal 2.9–10). In reciprocal relations with the assembly in Jerusalem, other nascent assemblies were to send economic assistance to the poor there. According to Paul's later rationalization, the nations should 'be of service' to Israel in material goods since they had come to share in Israel's 'spiritual blessings' (Rom 15.27; cf. Isa 56.7, about the nations bringing tribute in gratitude to Jerusalem at the final time of fulfillment).

Paul's instructions about the collection in 1 Cor 16.1–4 (and 2 Cor 8; 9) indicate that the network of assemblies had an 'international' political-economic dimension diametrically opposed to the tributary political economy of the empire. Even before Paul set out on his own independent mission into Asia Minor and Greece, the movement had developed its distinctive way of practicing international economic solidarity and (horizontal) reciprocity, the (relative) 'haves' sharing with the 'have-nots.' Besides belonging to a larger international movement, the local assemblies shared economic resources across the 'nations' and across considerable distances. Both the international character of the movement and its international economic reciprocity were unusual, perhaps unique, in the Roman empire or in any ancient empire.[15] By contrast with the vertical

14. For fuller treatment, see the suggestive study by Dieter Georgi, *Remembering the Poor: The History of Paul's Collection for Jerusalem* (Nashville: Abingdon, 1992).

15. The collection embodied the politics as well as the economics of the movement, with delegates chosen by the assemblies themselves designated to bring the resources to the assembly in Jerusalem. Surely one of Paul's motives in pressing the project was to demonstrate to the Jerusalem leaders he had alienated that his labors among the nations had indeed borne fruit.

and centripetal movement of resources in the tributary political economy of the empire, Paul organized a horizontal movement of resources from one subject people to another for the support of 'the poor among the saints at Jerusalem' (Rom 15.26).

The purpose and rhetoric of 1 Corinthians itself, finally, indicates how Paul is attempting to 'build up' his assemblies as independent communities over against the dominant society. As recent studies of Paul's rhetoric have shown, he uses the basic forms of Greco-Roman political rhetoric.[16] The arguments in 1 Corinthians are 'deliberative' rhetoric, attempting to persuade the group addressed about a particular course of action they should take. The key terms in the arguments, moreover, are those of political discourse, particularly terms focused on the unity, concord, best advantage, and mutual cooperation within the *polis*. Far from urging the Corinthian 'saints' to conform with Corinthian society, however, he insisted that they maintain their solidarity as an exclusive community that stands against the larger society.[17] First Corinthians and his other letters were Paul's instruments to shore up the assemblies' group discipline and solidarity over against the imperial society, 'the present evil age' (Gal 1.4), 'the present form of this world [that is] passing away' (1 Cor 7.31).

16. Mitchell, *Rhetoric*; Laurence L. Welborn, 'On the Discord in Corinth: 1 Corinthians 1–4 and Ancient Politics', *JBL* 106 (1987) 83–113. Cf. ch. 10 above.

17. We need be under no illusions, however, that in dealing with the divisiveness in the Corinthian assembly, Paul consistently implemented the ideal enunciated in the baptismal formula of Gal 3.28. On the 'slippage' and inconsistency, see Schüssler Fiorenza, *In Memory of Her,* esp. chs. 6 and 7, and Wire, *Corinthian Women Prophets.*

PART II
METHODOLOGICAL REFLECTIONS

Chapter 19

Sources: Use, Abuse, Neglect. The Importance of Ancient Popular Culture

Justin J. Meggitt

When I was returning from Greece to Italy and had come to Brundisium, after disembarking, I was strolling about the famous port. . . . There I saw some bundles of books exposed for sale, and I at once hurried to them. Now all these books were filled with miraculous tales, things unheard of, incredible. . . . Attracted by their extraordinary and unexpected cheapness, I bought a large number of them for a small sum and ran through all of them hastily in the course of the next two nights. But when writing the tales down, I was seized with disgust for such worthless writings, which contribute nothing to the enrichment or profit of life.[1]

A wasted couple of nights for Gellius? Perhaps. But it would not be for those who want to understand the Corinthian correspondence. If New Testament scholars wish to make sense of the preoccupations and expectations of both Paul and the Corinthian community, we must seek out just such material. By this, I do not mean paradoxographical literature specifically, although writings of this kind are valuable.[2] Rather, we should seek out those sources, both literary and nonliterary,

---

1. Aulus Gellius, *Attic Nights* 9.4.9ff.
2. For an example of paradoxographical literature see William Hansen, *Phlegon of Tralles' Book of Marvels* (Exeter: Exeter University Press, 1996).

that give voice to the world of the nonelite, that articulate what could be termed the *popular culture* of the first century, of which paradoxographical writing is but one example.[3] In so doing we would begin to go some way to dealing with a fundamental problem that hampers all interpretations of the Corinthian epistles to a significant extent: *the problem of dependence on elite sources* (written and nonwritten). Although most scholars use a variety of sources in their analysis of the letters, and believe that their employment of them is increasingly sensitive and sophisticated, failure to recognise the *atypical* and *unrepresentative* nature of much of the material that is employed to reconstruct the context within which the letters are interpreted renders much of what is written about them of little value. We must rethink our evidential presuppositions and undergo a significant change in perspective.

Interpreters of the Corinthian literature have been criticised for their inadequate use of evidence before. In 1992 Richard Oster noted that 'New Testament scholarship has proceeded throughout much of the century with little concern for and even less contact with the artefacts of the Graeco-Roman world'.[4] He ably demonstrated that not only has it neglected vital data but it also made many methodological mistakes in its use of those material remains to which it has attended. The examples he gives to illustrate his point should be sobering for any New Testament scholar. For instance, it is quite remarkable how many experienced and influential commentators continue to insist that the fragmentary inscription referring to the 'Synagogue of the Hebrews' found in Corinth belongs to a synagogue contemporary with the Pauline mission, despite the fact that it clearly dates from some centuries later.

This is not the place to repeat Oster's criticisms, although they do bear repeating. Rather, my complaint is of a different kind and degree: it is one that I believe can be leveled at New Testament scholarship more generally. Most studies of the Corinthian epistles assume that the basic beliefs and practices of the first-century world within which the church members lived are relatively easy to establish and describe, and that consequently one can discover with a significant degree of certainty such things as the causes of the conflict over the Lord's Supper in 1 Cor 11 or the origins of the disagreement over the nature and necessity of the resurrection body in 1 Cor 15. But confidence in such findings is both misplaced and misleading. Unless we begin by attempting to reconstruct a context of interpretation that rescues the nonelite of the first cenutry from the 'enormous condescension of posterity',[5] our interpretations, however sophisticated or useful, are bound to be fallacious. We must take account of the undocumented dead of antiquity, who, of course, constituted virtually all its inhabitants. We cannot allow our dialogue with the past to continue to be one where 'we are deaf to the

---

3. Meggitt, *Paul, Poverty*, 18–39.
4. Richard E. Oster, 'Use, Misuse and Neglect of Archaeological Evidence in Some Modern Works on 1 Corinthians (1 Cor 7,1–5; 8,10; 11, 2–16; 12, 14–26)', *ZNW* 83 (1992) 52–73.
5. E. P. Thompson, *The Making of the English Working Class* (London: Victor Gollancz, 1963) 12. This striking expression continues to be used in historical scholarship. See, for example, Eric Hobsbawm, *Uncommon People: Resistance, Rebellion and Jazz* (London: Abacus, 1998) viii.

great mass of those who lived and died in the period in which the New Testament was written and who left nothing, except perhaps their bones or ashes, behind them'.[6] To put it bluntly: it will not do to 'listen' only to those favourites of exegetes, such as Philo, Plutarch, and Quintilian (or even Junia Theodora), as we attempt our interpretations.

If we wish to find more representative sources with which to construct our understanding of the context within which the Corinthian correspondence was written and read, and to interpret such sources appropriately, it is necessary to look beyond New Testament scholarship. There is, of course, no point reinventing the wheel. Others have been driven by similar concerns in cognate disciplines. Perhaps most famously, George Rudé,[7] or Eric Hobsbawm,[8] initiated the study of 'history from below' some decades ago and, although their approach can now appear rather parochial, unnecessarily fixated with conflict, and too obviously ideological in its presuppositions and motivations, there is still much to learn from this branch of history and the reception of its ideas. Likewise, New Testament scholars could also gain much from debates surrounding new American historical archaeology, proponents of which claim that archaeology is in a unique position to restore to us the lost voices of the 'people without history'.[9] In this piece, however, I would like to argue that interpreters of the Corinthian letters have most to benefit from those who have made the study of 'popular culture' their central preoccupation. It is only after an active engagement with this particular branch of scholarship that we should revisit the question of how we determine and employ sources relevant to the study of the Corinthian correspondence.

POPULAR CULTURE

It is necessary to say a few things about the study of popular culture and New Testament scholarship before we return to the Corinthian correspondence and demonstrate how attention to its concerns can benefit our analysis of the texts.[10]

---

6. J. J. Meggitt, 'Response to Martin and Thiessen', *JSNT* 24 (2001) 85–94.

7. For a review of Rudé's work and a comprehensive bibliography see F. Krantz, 'Sans érudition, pas d'histoire', in *History from Below: Studies in Popular Protest and Popular Ideology in Honour of George Rudé* (ed. F. Krantz; Montreal: Concordia University Press, 1985) 3–40.

8. Eric Hobsbawm has published extensively in this field since his famous collaboration with Rudé (E. Hobsbawm and G. Rudé, *Captain Swing* [Harmondsworth: Penguin, 1973]).

9. Charles Orser, *A Historical Archaeology of the Modern World* (New York: Plenum Press, 1996) 178–79.

10. There are many introductions to popular culture available. Among the best are John Fiske, *Understanding Popular Culture* (London: Routledge, 1989); J. Storey, *An Introductory Guide to Cultural Theory and Popular Culture* (London: Harvester Wheatsheaf, 1993); David Strinati, *An Introduction to the Theories of Popular Culture* (London: Routledge, 1995). Some New Testament scholars have shown an awareness of the implications of cultural studies for the field. See, e.g., Stephen D. Moore, 'Between Birmingham and Jerusalem: Cultural Studies and Biblical Studies', *Semeia* 82 (1998) 1–32, and David Brakke, 'Cultural Studies: Ein neues Paradigma us-amerikanischer Exegese', *Zeitschrift für Neues Testament* 2 (1998) 69–77.

New Testament scholars may well consider an interest in popular culture misguided because it is anachronistic. Many associate the study of popular culture with the study of mass or media culture, and assume that it is a product of industrialisation or, more recently, globalisation. Indeed, the dominant concern of studies in this field remains the study of *contemporary* culture (and, in particular, media). Despite the protestations of publications such as the *Journal of Popular Culture*,[11] one need only look at the contents page of any volume to see that most of the current work being undertaken is of just such a kind. There are few studies by ancient historians that even begin to address the question (Jerry Toner's recent, polemical *Rethinking Roman History* is an exception),[12] although there are many historical studies of other epochs that do. Indeed, many of the most important theorists of popular culture have cut their teeth on the historical analysis of past cultures (Peter Burke, author of the seminal *Popular Culture in Early Modern Europe,* is just such an example[13]). So, a priori, there is no reason to ignore this perspective—unless, of course, New Testament scholars would like to claim to be historians (as a significant number do) but do not think that such a claim requires them to read the work of historians.

Some New Testament scholars may well believe that such an interpretive perspective is no more than an ideological Trojan horse that once employed is guaranteed to arrive at certain results hostile to their particular interests (results that they might claim are against 'common sense' and straight presentation of the 'facts'). Certainly, some of the formative studies of popular culture produced by Stuart Hall and Tony Bennett in the 1970s, from the British cultural studies perspective, assumed that popular culture is always an arena for class struggle—and even now many studies of popular culture employ a qualified Marxism that owes itself to Antonio Gramsci, and makes much of his notion of contested hegemony[14] (in which popular culture is the site of negotiation between dominant and subordinate classes). However, this need not be the case. J. M. Golby, the coauthor of an influential study of crowds in the premodern and modern period, has made a concerted case for conceptualising popular culture as the product of 'many social groups and interests',[15] and something that is not necessarily characterised by conflict.

In fact, a greater problem than either anachronism or ideological bias faced by those undertaking a study of ancient popular culture is the danger of cultural populism. This is particularly true of any analysis that does not attempt to try to

---

11. The recent collection of studies of popular culture and religion edited by Bruce Forbes and Jeffrey Mahan evidences just such a contemporary preoccupation. See B. Forbes and J. Mahan, eds., *Religion and Popular Culture in America* (Berkeley: University of California Press, 2000).

12. J. Toner, *Rethinking Roman History* (Cambridge: Oleander, 2002).

13. P. Burke, *Popular Culture in Early Modern Europe* (London: Temple Smith, 1978). For other examples of the study of popular culture in past societies see, for instance, Barry Reay, *Popular Cultures in England: 1550–1750* (New York: Addison Wesley Longman, 1998), and Eileen Yeo and Stephen Yeo, *Popular Culture and Class Conflict, 1590–1914* (London: Harvester, 1981).

14. J. M. Golby and A. W. Purdue, *The Civilisation of the Crowd. Popular Culture in England 1750–1900* (2nd ed.; Stroud: Sutton, 1999).

15. Golby, *Civilisation*, 6.

account for popular culture and the forces that shape it.[16] Too often scholars of popular culture are drawn to the exceptional or anomalous in their studies, providing fascinating but often narrow accounts of phenomena in past cultures that are striking or fascinating to ours but are otherwise unilluminating. Classical scholarship, upon which New Testament scholars are parasitic, contains examples of this kind (such as Carlin Barton's *The Sorrows of the Ancient Romans: The Gladiator and the Monster*).[17]

In one respect, the failure of New Testament scholars to take account of popular culture is understandable. The sources themselves have often been neglected and treated with disdain by those whose business it is to study them and make them available to others. For example, the most comprehensive treatment of paradoxography in recent years notes that it is a branch of literature that 'has hardly been able to attract the attention of more than a few scholars over the past century'[18] and then proceeds to observe that in reading such texts one inevitably senses 'the lowering of the temperature, the difference of "class", the loss of quality in style and content which it is tempting to ascribe to the poor intellectual capacities of their author or to their sole purpose to cater to the taste of the masses, interested in nothing else but cheap entertainment'.[19]

However, the neglect of popular culture, although understandable, is not defensible. Indeed, it is particularly regretable that those New Testament scholars who have spent considerable time claiming to apply the insights of cultural anthropology in their analyses of early Christian literature have not, to my knowledge, addressed the question of popular culture in any concerted way. Although I have yet to find a justification for this omission, it is likely that the homogenising, ahistorical view of ancient Mediterranean culture that characterises their work probably accounts for this.[20]

So much for popular culture and the New Testament. But what use can it be to someone trying to make sense of the Corinthian correspondence? In what follows I will sketch out four observations that are evident from studies of popular culture and that will be beneficial for exegetes of the letters to keep in mind as they seek to read them. These observations are not exhaustive but are indicative of the value of this approach in drawing our attention to aspects of first-century culture that we have previously ignored.

16. Strinati, *Introduction*, 255.

17. Carlin Barton, *The Sorrows of the Ancient Romans: The Gladiator and the Monster* (Princeton: Princeton University Press, 1992).

18. Guido Schepens and Kris Delcroix, 'Ancient paradoxography: origins, evolution, production and consumption', in *La letteratura di consumo nel mondo greco-latino* (ed. Oronzo Pecere and Antonio Stramaglia; Cassino: Universite degli Studi di Cassino, 1996) 375.

19. Schepens and Delcroix, 'Ancient paradoxography', 378. It is worth recalling, before one assumes poor intellectual capacity on the part of readers of popular literature, that according to the *Phaedo* 61b, one of Socrates' last acts was to versify some of Aesop's fables—an observation I owe to Ron Rembert. For a useful introduction to Greek popular literature see W. Hansen, *Anthology of Greek Popular Literature* (Bloomington: Indiana University Press, 1998).

20. See, e.g., J. J. Meggitt, 'Review of Bruce Malina, *The Social World of Jesus and the Gospels*', *JTS* 49 (1998) 215–19.

1. STUDIES OF POPULAR CULTURE SHOULD ALERT US TO THE IMPORTANCE OF THE INFORMAL, UNOFFICIAL, AND UNSANCTIONED.

Popular cultural studies have drawn attention to the significance of the informal, unofficial, and unsanctioned within cultures. We are now, for example, aware of the importance of the spontaneous moralities and hierarchies of crowds[21] and the longer-lasting solidarities and identities created by patrons of bars or gaming tables[22] or fans of actors or musicians, aspects of past societies that had been little noted by New Testament scholars but for their members were important in constituting the worlds they inhabited.[23] Awareness of popular culture alerts us to the presence and diversity of *lex non scripta* that existed between and within different social groups in the empire and that did not necessarily reflect those that were officially enforced or generally sanctioned.[24]

It is in their nature for the things that constitute popular culture to be ephemeral and leave little behind (in the case of gaming tables, little more than a few perpendicular scratches on paving stones; in the case of popular theatre we have only one surviving script of a pantomime—a form of theatre that dominated in the early empire but was largely improvised).[25] But our ignorance does not mean that such things were any the less real or important. Indeed, New Testament scholars should have expended more time on their study given the prominence of such practices in the culture: pantomime artists and their followers were, after all, more regularly repressed and banned from Rome in the first and second centuries than, for example, Jews or followers of Isis (vicious riots often seem to have resulted from the clash of partisan fans).[26]

Those studying the Corinthian literature have been overconcerned with the examination of the formal, official, and sanctioned in interpreting the beliefs and

---

21. The classic study is E. P. Thompson, 'The moral economy of the English crowd in the eighteenth century', *Past & Present* 50 (1971) 76–136, although there are more recent treatments of this phenomenon, such as A. Randall and A. Charlesworth, eds., *Markets, Market Culture and Popular Protest in Eighteenth-Century England* (Liverpool: Liverpool University Press, 1996).

22. J. P. Toner, *Leisure and Ancient Rome* (Oxford: Blackwell, 1996). See also Gerda Reith, *The Age of Chance: Gambling in Western Culture* (London: Routledge, 1999).

23. A rare exception is the recent article by L. L. Welborn, 'Paul's Appropriation of the Role of the Fool in 1 Corinthians 1–4', *BibInt* 10 (2002) 420–35. The significance of the spectacles and theatre among early Christians is evidenced from Tertullian's *On Spectacles* and the work of the same title authored by Pseudo-Cyprian. It is not widely known that as well as being, on occasion, the entertainment, Christians also appear to have found such events entertaining and were reluctant to cease attending them (indeed, they felt biblically justified in so doing).

24. Linda Ellis and Marius Tiberius Alexianu, 'Duplex ius', in *Confrontation in Late Antiquity* (ed. Linda Hall; Cambridge: Orchard Academic, 2003) 117–33.

25. See W. Beare, *The Roman Stage* (London: Methuen, 1955) 304–9.

26. Expulsions of Jews from Rome: Valerius Maximus 1.3.3 (139 B.C.E.); Josephus, *Ant.* 18.81–84; Suetonius, *Tib.* 36; Tacitus, *Ann.* 11.28; Cassius Dio 57.18 (19 C.E.) and Suetonius, *Claud.* 25 (49 or 41 C.E., though see also Cassius Dio 60.6.6). Expulsion of Isis worshipers: Josephus, *Ant.* 18.65; Tacitus, *Ann.* 2.85. For the repression of pantomime artists and their fans see Justinian, *Digest* 48.19.28.3; Cassius Dio 57.21; Tacitus, *Ann.* 4.14, 13.24; Suetonius, *Tib.* 37; Suetonius, *Nero* 16;

practices of the Pauline churches. We shall have to face the awkward fact that if we focus our analysis on, for example, conceptualisations of the household in first-century written sources, or literary presentations of, say, *Romanitas*, in order to elucidate a significant element of the context within which these texts were written, we may make interpretive claims that are unsustainable. Such things may be very differently experienced within the popular cultures of the empire. Indeed, we may have to admit that some of the things that have so preoccupied and dominated interpretation of the letters may not have actually been significant components of the lives of most Corinthians, as I believe is the case with patronage.[27]

All kinds of issues become problematic when we begin to take account of the informal and unsanctioned in the popular culture of the first century in our readings. Our most cherished assumptions may need revision. For example, it is commonly held that society within the Roman Empire was rigidly stratified, and that everyone was expected to know their place (something that, for many exegetes, is a significant factor in explaining the tensions within the Corinthian correspondence). Yet a consistent problem, to judge from legislation, literary evidence, and material artefacts, was the regular usurpation of status and its symbols.[28] Indeed, even the clear distinction between slave and free, surely something assumed to be obvious and central to first-century life (and early Christian rites—1 Cor 12.13) may not have always been obvious[29] or central. In the first-century slave biography the *Life of Aesop*, we find a telling exchange between Aesop and a poor farmer in which Aesop's disclosure that he is a slave meets with the response: "Did I ask you whether you are a slave or free man? What do I care?"[30]

2. WITHIN POPULAR CULTURES APPARENTLY MUTUALLY EXCLUSIVE PRACTICES AND CONVICTIONS CAN COEXIST.

Of course, for the cultured despisers of popular culture, most of it appeared inconsistent and irrational. The denial of rationality is a convention in descriptions of the other, particularly the socially inferior other in Greek and Roman literature. It was seen as an aspect of the brutish, fickle, and animal nature of the

---

Suetonius, *Dom.* 7; Pliny the Younger, *Pan.* 46. For further information on the pantomimes see E. Wuest; 'Pantomimus', in PW, 18.3 (1949) 833–69; Richard Beacham, *The Roman Theatre and Its Audience* (Cambridge: Harvard University Press, 1992) 116–53; and H. Leppin, *Histrionen: Untersuchungen zur sozialen Stellung von Bühnenkünstler im Westen des Römischen Reiches zur Zeit der Republik und des Principats* (Bonn: Habelt, 1992).

27. See Meggitt, *Paul, Poverty*, 167–69.

28. See M. Reinhold, 'The Usurpation of Status and Status Symbols in the Roman Empire', *Historia* 20 (1971) 275–302.

29. See, e.g., the incident recorded in Seneca, *Clem.* 1.24.1.

30. *Life of Aesop* 60. A useful analysis of the social-historical value of the *Life of Aesop* can be found in K. Hopkins, 'Novel Evidence for Roman Slavery', *Past & Present* 138 (1993) 3–27.

unlearned classes—a common topos.[31] Of course, what is depicted by elite sources as incoherent and immoral was far from necessarily so (for example, the practice of de facto marriages in seventeenth-century England is not evidence of immorality but a different, community-sanctioned morality, independent of the clerical critics who were so disturbed by it). However, while it is important to see irrationality as a topos in many pertinent elite sources, it is also important to take seriously the diversity and even inconsistency of popular cultures.[32]

Dale Martin's *Corinthian Body*, a work that is among the most innovative studies of the Corinthian letters of recent years and one that is, in some respects, sensitive to the concerns of this chapter,[33] unfortunately provides a good illustration of the consequences of failing to recognise this. In his analysis Martin contends that:

> the theological differences reflected in 1 Corinthians *all* resulted from conflicts between various groups in the local church rooted in different ideological constructions of the body. Whereas Paul and (probably) the majority of the Corinthian Christians saw the body as a dangerously permeable entity, threatened by polluting agents, a minority of those in the Corinthian church (which, following several scholars, I call the strong) stressed the hierarchical arrangement of the body and the proper balance of its constituents, without evincing much concern over body boundaries and pollution. . . .
>
> Furthermore, these positions correlate with socio-economic status, the strong being the higher status group, who enjoy a relatively secure economic position and high level of education, and Paul, like many members of the Corinthian church, being among the less educated, less well off inhabitants of the Roman Empire.[34]

A closer reading of the evidence demonstrates that Martin's assertions are unwarranted: elite authors often testify to a fear of external, polluting agents, as is evidenced by their use of apotropaic devices[35] and their fear of the power of magic (clear from such events as those surrounding the death of Germanicus, Tiberius's adopted son).[36] And likewise, the poor could have hierarchical views of the body[37] and a logic of 'balance' was central to many folk remedies.[38] Indeed, both groups also appear to have had room for naturalistic explanations of their

31. See, e.g., K. R. Bradley, 'Animalizing the Slave: the Truth of Fiction', *JRS* 90 (2000) 110–25.

32. E. Hobsbawm, *Primitive Rebels* (Manchester: Manchester University Press, 1959) 29. For further examples of this phenomenon see Rudé, *Ideology and Popular Protest*, 31–32.

33. As Horrell and Adams note (above, p. 22), Martin's refusal to interpret Corinthian views against any particular philosophical background but rather to understand them in the light of their exposure to philosophical commonplaces is an important contribution to our study of the correspondence.

34. Martin, *Corinthian Body*, xv.

35. Pliny the Elder, *Nat.* 30. Many such devices could be very costly. See M. Waegman, *Amulet and Alphabet: Magical Amulets in the First Book of Cyranides* (Amsterdam: Gieben, 1987).

36. See Tacitus, *Ann.* 2.69.

37. Humoral theory was probably important to many. See, e.g., *Philogelos* 184.

38. Such as many of those that Pliny recorded in *Nat.* 24.

predicaments (for example, they could be unaware of or uninterested in the origin of an illness and subsequently equivocal in their conceptions of their bodies and its boundaries).[39] Martin's fundamental interpretive premise is flawed: it is unlikely that there were two distinctive and conflicting ideological constructions of the body that correlated with socioeconomic status in Corinth.

This is not just a matter of evidence shipwrecking a good hypothesis. Martin's interpretive project was flawed from the outset by his failure to take into account the inconsistencies present within popular cultures and the multiple, incompatible constructions of the body individuals and groups within Corinth could reasonably be expected to possess. The studies of popular healing undertaken by Arthur Kleinman should help us to recognise the likelihood of this. He has demonstrated that even in quite static, traditional cultures (which first-century Corinth was not), explanations of illness by sufferers tend to be 'idiosyncratic and changeable. . . . They are partly conscious and partly outside of awareness, and are characterised by vagueness, multiplicity of meanings, frequent changes and lack of sharp boundaries between ideas and experience'.[40] Those in need of healing or in fear of illness commonly use methods that imply very different understandings of the body (so, for example, it is no surprise to find Soranus observing that women giving birth regularly employed amulets in addition to doctors and midwives).[41] Such actions could be justified and accounts rationalised (if this was required) in ways that did not lead to the acceptance or abandonment of any particular model, regardless of outcome.[42] All previous attempts at healing could be integrated into the sufferer's narrative of their own suffering (as we can see in Paul's explanation of his affliction in 2 Cor 12.7–9). Ironically, they are likely to have been integrated in ways that reinforced the validity of all the different models assumed.[43] It is clear that popular cultures can be pragmatically robust and can allow a degree of incompatibility between beliefs and practices, and our interpretations are problematic if we do not take this into account.

---

39. For the majority of the illnesses described in the New Testament, no particular explanation seems to be given or sought. See remarks in D. Amundsen and C. Ferngren, 'The Perception of Disease Causality in the New Testament', in *ANRW* 37.3 (1995) 2934–56. This is also true of other sources, such as Artemidorus's *Oneirocritica*.

40. Quoted in C. Helman, *Culture, Health and Illness* (4th ed.; London: Butterworth Heinemann) 85. The influential study is A. Kleinman, *Patients and Healers in the Context of Culture* (Berkeley: University of California Press, 1980).

41. Soranus, *Gynecology* 3.42.

42. Of course, people are not *necessarily* forced to create such rational narratives of their experience. An entry in the diary of Samuel Pepys in 1664 reads: 'So ends the old year . . . I bless God that I have never been in so good plight as to my health . . . as I am in this day and have been this four of five months. But I am at a great loss to know whether it be my Hare's foote, or taking a pill of Turpentine, or my having left off wearing a gowne'. See R. Porter, 'The Patient's View: Doing Medical History from Below', *Theory and Society* 14 (1985) 175–98.

43. For an example of this see S. H. Muela, J. M. Ribera, and M. Tanner, 'Fake malaria and hidden parasites—the ambiguity of Malaria', *Anthropology & Medicine* 5 (1998) 43–61.

3. STUDIES OF POPULAR CULTURE SHOULD ALERT US TO THE SIGNIFICANCE AND COMPLEXITY OF THE RECEPTION OF IDEAS AND PRACTICES.

A central feature of the study of popular culture has become the study of reception. Scholars of popular culture have been alert to the failings of textual determinism for some decades, although this came about as a consequence of empirical studies of reception as much as from engagement with any particular hermeneutical developments.[44] New Testament scholars have much to learn from such a preoccupation. To put it bluntly: it will not do to use our sources to establish the existence of a belief or practice in first-century Corinth and, in the light of this, interpret the Pauline texts. Rather, we must attend to the difficult task of establishing not just the presence of a belief or practice, but its significance and the nature of its interpretation by those who encountered it, before we can use it to aid our interpretation of the letters themselves.

It is helpful to illustrate the value of this by reference to a concrete example.[45] Many exegetes have stressed the importance of the imperial cult and the related ideology of imperial rule to the interpretations of the Corinthian correspondence (see, for example, Horsley's article in this collection: ch. 18).[46] However, few have attended in a systematic way to the dissemination and *reception* of either. But before we undertake any exegetical work that takes these phenomena into account, we must first establish that the imperial cult and imperial ideology were both known and active components of the culture within which the Corinthian Christians lived. This is actually quite difficult to do, even when we are dealing with data that by its nature appears very tangible. For example, the prolific number of inscriptions referring to the divinity of the emperor that were on public display throughout the empire, including Corinth,[47] do not necessarily indicate that the content of imperial ideology or the claims of the cult were understood or significant. We should not underestimate the capacity for public inscriptions to be unnoticed or misunderstood even by those who lived their lives surrounded by them. The fact that in the process of destroying Alexandrian

---

44. See, e.g., David Morley, *The Nationwide Audience* (London: British Film Institute, 1980), and the early essays produced by Stuart Hall, the influential director of the Centre for Contemporary Cultural Studies at Birmingham University and reproduced in Stuart Hall, *Early Writings on Television* (London: Routledge, 1997).

45. The one below is dependent on my essay 'Taking the Emperor's Clothes Seriously: The New Testament and the Roman Emperor', in *The Quest for Wisdom: Essays in Honour of Philip Budd* (ed. C. Joynes; Cambridge: Orchard Academic, 2002) 143–69.

46. R. A. Horsley, '1 Corinthians: A Case Study of Paul's Assembly as an Alternative Society', in *Paul and Empire: Religion and Power in Roman Imperial Society* (ed. R. A. Horsley; Harrisburg: Trinity Press International, 1997) 242–52.

47. E.g., there were thirteen such inscriptions to Augustus alone in the main market of Roman Athens; see A. Benjamin and A. Raubitschek, 'Arae Augusti', *Hesperia* 28 (1959) 65–85. For Corinth see M. E. H. Walbank, 'Evidence for the imperial cult in Julio-Claudian Corinth', in *Subject and Ruler: The Cult of the Ruling Power in Classical Antiquity* (ed. A. Small; Ann Arbor: Journal of Roman Archaeology Supplements Series, no. 17, 1996) 201–4.

Jewish prayer halls in 39 C.E., a mob of Gentiles seeking to promote the worship of Caligula actually destroyed dedications to previous emperors is indicative of this.[48]

Indeed, it is very difficult to find any evidence that can help us to determine the reception of literary sources that are central to many scholarly interpretations. That we can demonstrate that Virgil's conceptualisations of imperial ideology were popular and widely known, both in his day and subsequently, is extremely unusual.[49] Graffiti from Pompeii indicate that his readership went well beyond his own class,[50] and we are told (presumably plausibly) that some of his lines extolling the divinity of Augustus were rapturously received by a rowdy mob at an imperial games during his lifetime.[51] There is also evidence that his particular understanding of the divinity of the emperor continued to be influential long after his death.[52] For other authors of our period, however, the business of investigating their reception is almost impossible to undertake as the evidence is so scant.

To complicate matters further, it is important for exegetes to realise that the process of reception of an idea involves, to some extent, its transformation, something that is likewise a far from simple thing to examine. The elements of imperial ideology could be appropriated in ways that were clearly never intended by its proponents. For example, during Tiberius's rule, a woman followed the senator Gaius Cestius Gallus around Rome, hurling abuse at him while clutching a portrait of the emperor and thus avoiding prosecution (a practice that was far from uncommon).[53] Indeed, despite draconian legislation surrounding the treatment of representations of the emperor,[54] we should not assume that these were treated with respect by the general population: piss pots used by fullers in Rome were nicknamed *Vespasiani* after the emperor who introduced an unpopular tax upon them,[55] an illustration that shows something of the unpredictability of the reception of an image.

The study of reception should alert us to a more general issue to bear in mind as we examine the Corinthian literature. Paul and the Corinthian church may well be reacting to very different forms of the ideas and practices that we assume are central to their context than those that were officially propagated and are evidenced in accessible sources.

48. Philo, *Legat.* 133.
49. See A. K. Bowman, 'Literacy in the Roman Empire: Mass and Mode', in *Literacy in the Roman World* (ed. J. Humphrey; Ann Arbor: Journal of Roman Archaeology Supplement Series, no. 3, 1991) 119–31. Evidence for participation in literate culture can be seen in such details as Nero's use of placards to advertise his 'triumph' following his tour of Greece (Cassius Dio 62.20).
50. H. H. Tanzer, *The Common People of Pompeii. A Study of the Graffiti* (Baltimore: Johns Hopkins University Press, 1939) 83–84. The remarkable popularity of Virgil may be indicated by the fragments of the *Aeneid* found in letters as far apart as Vindolanda (*Tab. Vindol.* II. 118) and Masada (*Doc. Masada* 721).
51. Tacitus, *Dial.* 13.
52. Scriptores Historiae Augustae, *Albinus* 5.2.
53. Tacitus, *Ann.* 3.36.
54. *Acts of Peter* 11. See Justinian, *Digest* 48.4.4–6. Cf. also Cassius Dio 62.23.
55. Martial, *Epigrams* 6.93; Suetonius, *Vesp.* 23.3; Cassius Dio 65.14.

4. THE STUDY OF POPULAR CULTURE SHOULD MAKE US AWARE OF THE LIMITATIONS OF OUR KNOWLEDGE AND MORE CIRCUMSPECT IN OUR EXEGETICAL CLAIMS.

There is much we will never know. As Garnsey and Saller have said more generally of the study of the social and cultural life of the early Roman Empire, the evidence we have is limited in quantity and quality, and, 'while these deficiencies should not be allowed to determine what (historical) questions are asked, they do circumscribe the field of questions to which convincing answers can be given'.[56] Perhaps the greatest problem with the current use of sources by New Testament scholars, myself included, is that they infer too much, too easily.[57] It is important to remember that for all the claims some scholars make, we still have no idea of some of the most basic features of Greek and Roman life in the first century as it would affect the Corinthians. If we do not even know what a slave in Corinth *wore* should we really be so confident in assuming we can know what they *thought* or how they may have been expected to behave in different social contexts?[58] What do we really know of the Jewish community in Corinth in the first century apart from the fact that it existed? What kinds of Judaism did they practice, what convictions and conventions were common to their members?

Despite its obvious importance, we should not think that developments in archaeology will help us to overcome this problem in the future, as some might suppose. We know that much of what has been found at Corinth was redolent with meaning for the original inhabitants, and this is true of even the most humble domestic artefacts,[59] and access to those meanings would help us understand the dynamics that underlie the correspondence, but those meanings will always remain largely unknowable. The 'hidden voice' will always remain 'frustratingly elusive'.[60] When it comes to imparting information about the more complex aspects of human social life (beyond rudimentary inferences about the production and consumption of archaeological phenomena themselves),[61] 'the spade cannot lie' because it 'cannot even speak'.[62]

---

56. P. Garnsey and R. Saller, *The Roman Empire: Economy, Society and Culture* (London: Duckworth, 1987) 108.

57. G. Schöllgen, 'Was wissen wir über die Sozialstruktur der paulinschen Gemeinden?' *NTS* 34 (1988) 71–82.

58. Of course, elite literature assumed that one's identity as a slave was obvious from appearance alone but, paradoxically it is also clear that this was not actually so, as the story in Seneca, *Clem.* 1.24.1 indicates. For further discussion of this see Michele George, 'Slave Disguise in Ancient Rome', *Slavery & Abolition* 23 (2002) 41–54.

59. J. Hoskins, *Biographical Objects: How Things Tell the Stories of People's Lives* (London: Routledge, 1998) 196.

60. M. Hall, *Archaeology and the Modern World: Colonial Transcripts in South Africa and Chesapeake* (London: Routledge, 2000).

61. C. Hawkes, 'Archaeological Theory and Method: Some Suggestions from the Old World', *American Anthropologist* 56 (1954) 155–68.

62. P. Grierson, 'Commerce in the Dark Ages: A Critique of the Evidence', *Transactions of the Royal Historical Society* 9 (1959) 129.

I do not mean to end this discussion on a pessimistic note. There is much that can still be said. For example, the first comprehensive study of nutrition experience in antiquity, one that attends to material indicators of malnutrition, has argued that chronic malnutrition (endemic, *not* episodic) was the common experience (as my own analysis of the Corinthian literature argued).[63] Such a picture is hard for most scholars to accept[64] but should lead us to rethink some of our interpretive assumptions about Paul and the Corinthian church and revise some of the readings of the correspondence that currently dominate and are well represented in this collection.[65] More rigorous attention to relevant sources will allow us to sustain just such general inferences about the context of Paul and the Corinthians and address its consequences, even if some of our more complex reconstructions and tenuous speculations will be exposed as indefensible.

CONCLUSIONS

The study of ancient popular culture should not be regarded as a marginal concern for New Testament scholars: it should have a central place in our deliberations. Ultimately we may find that less can be said with certainty but what is said will be more valuable and of greater lasting significance than readings of the letters that fail to address it. To return to Gellius: to attend to the popular is far from worthless or without profit for those who wish to interpret the Corinthian correspondence, even though it may well be a disconcerting and disturbing experience.

What has been sketched here is only an indication of the implications of a popular cultural approach to the texts. There are many other ways in which it can assist our understanding of this material. It should be emphasised that its significance is not limited to the reexamination of those aspects of the correspondence that are, to most New Testament exegetes, more narrowly 'social' or 'cultural' in their character (such as the construction of gender among the Corinthians or the causes of the conflicts within the community). There are, in fact, few aspects of our understanding of the letters that would not be transformed by the application of this perspective. For example, our comprehension of the Christology, pneumatology, ecclesiology, eschatology, and even the understanding of God found in the epistles will be considerably altered if we begin, as I maintain we should, by taking seriously the 'enormous condescension of posterity'.

---

63. P. Garnsey, *Food and Society in Classical Antiquity* (Cambridge: Cambridge University Press, 1999).

64. Garnsey, *Food*, 3.

65. See further Meggitt, *Paul, Poverty*.

Chapter 20

The Methods of Historical Reconstruction in the Scholarly 'Recovery' of Corinthian Christianity

Bengt Holmberg

1. ON THE IMPORTANCE OF KNOWING ENOUGH ABOUT ANCIENT SOCIAL HISTORY

In his often-quoted criticism of my dissertation,[1] the Australian classicist Edwin A. Judge took up my own term, the 'idealistic fallacy' (interpreting historical phenomena as being directly formed by ideas), and turned it around, accusing me of committing the opposite mistake, the 'sociological fallacy'. This consists in 'the importation of social models that have been defined in terms of other cultures' and 'transposed across the centuries' without undertaking the painstaking fieldwork of finding the social facts of life characteristic of the world to which the New Testament belongs.[2] One of the things I had got wrong because of this error was the role and meaning of giving and receiving money in a Greco-Roman

---

1. B. Holmberg, *Paul and Power: The Structure of Authority in the Primitive Church As Reflected in the Pauline Epistles* (Lund: Gleerup, 1978). This was republished by Fortress Press, Philadelphia, in 1980; pagination differs slightly between these two editions.
2. E. A. Judge, 'The Social Identity of the First Christians: A Question of Method in Religious History', *JRH* 11 (1980) 210.

context. Judge pointed out that money was usually given downward, as it were, from the patron to support his clients, not from dependants or followers 'up' to their leader or patron in order to support him. In that culture receiving money is thus more likely a sign of being dependent than of having dependants, of being weak and bound to others rather than being strong and free.[3]

Judge was right about the lack of 'fieldwork' on my part. At that time, I knew almost nothing about patronage in ancient Mediterranean cultures, nor its financial implications. This is, however, not a 'sociological fallacy', as Judge would have it, a result of importing Weber's sociology of charismatic authority (which I used in that book and which says nothing much about the direction of money) into first-century Christianity and thereby distorting its true shape. I erred in supposing (or rather taking for granted) that the giving and receiving of money mean much the same in any culture as it does in the European–North American setting. But this is merely a common anachronism due to lack of historical knowledge and imagination, and hardly qualifies as a sociological model, inappropriate or not.

What difference does this lack of sociohistorical knowledge make in interpreting the New Testament? Actually, I was describing and discussing mainly one type of money flow that is clear enough in the sources: the right of a traveling missionary or 'apostle' to receive support from other believers. To begin with a fairly unnoticed phenomenon in this area, it is a fact that Paul expected the service of προπέμπεσθαι, 'to be equipped for travel', from his local churches, that is, being provided with food, (some) money, guides, and company when traveling. He expected this even from the church in Corinth, from which he emphatically vowed not to receive any support (1 Cor 9.15b; 2 Cor 11.9b, ἐν παντὶ ἀβαρῆ ἐμαυτὸν ὑμῖν ἐτήρησα καὶ τηρήσω). In the taken-for-granted service of apostolic προπέμπεσθαι from the congregations of believers that Paul had relations with, we meet 'an obligation to support missionaries so fundamental and indisputable that it does not even enter the discussion of the delicate question of why Paul did not avail himself of his apostolic rights (1 Cor 9; 2 Cor 11–12).'[4]

This obligated flow of money from local Christians to their traveling apostles is, however, only part of a more demanding package of 'rights' (ἐξουσίαι) of such people. We learn about three more such rights in 1 Cor 9.4–6:

(1) ἐξουσίαν φαγεῖν καὶ πεῖν, 'right to our food and drink',
(2) ἐξουσίαν ἀδελφὴν γυναῖκα περιάγειν, 'right to be accompanied by a believing wife',
(3) ἐξουσίαν μὴ ἐργάζεσθαι, 'right to refrain from working for a living'.

3. 'Generally in the Greco-Roman world, money was given downward on the social scale, whereas "honor" was given upward, in return for money' (Martin, *Corinthian Body*, 81, referring to E. A. Judge, 'Cultural Conformity and Innovation in Paul: Some Clues from Contemporary Documents', *TynBul* 35 [1984] 15). See further Chow, *Patronage and Power*, 30–33 and passim; and Clarke, *Secular and Christian Leadership*, 31–36.

4. Holmberg, *Paul and Power*, 1978, 89 = 1980, 87.

The conclusion is hard to avoid that an apostle exercising all his rights must have been a salaried person—given his living by other Christians. In other words, his apostolic authority is manifested also by the flow of money and support from the believers, even if the level of comfort experienced in such a life should perhaps only be termed (with Theissen) 'charismatic poverty'.

Theissen suggested in 1975 that the 'salaried apostle' was a behaviour pattern for missionaries from the Palestinian-Syrian parts of the earliest church ('the Jesus movement'), in which it was understood as a mark of apostolic authenticity. Because it did not fit very well into the somewhat different cultural setting of Asia Minor and Greece, with a stronger mistrust against religious charlatans and preachers who used their preaching to line their own pockets, it was abandoned by Barnabas and Paul when they took up Christian mission work in these areas. The apologetic argument of 1 Cor 9 was a result, then, of the clash between two different ideas about how real apostles of Christ should behave, actually a clash between two different, culturally conditioned Christian leadership role patterns.[5]

This reading of the text is actually a mirror-reading of it, that is, it operates on the assumption that anything affirmed in the text must have been denied or challenged in the historical situation it aims at. But as Margaret Mitchell showed in a stunning footnote, it is not possible to understand 1 Cor 9 as a true defence against actual charges against Paul for not having received money.[6] Paul does not have to defend his choice of working with his own hands to earn a living instead of choosing charismatic poverty.[7] Nor does this text give the impression that Paul is talking about something the Corinthians have never heard of before—apostles' rights of support. They know about other apostles and their customary ways and, as 2 Cor 11.20 shows, were quite prepared to pay apostles who demanded to be paid. In 1 Thess 2.6 Paul writes in passing that he and Barnabas could have made their weight felt, that is, exacted money, but chose not to. A flow of money from below to people with authority is thus not an anachronistic idea imported into the first century from our times, but a social fact in the world of the New Testament. To that degree Judge's generalisation about the direction of money in Greco-Roman culture needs to be nuanced from ancient evidence itself.

One problem in understanding this fact is Paul's remarkable reluctance to make use of this custom and receive money from his own congregations, and that is where my ignorance of patronage made a difference. When discussing possible reasons for this Pauline reluctance twenty-five years ago,[8] I reached the conclusion that the reason underlying the different arguments given by the apostle in

---

5. G. Theissen, 'Legitimation und Lebensunterhalt: Ein Beitrag zur Soziologie urchristlicher Mission', originally in *NTS* 21 (1975) 192–221, now in *Social Setting*, 27–67.

6. Mitchell, *Rhetoric*, 244–45 n. 330.

7. Lars Aejmelaeus, 'The Question of Salary in the Conflict between Paul and the 'Super Apostles' in Corinth', in *Fair Play: Diversity and Conflicts in Early Christianity. Essays in Honour of Heikki Räisänen* (ed. I. Dunderberg, C. Tuckett, and K. Syreeni; NovTSup 103; Leiden: Brill, 2002) 343–76.

8. *Paul and Power*, 1978, 92–95 = 1980, 89–93.

different letters was his policy of entering into financial relations only with ἐκκλησίαι with which he had developed a trusting κοινωνία relation. Corinth was the exception from the normal development of trust between the apostle and his congregation, and such a bitter experience that Paul did not believe that a trusting κοινωνία with them would ever materialise.[9] But because of my lack of apposite social-historical knowledge I was not aware of the invisible strings of sentiment and dependence that were attached to the receiving of money in Paul's social environment and that influenced his policy. In the Greco-Roman context, the classicists tell us, this was naturally understood as establishing something of a client-patron relation, where the receiver becomes the dependent party. It is therefore quite probable that Paul in his somewhat strained excuses to the Corinthians in 2 Cor 12 for not wanting their money, or in his laboured thanksgiving to the Philippians for their gift of money to him (Phil 4.10–20), was striving for a freer relation without telling us so. He wanted a relation where he did not have to carry the burden of gratitude and obligation incumbent on any client house-teacher toward a *patronus*-like individual or group. He much prefers them to be dependent on him than the other way round, which is why he emphasises his enduring role as their founding apostle and 'father' (2 Cor 12.14b; cf. 1 Cor 4.15) and spiritualises the gift he received from the Philippians.[10] In this regard (finding a realistic, adequate interpretation of Paul's reluctance to enter a relation of receiving money), better 'fieldwork' in ancient social history has improved the understanding of the New Testament texts.

Just to mention one more example of the importance of social history in the interpretation of 1 Corinthians, I would point to the discussion between Gerd Theissen and Justin Meggitt concerning poor people's attitudes to eating meat. Theissen notes that most people (i.e., poor people) in Mediterranean first-century society did not eat meat very often, and when it happened, they had not bought the meat themselves. It was distributed for free and eaten in the context of religious feasts, paid for by the authorities or some rich benefactor. And, generally speaking, much meat that was offered for sale in the city's *macellum* had been part of an animal sacrifice in one of the city's temples. Thus meat consumption for poor people was naturally associated with participation in religious activity, connected with 'the gods', and for poor Christians therefore somehow tainted by this numinous, idolatrous connection. For rich people, including the few rich Christians in Corinth, meat had no such associations with idolatry, but was rather an everyday phenomenon. So Theissen detects a stratum-specific difference in the attitude to food that had been in contact with 'idols', which explains the problem that Paul discusses in 1 Cor 8–10. The 'strong' are more or less the same as the rich and socially more elevated within the congregation, while

9. This is a conclusion reached also by Aejmelaeus, 'Salary', 364.
10. Martin, *Corinthian Body*, 79–86.

the 'weak' are situated at a lower social level. Social stratification is thus an important factor behind what looks at first like a purely religious or theological debate.[11]

Justin Meggitt criticises the social-historical basis for Theissen's reconstruction of the historical situation behind 1 Cor 8–10 and the following interpretation of the conflict. In Meggitt's opinion Theissen has overlooked that even poor people had much more everyday and non-numinous contacts with meat consumption through the well-attested *popinae* and *ganeae*, the ubiquitous cooking shops and eateries frequented by ordinary, poor people in towns and cities. Many of the urban population had no kitchens or cooking facilities at home, but bought their hot meal of the day in a local *popina*. Ancient authors tell us that meat was available at these places, although of low quality and coming from parts of the animal that one did not want to think about.[12]

Even without being competent to decide which one of Theissen and Meggitt has taken all relevant social-historical information about ancient eating habits into account and interpreted it correctly, one can recognise the immediate connection between the facts of ancient social history and the reconstruction of historical reality in the Corinthian church. A good knowledge of social history is indispensable for reaching secure conclusions about stratum-specific differences in attitude and mentality, which form the basis of textual interpretation in this case. This is the undeniably strong point in Judge's criticism against a too-facile sociological interpretation of first-century Christian texts.

2. INCREASED KNOWLEDGE OF SOCIAL HISTORY AND SOCIAL STRATIFICATION

In the last twenty-five to thirty years historical research on the New Testament has turned vigorously to investigation of social realities in Mediterranean societies and cultures. The demand for more and better fieldwork has been heeded. Among areas of special importance for the historical reconstruction of Corinthian Christianity one can point to:

- the social location of Paul and social stratification within his congregations (see below);
- class and status in the Roman Empire, and in Corinth specifically; the phenomenon of status dissonance (or status inconsistency) also belongs here;[13]

11. G. Theissen, 'Die Starken und Schwachen in Korinth' (originally in *EvT* 35 [1975] 155–72), now in *Social Setting*, 121–43.
12. J. J. Meggitt, 'Meat Consumption and Social Conflict in Corinth', *JTS* 45 (1994) 137–41.
13. Meeks, *First Urban Christians*.

- patron/client relations, social networks, relations to social elites;[14]
- specific status indicators (like property, ownership of slaves[15] and business, recognised social positions or offices,[16] eating habits,[17] attitudes to the human body,[18] litigation,[19] rhetorical education).[20]

From the work of Edwin Judge in 1960[21] and onward something that has been called a 'new consensus' about the social location of the first Christians emerged, in opposition to the image of them as mainly situated in the lowest strata of society, among the poor, uneducated, and unprominent majority of the empire's inhabitants, which was (thought to be) the 'old consensus' after Adolf Deissmann's influential writings at the beginning of the twentieth century.[22] Judge pictured Paul and his coworkers as a set of fairly well-educated, cosmopolitan, and cultured people who moved easily also in the upper strata of the Mediterranean cities in their Christian mission work. And this situated at least some early Christians quite a bit higher up in society than previously thought.

This perspective was developed in a number of groundbreaking studies by Gerd Theissen in 1973–75, in which he conducted a sociographic and especially a prosopographic investigation of named individuals in the Corinthian congregation, whose status indicators locate them in somewhat elevated social positions.[23] Through the work of Abraham J. Malherbe and Wayne A. Meeks this perspective was further developed into a deeper and more detailed awareness of status differences in ancient Greco-Roman society and in the Christian ἐκκλησίαι, and of the phenomenon of status inconsistency (Meeks put this to use in explaining the

14. See Chow, *Patronage and Power;* Clarke, *Secular and Christian Leadership*; and Philip A. Harland, 'Connections with Elites in the World of the Early Christians', in *Handbook of Early Christianity: Social Science Approaches* (ed. A. J. Blasi, J. Duhaime, P.-A. Turcotte; Walnut Creek, Calif.: AltaMira Press, 2002) 385–408.

15. D. C. Verner, *The Household of God: The Social World of the Pastoral Epistles* (Chico, Calif.: Scholars Press, 1983) 60–61, estimates that only one-fourth of the free families were wealthy enough to own even one slave. The presence of slave owners in Pauline Christianity tells us something, then, about the socioeconomic range of these congregations.

16. Theissen, 'Social Stratification in the Corinthian Community', from *Social Setting,* 69–119. Cf. ch. 6 above.

17. Theissen, 'The Strong and the Weak in Corinth: A Sociological Analysis of a Theological Quarrel', from *Social Setting,* 121–43.

18. Martin, *Corinthian Body*.

19. P. Garnsey, *Social Status and Legal Privilege* (Oxford: Clarendon Press, 1970) and discussed extensively in the works of Clarke, Martin, Winter, Witherington.

20. S. M. Pogoloff, *LOGOS AND SOPHIA: The Rhetorical Situation of 1 Corinthians* (SBLDS 134; Atlanta: Scholars Press, 1992).

21. E. A. Judge, *The Social Pattern of Christian Groups in the First Century: Some Prolegomena to the Study of New Testament Ideas of Social Obligation* (London: Tyndale Press, 1960).

22. Theissen points out that this conventional picture of the history of research into the social level of early Christians is not correct. There never was any consensus, nor is there now, but 'rather a renewed socio-historical interest with different results', in: 'The Social Structure of Pauline Communities: Some Critical Remarks on J. J. Meggitt, *Paul, Poverty and Survival*', *JSNT* 84 (2001) 66.

23. Now collected and translated in Theissen, *Social Setting*.

attractiveness of Christian groups to certain people).[24] In the writings of John Chow, Andrew Clarke, and Bruce Winter the picture is even further consolidated of first-century Christians in Corinth (and in the Mediterranean diaspora generally) as coming from low and high social strata in Greco-Roman society, excepting only the topmost aristocracy.[25] The latter three authors emphasise especially the importance of patronage and patronal networks in understanding how the surrounding society affected life inside the Christian community, often in a negative way. To put it briefly, the rich and socially more powerful Christians were the leaders in the Corinthian congregation, and they created most of the problems that the apostle addresses in his Corinthian correspondence. Thus what may look at first like theological and ethical problems and discussions are actually caused more by social factors like stratum-specific behaviour patterns operative in the everyday life of these Christians than by differing religious perspectives or theological traditions.

3. WHAT GUIDES THE INTERPRETATION OF ANCIENT SOURCE MATERIAL?

While there is no way of denying that our knowledge of the sociohistorical setting of Corinthian Christianity has increased generally through the research of the last decades, a remaining question is how this added material knowledge can and should be used and interpreted. New questioning will elicit new data and new insights, but these new questions are of course guided by and result in overarching interpretive perspectives of the reality investigated. These perspectives have to do with judgments on the representative nature of uncovered data—do they reflect more than a part of the historical situation we are looking at? The information assembled, for example, by John Chow on the working of patronage in Roman Corinth may be correct as far as it goes, but if patronage is not a ubiquitous social phenomenon, but only reflects social relations at a level of society where (almost) no Christian moved in the middle of the first century, it does not help us understand early Corinthian Christianity.[26] Sociohistorical data are only telling if they are put into 'an appropriate context of interpretation'. This is the main contention of a recent discussion concerning a realistic and responsible handling of ancient source material.

The 'consensus' sketched above that places Paul and dominant parts of Pauline Christianity in the social stratum just below the elite has been vigorously attacked by Justin J. Meggitt in his *Paul, Poverty and Survival*.[27] He claimed that scholars

24. A. J. Malherbe, *Social Aspects of Early Christianity* (2d ed.; Philadelphia: Fortress, 1983); Meeks, *First Urban Christians*.
25. Chow, *Patronage and Power*; Clarke, *Secular and Christian Leadership*; Winter, *After Paul Left Corinth*.
26. This is the opinion of, e.g., Aejmelaeus, 'Salary'.
27. Meggitt, *Paul, Poverty*.

in the 'new consensus' had uncritically accepted the information given in the extant, predominantly upper-class-based, ancient literature as trustworthy evidence of social realities. There are good reasons to doubt that this literature gives a true picture of what life was like for the 99 or so percent of the population that did not belong to the elite but struggled every day simply to survive the next day or week. Most people were poor and devoted their lives to survival. As no Christian in the first century belonged to the elite, we simply have to picture all members of the Pauline churches (including, of course, the apostle himself) as belonging to the poor 99 percent. Seen in this light the Pauline letters provide evidence of a conscious social strategy of cooperation and 'mutualism' advocated by Paul, where poor people help each other in an egalitarian reciprocity structure. This social location and this strategy for survival is then what Meggitt calls an appropriate context of interpretation, which is not produced by concentrating on information about the way the upper classes lived.

This is also the perspective of Ekkehard W. Stegemann and Wolfgang Stegemann (both German professors of the New Testament) in their work on the social history of the first Christians,which was published in English a year after Meggitt's book.[28] The Stegemann brothers also place the early Christians of the first century fairly low in society. They start, however, with a thorough description of ancient (agrarian) economy in the Roman Empire, after which they devote a full chapter to social stratification generally in this society, reviewing and discussing the positions of classical scholars such as Alföldy, Vittinghof, Christ, Schneider, and Garnsey-Saller (53–95). The Stegemanns find it necessary to subdivide the traditional two-tier divison of society into elite and nonelite (*honestiores* and *humiliores*). They divide the upper stratum into (a) people belonging to the three *ordines*—the senatorial, equestrian, and decurional, (b) rich people without *ordo*, and (c) retainers of the upper stratum (not themselves belonging to the elite). The lower stratum, which of course contains the large majority of the population, has to be divided into at least (d) the relatively prosperous and relatively poor (*penētes*), and (e) the absolutely poor (*ptōchoi*).[29] The Stegemanns actually lean toward dividing (d) further, inserting a group of people who live at 'minimum existence', just above the 'absolutely poor'. In striving to drive home the bleak reality of poverty, terminology becomes a bit fuzzy here: if the absolutely poor scrape along for a few decades of miserable life, they must after all be said to live at the minimum subsistence level, not below it. People who live *below* the minimum existence for more than a month are only found in graves.

In their chapter 10, the Stegemanns apply their stratification model to the early Christians in the urban societies of the Roman Empire, among which are also the Pauline communities, in the fifties and after 70 C.E.[30] The resulting pic-

---

28. E. W. Stegemann and W. Stegemann, *The Jesus Movement: A Social History of Its First Century* (Minneapolis: Fortress, 1999; translation from *Urchristliche Sozialgeschichte: Die Anfänge im Judentum und die Christusgemeinden in der mediterranen Welt* [Stuttgart: Kohlhammer, 1995]).

29. Ibid., 72 (figure).

30. 'The Social Composition of Christ-confessing Communities', *Jesus Movement*, 288–316.

ture is that the Christ-confessing communities of the first century had no *ordo* members, but a few rich people from the subdecurional stratum, and some retainers. The overwhelming majority of Christians in these communities (and Paul too)[31] belonged to the category (d) above, and many of them were slaves or former slaves. But the absolutely poor were apparently not represented in Pauline communities, neither in the fifties nor later in the first century.[32]

The important difference between the Stegemanns and Meggitt is that the former find it necessary to subdivide the large nonelite into three or four significantly different social strata, while Meggitt comes close to stating that everyone, except those in strata (a) and (b), is destitute and shares the plight of the desperately poor whose life is a continuous struggle to survive. In doing this, he certainly marshals large amounts of sociohistorical evidence and knows the ancient sources very well, but his interpretive perspective on the data is 'pauperistic', that is, he is determined to understand Paul and his Christian communities as really poor. For example, in his analysis of Paul's social standing, Meggitt dismisses everything that might point in other directions.[33] Paul was literate (like only 10 percent of the population); the style, structure, and content of his writings evidence a high level of education, both Jewish and Greek (probably even fewer had that); he was a Roman and Tarsian citizen; he traveled for years in the east, building networks of socially capable people, and so on. Yes, but none of these characteristics *needs* be taken as evidence of a well-to-do background, and they are therefore not allowed by Meggitt to accumulate into even a doubt or nuance concerning Paul's social lowliness. This consistent interpretion of data in one desired direction is what I call his pauperistic perspective. This is one way to interpret the data and it is quite possible to do so, but the adequacy of this interpretative perspective and the probability of its result are also quite open to discussion.

Meggitt's important book has challenged a majority of scholars writing on sociohistorical aspects of the New Testament, especially the Pauline area, and sparked a vigorous debate. Some of those attacked by Meggitt have replied to his charges and challenged his own use of sources and his reconstruction of the situation in the Corinthian church. The *Journal for the Study of the New Testament* devoted part of its first 2001 issue to a discussion of Meggitt's views on the handling of sources by Martin and Theissen, with a reply from Meggitt.[34]

---

31. The result of Stegemanns' analysis of Paul's own social standing (pp. 297–302) is quite similar to the picture given by Meggitt, but arrived at not by applying a pauperistic perspective, but by discounting the evidence of the Acts of the Apostles—Paul's Jerusalem education at Gamaliel's feet, commission from the high priest, Roman citizenship, socialising with and converting the rich—as purely Lucan fiction.

32. Summary, ibid., 303 and 316. This summary is quite similar to the one arrived at by Meeks in his *First Urban Christians*.

33. Meggitt, *Paul, Poverty*, 75–96.

34. D. B. Martin, 'Review Essay: Justin J. Meggitt, *Paul, Poverty and Survival*', *JSNT* 84 (2001) 51–64; and Gerd Theissen, 'The Social Structure of Pauline Communities' in the same issue, pp. 65–84. Justin Meggitt answers his critics in the same issue, pp. 85–94: 'Response to Martin and Theissen'.

Dale Martin commends Meggitt for his boldness in taking on a popular consensus in scholarship, and for his thoroughness in presenting ancient material. He also agrees with him that Pauline Christianity cannot be described as a movement made up of, or to a large extent controlled by, the elite, and also sides with him and others in disallowing the use of the too modern category of 'middle class' in description and analysis of the ancient Roman world.[35]

Martin is, however, sharply critical of many other aspects of Meggitt's work, beginning with his procedure of dividing the ancient Roman world into only two groups of socioeconomic importance: the elite (less than 1 percent of all people), and the rest, who are seen as uniformly poor, living at or near subsistence level, and therefore struggling for their survival day by day. Within this 99 percent Meggitt refuses to admit any differences in status, affluence, social influence, or power as important for understanding internal relations and conflicts within the early Christian groups. Their alleged common economic predicament—destitution and the ensuing daily struggle to survive—overshadows, not to say obliterates, any differences as regards status indicators adduced by other scholars: having a home of one's own, owning a house, hosting a Christian group, owning a business, owning a slave, being able to travel, showing evidence of rhetorical education, practising benefaction, and supporting poorer people. Differences in these respects are not denied by Meggitt but quickly passed over as socially insignificant, and of no help at all in explaining tensions and conflicts between the uniformly poor Christians.

Meggitt rightly criticises others for depending too unsuspectingly on the opinions of ancient upper-class writers as reflecting historical reality, but sometimes slips into the same habit himself. Martin also points out that Meggitt's objections against other scholars' opinions and hypotheses are often phrased with qualifiers like 'necessarily', 'firm grounds', 'direct correlation', 'invariably', 'unequivocally' that

> render his statements unassailable. How could anyone demonstrate that evidence taken by almost all of us to be partial, suggestive and circumstantial necessarily constitute proofs? Meggitt's rhetoric raises the bar for historical evidence to heights impossible for normal historiography. But normal his-

---

35. The warning that 'class' is an anachronistic concept of low explanatory value in ancient social history is something of a commonplace among social historians of the Roman Empire, as well as among exegetes who have worked in this field; see already my *Sociology and the New Testament: An Appraisal* (Minneapolis: Fortress, 1990) 22, and the literature quoted in that chapter. Nonetheless, Dale Martin finds the concept of class useful, indeed almost necessary, if one wants to give a true picture of the relation between higher and lower social strata. He adopts a definition of class from the classical historian G. E. M. de Ste. Croix, who defines 'class' as 'the collective social fact of exploitation, the way in which exploitation is embodied in a social structure'. Martin continues: 'Since class is a relation, those who live off the surplus labor value of others (no matter how wealthy or otherwise they are) are members of the propertied, or upper, class, whereas those whose labor provides the surplus value that supports the livelihood of others are members of the exploited class or classes' (Martin, *Corinthian Body*, xvi). If we use this understanding of 'class', we have to conclude that Paul (as well as other salaried apostles) was really an upper-class person in relation to his congregations.

toriography need not demonstrate what must be the case. It need only show what probably is the case—which is always accomplished by cumulative and complicated evidence.[36]

As for the 'mutualism' advocated as Paul's practical and practised solution to the survival problem of the poor, Martin questions the textual basis for it. It is hardly evidenced even within the New Testament (and then only really in regard to the collection for Jerusalem), and not at all outside it, which makes it suspiciously unique in ancient history. Here, remarkably, Meggitt refrains from an 'ideological' reading of Paul, or in other words from suspecting the apostle of wanting to mask the hierarchical meaning of the collection by using the language of reciprocity and κοινωνία about it, or not entertaining even the possibility that the spiritualising of the Philippian gift to Paul in Phil 4:10–20 is done to conceal the fact that their gift makes the apostle appear as their dependent 'client'.

Gerd Theissen's main criticism of Meggitt's work is directed against his thoroughgoing homogenisation of Roman society. By adamantly denying any other stratification than the one between the elite (senatorial, equestrian, and decurional *ordines*), which encompassed less than 1 percent of the total population, and on the other hand the uniformly poor remaining 99 percent (some 70 million people!), Meggitt has closed his eyes to sociohistorical reality and simplified it beyond historical belief.

But of course there must have existed further stratification of local types below the highest, imperial upper class among so many million people, says Theissen. Available information about wages of city employees and civil servants, about ownership of land, slaves, and businesses evidences noticeable differences in wealth and influence and status among the 99 percent that Meggitt depicts as simply destitute. The Acts of the Apostles tells us about Paul's Tarsian and Roman citizenship (according to many scholars a social distinction of sorts around the middle of the first century),[37] and this is accepted by Meggitt. So why, asks Theissen, does he not accept the same writer's information about highly placed people (especially women) becoming Christians? All information about upper-class believers can hardly be explained away on the basis of Lucan tendency. Pliny the Younger writes to the emperor Trajan and tells him that the Christian faith has invaded 'all orders, *ordines*', expressly mentioning women. Upper-class women found it easier than their husbands to become Christians, as they were not obliged to participate in city and imperial cults as part of holding a civic office. Just below the stratum of families from which men were admitted to become *decuriones* is found a subdecurional class of families, who were rich enough to qualify for such election but could not be admitted because of the *numerus clausus* of decurions. Theissen believes that Christianity spread especially in this subelite stratum,

36. Martin, 'Review Essay', 62.
37. Meggitt counters that Roman citizenship (according to P. A. Brunt, *Italian Manpower*, 1971) was held by some 6 million people at this time, of which maybe 2 million lived outside Italy. Most of these were, of course, poor (*Paul, Poverty*, 80–82).

already in the first century. Both the Epistle of James and the Shepherd of Hermas testify to the presence of rich persons in the church.

To counter, as Meggitt does in his reply to Theissen,[38] that the social life (location) of the Christian communities had moved upward during the period from Paul to the end of the first century (as new religious movements tend to do) amounts to giving up the main idea of a uniformly destitute 99 percent. He now seems ready to admit that there existed social stratification within this immense group, only delaying the advent of Christians into higher levels of society by a time span of forty to fifty years.

Theissen points to two further characteristics of the first-century Christian church that really break up the picture of its uniform poverty. This movement was a deviant social minority, with a type of inner cohesion across social boundaries and strata that we find evidenced in (a) the *familia Caesaris*, the greatly extended household and administrative staff of the Roman emperors made up of freemen, *liberti,* and even slaves, located in many places throughout the empire, (b) in the Jewish diaspora communities, and (c) the ancient clubs, *collegia*. All these, including then the early Christian communities, were socially distinct groups comprising both rich and poor, highly and lowly placed people, but which were held together by other factors of integration than belonging to the same social stratum.

Thomas Schmeller's data on ancient *collegia* also needs to be taken into consideration here, in order to help us characterise the early Christian groups. He has shown that professional clubs often had highly placed patrons, a large proportion of freemen, and that their leading positions were filled with long-time incumbents. Religious clubs, on the other hand, seldom had socially prominent patrons, but instead a high number of slaves, and constant changes in the incumbency of offices. The latter characteristic shows that members of these clubs normally were not affluent enough to carry the burden of being in (club) office for a long time. This financial burden had to be shared by many people, which is why the incumbency periods had to be short.[39] Early Christian groups seem to have had more permanent officeholders, and attempts at replacing them with others met strong resistance (*1 Clement*), a characteristic that indicates a level of moderate prosperity. Probably the Christian groups also had patrons who were themselves participating members of the life of the *collegium*. One exception might be the much-discussed οἰκονόμος of Corinth, Erastus. In his renewed prosopographical discussion of individual Christians in Corinth, Theissen finds it probable that Crispus, Stephanas, and Gaius belonged to the more socially elevated strata of the city, which corroborates the more general information of Acts mentioned earlier.

---

38. Meggitt, 'Response to Martin and Theissen', 91.
39. Thomas Schmeller, *Hierarchie und Egalität: Eine sozialgeschichtliche Untersuchung paulinischer Gemeinden und griechisch-römischer Vereine* (SBS 162; Stuttgart: 1995); cited from Theissen, 'Social Structure', 76ff.

As regards mutualism, Theissen does not agree that this specific ethos has to be intimately connected to social homogeneity. The probability of a one-to-one relation between a theological or ethical idea on the one hand and a specific structure of social interaction on the other is not very high. Even if the apostle Paul refers to and advocates mutualism or κοινωνία to his readers, this ideal could have functioned more as an interpretation or even as a challenge to change behaviour than as a symbolic depiction of a real behaviour pattern.[40] In Corinth, it could very well have been the case that the ethical ideal had to give way to the social realities of stratification. All are equal in Christ, but 'on the other hand, we find a stratified social reality in early Christianity, which transforms the original mutualism to love patriarchalism'.[41]

4. THE ROLE OF MODELS IN SOCIAL-SCIENTIFIC INTERPRETATION OF NEW TESTAMENT TEXTS

One important discussion between practitioners of New Testament exegesis with a heightened awareness of the social dimension of faith is about the role of social-scientific theory and models in the interpretation of New Testament texts and the historical situation behind them. It is presented in a fashion of general methodological interest in a recent scholarly exchange between Philip Esler and David Horrell.[42]

Both of them make a distinction between two different kinds of scholars in the field: (a) social-scientific interpreters, who make sense of biblical texts with the help of the social sciences (sociology, anthropology, social psychology, and economics), and (b) social historians, who are interested in social realities but not in social sciences, and refrain from or even advise against the use of social-scientific theory or models. Among the former can be mentioned especially scholars belonging to the Context Group—Bruce Malina, Jerome Neyrey, John Elliott, Philip Esler, Richard Rohrbaugh, who have focused on the development and application to the New Testament of anthropological models for understanding human behaviour in other societies, especially the biblical ones.[43] The counterpart farthest away from this approach on the other side would be scholars like Edwin Judge or Andrew Clarke, who see social sciences as rather distortive and unnecessary in the exegetical and social-historical task. A more common, mediating position would be scholars who

40. Cf. the argument in Holmberg, *Sociology and the New Testament*, 140–44, on the difficulty of reading a specific behaviour or concrete social situation from a theological or hortatory text.

41. Theissen, 'Social Structure', 84.

42. P. F. Esler, 'Review of D. G. Horrell, *The Social Ethos of the Corinthian Correspondence*' *JTS* 49 (1998) 253–60. This was answered by D. G. Horrell, 'Models and Methods in Social-Scientific Interpretation: A Response to Philip Esler', *JSNT* 78 (2000) 83–105. Esler responded to Horrell's countercriticism in the same issue: 'Models in New Testament Interpretation: A Reply to David Horrell', 107–13.

43. The approach is clearly described by J. H. Elliott, *What Is Social-Scientific Criticism?* (Minneapolis: Fortress; SPCK: London, 1993).

use and advocate a much more tentative use of social theory, eclectic and piece-meal. In this group we find some of the best-known 'sociological' exegetes, such as Gerd Theissen and Wayne Meeks, whose approach is closer to an 'interpretivist' anthropologist such as Clifford Geertz.[44] This approach is based on participant immersion in a culture, resulting in a thorough understanding from within and without, formulated in what Geertz calls a 'thick description'.

Esler is hesitant about the feasibility of an interpretivist stance in ancient social history, because of the scarcity of data, which does not allow anything even near a 'thick description'. In addition, every historian or exegete uses modeling—meaning the obvious set of presuppositions, guiding ideas, interpretive patterns used by anyone working to understand a text or set of data. And if we all use models in intellectual work, 'explicit modelling is preferable to implicit model-ling'.[45] The use of explicit models does not presuppose any determinism or view of human life as run by invisible iron laws. Models are only tools, 'heuristic devices, not social laws. The test for success is a pragmatic (and modest) one, namely, whether plausible historical results have been produced in the process'[46] of making sense of data through using models, preferably cross-cultural ones, that is, from the cultural context of the person or group one is investigating, and not from our own time and culture.[47]

Horrell does not agree with the idea implicit in Esler's text: that only scholars working with explicit cross-cultural models are social-scientific interpreters. There are more ways than one of being that, and the use of models is not neces-sary for anyone who wants to do sociologically informed exegesis. On the con-trary, using explicit models always runs the risk of flattening and generalising the evidence, not allowing the true, unkempt diversity of historical reality to appear. In my opinion, this can happen both in the work of scholars who shy away from the use of any 'model' (like Judge, who seems to be guided by his knowledge of patronage to disregard money moving in the 'wrong' direction), and of those whose methodology is based on a rigorous application of anthropologically based models (like Esler, for whom ancient honour-and-shame patterns must have shaped the behaviour of Paul and James into a game of one-up-manship, smart promise-breaking, and vindictiveness).

Further, the very term 'model' needs to be more precisely defined. It should not be used for just about any 'theory', 'ideal type', or perspective that a scholar wants to test on ancient material. This makes the term so wide that it amounts to no more than stating the widely accepted truth that human perception is never

44. Here one could also mention B. Witherington III, *Conflict and Community in Corinth: A Socio-Rhetorical Commentary on 1 and 2 Corinthians* (Grand Rapids: Eerdmans, 1994).

45. Esler, 'Review of Horrell', 255.

46. Ibid., 256.

47. I consider very helpful and clarifying Esler's discussion about models and their use, and social-scientific methodology generally, in his *Community and Gospel in Luke-Acts: The Social and Political Motivations of Lucan Theology* (SNTSMS 57; Cambridge: Cambridge University Press, 1987) 6–16.

purely objective or detached.[48] Models should not be seen as ideas that a scholar starts from and lets his research be guided by, but rather as the results of empirical research, which serve to simplify, abstract, or generalise the findings obtained, so that they can be further tested elsewhere.

Generally speaking, models are therefore 'based on a philosophy of human action that regards such behaviour as predictable and regular, presentable in generalised and typical patterns that occur cross-culturally, and that might, albeit tentatively, enable the formulation of (social) laws, or at least generalisations, concerning human behaviour.'[49] This point is where Esler and Horrell are deeply divided, not only as regards methodology, but also in their fundamental ideas about human social behaviour as such. Esler uses and defends the perspective of Peter Berger and Thomas Luckmann in their famous book, *The Social Construction of Reality* (1967), according to which social structures have a kind of objective or objectified existence, meeting the human agent as an external reality that steers action along certain predetermined channels. Against this Horrell holds the 'structuration' perspective of Anthony Giddens, which emphasises the participation of the human actor in both the maintenance and transformation of social structures. Such structures are not made of iron, but are constantly adapted and transformed by actors in the very act of behaving within the confines of structure. But in the opinion of Esler both Giddens and Horrell greatly overstate the extent to which human beings transform rather than reproduce the values and institutions of the social system they are part of.

This difference in the understanding of human freedom vis-à-vis social structures means that Horrell is prepared to reckon with a considerable degree of freedom and creative space for Paul and other social actors in early Christianity. Esler on the other side understands the same actors as to a large extent constrained and bound by the given structures of their social world, so that they do not have very much choice to act differently from what the prevailing social patterns prescribe. At this deep level, the controversy is no longer about method, but rather about 'social ontology', or the philosophy of human action and answers to questions about the scope and depth of social constraints on individual freedom of action.

5. CONCLUDING REFLECTIONS

To summarise my arguments above, I should first state that a detailed knowledge of the historical setting of the early Christians is indispensable for any historical reconstruction of their real life. Historiography cannot operate without historical data that can serve as evidence, nor can it neglect any available historical data, just because they cannot be easily fitted into one's own outlook or 'model'. Sociohistorical fieldwork is what hypotheses, models, and theories work on and are

48. Horrell, 'Models and Methods in Social-Scientific Interpretation', 85.
49. Ibid., 86.

constructed from. This means also that models or theories cannot substitute for evidence, by filling in gaps in the data, as it were. If a model is based on a considerable amount of data that are clearly analogous to what we are investigating in the New Testament, the model can serve as an abbreviated form of a probability judgment about what might have occurred in that situation, although the evidence for it is actually lacking. In other words, historically based models can turn a guess into an educated guess, but no more.

It is obvious that data of a historical nature are not transformed into 'historical facts' or even meaningful information by their sheer existence. Data are mute, until made to talk by being inserted in an interpretive framework. This is what the debate about perspectives reported in section 3 above is grappling with. To assemble general data about prosperity and poverty in first-century societies is of course needed for a sociohistorical reconstruction of social stratification in these societies. But even a well-researched picture of ancient stratification will in itself not answer the question of where early Christianity is to be located in the picture. That is decided by one's chosen interpretive perspective. And only when the argument between, say, a pauperistic perspective (as in Meggitt) or its opposite (as in Judge or Winter) has been fought out, can one go ahead and use sociohistorical knowledge to interpret and explain the presence or absence of stratum-dependent conflicts and behaviour patterns in these groups.

From the discussion between Esler and Horrell it is also clear that the very concept of a social-scientific model needs to be clarified, as well as its appropriate use. It cannot be used about any guiding idea or presupposition in research and interpretation—that would make the term too wide for any usefulness. When discussing models and their use a dozen years ago, I based myself on the works of Esler and John Elliott (with Thomas Carney and E. P. Thompson in the background).[50] In words quoted from Carney, 'a model is something less than a theory and something more than an analogy. . . . A theory is based on axiomatic laws and states general principles. It is a basic proposition through which a variety of observations or statements become explicable. A model, by way of contrast, acts as a link between theories and observations'.

I would now add the demand of Horrell that such models should be based on previous empirical research, thereby summarising real phenomena. They are simply more or less useful shorthand summaries of analogous social behaviour, aiding but not governing historical perception and explanation. One could also follow Horrell in being hesitant about Esler's claim that a model always introduces a dynamic element into an otherwise static classification or set of observations. The often-stated guideline that models should be used heuristically (help frame new questions and look for unnoticed evidence in answering them) is correct, but not always adhered to in practice, when the social-scientific model is allowed a predictive or prescriptive power in historical explanation.

50. Holmberg, *Sociology and the New Testament*, 12–17.

The concluding paragraphs of section 4 above refer to the philosophical debate between two differing philosophies of human action, found in Peter Berger and Thomas Luckmann behind Esler and in Anthony Giddens behind Horrell. This goes to show that social-scientific perspectives or toolboxes usually come with an ontology of their own, even if this is not visible to begin with. Those who want to use these toolboxes must be prepared eventually to grapple with the underlying philosophical issues about the nature of social reality.[51] Horrell and others have stated, and justly so, that the methodological distinction between social science and history is nonexistent.[52] Perhaps we should be prepared to extend this holistic perspective also to the relation between social science and philosophy and theology, even if the relation between these disciplines is rather more thorny. Ultimately social science contains a philosophy of social human reality too. Even biblical scholars should recognise the need to appraise critically the fundamental and philosophical bases of the approaches they take. This is not to say, however, that philosophical perspectives on the true character of human action could take the place of detailed historical study in the work of historical reconstruction. But it reminds us that historical interpretation is a wide-ranging and complex task, connected as it is to several other branches of scholarly research into social action and human reality.

51. Cf. my remarks on this in *Sociology and the New Testament*, 150–55.
52. Horrell, 'Social Sciences Studying Formative Christian Phenomena: A Creative Movement', in *Handbook of Early Christianity: Social Science Approaches* (ed. A. J. Blasi, J. Duhaime, P.-A. Turcotte; Walnut Creek, Calif.: AltaMira Press, 2002) 12–13. Revised version of the original in D. G. Horrell, ed., *Social-Scientific Approaches to New Testament Interpretation* (Edinburgh: T. & T. Clark, 1999).

Chapter 21

The Shifting Centre: Ideology and the Interpretation of 1 Corinthians

Margaret Y. MacDonald

The concept of 'ideology' is increasingly being employed by biblical scholars in considering the nature of the biblical record itself and in discussions of methodology and theoretical approach. In common usage, however, it is a term with a wide variety of associations, sometimes including pejorative overtones. It has been frequently linked with economic and political theory (especially in Marxist thought), but also with political propaganda, invective, and distortion. The influential critique of ideology by Karl Marx and Friedrich Engels (*The German Ideology*, 1846) has resulted in a legacy of associating ideology with class struggle and the production of 'false consciousness in the perception of social reality by those living under the dominant ideology'.[1] There has been an attempt in social-scientific scholarship, however, to employ the concept in a more neutral sense to refer to a range of social phenomena. The sociologist Edward Shils, for example, described ideology as one type of comprehensive pattern of cognitive and moral belief about humanity, society, and the universe. According to Shils, ideology should be distinguished from other patterns such as outlooks, creeds, and systems

---

1. R. P. Carroll, 'Ideology', in *A Dictionary of Biblical Interpretation* (ed. R. J. Coggins and J. L. Houlden; London: SCM; and Philadelphia: Trinity Press International, 1990) 309.

of thought, and is characterized by a demand for complete subservience to its principles and a sense of alienation from existing society: Ideologies 'recommend the transformation of the lives of their exponents in accordance with specific principles; they insist on consistency and thoroughgoingness in their exponents' application of principles; and they recommend either their adherents' complete dominion over the societies in which they live or their total, self-protective withdrawal from these societies'.[2]

Shils's work on ideology has actually substantially influenced New Testament scholars employing social-scientific methods in analyzing the formation of the Jesus movement and the interaction between church groups and society.[3] But in this essay I will employ the much more general definition offered by Robert P. Carroll of ideology as 'a term for a system of ideas providing a framework for perceiving social reality and generating practical concerns'.[4] According to Carroll's definition ideology may refer to a worldview that leads people to a particular set of actions (e.g., the formation of a new religious movement), but it may also describe a set of ideas of a specific individual (i.e., the ideology of Paul or a particular biblical interpreter). In short, in all areas where ideas are present, there exists ideology.[5]

My primary goal in this essay is to examine the ideologies adopted by biblical scholars in their interpretation of 1 Corinthians. Although it is not my main concern here, it should, however, be noted that how the Bible itself functions 'as an ideological system or set of ideological systems' is a related issue that increasingly shapes biblical scholarship.[6] The very use of the term 'ideology' by biblical interpreters to refer to the content of the biblical text bespeaks an ideological stance on the part of interpreters: a general tendency to view the 'religious' content of texts as fundamentally related to, and sometimes indistinguishable from, political, social, and rhetorical features of the text and the cultural world it presumes. Thus one of the concepts employed by J. M. G. Barclay in his exploration of the possible correlations between the symbolic world of the Corinthians and the character of their social experience is 'the influence of a newly adopted ideology'.[7] Similarly, Stephen C. Barton speaks of the ideology of the Corinthians as 'no mere epiphenomenon of the churches' social life', but rather a 'thought-world in

---

2. E. Shils, 'The Concept and Function of Ideology', in *International Encyclopedia of the Social Sciences* (ed. D. L. Sills; New York: Macmillan, 1968–91) 7:68.

3. See, for example, J. H. Elliott, *A Home for the Homeless: A Sociological Exegesis of 1 Peter: Its Situation and Strategy* (London: SCM, 1981) 104–5, 267–68; M. Y. MacDonald, *The Pauline Churches: A Socio-historical Study of Institutionalization in the Pauline and Deutero-Pauline Writings* (Cambridge: Cambridge University Press, 1988) 36–37.

4. Carroll, 'Ideology', 309.

5. Carroll, 'Ideology'. Carroll discusses the work of major thinkers concerning ideology including K. Mannheim and P. Ricoeur (309–11).

6. Carroll, 'Ideology', 309. Noting their very different approaches, Carroll has drawn attention especially to N. K. Gottwald, *The Tribes of Yahweh* (London: SCM, 1979), and N. Sternberg, *The Poetics of Biblical Narrative* (Bloomington: Indiana University Press, 1985).

7. Barclay, 'Thessalonica and Corinth', 68 (above, p. 193).

the light of which a social world could be constituted or reconstituted'.[8] The term 'ideology' is frequently employed when the term 'theology' seems too narrow or misleading. This can be seen in Elizabeth Castelli's discussion of Paul's thought on women and gender where she describes Paul's texts speaking for 'history and ideology' in a variety of contexts and explains such key passages as 1 Cor 7, 1 Cor 11.2–16, and Rom 1.18–32 under the rubric of 'sexuality, ideology, and gender trouble'.[9]

How the use of the concept of 'ideology' to describe the thought of biblical authors or communities can itself serve as an indicator of the ideologies of the interpreters will be illustrated further below. But before I begin a detailed discussion of the ideologies shaping scholarship on 1 Corinthians, it is important to comment briefly on the relationship between methodology and ideology. It is impossible to avoid issues of methodology when considering the ideologies of interpretation. While in the first instance methodology refers to the common ways employed by interpreters to analyze texts, particular methodological approaches rest upon ideological presuppositions that are sometimes explicit, but most often remain implicit or are insufficiently acknowledged. In his discussion of methodology in biblical interpretation, John Riches has drawn attention to this fact, noting a deep division between those scholars who believe that the Bible should be analysed with the same methods as any other ancient text and others who feel that the Bible requires a special way of reading on account of its character as divinely inspired and infallible Scripture.[10] Even among scholars who function within the same broad historical-critical framework, choices of different methods rest upon different ideological underpinnings. For example, as discussed further below, some social-scientific analysis of 1 Corinthians reveals substantial confidence in the possibility of an objective reconstruction of the historical past and a tendency to distance ancient society from contemporary concerns. According to some feminist scholars, however, such aspirations are not only illusory, but contrary to what should be the ultimate goals of biblical scholarship. For example, in setting forth her fourfold methodology for rhetorical-critical analysis of 1 Corinthians, Elisabeth Schüssler Fiorenza has identified a fourth stage where the essence of rhetoric as political discourse leads to critical assessment: 'New Testament rhetorical criticism, therefore, cannot limit itself to a formalistic analysis of 1 Corinthians, nor to an elucidation of its historical-social context; rather it must develop a responsible ethical and evaluative theological

8. Barton, 'Paul's Sense of Place', 233.

9. Elizabeth A. Castelli, 'Paul on Women and Gender', in Women and Christian Origins (ed. Ross Shepard Kraemer and Mary Rose D'Angelo; Oxford and New York: Oxford University Press, 1999) 222, 226–30. Castelli appears here to be influenced especially by the work of Bernadette Brooten ('Early Christian Women and Their Cultural Context: Issues of Method in Historical Reconstruction', in Feminist Perspectives on Biblical Scholarship [ed. Adela Yarbro Collins; Chico, Calif.: Scholars Press, 1985] 65–91; idem, Love Between Women: Early Christian Responses to Female Homoeroticism [Chicago: University of Chicago Press, 1996]).

10. J. K. Riches, 'Methodology', in A Dictionary of Biblical Interpretation (ed. R. J. Coggins and J. L. Houlden; London: SCM; and Philadelphia: Trinity Press International, 1990) 449.

criticism.'[11] Fiorenza's statement vividly illustrates the close relationship between ideologies of biblical criticism and methodological approaches; this relationship will surface frequently in the discussion that follows.

As is the case with Fiorenza's work on 1 Corinthians (and much feminist or liberationist interpretation), ideologies can sometimes be identified readily by readers based on explicit statements made by authors. In addition, some ideologies are linked quite obviously to the personal histories and religious commitments of interpreters.[12] Yet in discussing the ideologies of biblical criticism, it is important to be aware of the fact that we are talking about systems of ideas with varying degrees of formality, cohesiveness, and comprehensiveness—loose collections of assumptions (often unexamined), as well as articulated positions and schools of thought. In this essay I am especially interested in exploring how ideologies have shaped scholarship on the Corinthian correspondence in ways that would not be immediately obvious to readers, such as presuppositions about the nature of the relationship between Paul and the community, including subtle (and not so subtle) tendencies for interpreters to side either with Paul against the Corinthians or with the Corinthians against Paul.

In what follows I will discuss how scholarship has frequently been shaped by decisions to privilege Paul's ideas as a window into reality as opposed to cultural values and socially bound motives that may also have influenced teaching and behaviour. In addition, it will be important to consider how the presentation of opponents in Corinth is related to ideological considerations, including the treatment of Judaism and the Gentile world, and the desire to identify a central historical problem in Corinth. It is interesting to examine to what extent the Corinthian church has sometimes been seen as a reflection of 'Christianity' with a separate and distinct identity that can be permeated by influences from the outside. There is great variation with respect to whether the Corinthian correspondence is seen largely as a reflection of life in the *ekklesia* or whether it is located much more broadly within the social-religious-political framework of the Roman world. In examining the implicit ideological influences on Corinthian scholarship, I will pay close attention to how methodological approaches are related to assumptions about such issues as the cultural distance between the ancient world and the modern world. I will also consider how sometimes the ideologies of very recent scholarship may be limiting the purview of interpretive questions at the expense of promising earlier trends. Finally, paying particular attention to the contribution of feminist interpreters of the Corinthian correspondence, I will

---

11. Fiorenza, 'Rhetorical Situation', 389 (above, p. 148).

12. E.g., we might consider the preface by the editor, Daniel J. Harrington, S.J., to the new Sacra Pagina series of NT commentaries (Collegeville, Minn.: Liturgical Press) written by a team of Catholic biblical scholars: 'The goal of *Sacra Pagina* is to provide sound critical analysis without any loss of sensitivity to religious meaning'. In practice, however, there is much overlap between the results of such an interpretive exercise and other commentaries that do not share the same perspective. On the nature of this overlap see John Riches's discussion of differences of perspectives between reading the Bible from the standpoint of a theist or a humanist ('Methodology', 450).

discuss the need for more open discussion about matters that frequently lie beneath the surface of interpretation.

THE IMPORTANCE OF BAUR

In reading the collection of essays included in this volume, it becomes immediately clear that the nineteenth-century work on Corinthian Christianity by F. C. Baur set the stage for later work and continues to influence scholarly enquiry even today (though many of Baur's particular conclusions have been abandoned or questioned). The extract from Baur's book, *Paul: The Apostle of Jesus Christ*, included in this volume reproduces much of the German article, 'Die Christuspartei in der korinthischen Gemeinde' (1831), which is widely recognized as having inaugurated the Tübingen reconstruction of early Christianity involving conflict between Jewish (Petrine) and Gentile (Pauline) parties. In Baur's view the four-party division suggested by 1 Cor 1.12 was in reality a two-party division with the Paul and Apollos (Pauline) party on one side and the Cephas and Jesus (Petrine) party on the other. The focus on conflicts and their resolutions by Baur, a philosophical theologian by training, has often been seen as a reflection of Hegelian influence upon him, especially with respect to the pattern of thesis and antithesis leading to synthesis. But according to Robert Morgan, it is important to remember that conflict was an indisputable part of the life of early churches and that Baur may well have been prepared to identify it by his own experience of theological oppositions (especially between Protestantism and Catholicism) even before he read Hegel.[13] Baur's great impact on the future historical-critical scholarship is beyond question. According to Morgan, Baur's historical reconstruction became 'a symbol of the uncompromising search for the historical truth about Christianity', and, with a method that outlived particular conclusions, 'elements of his construction remained visible throughout the period of 150 years, during which the historical-critical paradigm in NT studies retained its hegemony, largely unchallenged by other methods.'[14] It is indeed instructive to read Baur's work on Corinth in light of the subsequent development of scholarship on the Corinthian correspondence. Many of his insights were taken up by scholars engaged in historical work, but his ideas also anticipated the preoccupations of scholars adopting methods and interpretive techniques, such as rhetorical criticism and social-scientific criticism, that have gained currency only very recently. Reading Baur's work, however, also brings to the fore some key ideological corrections that have profoundly changed the discourse about Paul and the Corinthians over the past quarter century.

In Baur's work one immediately notices the recognition of the historical problems of the church in Corinth that continue to fascinate interpreters. Baur believes that the epistles to the Corinthians offer a window into 'the full reality

13. Morgan, 'Tübingen School', 711.
14. Morgan, 'Tübingen School', 712–13.

of concrete life, with all the complicated relations which must have existed in a Christian church of the earliest period'.[15] Related to this is the recognition that even within churches under Paul's direct influence, other players such as Apollos had a significant role.[16] In his discussion of the parties mentioned by Paul in 1 Cor 1.12, Baur acknowledges a probable divergence between the parties' views of the leaders and the opinions the leaders held of one another. Anticipating the questions of later practitioners of rhetorical analysis of the Corinthian epistles, Baur refers to the argumentative strategies of Paul, who may well have multiplied the party names 'in order to depict the overbearing party-spirit of the Corinthian Church'.[17] Baur's linking of the situation of 1 Corinthians and 2 Corinthians is in keeping with recent works that seek to read these two documents together.[18] Moreover, his attention to apostolic authority calls to mind later systematic studies of the topic, including those from a social-scientific perspective.[19] Yet, despite significant points of contact with later scholarship, it is also important to acknowledge that the ideological basis of some of Baur's assertions would not be considered acceptable by the scholarly community today.

There is no question that Baur's reconstruction of early Christianity involving conflict between Jewish (Petrine) and Gentile (Pauline) parties has had a major impact on many subsequent interpreters debating with Baur and taking up and/or questioning particular aspects of his thesis. Despite a general tendency of late to reject Baur's thesis as a major explanatory model for the Corinthian situation, there has been a recent attempt to revive Baur's theory of two major divisions in Corinth by Michael Goulder (incorporating modern research on the diversity of first-century Judaism).[20] It is clear, however, that the vision of the relationship between Judaism and Christianity that underlies Baur's specific reconstruction would not be accepted today in most circles. Baur presents Paul as opposing 'proud' Jewish Christians who, with somewhat devious motives, infiltrate the Corinthian church comprised of a Gentile membership:

> The special zeal of the Jewish Christians for the Mosaic law, may . . . be essentially the actuating motive, but since in a Church of Gentile Christians, such as was the Corinthian, they could not expect favourable reception, if they had immediately brought forward their principles, they fell back on the special ground of their Judaistic opposition, they attacked the apostolic authority of the Apostle, and endeavoured in this way to work against him.[21]

---

15. Baur, *Paul*, 268.

16. Baur, *Paul*, 270 (above, p. 52–53).

17. Baur, *Paul*, 275. See also Baur's discussion of the first section of the epistle as apologetic (278–79) and his discussion of Paul's strategies in dealing with the question of food sacrificed to idols (279) (above, pp. 57–58).

18. Baur, *Paul*, 277. See, e.g., Ben Witherington III, *Conflict and Community in Corinth: A Socio-Rhetorical Commentary on 1 and 2 Corinthians* (Grand Rapids: Eerdmans, 1995) (above 57).

19. Baur, *Paul*, 276. See B. Holmberg, *Paul and Power: The Structure of Authority in the Primitive Church as Reflected in the Pauline Epistles* (Philadelphia: Fortress, 1980) (above 55).

20. Goulder, 'Σοφία' (above ch. 13).

21. Baur, *Paul*, 277 (above, p. 57).

We might also consider his summary of the contents of 2 Cor 5 with a particular interest in the meaning of the phrase Χριστὸς κατὰ σάρκα ('Christ according to the flesh', 2 Cor 5.16), which he views as a reference to the Messiah of Judaism and associates with both Paul's opponents who pride themselves on being of the Christ party and with the Apostle's own previously inferior stage of spiritual life. In the following statement Baur assumes the voice of the Apostle: 'I have freed myself from all prejudices, from all the material ideas and expectations which had naturally taken hold of me from my nationality—which had devolved upon me as a born Jew'.[22] Baur's blatantly negative characterization of Judaism alerts us to the need for critical analysis of the presentation of Judaism in the work of other scholars on the Corinthian letters and to seek out presuppositions that may be more subtle, but equally dangerous and misleading.

There are strong ideological components in Baur's presentation of Paul's spiritual transformation and mastery. He discusses Paul's waiver of various apostolic rights in 1 Cor 9, including the apostolic right to be accompanied by an ἀδελφὴν γυναῖκα ('a sister as wife/woman'; 1 Cor 9.5), and explains the basis of such rights including common cultural practices, the precepts of the Mosaic law, and the customs of Mosaic sacrificial worship. Linking fleshly limitations implicitly and explicitly with the other apostles, the opponents who attack him, and ultimately with Judaism, Baur reads Paul's discourse in 1 Cor 9.15–17 as follows: 'his carnal nature he held in such subjection that it was forced to yield to the power of his spirit'.[23] Baur's attention is by no means here directly on Paul's views on women. Yet the fact that he describes Paul's relinquishing of apostolic rights in such terms (having previously mentioned the apostolic right to be accompanied by a woman) suggests that we should be including contact with female flesh as part of the carnal nature that, in Baur's view, the Apostle must hold in subjection. As we consider the views of subsequent interpreters of Paul, it will be interesting to see where women stand in relation to forces that the Apostle is said to be opposing.

PAUL AT THE CENTRE

Underlying Baur's views on Paul is the notion that the Apostle triumphs where others fail or at least reach the limits of their carnal capabilities. In examining the interplay between Paul and the Corinthians themselves or the Apostle's opponents in Corinth, interpreters have been most interested in Paul's position and have frequently sided with Paul against these others. This state of affairs has led Fiorenza to comment: 'A cursory look at scholarship on 1 Corinthians indicates that Paul is a skilled rhetorician, who, throughout the centuries, has reached his

---

22. Baur, *Paul*, 283.
23. Baur, *Paul*, 280; see esp. 279–80 (above, p. 59).

goal of persuading his audience that he is right and the "others" are wrong'.[24] It is not difficult to find examples to support Fiorenza's conclusions. We might consider the following statement by C. K. Barrett: 'we learn much of what Paul thought right from what the Corinthians got wrong'.[25] Barrett has offered much valuable exegetical work through his various studies and commentary on 1 Corinthians, and has in fact set out to understand the positions of the Corinthian parties (in contrast to Baur, he argues that 1 Cor 1.12 reflects the existence of four distinct groups) with great attention to the literary issues involved in seeking to extract historical information from biblical texts.[26] But, typical of scholarship of the 1950s and 1960s, the interest in factions, groups, and opposing parties in Corinth in Barrett's work is shaped by the predominant interest in Paul's thought rather than by a desire for a full understanding of the Corinthian community as a whole, or the particular groups who opposed Paul *on their own terms*.

From about the same period, the work of N. A. Dahl exhibits similar tendencies. In the midst of the discussion of 1 Cor 1–4 where he calls for a reconsideration of Baur's view that the text serves as an *apology* for Paul's authority as an Apostle, he sets out several methodological statements to guide historical construction, including the following: 'Due account must be taken of the perspective under which Paul envisages the situation at Corinth. But as far as possible, we must also try to understand the Corinthian reaction to Paul'.[27] This call for balance in analysis between Paul's position and the Corinthian reaction was fulfilled in much subsequent scholarship. Dahl moved in that direction himself, but one nevertheless finds in Dahl's work subtle evidence of the author siding with Paul. The Corinthians are depicted as 'assertive and quarrelling', and Paul himself 'does not, as his adherents are likely to have done, deny the facts which his opponents alleged against him'.[28] Dahl states that the chief task of the historian 'must be not to express sympathy or antipathy or to evaluate virtues and shortcomings, but to try to understand Paul as he wanted to be understood, as an apostle of Jesus Christ'. But in the end he paints a picture of an apostle (described as 'an amazing person') who is completely immune to human judgments, including the tribunal of history.[29] In Dahl's work there is a certain tension between the desirability of historical neutrality and the notion of an apostle who somehow transcends the limits of human weakness and history.

As Elisabeth Schüssler Fiorenza has pointed out, the general tendency for interpreters to side with Paul against the Corinthians is related to the canonical authority of Paul's teaching in the Christian tradition. According to Fiorenza, one must look behind the canonical status and ask the historical question whether Paul's authority may have been interpreted differently in a first-century context

24. Fiorenza, 'Rhetorical Situation', 390 (above, p. 149).
25. Barrett, 'Christianity at Corinth', 269 (above, p. 80).
26. Barrett, 'Christianity at Corinth', 270–74 (above, pp. 82–84).
27. Dahl, 'Paul and the Church at Corinth', 44 (above, p. 87).
28. Dahl, 'Paul', 54–55 (above, p. 94).
29. Dahl, 'Paul', 61.

than it would first appear on the basis of the implied author's claim to apostolic authority (here Fiorenza draws upon reader-response criticism in elucidating her first stage of rhetorical-critical analysis to note that the implied author encompasses the perspective of the contemporary interpreter): 'In other words, does Paul's power of persuasion rest on his presumed authority or did it have the same effect in the historical situation in which such canonical authority cannot be presupposed?'[30] It may appear at first glance that Fiorenza is separating historical investigation from theological preoccupations, and, indeed, some interpreters have purposefully located their historical studies of Paul's letters outside the theological realm. But for Fiorenza herself, the discovery of alternate voices and perspectives among the Corinthians becomes part of responsible ethical and evaluative theological criticism. According to Fiorenza's reconstruction, Paul becomes one of several missionaries whom the Corinthians consult on the meaning of 'new life' in Christ; such a consultative process does not mean that the community would immediately accept Paul's advice, but rather would evaluate it in terms of their own pneumatic self-understanding.[31] In Fiorenza's work the Corinthians' own pneumatic understanding becomes an equal conversation partner with Paul's theological understanding of the cross and resurrection.[32]

The move of Paul away from the centre of interpretation of the Corinthian correspondence can be seen most clearly in the work of feminist scholars and perhaps most dramatically in the study of 1 Corinthians by Antoinette Clark Wire (discussed in detail below), where one senses that she is siding with the Corinthians against Paul. Yet it is also clearly evident in recent scholarship on 1 Corinthians that seeks to locate the community within the broader context of the Roman world and to understand it as distinct from other Pauline groups such as the Thessalonian church. A desire to understand the particular circumstances of the church at Corinth, for example, leads Barclay to remind interpreters to be aware of the tendency for Paul's perspective on the Corinthians to control our description of them.[33]

Related to this tendency to move Paul away from the centre of interpretation is a general inclination to remove Paul from his apostolic 'pedestal' and to see him as influenced by a variety of cultural, political, and interpersonal factors. In contrast to much earlier scholarship, in Michael Goulder's 1991 article there is a notable absence of a privileging of Paul's theological position and a more definite attempt to balance the Apostle's viewpoint against alternate opinions that surfaced in the early church. Within the Corinthian context Paul becomes a pragmatic missionary/pastoral strategist. In explaining why Paul may have complicated the situation involving the Corinthian parties by representing the two parties as four (reviving Baur's thesis), Goulder states: 'He does it, as my old Theological College

---

30. Fiorenza, 'Rhetorical Situation', 390; see 389–90 (above, p. 149).
31. Fiorenza, 'Rhetorical Situation', 398 (above, p. 158).
32. Fiorenza, 'RhetoricalSituation', 398–99 (above, p. 158).
33. Barclay, 'Thessalonica and Corinth', 64 (above, p. 189).

Principal used to say, from holy guile: he is trying to avoid a confrontation.'[34] In fact, in addressing the issue of motives, Goulder comes close to casting Paul in a negative light in assessing his treatment of the issue of non-kosher meat: 'It takes all Paul's artificial even-handedness to pour oil on these troubled waters'.[35]

That Paul's actual agenda may have been quite different from his stated position is suggested by L. L. Welborn in his interesting analysis of how Paul's treatment of the divisions in Corinth reflects the language of ancient politics. By drawing special attention to Paul's terminology in 1 Cor 1.26–27, Welborn distinguishes between Paul's "official" reaction in 1 Cor 1–4 and 11.17–34 that high status does not mean being distinguished in 'the true spiritual sense' and that the divisions in the circumstances of the community are ultimately a sign of God's grace, and what the Apostle knew to be the case in reality: 'It is, at any rate, clear that, whatever he says, Paul *knew* better. Like Aristotle he knew that feelings of inequality arising from distinctions of wealth, noble birth, and higher learning are the ἀρχαὶ καὶ πηγαὶ τῶν στάσεων (Arist. *Pol.* 5.1 1301b5).'[36] For Welborn, Paul's ironic use of terminology associated with the ancient economy in 1 Cor 1.26–27 stops short of direct opposition of the societal state of affairs: 'Paul is more subtle and evasive; he translates the existing value terms without penetrating and unmasking them.'[37] It is interesting to note that in creating a more human picture of Paul, scholars have frequently made assertions about the Apostle's motives (often at variance with what he states explicitly). Even in the case where such 'psychological' profiles are informed by a sophisticated understanding of ancient society, one should be aware of the risks of projecting the 'Introspective Conscience of the West'—to quote from the title of Krister Stendahl's famous essay—upon the Apostle.[38]

A final aspect of placing Paul at the centre of interpretation involves making his ideas and/or intellectual debates with his opponents the most important determining factors in understanding the situation in Corinth. Social-scientific interpreters of the New Testament have been especially vocal in pointing to the dangers of 'the history of ideas' approach that dominated so much historical-critical research prior to the 1980s—where the issues in New Testament communities tend to be presented in highly conceptual terms with little attention being given to the reciprocity between religious symbolism and social realities.[39] It is possible to speak to some degree of a shift in recent scholarship away from a

---

34. Goulder, 'Σοφία', 520 (above, p. 177).

35. Goulder, 'Σοφία', 530. Although he is speaking generally about the Corinthian context, with this statement Goulder is speaking specifically about Rom 14.2–3.

36. Welborn, 'On the Discord at Corinth', 96 (above, ch. 10).

37. Welborn, 'On the Discord at Corinth', 98.

38. Krister Stendahl, 'Paul and the Introspective Conscience of the West', in *Paul Among Jews and Gentiles* (Philadelphia: Fortress, 1978) 78–96. The dangers of projecting modern individualistic ideas upon NT authors have been highlighted by those scholars incorporating insights from cultural anthropology within their work; see, e.g., Jerome H. Neyrey, *Paul in Other Words: A Cultural Reading of His Letters* (Louisville: Westminster/John Knox, 1990).

39. See, e.g., Robin Scroggs, 'The Sociological Interpretation of the New Testament: The Present State of Research', *NTS* 26 (1979–80) 165; Elliott, *Home for the Homeless*, 4.

main focus on ideas toward 'ideas in context'. One might consider, for example, the evolution in the approach to the study of Corinth by R. A. Horsley. Responding to the Gnostic or 'proto-Gnostic' theories to explain the Corinthians' religious outlook, in his 1981 study Horsley looked beyond Christian works to investigate Hellenistic Jewish literature and to suggest that the emphasis on 'wisdom' in Corinth is best understood in light of a Jewish sapiential background. The move toward consideration of context in Horsley's work stands out especially clearly in his reaction to what he terms as Conzelmann's 'philological approach' (with a strong focus on comparison of words and phrases from various ancient sources), which fails to consider 'broader patterns of thought'.[40] Horsley's focus is mainly on concepts and principles to which Paul objects when he states: 'On the basis of the analogous use of language and ideas in Wisdom and Philo it is clear that the Corinthian *gnosis* is part of a whole pattern of religious self-understanding'.[41] Although the operative notion of context in Horsley's 1981 study is mainly a 'thought world', his more recent work on the Corinthian church emphasizes a political setting within Roman imperial society and the social impact on 1 Corinthians to a greater extent. Rhetorical analysis of Paul's arguments in 1 Corinthians leads ultimately to 'at least two discourses that stand opposed to the Roman imperial order and its culture'.[42] Horsley is certainly interested in the shape of Paul's particular argument, but, in keeping with the work of Fiorenza and Wire, he makes use of rhetorical analysis to uncover the other voices of the newly founded church in Corinth, especially the voices of the Corinthian *pneumatikoi*. Paying particular attention to the function of public rhetoric in the Roman imperial world and its relationship to societal power relations, Horsley notes that the concrete rhetorical situation that Paul addressed in 1 Corinthians was more complex than has been previously admitted.[43]

While by no means always explicitly drawing upon specific concepts borrowed from the sociology of knowledge, much recent work on the Corinthian correspondence seems to have an underlying conviction that the relationship between the 'symbolic universe' of the Corinthian community and the social life of the community is dialectical.[44] Yet there is no consensus about the precise weight that

40. Horsley, 'Gnosis in Corinth', 33 (above, p. 121).

41. Horsley, 'Gnosis in Corinth', 48.

42. R. A. Horsley, 'Rhetoric and Empire—and 1 Corinthians', in *Paul and Politics* (ed. R. A. Horsley; Harrisburg: Trinity Press International, 2001) 101.

43. Horsley, 'Rhetoric and Empire', 82. Horsley believes that recent studies adopting the perspective of rhetorical analysis can supplement and refine earlier work on the theology of the Corinthian community. He includes his own essays on Corinth published from 1976 to 1980 in a list of these earlier works. See pp. 85–86 including n. 45.

44. Peter L. Berger and Thomas Luckmann's *The Social Construction of Reality* (Garden City, N.Y.: Doubleday, 1967) has had a broad impact on NT scholars beyond those employing specifically social-scientific approaches. See, e.g., the discussion by Barclay, who raises the question of a possible correlation between the structure of the symbolic world and social experience ('Thessalonica and Corinth', 66, 73 [above, p. 191]). More generally, see D. G. Horrell, 'Berger and New Testament Studies', in *Peter Berger and the Study of Religion* (ed. L. Woodhead with P. Heelas and D. Martin; London and New York: Routledge, 2001) 142–53.

should be assigned to ideas as opposed to other aspects of community and societal life such as social status, physical environment (including housing), and various cultural values (e.g., honour and shame). Even in discussions of such matters as the social status of the Corinthians, it is interesting to observe how Paul's ideas and theological concepts continue to challenge interpreters. In questioning the 'new consensus' concerning the socioeconomic picture of the Corinthians evident in the work of scholars such as Gerd Theissen and Wayne Meeks, Justin J. Meggitt has argued against the notion that Erastus came from privileged circles (with Rom 16.23 usually understood as a reference to his role as 'city treasurer' and read in relation to the famous Corinthian Erastus inscription). At one point in his argumentation, Meggitt questions the usual reading of Rom 16.23 on the basis of Paul's thought, noting that this reading 'presupposes that Paul would take special pride in having a powerful convert—yet the apostle, if anything, shows antipathy to the notion of secular prestige in his epistles'.[45] Whether Paul's expressions of antipathy to the notion of secular prestige should be taken as a window into the reality of his dealings with particular individuals is certainly a matter for debate. Yet Meggitt's critique in this instance does raise the question whether the great emphasis on broader societal and material evidence in the interpretation of early church life may sometimes now be running the risk of neglecting evidence expressed in ideational-theological terms that is difficult to evaluate under the rubric of social phenomena.

Beyond the general agreement that exists among many scholars that the interpretation of the Corinthian epistles needs to be informed by the broader societal context of the Roman world, there has been surprisingly little discussion of how much emphasis to place upon Paul's ideas in this composite picture—ideas that at face value sometimes challenge societal ideals substantially. This is one area of investigation that could definitely benefit from open methodological debate, for decisions about such matters now appear sometimes to rest more upon underlying ideological standpoints rather than well-articulated ideological positions. Moreover, the growing interest in rhetorical analysis and the tendency for Paul and/or the Corinthian Christians' thought to be explained in relation to a school or branch of Greco-Roman philosophy (such as Stoicism and Cynicism) means that debate about the importance that should be attached to intellectual exchange in interpreting Paul's letters is bound to continue well into the future.[46]

---

45. Justin Meggitt, 'Social Status of Erastus', 218–19 (above, p. 221). On the issue of social status see also the review essays on Meggitt's work and response by Meggitt himself: Dale B. Martin, 'Review Essay: Justin J. Meggitt, *Paul, Poverty and Survival*', *JSNT* 84 (2001) 51–64; Gerd Theissen, 'The Social Structure of Pauline Communities: Some Critical Remarks on J. J. Meggitt, *Paul, Poverty and Survival*', *JSNT* 84 (2001) 65–84; Justin J. Meggitt, 'Response to Martin and Theissen', *JSNT* 84 (2001) 85–94.

46. On Paul and stoicism see the essay by T. Paige reproduced in this volume (ch. 16 above). See also W. Deming, *Paul on Marriage and Celibacy: The Hellenistic Background of 1 Corinthians 7* (Cambridge: Cambridge University Press, 1995). On Cynicism see F. G. Downing, *Cynics, Paul and the Pauline Churches. Cynics and Christian Origins II* (London and New York: Routledge, 1998).

CHRISTIANITY AT THE CENTRE

When Paul's theological thought emerges as the most important feature of his letters and the central determining factor for community developments in scholarship on the Corinthian epistles, we frequently find the closely related interest in the shape of Christianity as a distinct religion. One might consider, for example, the following statement by C. K. Barrett: 'In the Corinthian epistles Paul deals with an exceptionally large number of practical problems, always on the basis of a theological grasp of the situation, so that there is in fact no more important source for Paul's conception of the Christian way of life.'[47] Similarly, in his comments concerning 1 Cor 5–6 Anthony C. Thiselton ascribes to Paul a definite vision of Christianity which he believes reflects the notion of eschatological destiny: 'Christians must strive to be now what they are to *become*'.[48] In the scholarship of the 1960s and 1970s the idea that the *ekklesia* of first-century Corinth represents 'Christianity' is largely unquestioned. Subsequent work on the diversity of first-century Judaism, the complexity of Greco-Roman religions, and the variety of early church communities, as well as a heightened awareness of the problem of anti-Judaism in New Testament scholarship, has meant that the label 'Christianity' is now applied to early church communities much more cautiously and is sometimes avoided altogether. This cautious use of Christian terminology is evident in Horsley's 1981 study. He argues that Paul employs language originally belonging to Sophia in Hellenistic Judaism to make claims about Christ countering the Corinthians' *gnosis,* allowing us to observe 'the syncretistic process by which the religious movement eventually known as Christianity developed'.[49] In Horsley's later work on 1 Corinthians, however, his caution with respect to terminology extends even to the translation of the term *ekklesia* as 'church', which he views as a reflection of Paul's discourse being 'subjugated by modern Western cultural hegemony when discussed only in terms of religion'. Horsley warns strongly against the assumption that Paul and the Corinthians were involved in the religion that we call now call Christianity.[50]

Many scholars today who use the terms 'early church' or 'Christianity at Corinth' to speak about the assembly/community there are aware that they are talking about Christian origins very different from what later became an institutionalized Christian religion. Yet Horsley's remarks do raise the issue of how the language we use may impose unconscious assumptions about the nature of the reality we are discussing, including (and particularly relevant for Horsley's work) ideas about what constitutes a 'religious' movement as a opposed to a 'political' movement. It is also interesting to consider how underlying notions of a Christian identity have contributed to the tendency to depict the community as a well-defined

47. Barrett, 'Christianity at Corinth', 269 (above, p. 80).
48. Thiselton, 'Realized Eschatology at Corinth', 517 (above, p. 113).
49. Horsley, 'Gnosis in Corinth', 51.
50. Horsley, 'Rhetoric and Empire—and 1 Corinthians', 86.

entity which can be penetrated by Paul's opponents or influences from the outside. The work of W. Schmithals offers an especially clear example of this. Schmithals's influential thesis is that Paul faced a singular opponent in Corinth which came into the community from the outside: Jewish Gnosticism. While the particular theory of Paul's opposition to Gnosticism (or according to other scholars, proto-Gnosticism) has largely fallen out of favor, there is much about the way Schmithals presents the relationship between Paul, community, and opponents that resonates throughout studies of the Corinthian correspondence. One senses in Schmithals's analysis a notion of 'hard lines' around the community which nevertheless are sometimes penetrated by opposing forces. There is an underlying distinction between true Christians and the 'Christians' who subscribed to a Gnostic Christology. In the passage below Schmithals is concerned with the meaning of the phrase 'Let Jesus be accursed' (1 Cor 12.3), which he believes reflects this Christology:

> Since in no case could ecstasy excuse a cursing of Jesus on the part of baptized people, it is to be presumed that one certain understanding of Christianity—precisely the one disputed in Corinth—did not rule out an ἀνάθεμα 'Ιησοῦς. But since on the other hand no one at that time could have been called a Christian or could have appeared as such to the Corinthians without a confession of the proclaimed Christ, there results the paradoxical fact that there were in Corinth people for whom it was not a contradiction to confess Χριστός and to cry ἀνάθεμα 'Ιησοῦς.[51]

According to Schmithals these people were likely a group of Jews (probably the same ones referred to as 'Hebrews' in 2 Cor 11.22). In the sense that they confessed Christ as the Son of God they qualified as Christians, but they denied that Christ was truly born of woman (Gal 4.4) and expressed this with the phrase, 'Let Jesus be accursed'. In this separation of the man Jesus from the heavenly spiritual Christ, these 'Christians' expressed a 'genuinely Gnostic Christology'.[52]

Schmithals's work reflects a common approach in the study of the letters to the Corinthians: the desire to explain the content of the letters by linking all elements to an overarching problem. This approach may often be related to the tendency to use a vision of Christianity as a starting point for analysis and to look for conflict or opposing visions in monolithic terms—clearly in opposition to the truth presented by the Apostle. Baur's legacy of concentration on conflicts and their resolutions has taken on many permutations in scholarship on the Corinthian correspondence with the theories concerning such all-encompassing issues as Gnosticism (or proto-Gnosticism; e.g., Schmithals), a struggle against a Jewish Petrine party (e.g., Baur, Goulder), overrealized eschatology (e.g., Thiselton), or Stoic ideas (e.g., Paige). The great variety in these theories, including differences with respect to whether the community at Corinth fell victim to influences

---

51. W. Schmithals, *Gnosticism,* 127 (above, pp. 74–75).
52. Schmithals, *Gnosticism,* 129; see 127–29 (above, p. 77).

that originated in church circles or infiltrated the community from the outside, points to the inadequacy of the type of analysis that seeks to link the various issues at Corinth to a single source. Recent work seeking to situate the community at Corinth within the Roman world has highlighted the complexity of the setting and influences on the life of the congregation.

With careful analysis of the social and intellectual life of the Corinthians, Dale B. Martin has critiqued many of these overarching theories as overly simplistic, drawing attention to broad parallels between the ideas in 1 Corinthians and the intellectual climate of the ancient world, and also noting a tendency among scholars to read later church realities back into the life of the Corinthian congregation.[53] Martin's response to theories that seek to explain the perspective of the Corinthians in terms of an 'overly-realized eschatology' offers a particularly instructive example of a tendency to move 'Christianity' away from the centre of interpretation. Martin responds to the frequently espoused view that the Corinthians believed that they had already been raised, to which Paul replied with his own 'reserved' eschatology linking the benefits of salvation, status, and glory to the Parousia of Christ: 'The problem with this interpretation is that there is no evidence that the Corinthians claim these benefits as a result of first learning about such eschatological benefits through Christian preaching and then transferring them to present experience'.[54] In explaining the significance of Paul's apocalyptic concepts, he draws the important distinction between what Paul might cast in eschatological terms as an apocalyptic Jew and the actual origins of the beliefs of the 'strong' in Corinth. With reference to the Corinthian conflict over the nature of the resurrected body in 1 Cor 15 and the Corinthian claim to have knowledge of 'all things' (e.g., 1 Cor 1.5), he suggests that the stance of the Corinthians can be understood in terms of a claim of 'status symbols that popular philosophy and upper-class ideology attributed to those who were wise' and notions of despising the body current in popular philosophy. Noting that realized eschatology is a position that emerges in Pauline Christianity with the deutero-Pauline works of Colossians, Ephesians, and the Pastoral Epistles, he argues that the realized eschatology theory is a more complicated one than is actually warranted by the textual evidence from 1 Corinthians and represents a projection of later Christian developments upon an earlier time.[55]

SOCIETY AT THE CENTRE

Martin's work offers a good example of the scholarly trend to investigate the Corinthian letters within their Greco-Roman context. This attempt extends far

53. Martin has critiqued the tendency to explain the position of Paul's 'opponents' in Corinth by appealing to Gnostic (or proto-Gnostic) influences, Stoic-Cynic circles, and the perspective of 'overly-realized eschatology' (*Corinthian Body*, esp. pp. 70–73, 105–6).

54. Martin, *Corinthian Body*, 105.

55. Martin, *Corinthian Body*, 106.

beyond simply noting a few social or community issues or a brief consideration of 'background', but goes further by taking into account the relationship between the text and the cultural values, political practices, physical environment, and social networks of the ancient world. This move toward society at the centre sometimes also includes sophisticated analysis of how texts reflect rhetorical conventions of the ancient world and thematic interests of major schools of thought, crossing the boundaries of philosophy, religion, and moral-political invective. It is interesting to note that in arguing against Baur's theory of conflict between parties with distinct theological positions in a favour of a Corinthian community engaged in bickering based on influences from the Hellenistic world (including an emphasis on rhetoric), the work of Johannes Munck in the 1950s anticipated many future studies. Munck emphasized that divisions in Corinth could arise for nontheological reasons.[56] More recently some scholars have been vocal about how a preoccupation with 'religious' issues and the adoption of theological perspectives have obscured our understanding of the Corinthian situation. With a specific interest in how 1 Corinthians reflects the language of ancient politics, Welborn identifies the real issue reflected in 1 Corinthians 1–4 as partisanship and the struggle for power and describes the notion of dogmatic controversy which characterized so much earlier scholarship as having 'collapsed under its own weight'.[57] Particularly revealing in light of the interests of this essay is Welborn's ideological critique (and quite rare among interpreters of the Corinthian correspondence) of scholarship that has ignored class struggle in a manner that 'attests the scholars' own sympathies and inclinations'.[58]

Employing a variety of methodological approaches, including sociohistorical methods, social-scientific interpretation, rhetorical criticism, and even archaeological approaches, scholars who focus on the social context of the Corinthian correspondence have introduced a series of fresh questions and hypotheses where traditional historical methods have run into dead ends. Perhaps no scholar's work has been more influential in this regard than that by Gerd Theissen on social stratification in Corinth. Among Theissen's major goals is to disprove 'the romantic idea of a proletarian Christian community'.[59] Theissen calls for more rigorous and sociohistorically informed scholarship, drawing special attention to the 'sociological implications' of the concepts Paul uses to describe the makeup of the Christian community in 1 Cor 1.26–29 and rejecting utopian, idealistic, or highly speculative reconstructions. According to Theissen caution is required when evaluating statements about individuals in the New Testament with exegesis conducted on the basis of 'methodical criteria'.[60]

56. Munck, 'The Church without Factions', 138–39 (above, p. 65).
57. Welborn, 'On the Discord at Corinth', 89 (above, p. 143).
58. Welborn, 'On the Discord at Corinth', 94. See also p. 86.
59. Gerd Theissen, 'Social Stratification in the Corinthian Community', in *Social Setting*, 70; see pp. 69–70 (above, p. 99).
60. Theissen, *Social Setting*, 73 (above, p. 101).

With respect to the use of sociological concepts by Theissen and others to analyze the Pauline churches, it is important to note that employing social-scientific
insights and models in New Testament scholarship has sometimes proven to be
controversial on both methodological and ideological grounds.[61] Confidence in
value-neutrality, for example, has been subject to ideological critique by feminist
scholars. They have warned that in the desire to disengage from modern concerns, influences, and value judgments, some practitioners of social-scientific
criticism have been overly confident in 'scientifically-tested' models from sociology and anthropology and have questioned whether such 'disengaged' scholarship is laudable in the first place.[62] With respect to the relationship between the
Bible and context, Elisabeth Schüssler Fiorenza has stated that it is not enough
for scholars to uncover the original intention of biblical authors or even to elucidate the ethical consequences and political functions of biblical texts in their
ancient historical contexts—scholars must also elucidate such consequences and
functions within their own contemporary sociopolitical contexts.[63]

While it has not gone unquestioned, there can be no denying the major
impact of Theissen's thesis concerning social stratification in Corinth: the majority of the members of the Corinthian congregation known to us by name demonstrate high social status. These are the people who exercise influence in the
community and within Paul's broader mission enterprise. Those of lower strata
(the majority of the congregation) rarely appear as named individuals.[64] In reading the essays included in this volume, the influence of this picture of a stratified
community that included some well-to-do members is unmistakable. The notion
that there were elite members of the community is central to Paige's theories concerning the effect of Stoicism upon the group; to Chow's argument that the
immoral man of 1 Cor 5.1–13 was a wealthy patron; to Welborn's arguments
concerning Paul's use of the categories of ancient politics to address factions; and
to Murphy-O'Connor's interpretation of the archaeological evidence to describe
the daily life of house churches.[65] Yet the great interest in the social status of the

---

61. For the influence of Theissen on method in the study of Pauline communities see, e.g., Meeks,
First Urban Christians; MacDonald, *Pauline Churches.* For critique of the use of sociological concepts
in scholarship on 1 Corinthians see esp. Clarke, *Secular and Christian Leadership,* 3–7.

62. See Mary-Anne Tolbert, 'Social, Sociological, and Anthropological Methods', in *Searching
the Scriptures,* vol 1: *A Feminist Introduction* (ed. Elisabeth Schüssler Fiorenza; New York: Crossroad, 1993) 268; see also Elisabeth Schüssler Fiorenza, *Feminist Practices of Biblical Interpretation*
(Boston: Beacon, 1992) 83–86. But in my response to this critique I argue that it is possible to com-
bine social-scientific interpretation of the NT with a feminist approach (Margaret Y. MacDonald,
Early Christian Women and Pagan Opinion: The Power of the Hysterical Woman [Cambridge: Cambridge University Press, 1996] 22–27).

63. Elisabeth Schüssler Fiorenza, 'The Ethics of Biblical Interpretation: De-centering Biblical
Scholarship', *JBL* 107 (1988) 15.

64. Theissen, 'Social Stratification in the Corinthian Community', 95–96 (above, p. 105).

65. Paige, 'Stoicism, ἐλευθερία and Community at Corinth', 182–92 (above, ch. 16);
J. K. Chow, 'Patronage and Power in the Corinthian Church', in *Patronage and Power,* 131 (above,
ch. 15); Welborn, 'On the Discord at Corinth', 98–99; Jerome Murphy-O'Connor, 'House-Churches
and the Eucharist', in *St. Paul's Corinth* (see above, ch. 9).

Corinthians, and especially the use of Theissen's theory to anchor further theories about the social setting of the epistles, should lead to a more self-conscious examination on the part of scholars of the interests and presuppositions that shape our work. A few questions come immediately to mind: Is the concentration on status simply a matter of accurately reading the sources, or is the issue of such relevance to our own time and struggles that we wish to bring it to the centre as a major interpretive priority? Should scholars be much more explicit in discussing how interpretation of the issue of status within the New Testament may have ethical and political consequences within a contemporary setting in the manner suggested by Fiorenza above? What might the scholarly community have invested in the theory that there were some members of the Corinthian community of high social status? Does acceptance of such a theory, for example, open up a whole range of Greco-Roman textual and material evidence associated with the elite (including housing evidence) that would otherwise not be relevant? Have studies of the social status of the early Christians been unduly influenced by male patterns of social mobility and prestige at the expense of the potentially very different circumstances of women?[66] This is not a critique per se of the work of any particular scholar, but a general call for more self-conscious awareness on the part of interpreters of the consequences of adopting particular theories and concentrating on specific features of texts.

A general question that has arisen as a result of the move of society 'to the centre' in the work of many scholars (but which often remains unarticulated) is how one assesses similarities between language and concepts in the *ekklesia* and in other groups and associations in the Roman world, and how one deals with the question of the formation of a distinct identity.[67] Although it is not always the case, there has been a general emphasis on continuity in comparison, rather than on noting differences and unique features. This tendency has been bolstered to a certain extent by social-scientific methodologies that tend to seek out generalities and patterns.[68] Moreover, in recent years scholars have offered valuable evidence to measure against claims of Christian 'uniqueness' and against making assumptions about divisions among the political, religious, and social realms based on modern conceptions. But with so much focus on norms and cultural values, one wonders if the pendulum may have swung too far, so that aspects of

66. The notion of 'dissonant status' (i.e., high status according to some criteria, but low status according to others) does allow to a certain extent for different patterns for men and women (see Meeks, *First Urban Christians*, 22–23). Moreover, in Theissen's recent work he discusses some of the different circumstances of women, locating women among exceptional early Christians of elite status ('The Social Structure of Pauline Communities', 70–71).

67. One aspect of Meggitt's critique of 'the new consensus', for example, raises this question. In discussing the usual understanding of Erastus as the city treasurer (Rom 16.23), he notes the possibility that the civic terminology could be referring to an office within the church in keeping with practices of *collegia* with respect to their own offices ('The Social Status of Erastus,' 219; above, p. 221).

68. On the dangers of harmonization and standardization in the use of social-scientific methodologies see Bengt Holmberg, *Sociology and the New Testament: An Appraisal* (Minneapolis: Fortress, 1990) 155; further Horrell, *Social Ethos*, 22–26.

life in the ancient world that approach what we conceive as 'religious' (making claims about the ultimate meaning of life and/or beliefs concerning divinities) are sometimes unduly neglected. Has work on the Jewish thought world as a background for understanding the Corinthian correspondence—evident, for example, in Goulder's work or in Horsley's earlier studies—been receiving the attention it deserves in recent years? With respect to issues of distinctiveness, more work needs to be undertaken on the simultaneous appropriation and reinterpretation of culture to create identity in the Corinthian *ekklesia*. But as Barclay's study makes clear, one cannot assume that the lines of identity were always drawn in the same way in the Pauline churches, whether we are talking about attitudes to nonbelieving individuals or openness to and interpretation of cultural influences in a variety of forms, including education.[69]

WOMEN AT THE CENTRE

There is no question that scholars investigating the place of the Corinthian letters within their Greco-Roman context will make significant contributions for some time to come. An interest in context has also been central to the work of many feminist scholars who have placed women at the centre of their interpretive efforts, but who have also offered interesting critiques of many of the dominant theories and approaches of various 'societal' readings of 1 and 2 Corinthians, drawing attention to a sustained reluctance on the part of many interpreters to take up the challenges of feminist readings.[70] Even the influential and recent readings of Paul's work in light of Roman imperial ideology have been criticized for maintaining the traditional tendency for Paul's voice to be placed 'at the authoritative centre' of a letter at the expense of other voices, and for highlighting Paul's radical stance within an imperial context without paying due attention to how Paul's language echoes and reintroduces imperial power relations in various ways.[71]

In general, feminist scholarship on the Corinthian correspondence has followed two major lines of enquiry. First, women have been brought to the centre in the sense that attention shifts from male attitudes to women to the recovery of the lives of the women themselves, using historical and sociohistorical methods. For example, my study of 1 Cor 7 identifies women as among the main proponents of sexual asceticism in Corinth and seeks to understand their theology within their social context.[72] Second, feminist scholars have engaged in rhetorical

---

69. Barclay, 'Thessalonica and Corinth', 68 (above, p. 193).

70. See Fiorenza's critique of Theissen's conclusions concerning Chloe ('Rhetorical Situation', 394–96, above, pp. 154–56). See also the feminist critique of the use of social-scientific models discussed above.

71. See Cynthia Briggs Kittredge, 'Corinthian Women Prophets and Paul's Argumentation in 1 Corinthians', in *Paul and Politics*, 104–9. See also Antoinette Clark Wire, 'Response: The Politics of the Assembly in Corinth', in *Paul and Politics*, 124–29.

72. MacDonald, 'Women Holy' (above, ch. 12).

analysis seeking to elucidate the rhetorical situation created by Paul's arguments, thereby expanding and sometimes questioning or rendering more complex what has traditionally been viewed as the historical circumstances of the letters. As is the case in the study of 1 Corinthians by Fiorenza discussed above, scholars adopting this method have both drawn upon the insights of modern rhetorical theory and sought to evaluate Paul's arguments informed by the conventions of ancient rhetoric. One of the most valuable aspects of this approach is that in its sustained effort to recover other voices, it has opened up discussion of the implications of texts for women in the community even where women are not specifically named. In other words, feminist analysis of the Corinthian correspondence has expanded far beyond such well-known and controversial texts as 1 Cor 11.2–16 and 14.34–36.

The most extensive and influential feminist study to date of the Corinthian correspondence is unquestionably Antoinette Clark Wire's *Corinthian Women Prophets: A Reconstruction through Paul's Rhetoric* (1990). Wire's study combines the two lines of enquiry above and departs significantly from other works on 1 Corinthians in both conclusions and approach. To appreciate the impact of Wire's work as fully as possible, it is important to read it against a background of earlier studies. Two dominant themes that surface in discussions of women and 1 Corinthians prior to (and to a certain extent continuing even beyond) Wire's study are fragmentation and incongruity. For example, scholars have sometimes recognized Paul's arguments in 1 Cor 11.2–16 as convoluted, and one senses a general discomfort about patterns of argumentation that seem to depart from Paul's usual approach or are highly culture-bound. But according to Thiselton, such efforts were deliberate on Paul's part:

> Some of the commentators who wish to defend Paul's methods of argument find these verses embarrassing, on the ground that they are entirely relative to highly time-bound considerations. But this is no accident. Paul is concerned to show that the eschatological status of the Christian does *not* raise him above everyday questions about particular times and particular places. . . . Paul, however, does not accept uncritically either the Corinthians' eschatology or their theology of the Spirit.[73]

Thiselton responds in part here to the arguments of W. O. Walker to the effect that 1 Cor 11.2–16 constitutes a non-Pauline interpolation.[74] Even more widely accepted by scholars is the theory that 14.34–35 constitutes a later interpolation, based in part on perceived incongruity between Paul's quasi acceptance of the prophetic activities in 11.2–16 and his call for silencing in 14.34–35, as well as similarities between 14.34–35 and the treatment of women in the Pastoral Epistles. While it is beyond the scope of this discussion, theories concerning interpolation and Paul's treatment of women would benefit from a detailed ideological

---

73. Thiselton, 'Realized Eschatology at Corinth', 521 (above, p. 117).
74. William O. Walker Jr., '1 Corinthians and Paul's Views Regarding Women', *JBL* 94 (1975) 94–110.

critique, including an examination of the evidence that leads to such theories and the propensity on the part of scholars to view Paul's thought as a harmonious system or as fragmentary and impulsive 'reactions'. Wire's own approach to this background of discussion of textual and theological anomalies is to read 1 Corinthians as a whole (arguing in favor of the textual integrity of the work, including 14.34–35), offering a rhetorical commentary that aims to bring the perspective of the Corinthian women prophets to bear on every part of Paul's letter.

In contrast to Thiselton's comments above that seek to demonstrate the challenge posed by Paul to the Corinthians' theology of the Spirit, it is precisely the theology of the Spirit of the Corinthian women prophets that Wire presents as a challenge to Paul: 'the Corinthian women prophets claim direct access to resurrected life in Christ through God's spirit. Being thus filled, rich and ruling, they take part in Christ's joyful meal and God's word goes forth from them to each other in ever-widening circles'.[75] Robin Scroggs has called Wire's work 'the most striking defense of the Corinthian theology against Paul's theology of the cross'.[76] Like other feminist studies, Wire offers an example of ethically and politically engaged scholarship, and sometimes her defense of the theology of the Corinthian women prophets against Paul is expressed with very strong language. For example, she describes Paul's response in the final two verses of 1 Corinthians 14 as Paul throwing 'the blanket of propriety over this attempted rape of the women's divine gifts'.[77] As is typical of feminist work, Wire's scholarship exposes the folly of interpretation that masks the interpreter's own interests, and takes risks in the process of reconstruction. Her investigation rests explicitly upon the presupposition that 'the women prophets in Corinth's Church have a place in the group Paul is addressing, some role in the rhetorical situation'.[78] Reviewers have critiqued Wire for assuming that the women prophets of Corinth are always in Paul's purview and for giving these women prominence when it is not warranted by the sources.[79] A feminist response to such a critique might be that the assumption that women are absent from Paul's purview (without explicit evidence of this) is itself problematic. There is much in the history of women to suggest that they were very often present even when not explicitly acknowledged and were oppressed by subtle, as well as blatant, measures.

The issue of what is actually warranted by the sources does, however, offer an important historical challenge to feminist work that often results in highly plausible but ultimately hypothetical *reconstructions*. It is precisely on historical grounds that Jewish feminist scholars have questioned the ideological presuppositions of some feminist reconstructions of Christian origins that identify a liberating component in the earliest Jesus movement, speaking to leadership concerns in contemporary Christian communities. Warning about how modern

---

75. Wire, *Corinthian Women Prophets*, 185.

76. Robin Scroggs, 'Review of Wire, *The Corinthian Women Prophets*', *JBL* 111 (1992) 557.

77. Wire, *Corinthian Women Prophets*, 156.

78. Wire, *Corinthian Women Prophets*, 9.

79. See reviews of Wire's book by Robert H. Gundry, *JAAR* 61 (1993) 392–95; Beverly Gaventa, *Int* 66 (1992) 412–13; Barbara E. Reid, *CBQ* 54 (1992) 594–96; Scroggs, *JBL* 111 (1992) 546–48.

preoccupations can skew historical reconstructions, such scholars have called for careful attention to the varied lives of Jewish women in the Hellenistic and Roman periods and have questioned the assumption that Jesus liberated Jewish women from a repressive patriarchal system.[80] In my work, I have discussed how a desire to find an emancipatory element in early Christianity may have created an 'anti-married woman' bias in some scholarship on early Christian women leading to a false dichotomy between the celibate/liberated woman and the oppressed/married woman in early church circles.[81] Feminist scholars are increasingly conscious that arguments concerning the oppression/liberation of women must be critically examined for what is being implied about the identity of the oppressors and the motives of the liberators/liberated with an awareness of the impact of their reconstructions for depictions of both ancient peoples and modern communities.

Placing women at the centre of interpretation has influenced and will continue to influence the interpretation of the Corinthian correspondence in significant ways. Central paradigms with respect to the status of the Corinthians have been challenged and qualified by feminist interpreters.[82] Feminist work on the virgins, widows, and wives of 1 Cor 7 has highlighted the countercultural and potentially offensive initiatives of women in relation to society and raises doubts about theories of an unproblematic integration of the community within the broader society.[83] New research on house churches, the family, and the physical conditions of city life in the Roman world should prove especially valuable in understanding the role of women in negotiating society-*ekklesia* boundaries and in illustrating the centrality of the experience of women to the complicated and fascinating exchanges between members of the Corinthian community themselves and between the community and Paul.[84] But it is in its uncovering and critique of the ideologies of interpretation, and in its own defenses of particular ideological stances, that feminist work has had the greatest impact on the Corinthian interpretive enterprise. By making us conscious of our own voices and by seeking to uncover alternative voices that have been marginalized by the dominant structures of power in ancient society and beyond, feminist scholarship has ensured that self-critical reading of the Corinthian correspondence will remain a priority in the twenty-first century.

---

80. See Amy-Jill Levine, *'Women Like This': New Perspectives on Jewish Women in the Greco-Roman World* (Atlanta: Scholars Press, 1991) xvi–xvii; Ross Shepard Kraemer, *Her Share of the Blessings: Women's Religions Among Pagans, Jews, and Christians in the Greco-Roman World* (Oxford and New York: Oxford University Press, 1992) 133.

81. MacDonald, *Early Christian Women and Pagan Opinion*, 183–89.

82. Wire, 'Response: The Politics of the Assembly in Corinth', 125.

83. On social harmony and especially the absence of social alienation in Corinth see Barclay, 'Thessalonica and Corinth', 57 (above, pp. 184–85). For how a focus on women may offer evidence of social dislocation in relations between believers and outsiders see MacDonald, 'Women Holy in Body and Spirit'; idem, *Early Christian Women and Pagan Opinion*, 133–44, 189–95.

84. See, for example, Carolyn Osiek and David L. Balch, 'Gender Roles, Marriage, and Celibacy', in *Families in the New Testament World: Households and House Churches* (Louisville: Westminster John Knox, 1997) 103–55.

Chapter 22

Reconstructions of Corinthian Christianity and the Interpretation of 1 Corinthians

James D. G. Dunn

INTRODUCTION

The task of this essay is not to recount afresh the various attempts to fill in the background of Paul's letter to the church in Corinth, or to reconstruct the church's brief history and explain its tensions. The task is rather to reflect on how these different reconstructions affect our understanding of the theology and message of 1 Corinthians in particular.

We should acknowledge at once that there is a chicken-and-egg problem here. Since our knowledge of the Corinthian church is almost wholly derived from the New Testament, and mostly from Paul's Corinthian letters, any hypothesis regarding the situation addressed by Paul *must already presuppose an understanding of the letters themselves*. The problem is nicely illustrated and posed by the decision that translators have to make as to whether the opening sentence of ch. 7, 'It is well for a man not to touch a woman' (1 Cor 7.1b), should be placed in quotation marks, as a quotation by Paul of a *Corinthian* slogan, or left as an assertion of Paul's *own* views. The consequences are far-reaching, since on this decision will turn our whole understanding of Paul's view of sexual relations and marriage, perhaps even through a complete 180 degrees!

We should not, however, shy away from the problem. For it is simply another example of the hermeneutical circle familiar to all interpreters. All understanding of any text has to move round and round the circle, from part to whole, from whole to part, in order to increase understanding of the text (illuminating the individual verse from the section or letter as a whole; illuminating the whole from particular verses). And in the case of a historical text, written in an ancient language, the 'whole' cannot be limited to the complete text. For the language of the text is the language of a whole society. And we today will only begin to understand the use of the language *in* the text if we understand the use of the language *of* the text, that is, the language in its vocabulary, syntax, and idiom as it was familiarly used and heard by the writer and listeners to the text.

Moreover, a text like a letter is a context-specific text. That is, more than any other text it functions as one half of a dialogue. It was intended to address particular people in particular situations. It sought to evoke a response from these people. All the while, then, it makes references and allusions which the author could confidently expect the letter recipients to recognize and respond to, but which are unclear to those who read the letter later or outside that context. In those cases the hermeneutical circle embraces not only language particular to the text (the part) and its wider use (the whole), but language addressed to particular social situations (the part) and the social context itself (the whole). Difficult though it is, the reconstruction of social context is necessary for any full understanding of the letter.

This is the case with 1 Corinthians. A tentative easing round and round the hermeneutical circle asks of particular words or sentences how they would have been understood at the time, and asks of particular assertions or arguments how they would have been heard in the church of mid-first-century Corinth. What we know of the history, culture, and religions of Corinth itself provides various pointers and checks; and interplay with other texts (co-texts), New Testament or other ancient religious writings, provides other resonances and controls. So the hermeneutical circle is not confined within the Corinthian letters themselves and a real interpretive process can take place, in which the text contributes to a hypothesis about the context, and hearing the text within that hypothesized context enriches the understanding of the text. Or hearing the text may call for some revision of the hypothesis and a fresh reading of the text, and so on—the hermeneutical process, in dialogue with others proceeding round the same circle, requires constant reassessment and refinement.

It is this process I will illustrate from the history of the hypotheses reconstructing the Corinthian church. It will quickly become apparent that there are certain key texts in the letter on which particular hypotheses hang, and that these texts are being allowed to determine the interpretation of whole chapters or even the whole letter. In other cases, passages are not sufficiently context-specific for us to be confident regarding the situation addressed, and with the 'mixed signals' the interpreter can quickly become disoriented. And in still others, we will find a too narrowly based hypothesis running aground on the implausibilities it forces upon other parts of the letter.

F. C. BAUR: CONFLICT FROM THE FIRST

It was Ferdinand Christian Baur who determined that 1 Cor 1.12 would be the key to unlock the context and interpretation of 1 and 2 Corinthians. Paul's itemizing of what reads like four party slogans ('I am of Paul'; 'I am of Cephas'; 'I am of Apollos'; 'I am of Christ') certainly invites the hypothesis that Paul was writing in support of his faction ('I am of Paul') to resist or rebuke the others. Baur focused his attention on 'the Christ party', arguing that it was the claim made also by the Cephas party; that is, the *Christian Judaists* claimed special or even exclusive relation to Christ.[1] Key features of the resulting interpretation of the rest of the Corinthian letters were that 2 Cor 10–13 must be read as a sharp rebuke to this party, and 2 Cor 5.16 as an indication that Paul had moved on from his former reckoning of Christ as 'the Messiah of Judaism'. For Baur, Paul was the proponent of Christianity as a new spiritual reality that had left its Jewish origins behind. The ramifications of such an interpretation are considerable, not least the boost it gives to interpreting Christianity as an antithesis to Judaism, and perpetuating the idea of Christianity as a universal spiritual ideal now (being) stripped (by Paul) of its restrictively particularistic Jewish characteristics.

The interpretation of 1 Cor 1.12 remained a much disputed crux, because it so much established the context in which the rest of the letter should be read. Two of the most effective responses, both as it happens from Scandinavians, are included in the accompanying extracts. Johannes Munck argued that established parties are not in view in 1.12, let alone a particular Jewish-Christian party, but only 'bickerings' among church members. Thereby he shifted the interpretation away from Paul confronting a single other party to Paul rebuking the whole church.[2] Nils Dahl, by arguing that the other slogans all indicated opposition to Paul in varying degrees, reasserted the importance of reading 1 Corinthians as Paul's apology for his apostolic ministry.[3] In fact, in all this the consequences for interpreting the rest of 1 Corinthians were not substantial (more so with 2 Corinthians in Baur's case); the main effect was on the immediate context of 1 Cor 1–4. But of course it makes a difference to our own reading of 1 Corinthians whether Paul was responding to a particular faction in the church of Corinth, or was exhorting the whole congregation. The text then provides precedents for either confrontation or pastoral exhortation in the face of similar challenging situations in other times and places.

In recent years Michael Goulder has revived the Baur hypothesis, but endeavours to show how it applies more widely in the Corinthian letters. For example, the 'wisdom' criticized in 1 Cor 1–4 is 'a wisdom of the works of the law'; in 1 Cor 7 Paul counsels against Petrine asceticism; in 1 Cor 15 it was the Petrines who believed the 'spiritual' had already come.[4] Such interpretation can amount to

1. See Baur extract (ch. 1 above).
2. See Munck extract (ch. 2 above).
3. See Dahl extract (ch. 5 above).
4. M. D. Goulder, *Paul and the Competing Mission in Corinth* (Peabody, Mass.; Hendrickson, 2001), extending the thesis of the earlier extract (ch. 13 above); phrase quoted from p. 63.

little more than attaching the label 'Petrine' to a feature of 1 Corinthians for which some parallel in Jewish sources can be cited. The real question is whether so attaching the label makes much difference to our perception of how the issue was addressed by Paul. Goulder's reconstruction certainly affects the big picture of early Christianity (driven by two competing missions). So far as 1 Corinthians itself is concerned, however, it might be enough simply to note that in 1.22 it is the Greeks who seek wisdom, not the Jews (or the Petrines); and in 7.19 the argument that what matters is not circumcision but 'keeping the commandments of God' hardly suggests a hostility to Torah or to a Jewish Christianity that equally emphasized the commandments of God.

The lasting effect of Baur's reconstruction of Christianity's beginnings was its disruption of the traditional image of a primitive church united and operating in complete apostolic harmony. Since then it has not been possible to read any New Testament writing, particularly Paul's letters, without an ear cocked for echoes of disharmony and disagreement. When polemic, as in 2 Cor 10–13, has to be read as directed not outside the church but against *fellow Christians*, the precedent provided for subsequent apologetic and internal dispute reads rather differently.

HISTORY OF RELIGIONS: PARALLELS AND PRECEDENTS

The next major challenge to traditional interpretation of 1 Corinthians came a century ago with the 'history of religions school', which argued that the New Testament should not be read simply as a book of doctrinal teaching. Rather, the beginnings of Christianity should be seen within the context of the religions and philosophies of the day, with a view to discerning what and how much of New Testament teaching and the Christianity it described had been influenced by these other religions and philosophies.

The initial impact was on the understanding of Paul's teaching on *baptism and the Lord's Supper*, not least in 1 Corinthians, as influenced by contemporary mystery cults. In particular, Wilhelm Heitmüller argued that the very use of the formula 'in the name of' in the baptismal ritual (implied in 1 Cor 1.13) reflects the widespread belief in the religions of the time that the 'name' was a bearer of power and magic; and that the Eucharist (10.16–21; 11.24–26) reflects the primitive concept of devouring the godhead, most clearly attested in the Dionysiac mystery cult.[5] After all, 12.2 seems to allude to the kind of ecstatic frenzy that typified celebration of the Dionysiac mystery. Should then we see the 'party spirit' of 1.12 as derived from a sense of mystical bond established by baptism between the bap-

---

5. W. Heitmüller, *"Im Namen Jesu": Eine sprach-und religionsgeschichtliche Untersuchung zum Neuen Testament, speziell zur altchristlichen Taufe* (Göttingen, 1903); also *Taufe und Abendmahl bei Paulus: Darstellung und religionsgeschichtliche Beleuchtung* (Göttingen, 1903). Extracts are accessible in W. G. Kümmel, *The New Testament: The History of the Investigation of Its Problems* (1970; ET Nashville: Abingdon, 1972; London: SCM, 1973) 255–57.

tizer and the baptisand? Does Paul give ground to the idea of the eucharistic elements conveying Spirit to the participants ('spiritual food/drink'), while warning against regarding them as a prophylactic against divine judgment (10.1–13), but warning also that 'unworthy' participation can have the opposite effect (11.27–30)? At what point does awe before the holy become superstitious fear?

No doubt Heitmüller and others pressed too hard the possible parallels between the Christian sacraments and mystery cult initiation rites and shared meals. Analogy should never be confused with genealogy. At most of the key parallel points such influence as can be discerned is from Jewish tradition and precedents (cf. 6.11; 10.1–4, 18). Nonetheless, we should recall that Paul would have angled his instruction at these points, bearing in mind that such resonances between earliest Christianity and its religious environment would have influenced his audience's hearing of his letter. And the question remains whether the strong sacramental theology traditionally derived from such passages owes more to magical conceptions of the ancient mysteries than most twenty-first-century Christians would be wholly comfortable with. On any showing, we still do not know quite (Mormons excepted!) what Paul had in mind by his reference to 'those who are baptized on behalf of the dead' (15.29); nor is it clear whether Paul approved or disapproved of the practice!

THE QUEST FOR PRE-CHRISTIAN GNOSTICISM

The major impact made by the history of religions school was its claim that in many of the Pauline distinctives we should discern the influence of pre-Christian Gnosticism. Previously Gnosticism had been understood to be a second-century Christian heresy. But now the parallels between features of Paul's teaching and Gnostic sources, particularly the Corpus Hermeticum, suggested that Paul, or the Corinthian Christians, were influenced by Gnostic thought. The possible illumination to be shed on 1 Corinthians in particular was extensive. The classification of some Christians as 'spirituals (*pneumatikoi*)', as opposed to 'soulish (*psychikos*)' (2.13–15), was a Gnostic categorization.[6] The same source could have provided Paul with his characteristic 'in Christ' formula[7] and his concept of 'the body of Christ', so influential in chs. 10, 12, 14.[8] Rudolf Bultmann, seeking evidence of the pre-Christian Gnostic Redeemer myth within Paul's letters, found it in chs. 8 and 15: the role in creation attributed to Christ in 8.6 reflects the cosmological speculation of Gnosticism; Christ was the Man (Adam), the spiritual man, who overcomes the damage done by the psychic man (the first Adam) (15.44–49).[9]

---

6. R. Reitzenstein, *Hellenistic Mystery Religions: Their Basic Ideas and Significance* (1910; ET Pittsburgh: Pickwick, 1978).

7. W. Bousset, *Kyrios Christos* (2nd ed. 1921; ET Nashville: Abingdon, 1970) ch. 4.

8. E. Käsemann, *Leib und Leib Christi: Eine Untersuchung zur paulinischen Begrifflichkeit* (Tübingen: Mohr, 1933).

9. R. Bultmann, *Theology of the New Testament*, vol. 1 (ET London: SCM, 1952) 132, 174.

The consequences for interpretation of Paul, 1 Corinthians in particular, are far-reaching. In making use of the language of 'spirituals', does Paul validate any idea of a spiritual elite? Does his 'in Christ' formula have to be interpreted in mystical terms? Whatever its practical application, is an imagery of 'the body of Christ', derived from a quaintly archaic notion of a macrocosmic primal man, whose body of light has been fragmented and scattered throughout the material world, flawed beyond continued use? Was Paul's teaching on Christ a fresh revelation, or simply the adaptation of a myth, then very apposite, but now scarcely credible? Or can the interpreter strip away or penetrate through such mythical imagery to a substantive core that remains valid and communicable in other contexts? Here is another form of the hermeneutical circle, a movement back and forth between the *Sache* and the *Sprache*, the Word and the words, the substance and its expression in particular contexts. The trouble is always that we have to know as much as possible about the original context; otherwise we will be unable to distinguish the *Sache* from the *Sprache*, and may either throw out the baby with the bathwater, or, alternatively, drown the baby in the bathwater!

Attempts later in the twentieth century to illuminate the Pauline letters from a Gnostic milieu focused less on Paul himself than on his opponents; it was they who were influenced by Gnostic thought.[10] Where Baur could characterize all Paul's opponents as 'Judaizers',[11] now they were to be characterized as 'gnostics'. The light potentially to be shed on 1 Corinthians was almost blinding. Not only did it make sense of Paul's rebuke of the Corinthian 'spirituals' (3.1–4), but another key Gnostic term immediately became luminous—those Corinthians who claimed 'we all have knowledge (*gnōsis*)' (8.2). The gross libertine sexual behaviour indicated in 5.1 and ch. 6 could be explained by Gnostic dualism, which sharply distinguished spirit from body, so that the body could be sated without affecting the spirit. Paradoxically, the asceticism seen to be implied in ch. 7 could be explained equally on the same logic: bodily appetites could be starved since the spirit was unaffected. Most striking of all, the denial of the resurrection in 15.12 (another crux verse) could be explained as a Gnostic sense of present fulfilled salvation not dependent on a future resurrection (cf. 4.8), or at least not requiring a resurrection of the hateful body (15.35).

These early attempts to reconstruct the intellectual milieu of 1 Corinthians in terms of pre-Christian Gnosticism are generally reckoned to have been pushed well beyond what the evidence can safely bear. What the evidence for the time actually attests is a melting pot of religious ideas and philosophies, many of them Jewish in origin (the myth of Wisdom, as in Sir 24 and *1 En.* 42), others common in different religious systems (e.g., 'knowledge', ascetic practice).[12] None-

---

10. Schmithals, *Gnosticism*; see extract (ch. 3 above).

11. At the time of Paul 'judaize' was a term used for Gentiles who sympathized with Judaism and adopted Jewish customs, that is, lived as a Jew (see, e.g., BDAG, 478); the usage introduced in the nineteenth century and dominant since (Jews or Jewish Christians who urged Gentile Christians to proselytize) was unknown in the first century.

12. See Horsley extract (ch. 8 above).

theless, the significance of the whole debate is that it shows Paul to have been articulating a Christian teaching, not pristine and distinct from all other religious vocabulary of the time, but engaged with the religious debates and controversies of the time, his language reflecting in greater or lesser degree these debates and controversies. The extent to which he shaped or slanted his teaching to the particularities of the Corinthian situation can never be certain. But it does mean that contemporary interpretation and use of 1 Corinthians has to make allowances for that uncertainty and has to avoid the impression that Paul was dealing in absolutes clearly distinct and disconnected from other religious teachings of the time.

ENTHUSIASTS AND CHARISMATICS

An early variation of the Gnostic hypothesis took reconstruction of the thought world of the Corinthians on a different tangent. W. Lütgert argued that the early Christian community was confronted with a twofold challenge: not simply that of the nomistic Jewish Christians seen everywhere by Baur, but also, in Corinth in particular, by 'antinomian Gnostics', 'libertine pneumatics'. That is how 'the Christ party' should be identified. The parallel he cites is the Reformation caught between the old church and the '*enthusiasts*' (*Schwärmern*) of the Radical Reformation.[13] This recourse to the old Reformation 'bogey-man', the 'enthusiast', presumably influenced Ernst Käsemann in his reconstruction of Christianity's beginnings. 'Enthusiasm' was a mark of these beginnings. But whereas the 'post-Easter enthusiasm' of the primitive community was apocalyptic and future-looking in character, the enthusiasm of the dominant group in Corinth had a realized character: they 'believed themselves to have reached the goal of salvation already'.[14] In each case Paul is understood to have distanced himself from such enthusiasm.

Here it is 1 Cor 4.8 that proved to be the linchpin, with its repeated 'already' ('Already you are filled! Already you have become rich!'). If one linked 4.8 to 15.12 ('some of you say there is no resurrection of the dead') it was easy to detect an overrealised emphasis in Corinthian convictions. Anthony Thiselton attempted to demonstrate how an overrealised eschatology did not depend solely on these texts; on the contrary, it could lie behind and explain each of the problems that Paul confronted in 1 Corinthians.[15] The problem is that once a hypothesis is accepted, at least as a working hypothesis, the text can be read in its light, and, so long as the speculative reconstruction of the Corinthian attitudes is not too forced, there is little to enable the reader operating without that hypothesis to decide for or against it. The question is whether a verse like 11.26 ('you proclaim the Lord's death until he comes') should be regarded as an expression of 'eschatological

---

13. Lütgert, *Freiheitspredigt*, 96, 86, 8.
14. E. Käsemann, 'The Beginnings of Christian Theology' (1960), *New Testament Questions of Today* (ET London: SCM, 1969) 82–107 (here pp. 105–6); idem, 'On the Subject of Primitive Christian Apocalyptic' (1962), 108–37 (here pp. 114, 125).
15. See Thiselton extract (ch. 7 above).

reserve' (Käsemann), the Lord's Supper as having an 'interim character' (Thiselton), in order to correct overenthusiastic interpretation of the Lord's Supper. And if so, whether this is a note fundamental to Paul's teaching, or only contingent on addressing a challenge of overrealised eschatology.

The line of reconstruction in terms of spiritual enthusiasts readily blends into that which finds a more obvious meeting point between history and interpretation in the discussion of charisms (spiritual gifts) in 1 Cor 12–14. Paul's account of the body of Christ as 'charismatic community', with attention given particularly to speaking in tongues and prophecy, had traditionally been seen as something of an embarrassment, as evocative too much of Reformation *Schwärmerei* for comfort. But the emergence of Pentecostalism at the beginning of the twentieth century, and the subsequent spread of 'the charismatic movement' into the mainline Christian denominations, removed much of the exotic strangeness from the phenomenon of glossolalia. More important here, these twentieth-century developments provided a hermeneutical constituency more understanding of what Paul was probably dealing with, and more open and sympathetic to Paul's own teaching on the subject.[16] The hermeneutical principle of note is the relative difficulty in interpreting Paul's treatment of phenomena with which the interpreter has little familiarity or sympathy.

More specific questions of interpretation are numerous. For example, should the reconstruction of the Corinthian assembly and its inspired speech simply assume that twentieth-century experience of prophecy and glossolalia is the same as the Corinthian experience? What did Paul have in mind when he identified the charisms of 'word of wisdom', 'word of knowledge', of 'faith' and 'discerning of spirits' (12.8–10)? What did Paul understand glossolalia to be; should we speak of it as 'ecstatic speech' (NEB)? What did he mean when he asserted that 'we all have been baptized in one Spirit' (12.13)? Is his characterization of 'the body of Christ' as charismatic community, its members each as charismatically gifted, intended as a universal description of every Christian congregation? Or was his treatment of the subject determined by the fact that he was addressing the enthusiastic peculiarities of a particular church, so that his teaching has to be discounted, if its wider relevance is to be properly appraised? Alternatively, should Paul's final exhortation, that 'all things are to be done decently and in order' (14.40), be seen primarily as an attempt to quieten Corinthian overenthusiasm, or can it serve as a blueprint of church order in situations where there is little or no enthusiasm (of any kind!)?

SOCIAL-SCIENCE PERSPECTIVES: THE IMPORTANCE OF SOCIAL CONTEXT

The next major development in reconstruction of the Corinthian church's situation and beliefs was the application of the methods and perspectives of the social

---

16. Best illustrated by the commentary of Fee, *First Epistle*.

sciences. Here the main breakthrough was provided by Gerd Theissen.[17] As noted in the introduction to the extract, Theissen successfully challenged the prevailing view that the earliest Christians came from among the poor. In contrast, by assembling all that can be known about the individuals actually named in the church of Corinth, it would appear that they came from the upper strata of society. 'Not many of them were wise, powerful, or of noble birth' (1.26), but these seem to have been the most prominent, so that the church itself was marked by social stratification.

The light shed by this insight on the problems addressed in the letter is considerable. The tension between the 'weak' and the enlightened in ch. 8 should not be seen simply as an ideological clash between Jewish inhibition before idolatry and Gentile tolerance of it. The weak were probably the poorer members who could only hope to eat meat at public, religious ceremonies; and the enlightened would have been of higher social status, with a public role to play in city life where participation in public functions and feasts was expected. Again, the tension in ch. 9 (should Paul depend on support from the Corinthians?) was not simply about liberty of (Paul's) conscience. It was occasioned more by the need for an itinerant charismatic like Paul to depend on local residents for hospitality and provision, the problem being that he might thereby become too dependent on one particular high-status figure. For many, the most illuminating of Theissen's insights was his recognition that the main problems regarding the Lord's Supper in ch. 11 were *not theological but social*. The conflict was basically between rich and poor, between those who had enough and those who had nothing (11.22). The rich were going ahead with their meal before the poor had even arrived (11.33). 'Discerning the body' (11.29) was more about social sensitivity than theological acumen.

This further reminder that a text like 1 Corinthians should not be read simply as a clash between ideas or over doctrines is very healthy for the interpreter. Of course Theissen's particular reconstruction is open to criticism, as the extract from Justin Meggitt illustrates (see ch. 17 above). But it is the fact that social context is bound to have influenced Paul's advice and instruction that interpretion has to allow for. The interpretive issue is nicely highlighted by Theissen's categorization of Paul's solution to the fiasco of the Lord's Supper in Corinth in terms of 'love-patriarchalism'.[18] That is, the well-to-do could behave according to the norms of their social class in their private gatherings, but at the Lord's Supper they should behave as equal members of the body of Christ—patriarchy transfused with love. But should Paul's counsel here and elsewhere be read as socially conservative, legitimating the values and status hierarchy of the dominant social order, or is his criticism of the socially strong being too muted by the phrase?[19] In other words, interpretive decisions on a point like this could determine whether

17. See Theissen extract (ch. 6 above).
18. Theissen, *Social Setting*, 107–10.
19. See particularly Horrell, *Social Ethos*, ch. 4.

Paul is to be regarded as a supporter of a status quo characterized by grotesque disparity of wealth and power, the church to be seen as only ameliorating but not challenging it; or whether the church forms in any significant degree a counter-culture, its members expected to live by a different system of values beyond as well as within the weekly assembly.[20]

Taking seriously the social realities of the church in Corinth prompted a whole series of insights and perspectives, all with challenging interpretive corollaries. For example, many of the above reconstructions of the Corinthian church pre-suppose a large church with different factions of varying strengths. But it has long been recognized that the early churches must have met in private homes, not in purpose-built chapels. According to Rom 16.23 'the whole church [in Corinth]' met in the house of Gaius (presumably the Gaius mentioned in 1 Cor 1.14).[21] But if, as archaeological findings suggest, the houses of even the well-to-do in Corinth (we can suppose Gaius was one such) would have been hard-pressed to accommodate more than about forty people, then the group dynamics that Paul envisages in his letter were significantly different.[22] First Corinthians as a letter to a small back-street home-church reads differently from one written to a major ecclesiastical structure in Front Street.

Again, we need to recall that Corinth was a Roman (re)foundation and that Roman society was largely built round a patron-client structure. In this relation-ship patron and client bound themselves to each other, the patron to provide financial resources, employment, protection, influence, and so on, the client to give the patron his support, providing information and service, and acting on the patron's behalf. The relation was obviously hierarchical, the balance of power heavily weighted on the patron's side; the client was a dependent. What would happen, then, if a patron and some of his clients were members of the church in Corinth? And what would happen if it was the patron who was acting selfishly and irresponsibly in the situations portrayed in 1 Cor 5–6? This is the situation that John Chow envisages.[23] It would certainly explain the unwillingness of the Corinthian congregation to condemn the profligate of 5.1 and their readiness to support him (5.2, 6), as also Paul's unwillingness to take on a client's dependence, and obligations to a patron, in ch. 9. If Paul was so bold as to call for the man's expulsion, then his willingness to outface the powerful is strikingly attested.

A sociological perspective alerts the twenty-first-century interpreter to the fact that group identity involves a sense of boundary (marking off the insider from the outsider). A major part of the problem with the Corinthian church was not only lack of internal cohesiveness, but also lack of clear boundaries. The obvious boundaries of baptism and Lord's Supper were not functioning sufficiently to

---

20. See particularly Horsley's second extract (ch. 18 above).

21. It is generally accepted that Paul must have written his letter to the Christians in Rome from Corinth.

22. See Murphy-O'Connor extract (ch. 9 above).

23. See Chow extract (ch. 15 above).

mark out the Christian group in its ethos and lifestyle. Hence the pleas of chs. 6 and 10. Wayne Meeks analyses the situation in terms of boundaries with 'gates' in them; Paul did not want his converts in Corinth to 'go out of the world' (5.10).[24] John Barclay helpfully contrasts the churches of Thessalonica and Corinth, in that the boundary was too clear in the first case, but not clear enough in the latter.[25] Charles Robertson develops the model of 'overlapping networks'— the problem being that the church was not the only group with which the Corinthian believers could and wanted to identify—and takes up L. A. Coser's observation that 'a certain degree of conflict is an essential element in group formation and the persistence of group life'.[26] In each case the sense of a congregation living between two worlds helps sensitize modern readers to the combination of tact and boldness with which Paul confronted the tensions and ambiguities of complex social relationships. It also helps them read the precedents provided by 1 Corinthians for contemporary handling of the equally complex but different social relationships of Christians in the twenty-first century in a much more carefully nuanced and circumspect way.

FEMINIST STUDIES: THE STATUS AND ROLE OF WOMEN

A particular aspect of attempted reconstructions of Corinthian Christianity that caught fire in the last quarter of the twentieth century is the status of women in the church of Corinth. As the introduction to the extract from Margaret Mac-Donald indicates, many scholars have been persuaded by the contributions of such as Elizabeth Schüssler Fiorenza and Antoinette Wire that women played a prominent role in Corinthian Christianity.[27] The consequences of such a reassessment of the church at Corinth for the interpretation of 1 Corinthians could be considerable. What if, for example, as MacDonald suggests, the ascetics addressed in ch. 7 were the/some women of the congregation, who translated the assertion that in Christ 'there is neither male nor female' (Gal 3.28) into a claim to the right to remain celibate?[28] In a society where marriage in order to bear children was the norm, the alternative lifestyle being advocated would be shocking. Paul's response in 7.2–5 would be firm but temperate, and the absence of the final clause (about male and female) from the parallel in 12.13 to Gal 3.28 would then gain a heavy overtone of disapproval. The trouble with this interpretation is that Paul

24. Meeks, *First Urban Christians,* 100, 105–7.

25. See Barclay extract (ch. 14 above).

26. C. K. Robertson, *Conflict in Corinth: Redefining the System* (New York: Peter Lang, 2001), citing L. A. Coser, *The Functions of Social Conflict* (New York: Free Press, 1956), here p. 31.

27. E. Schüssler Fiorenza, *In Memory of Her: A Feminist Theological Reconstruction of Christian Origins* (London: SCM, 1983); Wire, *Corinthian Women Prophets.*

28. M. Y. MacDonald extract (ch. 12 above). This is a contemporary variation of the older view that what is in view in 7.36–38 is a celibate marriage—'partner in celibacy' (NEB).

seems to be thinking in terms of *male* celibacy (7.1, 36–38). Even so, however, Paul's own discouragement of marriage is clear (even if 7.1b is a quotation from the Corinthians' letter) and does not make for a strong doctrine of Christian marriage. Or does the possibility that Paul thought the return of Christ to be imminent (7.29–31) mean that his teaching at this point can be discounted? Chapter 7 provides an excellent example of the difficulties in achieving a clear or convincing line of interpretation precisely because the circumstances envisaged in and behind the text are unclear.

The main focus for clarification of the situation addressed by Paul and for the consequent interpretation of what Paul says in regard to Christian women are the two passages 11.2–16 and 14.34–36. Paul was evidently influenced by the social mores of the time—the belief that it was improper for a woman to wear her hair short, and the appeal to conventions of shame and honour (11.5–6, 13–15). Prophesying with unbound and disheveled hair could also have been regarded as too similar to the ritual practices of the Dionysiac or Isis cult for Paul's comfort (Fiorenza). Should such considerations be given the same weight as the theological principles Paul evokes in 11.3 and 7—that the husband is head (or source?) of the wife, and that the woman (or wife) is the glory of man (or her husband)—both evidently drawing on the creation narratives of Gen 1–2? In this case the fuller knowledge that sociological and anthropological studies give us of the conventions and cults of the time only sharpen the interpreter's dilemma. For they may help us to understand better why Paul reacted as he did, although the details are still somewhat speculative. On the other hand, the theological principles arguably are equally as time-bound as the social conventions, interpretations of creation narratives appropriate to a patriarchal society but questionable otherwise.

As for 14.34–36, a major problem is whether the verses belong to the original letter or were added later. Here the issue is not dependent so much on historical reconstruction, but historical reconstruction can still help shed light on the issue. If, for example, the key term *gynē* is translated 'wife' rather than 'woman', as is entirely appropriate, then the instruction can be seen as governed less by concerns for church order and more by concerns for household order— that it would be regarded as improper for a wife to sit in judgment on the prophecy offered by her husband (14.29). The illumination that comes from the social context is that the family was regarded as the basic unit of society, and that it was characteristically patriarchal in character, with the implication that Paul would not want his churches to be seen as a threat to that social order (14.33b, 36). Stephen Barton sharpens the point by noting that a 'sense of place' was involved.[29] Since the church met in a home, which of the two was to be given priority—the prophetess's (wife's) liberty to prophesy, or the wife's (prophetess's) subordination to the paterfamilias, the head of the family/house?

---

29. Barton, 'Paul's Sense of Place'.

RHETORIC AND INTERPRETATION

Finally, another strand that grew out of the history of religions school's concern to locate early Christianity within the religious and philosophical currents of the day was the recognition of the importance of rhetoric in the ancient world. Johannes Weiss, in his magisterial commentary on 1 Corinthians, was the first to draw extensively on sources contemporary with Paul in a thoroughgoing attempt to elucidate the letter. In so doing he was able to demonstrate more clearly than before that the 'wisdom' Paul was talking about in 2.1–5 was rhetorical wisdom, the effective art of persuasive speech. His insight is well illustrated by his observation that when Paul spoke of 'the demonstration (*apodeixis*) of Spirit and power' (2.4) he was using a technical term in rhetoric for a compelling conclusion drawn out from accepted premises.[30] The implication is that Paul was no mere beginner himself in knowledge of rhetoric and in use of rhetorical techniques. The corollary for interpretation is important: that despite his attack on 'the wisdom of words' and his self-deprecation ('my speech and my message were not in plausible words of wisdom'—2.4), Paul was quite capable of composing a rhetorically pleasing phrase. Indeed, he was quite capable of using the rhetorical techniques that he here played down. Such recognition of a *rhetorical* 'put-down' of *rhetoric* should at once alert us to the danger of reading passages like 1.18—2.5 simply at face value. The ear that is not attuned to irony and wordplay will miss significant dimensions of the text.

This early insight was swamped by the Gnostic hypothesis of the middle decades of the twentieth century, although C. K. Barrett's perception that Paul was using the term 'wisdom' in four different ways, two good and two bad, helped stem the tide of Gnostic interpretation.[31] But it was not until the latter decades of the twentieth century that the interpretation of 1 Corinthians as rhetoric, and knowledgeable rhetoric, revived.[32] Nor is it to be seen as simply a clash of rhetorical systems, as Duane Litfin tends to assume, theological rhetoric over against the rhetoric of eloquence.[33] The value of recognizing the rhetorical dimension of 1 Corinthians can only be seen with full effect when it is integrated with an equal recognition of the sociological perspective already elaborated. For it is not simply the case that sociological and rhetorical perspectives illuminate the background to the letter, the situation addressed by the letter. Nor is it the case that we can simply read off the background or situation from the letter itself. For the letter does not provide a dispassionate description of that situation. On the contrary, the intention in writing was to influence the situation, and to do so the rhetor may well have found it necessary to turn a blind eye here, focus on a point amenable to his case there, and in some degree manipulate the perception of the

30. J. Weiss, *Der erste Korintherbrief* (Göttingen: Vandenhoeck & Ruprecht, 1910) 50.
31. See Barrett, 'Christianity at Corinth'.
32. As also with the question of Stoic influence on Paul, which was also pioneered by Weiss; see, e.g., the extract from T. Paige (ch. 16 above).
33. Litfin, *St. Paul's Theology.*

situation to his own ends. This does not mean that we should see Paul as purely manipulative.[34] But it does mean that the modern interpreter has to be rhetorically aware and alert, otherwise a distorted picture of the Corinthian church may well emerge, the point of the letter will be clouded, and the subtlety of Paul's pastoral technique will be largely missed.[35]

L. L. Welborn can be credited with bringing out the extent to which the rhetoric involved in 1 Cor 1–4 was *political* rhetoric. The terms used by Paul in these chapters had been familiar in Greco-Roman historians to characterize conflicts within city-states: *schisma* ('schism'), *eris* ('strife'), *meris* ('party'); 'puffed up' (4.6), echoing 'the caricature of the political windbag'. What is in view, then, is not so much theological disagreement as political partisanship, a power struggle, not a theological controversy. Paul sought not so much to refute false teaching as to prevent *stasis* ('strife and discord').[36] It was principally on Welborn's findings that Margaret Mitchell built her highly effective reading of 1 Corinthians as an appeal for unity. Taking up Munck's older argument drawn from the letter itself, Mitchell was able to demonstrate from the richness of contemporary usage that Paul's language constituted a plea to the Corinthians to end their factionalism and to be reconciled to one another. In formal terms, the letter is an example of deliberative rhetoric, in which the appeal is presented as for the audience's advantage and proofs are adduced by way of example. Throughout the body of the letter she finds regular use of terms and phrases appropriate to an ancient discussion of factionalism and concord.[37]

Here again the benefit to twenty-first-century interpreters is twofold. They are alerted to the resonances of the language; they can enter a little more fully into the dialogue of which the text was part, recognizing the particularities and subtleties of what Paul actually said. So their awareness of the text's contextuality and historical reference becomes more acute. This also means that they are prevented from reading the text as though it was pristine, uncontaminated by the infighting and name-calling of political dispute. The text cannot be read as though it was permanently six feet above the real world, or consisted of absolute pronouncements applicable in every and any circumstance. Even those who want to affirm the text's Word of God status have to acknowledge that Paul was quite ready to 'mix it' when countering the factionalism of the Corinthian church.

CONCLUSIONS

In the introduction I argued that an ancient text like 1 Corinthians cannot be properly understood unless it is read against the background of its historical con-

34. As G. Shaw, *The Cost of Authority: Manipulation and Freedom in the New Testament* (London: SCM, 1983); contrast H. Chadwick, '"All Things to All Men" (1 Cor. 9.22)', *NTS* 1 (1954–55) 261–75.

35. See Fiorenza extract (ch. 11 above).

36. See Welborn extract (ch. 10 above).

37. Mitchell, *Rhetoric,* summary on 180–81.

text and as part of a dialogue with the Corinthian church itself. The trouble is that the historical context is still hard to reconstruct and the other side of the dialogue difficult to overhear. There is no single reconstructed context of those illustrated above that commands universal consent, although some that have been too narrowly based or too overdependent on specific verses like 1.12 or 4.8 have tended to lose support after their initial impact. Does that mean, then, that the task of interpretation is flawed from the outset, that no clarity of consensus can ever be achieved?

That may indeed be the case. For each interpreter or group of interpreters is in effect going round their own hermeneutical circle. The hermeneutical circles of different twentieth- or twenty-first-century interpreters will no doubt often overlap to a substantial extent, but they do not coincide. Alternatively expressed, a proper dialogue with the text involves a simultaneous dialogue with others asking questions of or listening to the text. Or again alternatively expressed, the above survey clearly reminds us that understanding of the text inevitably shifts and develops as perception of the reconstructed context shifts and develops. This does not mean that 'anything goes'. For every reading of the text is constrained by the actual wording of the text. But it does mean that as different reconstructions are proffered, or as different facets of the complex historical context of 1 Corinthians are illuminated, so different emphases and facets of the letter itself will be thrown into prominence (and others into shadow).

Is this tantamount to saying that there is no single 'correct' meaning of the text? Yes! In a multiparticipant dialogue different aspects and emphases are bound to be heard by different participants. But this was ever the case. The original recipients of the letter would have heard it differently as it was read to them, depending on their own different situations, and depending not least on how the reader of the letter phrased, intoned, and emphasised the words Paul had dictated. Even so, however, there must have been general agreement as to the value of the letter, as to its authority, which ensured that the letter was preserved, circulated, and began to be accorded that widening circle of authority which in due course ensured that it was included within the New Testament canon. The point is that the general agreement would not necessarily have been agreement on all the individual arguments made by the letter; the agreement need only have been that the letter was inspired and of apostolic weight, such that it must continue to serve as a resource for the faith and praxis of the early Christians.

The consequences of this recognition are twofold. First, it means that the various reconstructions of Corinthian Christianity do not help us to get to *the* meaning of the letter, as though there was only one correct meaning. What they do is help us to overhear more clearly the dialogue of which the letter was a part; and also help us, in at least a small degree, to enter into that dialogue for ourselves— as though the twenty-first-century interpreters of the letter are an outer circle of the Corinthian church, listening to the letter as it was read, joining with its members as they discussed how the letter spoke to them. Second, it means that we allow the text of the letter to function in an open-ended way; that is, we acknowledge its capacity to speak to us in different ways as different questions and issues are raised in regard to it. We could say that we acknowledge its power to speak to us of the twenty-first century with the authenticity of God's word which the first Corinthian Christians experienced and which made the letter so important for them. But we must not insist that *our* meaning is the *only* legitimate meaning.

Index of Ancient Sources

Index of Subjects and Modern Authors